FRENCH AND FRANCOPHONE STUDIES

'Taking Up Space'

Series Editors

Hanna Diamond (Cardiff University)
Claire Gorrara (Cardiff University)

Editorial Board

Kate Averis (Universidad de Antioquia)
Natalie Edwards (University of Adelaide)
Kate Griffiths (Cardiff University)
Simon Kemp (University of Oxford)
Margaret Majumdar (University of Portsmouth)
Debarati Sanyal (University of California, Berkeley)
Maxim Silverman (University of Leeds)

Other titles in the series

FRENCH AND FRANCOPHONE STUDIES

'Taking Up Space'

Women at Work in Contemporary France

Edited by

SIHAM BOUAMER
AND SONJA STOJANOVIC

UNIVERSITY OF WALES PRESS
2022

www.uwp.co.uk

British Library Cataloguing-in-Publication Data
A catalogue record for this book is available from the British Library.

ISBN   978-1-78683-907-7
eISBN   978-1-78683-908-4

The rights of the Contributors to be identified as authors of this work have been asserted in accordance with sections 77, 78 and 79 of the Copyright, Designs and Patents Act 1988.

The University of Wales Press gratefully acknowledges the financial assistance of the Nanovic Institute for European Studies in publication of this book.

Typeset by Mark Heslington Ltd, Scarborough, North Yorkshire
Printed by CPI Antony Rowe, Melksham

Contents

Part II. Revolving Doors: Liminal and Precarious Spaces

Part III. From Opening a Few Doors to Blowing the Doors Off

Series Editors' Preface

This series showcases the work of new and established scholars working within the fields of French and francophone studies. It publishes introductory texts aimed at a student readership, as well as research-orientated monographs at the cutting edge of their discipline area. The series aims to highlight shifting patterns of research in French and francophone studies, to re-evaluate traditional representations of French and francophone identities and to encourage the exchange of ideas and perspectives across a wide range of discipline areas. The emphasis throughout the series will be on the ways in which French and francophone communities across the world are evolving into the twenty-first century.

Hanna Diamond and Claire Gorrara

Acknowledgements

The editors wish to thank all the contributors for their work and commitment to this project, especially during these challenging times. We also wish to thank the anonymous reader for their generous reading and comments for the volume. We are grateful for all the work of the University of Wales Press staff, particularly Adam Burns, Dafydd Jones, Maria Vassilopoulos, Elin Williams, as well as the many others whose names we do not know, but whose labour we wish to acknowledge. We would like to also express our appreciation for Sarah Meaney, who copy-edited this massive volume. Finally, we would like to extend a special thank you to Sarah Lewis, Head of Commissioning, at the University of Wales Press for her guidance and patience throughout this process. This volume is in part made possible by a publication grant from the Nanovic Institute for European Studies, Keough School of Global Affairs, University of Notre Dame.

Notes on Contributors

Mercédès Baillargeon is associate professor of French and francophone studies at the University of Massachusetts Lowell. She specialises in literary, feminist and queer theory as well as reception studies, and is particularly interested in the relationship between aesthetics and politics in women's literature and the 'renouveau du cinema québécois'. She has published several articles and co-edited two special issues on Québec cinema. Her book, *Le personnel est politique: Médias, esthétique et politique de l'autofiction chez Christine Angot, Chloé Delaume et Nelly Arcan* was published by Purdue University Press in April 2019.

Siham Bouamer is assistant professor of Global French studies at the University of Cincinnati. Her research focuses on transnational movements from and to the Maghreb in literature and film. She is currently working on her first monograph tentatively titled *Colonial Tourists: French Women's Travel Narratives on Morocco*. She has co-edited a volume titled *Abdellah Taïa's Queer Migrations: Non-places, Affect, and Temporalities* (Lexington Books, 2021) and *Diversity and Decolonization in French Studies* (Palgrave, 2022).

Loïc Bourdeau is lecturer in French Studies at National University of Ireland, Maynooth. His research lies in twentieth and twenty-first-century global French studies. His publications include, among others, *Horrible Mothers: Representation across Francophone North America* (University of Nebraska Press, 2019) and *ReFocus: The Films of François Ozon* (Edinburgh University Press, 2021). He has also co-edited *Revisiting HIV/AIDS in French Culture: Raw Matters* (Lexington Books, 2022) with V. Hunter Capps and *Diversity and Decolonization in French Studies* (Palgrave, 2022) with Siham Bouamer. He launched and serves as series editor of *New Directions in Francophone Studies: Diversity, Decolonization, Queerness* (Edinburgh University Press).

Jennifer Carr holds a PhD in French from Yale University and an MA in cultural translation from the American University of Paris. Her research interests include contemporary French and francophone literature, feminist theory, experimental writing practices, translation and material culture. She currently teaches at Wellesley College.

Amaleena Damlé is associate professor in French at Durham University. Her research interests reside predominantly in questions of embodiment, affect, gender, sexuality and race in contemporary French and francophone literature and philosophy. She is the author of *The Becoming of the Body: Contemporary Women's Writing in French* (Edinburgh University Press, 2014), and has co-edited, with Gill Rye, three books on twenty-first-century women's writing in French. Amaleena is currently working on a monograph on the politics of consumption in Ananda Devi's writing, and a cross-cultural project on contemporary narratives of birth, including scholarly and creative writing.

Sandra Daroczi is a lecturer in French studies at the University of Bath. Her research focuses on contemporary women's writing, feminisms and the intersection of sociopolitical change, literature and the visual arts. She has contributed articles and chapters on the work of Marie Darrieussecq, Julia Kristeva, Tatiana de Rosnay and *le Mouvement de Libération des Femmes*. She is working on a monograph examining the reading dialogues put forward by Monique Wittig's fiction. She is interested in bridging the gap between academia and the public. Her most recent contribution was co-organising a workshop for the *Shameless! Festival of Activism against Sexual Violence* (November 2021).

Valentina Denzel is an associate professor of (seventeenth and eighteenth century) French literature with the department of romance and classical studies at Michigan State University. In her book *Les mille et un visages de la virago: Marfisa et Bradamante entre continuation et variation* (Classiques Garnier, 2016), she analyses the evolution of the representation of the woman warrior in French and Italian literatures from the Middle Ages to the Enlightenment. Her second book project examines the impact of the Marquis de Sade on punk and feminist movements, as well as on comic books in France, the United Kingdom and the United States.

Maxime Foerster is associate professor of French at SMU, Dallas. His encounter with Marie-Pierre Pruvot (Bambi) inspired him to publish *Une histoire des transsexuels en France* in 2006 and, more recently, 'Les femmes transgenres face au sida dans *Le Gai cimetière*' (*Contemporary French Civilization*, 46/2 (2021)).

Dorthea Fronsman-Cecil is visiting assistant professor of French at Lafayette College. Her research examines the integration of scholarly and activist discourses of the good life within French cultural productions representing labour and leisure. She is working on her first book, *'Nous bâtirons un monde nouveau': Punk Polemics, Aesthetics, and Everyday Life in Metropolitan France*, of which a draft won the 2019 Peter Lang Young Scholars Competition in French Studies.

Polly Galis is currently an Independent Scholar and was a teaching associate in French at the University of Bristol, where she recently conducted research into 'Narratives of Pleasure and Protest by Francophone Sex Workers' funded by the SFS Postdoctoral Prize Fellowship. Polly has a monograph forthcoming with Peter Lang, *Frank French Feminisms: Sex, Sexuality and the Body in the Work of Ernaux, Huston and Arcan* (2022), as a winner of the Young Scholars Competition. Previous publications include a special journal issue for *L'Esprit Créateur* (2020) and edited volume with Peter Lang (2021), both focused on the body in twentieth and twenty-first-century francophone culture.

Ciara Gorman is a PhD candidate in French at Queen's University Belfast, funded by the AHRC Northern Bridge Doctoral Training Partnership. Her doctoral research investigates the representation of criminal women in contemporary French crime fiction, from the figure of the killer nanny to the female serial killer and female gangster. She was awarded the Women in French UK-Ireland Postgraduate Prize in 2021.

Leslie Kealhofer-Kemp is associate professor of French and film at the University of Rhode Island. She is the author of *Muslim Women in French Cinema: Voices of Maghrebi Migrants in France* (Liverpool

University Press, 2015) and co-editor of *ReFocus: The Films of Rachid Bouachareb* (Edinburgh University Press, 2020). Her writing has been published in journals such as *The French Review, Modern and Contemporary France, Studies in French Cinema* and *Contemporary French Civilization.*

Johanna Montlouis-Gabriel is an assistant professor at North Carolina State University. Her work figures in *Essays in French Literature, Etudes Littéraires Africaines* and *The French Review* and Routledge Press. Her sole-authored book manuscript titled *The Afro-Feminist Creative Praxis of Black French Women* is under contract at the University of Nebraska Press in the 'Expanding Frontiers: Interdisciplinary Approaches to Studies of Women, Gender, and Sexuality' series. Her research focuses on the articulation of French-specific afro-feminism in contemporary France in creative realms ranging from literature, performance, film and digital and visual media broadly. She is a Camargo Foundation Fellow (Spring 2022).

Blase A. Provitola is assistant professor of language and culture studies and women, gender and sexuality at Trinity College (Hartford CT, United States). They have published on lesbian and queer activism and cultural production, postcolonial literature and transgender-inclusive pedagogy.

Rebecca Rosenberg is a final-year part-time doctoral student in the French department at King's College London. Her research examines autofictions representing suicidal ideation, mental illness and psychological suffering by francophone authors Nelly Arcan, Chloé Delaume, Linda Lê and Chahdortt Djavann. She has had research published on bibliotherapy and graphic medicine in depression memoirs and comics. She has research due to be published on fairy-tale mythology, trauma and Marie Nimier, and psychological pain in works by Delaume.

Sonja Stojanovic is assistant professor of French and francophone studies, concurrent faculty in the gender studies programme and faculty fellow at the Nanovic Institute for European Studies at the University of Notre Dame. She is the author of *Mind the Ghost: Thinking Memory and the Untimely through Contemporary Fiction in French*

(Liverpool University Press, 2023). Her current book project focuses on the figure of the cashier in contemporary French culture.

Amy Wigelsworth is a senior lecturer in French at Sheffield Hallam University. Her main area of expertise is French popular culture. She is the author of the monograph *Rewriting Les Mystères de Paris: The Mystères Urbains and the Palimpsest* (Legenda, 2016), as well as several articles and a book chapter on French urban mysteries and French crime fiction, and is also co-editor, with Angela Kimyongür, of *Rewriting Wrongs: French Crime Fiction and the Palimpsest* (Cambridge Scholars Publishing, 2014). Her current research is on work and culture, with a particular focus on representations of work in francophone fiction and film.

Jennifer Willging is associate professor of French at the Ohio State University. She specialises in twentieth and twenty-first-century French literature and culture with particular interests in post-World War II narrative, French-American cultural relations, theories of everyday life and representations of neoliberalism in the contemporary novel. She has published a book on expressions of narrative anxiety in post-war women's writing (*Telling Anxiety*, University of Toronto Press, 2007) and numerous articles on narrative voice and reliability, intertextuality and French intellectuals' reactions to contemporary cultural change. Her current book project treats contemporary French critiques of happiness as transcendent cultural value.

Introduction

SIHAM BOUAMER AND SONJA STOJANOVIC

From the second half of the twentieth century, major developments for women's rights have been underway in France: from the right to vote in 1944 to, more recently, equal rights (same-sex marriage and adoption in 2013) and anti-discrimination laws (2016). Most significantly, on the question of work, are the landmark decisions regarding reproductive rights (birth control, 1967; abortion, 1975), which recognise women's agency over their own bodies and thus help smooth their paths towards further education and career advancement. All these sociopolitical developments have been accompanied by a growth in women's labour in proportions previously unseen.[1] In their expansive study of (un)employment statistics through which they tease out a history of women's labour from the twentieth century onwards, Margaret Maruani and Monique Meron indicate that it is a phenomenon that dates back to the '"trente glorieuses" et qui se poursuit aujourd'hui encore en pleine crise économique et financière' ('"glorious thirty" and which continues today in the midst of an economic and financial crisis') (p. 50). In their study, they also demystify certain received ideas about women's work, particularly the notions that it constitutes a 'side-note' or that it is always viewed with suspicion as to the real value of this work (p. 9).

Even though France signed *The Universal Declaration of Human Rights* in 1948, in which article 23 stipulates 'equal pay for equal work',[2] pay discrimination remains a reality for many. As a matter of fact, the path to equality is never without challenges. For instance, while certain laws made it possible for women to seek gainful employment, their husband's consent remained a condition until 1965.[3] When it comes to contemporary contexts, Françoise Vergès has noted a recent wave of setbacks brought forth or emboldened by the election of far-right extremists, targeting specifically 'les minorités, les trans, les queers, les travailleuses/travailleurs du sexe, les racisé·es, les migrant·es, les musulman·es' ('minorities, trans and queer people, sex workers, racialised individuals, migrants and Muslims').[4] Indeed, at this moment in time, there is still a lot to be achieved when it comes to matters of accessibility, diversity, inclusivity, as well as regarding issues of career advancement, discrimination, precarity and sexual harassment in the workplace, to name a few. Nevertheless, what each debate on a setback or a law has brought back to the public sphere is the question of representation, both political and public (in press and screen media) – as seen, for example, through the debates for parity in politics. Furthermore, many social movements, political struggles and victories for labour rights have been, as Jeremy Lane points out, 'mirrored' in French cultural productions, leading to 'a profusion of ... depictions of the contemporary workplace'.[5]

Considering the question of women and labour goes beyond the notion of work. As Maruani and Meron discuss, '[l]'activité professionnelle des femmes est à la fois une réalité économique et une construction sociale' ('Women's professional activity is both an economic reality and a social construct').[6] As a matter of fact, women's labour – its realities or the way that it is imagined – can become 'un fil rouge pour lire la place des femmes dans la société' ('a common thread to understand the place of women in society') (p. 16). In this volume, we want to probe what this construction of women's work says about contemporary France through an investigation of a wide range of cultural – cinematic, literary, artistic, media – productions. As such, the two parts of the title of this volume, 'Taking Up Space': Women at Work in Contemporary France, intend to reflect the directions (the 'fil rouge') that guide the general scope of this study.

First, the expression 'Women at Work', which simultaneously aims to highlight the importance of women's roles in work spaces and the processes involved, allows us to enter into conversation with existing scholarship in broader disciplinary, geographical and historical contexts. In the specific context of France, several recent studies have focused on historico-sociological frameworks to approach this topic,[7] and a focus on the representations of women's experiences at work in contemporary cultural productions is certainly complementary. In that vein, Barbara Mennel's *Women at Work in Twenty-First Century European Cinema* (2019) is of particular interest. Beyond sharing a similar title with our volume, the study aims to analyse 'the cultural imagination of labor'[8] in European cinema (including France), a form of representation that some contributions address in our volume. Mennel also discusses pertinent questions relevant to women's labour, namely 'domesticity', 'precarious work', 'industrial labor', 'labor migration', 'care work' and 'reproductive labor'. Stepping away from 'the romanticization of labor relations' (p. 13) and echoing Maruani and Meron, the book argues that '[f]ilms do not simply reflect social reality; they also imagine alternatives and offer commentaries on the way we work' (p. 5). As such, the increasing depiction of women's work on screen, Mennel notes, opens the possibility to consider 'feminist approaches to the representation of women's work' (p. 7) within a transnational and neoliberal gendered economy.

The first part of the title, 'Taking up Space', which shapes the core of our theoretical framework, allows us to expand the question of 'women at work' by privileging the question of movement and space within a feminist praxis. We draw on Sara Ahmed's *Queer Phenomenology: Orientations, Objects, Others* (2006), where she explores the positionality of bodies in space, time and everyday life in relation to certain objects. More specifically, she questions 'how we inhabit spaces as well as "who" or "what" we inhabit spaces with'.[9] Such a dynamic, adds Ahmed, 'involves hard work ... [and] painstaking labor for bodies to inhabit spaces that do not extend their shape' (p. 62). Expanding on Ahmed's lexical use of labour, this volume enquires how women have 'take[n] up spaces' at work and address how women's bodies orient themselves in work 'spaces [that] are already occupied' (p. 62). Keeping in mind the importance of considering these often-invisible experiences as constitutive of 'work', we choose the expression 'work spaces' rather than 'workplaces', a word that does not reflect the scope of women's labour that we intend to include in the volume.[10]

It is important at this time to outline additional key definitions for the volume, in particular our understanding of the categories 'women' and 'work'. While we recognise that Ahmed specifically focuses on queerness in her analysis of disruptive bodies in space and we do include such representations in our volume, we also expand her framework by considering all women as potential deviant social subjects within the work space. As such, we cover diverse socio-economic and ethnic backgrounds; some of our contributors tackle salaried work in the academic, artistic, corporate and working-class worlds, but we also consider unpaid (i.e., reproductive, domestic) labour, illegal activities and activism. The inclusion of a vast array of categories seeks to contrast various experiences, while at the same time highlighting how much certain forms of labour, or workers, are often 'invisibilised'. For instance, Françoise Vergès points out the oft-devalued roles of cleaning ladies, despite their crucial roles to the functioning of economic, cultural and political institutions. She underlines the fact that this burden is kept invisible, particularly to avoid acknowledging the exploitation of racialised women, especially given the fact that this type of labour 'est considéré comme relevant de ce que les femmes doivent accomplir (sans se plaindre) ... le travail féminin de soin et de nettoyage constitue un travail gratuit' ('has been considered what women must do (without complaint) ... women's caring and cleaning work is free labour').[11]

Yet the additional work that falls to women should be understood not only in terms of domestic or care work, but also in the form of emotional work. The recent viral success of the comic strip by French artist Emma on the question of 'la charge mentale' ('mental load')[12] shows that there is growing public consciousness of these issues. While this particular burden has been made visible and has been widely mediatised,[13] it should also be noted that it often falls to activists and members of certain minoritised communities to educate the wider public. As they often do not have direct access to mainstream media and publishing, they must seek alternative paths (e.g., social media) to bring important issues to the fore. For instance, as a response to the dearth of representations of disabled people in French cultural productions and the lack of accessibility of many (work)spaces, activist Marina Carlos recently self-published (in both French and English) the book *Je vais m'arranger: Comment le validisme impacte la vie des personnes handicapées* ('*I'll Figure it Out: How Ableism Impacts Disabled People's Lives*') (2020).

Furthermore, there are aspects of invisible emotional work that are directly linked to the fact that France is a country adamant about its universalist colour-blind principles. This ideology has as an effect what Maboula Soumahoro has termed 'la charge raciale' ('racial load'), which involves the arduous task of 'endurer' ('suffering') systemic racism as well as bearing the burden 'd'expliquer, de traduire, de rendre intelligibles les situations violentes, discriminantes ou racistes' ('to explain, translate, make comprehensible violent, discriminatory or racist situations').[14] This is echoed by Vergès, who emphasises the labour 'd'accumuler les faits, les chiffres alors que faits et chiffres ... ne changent quoi que ce soit au rapport de force' ('[to] accumulate the facts and figures, while neither facts, [nor] figures ... change anything in the balance of power').[15] Subsequently, the topic of women at work, as we envisage it in this volume, transcends reflections on the representation of women in what is traditionally understood as the workplace. Sarah Waters, drawing from research on work suicides, has noted that women's identities are not necessarily completely 'bound up with' their occupations, but rather 'influenced by other factors including family relationships, parenthood and community'.[16] In this volume, we expand on the definition of 'work' to include analyses of the labour that women perform regardless of employment status and remuneration, that is, the labour that often intersects with these other factors – whether it manifests itself as care work, emotional labour or activism.

As a response to the invisibility and devalued role of women's labour highlighted in this introduction, we privileged the inclusion of contributions focusing on women 'writing' women,[17] because, and as Amaleena Damlé reminds us, '[i]f female voices and female authors make up a great part of the mainstream today, it seems vital to remember the relatively recent nature of this achievement and the struggles it has taken for women writers to obtain such recognition'.[18] Our focus on contemporary France (which we delimit as starting around May 1968) coincides with the 'sudden outpouring of new voices [that] rushed forth [starting in the 1970s], eager to speak women's lives and experiences, particularly in writing'.[19] This period is also witness to a social revolution that opened many doors for (working) women, a metaphor that guides the overall organisation of the volume. While a chronological examination of the topic would have perhaps shown an evolution in the ways that women at work are represented in the French cultural landscape, we chose to adopt a thematic approach to show points of convergence between the various chapters; they enter into productive dialogues with one another and bring to the fore intertwined and recurrent movements of resistance and strategies of survival in work spaces and contemporary French society alike. Drawing on Ahmed's phenomenological use of objects as key elements in bodily orientations, we explore women's experiences through different metaphors of the door used in colloquial expressions related to work. Doors, Ahmed describes in her recent work *On Complaint* (2021), 'teach us about power' and serve as a tool to assess 'who is enabled by an institution, who is stopped from getting in or getting through'.[20] Indeed, although the door appears to be an image cultivating ideas of immobility and lack of access, we exploit it to observe how women 'are let "out" or kept "in," thereby creating lines between public and private spheres'.[21] More importantly still, the door likewise signifies the potential of an opening, it can be opened willingly as a sign of hospitality, but it can also be forced open. In this volume, contributors show that doors are not only closed or open, but that they also serve as a threshold or are meant to be blown off.

Part I begins this volume with an examination of how women navigate work 'Behind Closed Doors'; namely, 'intimate' spaces, ranging from the household to the therapy room. Together, the chapters challenge the centrality of 'the male breadwinner and head of family … a role institutionalised [in post-war France] in the form of the generous child benefits that encouraged women to adopt subordinate roles as mothers and housewives'.[22] Rather than postulating that women are viewed eternally as passive objects, the contributions that constitute this section offer, on the one hand, a commentary on the structural oppression associated with domestic work, or what Barbara Mennel calls 'the specter of domesticity',[23] be it paid or unpaid, and highlight, on the other hand, the possibilities of women's agency and mobility within confined spaces.

Focusing on the domestic space, we begin with an analysis of the dynamics of exploitation within different spaces of confinement (housework, prison, prostitution) and the various strategies that these workers use to break out. Offering a transtemporal and transmedial reading of Albertine Sarrazin's autofictional novel *L'Astragale* ('Astragal') (1965), Polly Galis explores the negotiation of domestic work, sexual labour and criminality. The recent adaptations of the novel (Anne-Caroline Pandolfo and Terkel Risbjerg's 2013 graphic novel and Brigitte Sy's 2015 film), Galis argues, show the continuous prevalence of those issues in contemporary France, as well as their recasting within an intersectional framework. Ciara Gorman further explores the question of housewifely care and criminality, with a reading of Leïla Slimani's *Chanson douce* (*'Lullaby'*) (2016). Considering the crime fiction subgenre of domestic noir, Gorman contrasts the potential of domestic labour to create a harmonious home with the criminality of the seemingly 'perfect nanny' Louise.

We then shift the question of women's labour and domesticity to a different socio-economic status, specifically the negotiation of womanhood and intellectual life. Jennifer Willging turns to Paule Constant's 1998 *Confidence pour confidence* (*'Trading Secrets'*), a novel in which four middle-aged women spend the morning after an academic conference in the closed space of the organiser's home. Focusing on the consequences of ageing and dysfunctional family relationships, Willging argues that the novel uncovers the failures of second-wave feminism in the neoliberal era. Amaleena Damlé probes the question of the relationship between women and birth – as inarticulable and invisible labour – in the short-story collection *Naissances* (*'Births'*) (2005). Specifically, the chapter brings light to narratives that represent acts of feminist-embodied and epistemological labour and that allow to challenge restrictive discourses of unproductiveness surrounding reproductive and creative labour.

Fundamentally, the two contributions aim to problematise the question of emotional and psychological labour, which the last two chapters of this section also investigate. Blase Provitola underlines the relationship between labour and same-sex desire in Mireille Best's *Il n'y a pas d'hommes au paradis* (*'There Are No Men in Heaven'*) (1995), specifically the negotiation of sexual subjectivity – and its disclosure – within a working-class environment as a form of labour that disproportionately burdens women. Reflecting on Chahdortt Djavann's autofictional text *Je ne suis pas celle que je suis* (*'I Am Not Who I Am'*) (2011), Rebecca Rosenberg explores the strenuous nature of psychoanalytical work in the context of exile and bearing in mind the impact of trauma, linguistic barriers and financial precarity. Rosenberg also suggests that the polyphonic structure of the text reflects the psychoanalytic labour of the author whose own experiences are shared between the different voices of the text.

Part II, framed around the metaphor of 'Revolving Doors', focuses on the negotiation of liminal and precarious spaces – understood as both oppressive and productive spaces. Thinking specifically about the gendering of labour, these contributions explore how women interact with various spaces often deemed inhospitable. Identifying the figure of the *'femme forte'* ('strong woman') as an archetype of sorts, Jeremy Lane has argued that 'depictions of the contemporary French workplace have struggled to represent the reality of its increased feminisation as anything other than an aberrant departure from traditional and allegedly natural gender roles'.[24] The *femme forte* is often portrayed either as an 'executive woman' who is an 'unnatural hybri[d] ... renouncing marriage and motherhood to pursue her career', or, as a working-class mother 'struggling to keep family and community together in a context of mass male unemployment' that 'can be reconciled with more traditional notions of femininity and care-giving' (pp. 171–2). The 'strong women' discussed in this part both challenge and, to a certain extent, expand the realities presented by Lane.

We first continue the discussion of migrants' labour explored in Rosenberg's chapter by considering the social entrapment of the body, more specifically how economic pressures, gender norms, and racist and ableist views relegate marginalised communities to precarious living and working spaces. Through Sara Ahmed's concept of the 'affect alien', Siham Bouamer examines how Philippe Faucon's film *Fatima* (2015) showcases the title character's alienation of labour as a cleaning lady – mainly as a consequence of her linguistic shortcomings and the stereotypical perceptions she faces – while at the same time exploring the process through which Fatima reaches a certain consciousness of her estrangement through poetry writing. Sonja Stojanovic argues that in a French social imaginary that often describes cashiers as lacking intellect, their bodies are meant to take centre stage. Focusing on the representation of cashiers in Marie-Hélène Lafon's *Gordana* (2012) and *Nos vies* ('*Our Lives*') (2017), Stojanovic suggests that this intense focus on the body – cast as chimerical, foreign and disabled – speaks to fears associated with migrant labour.

We then turn to the difficulties and strategies to resist the oppressive nature of certain heteropatriarchal work spaces, both in the corporate and working-class worlds. Dorthea Fronsman-Cecil traces the progressive demise of an executive woman in Delphine de Vigan's novel *Les heures souterraines* ('*Underground Time*') (2009) arguing that the mental harassment to which she is subjected at work also manifests itself through metaphors of being 'below'. Pondering the similarities to several other contemporary texts, Fronsman-Cecil questions the inability of 'corporate fictions' to imagine a different – and positive – ending for its women protagonists. Through an analysis of Anne Garréta's *Dans l'béton* (*'In Concrete'*) (2017), Jennifer Carr argues that the novel playfully subverts both paternal authority and the oftentimes masculinised physical work of 'modernisation'. Meanwhile, it reads the novel's nebulously post-war temporality as a further troubling of filiation and the gendered divisions that it perpetuates through bodies and language.

Finally, we focus on narratives that challenge what Sara Ahmed identifies as 'the scripts of heteronormative culture',[25] shaping alternate career paths for women that are 'no longer ... secured by the categories of "women" or "gender"' (p. 177). Amy Wigelsworth considers the question of space as it relates to work in Catherine Poulain's *Le grand marin* (*'Woman at Sea'*) (2016) and the protagonist's efforts to impose herself in the male-dominated spaces of the Alaskan fishing world. In parallel, the chapter highlights the extra-diegetic literary echo of the novelist's navigation of the French literary landscape. In the last chapter, Maxime Foerster focuses on the career of Marie-Pierre Pruvot, and her transition from a career as an artist performing in a Parisian transgender cabaret to becoming a teacher of French in a middle school in the suburbs of Paris. Through the analysis of a documentary about Pruvot's life and her published memoirs, the chapter foregrounds trans women at work in contemporary France.

In Part III, titled 'From Opening a Few Doors to Blowing the Doors Off', we explore the ways in which women take over and inhabit work spaces from which they are rejected – from subtle to overtly revolutionary acts. While the preceding chapters also involve position taking within work spaces and reassert that the personal is indeed political, this last section focuses more forcefully on movements or personal engagements that call for collective and public actions and changes, or that critique certain institutions.

We begin by examining the manifestations of activism and feminist engagements and communities to dismantle power structures restraining women's work in the decade following the events of May 1968. Considering women's *bénévolat militant* ('militant voluntary work'), Sandra Daroczi explores the successes and challenges of three specific activities: the publication of the French feminist journal *Le Torchon brûle* (*'The Burning Rag'*) (1971–3); the organisation of neighbourhood groups; and the creation of alternative childcare. Focusing on the last issue of the French feminist comic magazine *Ah! Nana* (1976–8), Valentina Denzel examines two illustrations by artist Chantal Montellier to show how they challenge the objectification, marginalisation and invisibility of women in the workforce; an act even more subversive considering the male-dominated state of the comic industry.

The next two contributions turn to women's activism in the media. Within the context of the fraught reception of the mediatisation of the #MeToo movement in France, Mercédès Baillargeon examines how author Vanessa Springora, in her book *Le Consentement* ('*Consent*') (2020), uncovers a culture of silence around powerful men's abuses in the context of the literary and cultural establishment, exposing some of France's deep-seated sexist biases. Through the study of interviews and television appearances, Leslie Kealhofer-Kemp focuses on the career and activism of actress Aïssa Maïga, in particular her discourse on the obstacles to accessing the French film industry. Considering the potential limitations of the interview platform as an activist space, the chapter assesses the shaping of leveraged spaces to advocate for change.

Finally, the closing section aims to literally assert women's visibility by reflecting on the significance of representing working women 'on screen' and to offer a lens through which future generations can re-imagine and contemplate what it means to be a woman at work in contemporary France. Loïc Bourdeau analyses two 'imperfect' character types – the lesbian and the 'old' woman – who are deemed 'selfish' by patriarchal standards in *Dix pour cent* ('*Call My Agent*') (2015–). The chapter argues that screening the 'taking up [of] space' of these women on television is, in itself, a 'militant' act. Johanna Montlouis-Gabriel's chapter closes the volume by proposing the forging of alternative paths she terms '*tracées*'. Examining Mame-Fatou Niang and Kaytie Nielsen's *Mariannes Noires* ('*Black Mariannes*') (2016), Montlouis-Gabriel investigates how the documentary highlights the strategies deployed by Black women to create pathways for themselves, while also showcasing the normality of 'Black [women's] Excellence' at work.

Taken together these contributions convey how women's experiences at work can range from states of exhaustion and oppression to survival and celebration. At the same time, they show how, through deliberate stances and actions, various work spaces can also become sites of liberation, justice and revolution. Offering a large scope of representations of women at work, this volume opens the door for further research and dialogues in gender and labour studies. The volume also speaks to the importance of cultural productions in highlighting and calling out issues that women face within various work spaces, as well as in offering a platform that allows us to imagine a future where inclusive and equitable work spaces are the norm.

Works Cited

Ahmed, Sara, *The Cultural Politics of Emotions* (Edinburgh: Edinburgh University Press, 2004).

—— *On Complaint* (Durham NC: Duke University Press, 2021).

—— *Queer Phenomenology: Orientations, Objects, Others* (Durham NC: Duke University Press, 2006).

Battagliola, Françoise, *Histoire du travail des femmes* (Paris: Éditions La Découverte, 2008).

Carlos, Marina, *I'll figure it out: How Ableism Impacts Disabled People's Lives* (2020), *www.marinacarlos.com/livre-book* (accessed 31 December 2021).

—— *Je vais m'arranger: Comment le validisme impacte la vie des personnes handicapées* (2020), *www.marinacarlos.com/livre-book* (accessed 31 December 2021).

Chrisafis, Angelique, 'Drawn from experience: meet the feminist author whose comic strips hit home', *Guardian*, 2 November 2018, *www.theguardian.com/books/2018/nov/02/drawn-from-experience-meet-the-feminist-author-whose-comic-strips-hit-home* (accessed 31 December 2021).

Damlé, Amaleena, *The Becoming of the Body: Contemporary Women's Writing in French* (Edinburgh: Edinburgh University Press, 2014).

Emma, 'Fallait demander' [blog], 9 May 2017, *https://emmaclit.com/2017/05/09/repartition-des-taches-hommes-femmes/* (accessed 31 December 2021).

Hafter, Daryl M., and Nina Kushner (eds), *Women and Work in Eighteenth-Century France* (Baton Rouge LA: Louisiana State University Press, 2015).

Lane, Jeremy F., *Republican Citizens, Precarious Subjects: Representations of Work in Post-Fordist France* (Liverpool: Liverpool University Press, 2020).

Lane, Jeremy F., and Sarah Waters (eds), 'Work in crisis: film, fiction and theory', special issue of *Modern & Contemporary France*, 26/3 (2018).

Maruani, Margaret, and Monique Meron (eds), 'Introduction', in *Un siècle de travail des femmes en France 1901–2011* (Paris: Éditions La Découverte, 2012).

Mennel, Barbara, *Women at Work in Twenty-First Century European Cinema* (Urbana IL: University of Illinois Press, 2019).

Soumahoro, Maboula, *Le Triangle et l'Hexagone: Réflexions sur une identité noire* (Paris: Éditions La Découverte, 2020).

'Universal Declaration of Human Rights', The United Nations, *www.un.org/en/about-us/universal-declaration-of-human-rights* (accessed 31 December 2021).

Vergès, Françoise, *A Decolonial Feminism*, translated by Ashley J. Bohrer with the author (London: Pluto Press, 2021).

—— *Un féminisme décolonial* (Paris: La Fabrique éditions, 2019).

—— *Une théorie féministe de la violence: Pour une politique antiraciste de la protection* (Paris: La Fabrique éditions, 2020).

Waters, Sarah, *Suicide Voices: Labour Trauma in France* (Liverpool: Liverpool University Press, 2020).

Notes

1 Margaret Maruani and Monique Meron (eds), 'Introduction', in *Un siècle de travail des femmes en France 1901–2011* (Paris: Éditions La Découverte, 2012), p. 50.

2 'Universal Declaration of Human Rights', *The United Nations*, *www. un.org/en/about-us/universal-declaration-of-human-rights* (accessed 31 December 2021).

3 Maruani and Meron, *Un siècle de travail des femmes en France*, p. 58. For an outline of laws and policies regarding women's work in France, see pp. 57–9.

4 Françoise Vergès, *Une théorie féministe de la violence: Pour une politique anti-raciste de la protection* (Paris: La Fabrique éditions, 2020), pp. 10–11.

5 Jeremy F. Lane, *Republican Citizens, Precarious Subjects: Representations of Work in Post-Fordist France* (Liverpool: Liverpool University Press, 2020), p. 2.

6 Maruani and Meron, *Un siècle de travail des femmes en France*, p. 7.

7 In addition to Maruani and Meron, see, for instance, Daryl M. Hafter and Nina Kushner (eds), *Women and Work in Eighteenth-Century France* (Baton Rouge LA: Louisiana State University Press, 2015); and Françoise Battagliola, *Histoire du travail des femmes* (Paris: Éditions La Découverte, 2008).

8 Barbara Mennel, *Women at Work in Twenty-First Century European Cinema* (Urbana IL: University of Illinois Press, 2019), p. 5.

9 Sara Ahmed, *Queer Phenomenology: Orientations, Objects, Others* (Durham NC: Duke University Press, 2006), p. 1.

10 We draw this conceptualisation from Jeremy Lane and Sarah Waters who propose that 'the workplace is a space [and] … also a prism through which to look inwards towards subjective, intimate and material experiences of work'. Jeremy Lane and Sarah Waters, 'Introduction', in 'Work in crisis: film, fiction and theory', special issue of *Modern & Contemporary France*, 26/3 (2018), 225.

11 Françoise Vergès, *Un féminisme décolonial* (Paris: La Fabrique éditions, 2019), p. 8. Françoise Vergès, *A Decolonial Feminism*, translated by Ashley J. Bohrer with the author (London: Pluto Press, 2021), p. 2.

12 Emma, 'Fallait demander' [blog], 9 May 2017, *https://emmaclit. com/2017/05/09/repartition-des-taches-hommes-femmes/* (accessed 31 December 2021).

13 See, for instance, Angelique Chrisafis, 'Drawn from experience: meet the feminist author whose comic strips hit home', *Guardian*, 2 November 2018, *www.theguardian.com/books/2018/nov/02/drawn-from-experience-meet-the-feminist-author-whose-comic-strips-hit-home* (accessed 31 December 2021).

14 Maboula Soumahoro, *Le Triangle et l'Hexagone. Réflexions sur une identité noire* (Paris: Éditions La Découverte, 2020), p. 135.

15 Vergès, *Un féminisme décolonial*, p. 43. Vergès, *A Decolonial Feminism*, p. 26.
16 Sarah Waters, *Suicide Voices: Labour Trauma in France* (Liverpool: Liverpool University Press, 2020), p. 55.
17 Siham Bouamer's chapter focuses on Philippe Faucon's *Fatima* (2015), but as she explains in the introduction, the film is an adaptation of Fatima Elayoubi's *Prière à la lune* (2006).
18 Amaleena Damlé, *The Becoming of the Body: Contemporary Women's Writing in French* (Edinburgh: Edinburgh University Press, 2014), p. 3
19 Damlé, *The Becoming of the Body*, p. 3.
20 Sara Ahmed, *On Complaint* (Durham NC: Duke University Press, 2021), p. 26.
21 Ahmed, *Queer Phenomenology*, p. 175.
22 Lane, *Republican Citizens, Precarious Subjects*, p. 106.
23 Mennel, *Women at Work*, pp. 24–51.
24 Lane, *Republican Citizens, Precarious Subjects*, p. 248.
25 Sara Ahmed, *The Cultural Politics of Emotions* (Edinburgh: Edinburgh University Press, 2004), p. 149.

Part I
Behind Closed Doors: Work and Intimate Spaces

Chapter 1
A Transmedial and Transtemporal Reading of Labour on the Run in Albertine Sarrazin's *L'Astragale*

Albertine Sarrazin's biography is marked by spatial confinement, being interned in a reformatory school at sixteen years old and imprisoned for almost a decade.[1] She completed her baccalaureate while incarcerated and escaped from the Institute Bon Pasteur (1953) and Doullens prison (1957), turning to sex work to survive.[2] This second escape is fictionally recounted in her 1965 novel *L'Astragale* ('*Astragal*'), in which the heroine Anne breaks her talus bone while jumping from the prison ramparts. She is rescued by her soon-to-be-lover Julien who funds her medical treatment and pays relatives and acquaintances to conceal and care for her. Few forms of labour can be freely chosen by Anne in the circumstances. First, she is doubly restricted as convict and convalescent, with limited access to legal or physical employment. Second, she is expected to work for free to repay her hosts, despite remuneration from Julien. Third, once (literally) back on her own two feet, Anne vows to reimburse Julien, instigating a reluctant return to sex work. These contextual contingencies notwithstanding, Anne exerts agency by rejecting or modifying various types of work, and bases decisions on her surrounding environment and entourage. This chapter provides a transmedial and transtemporal reading of these responses to labour,

specifically domestic and sex work, that are shown to have a disproportionate impact on women.[3] I make a case for this novel's lasting
relevance for feminist studies, several decades on from its first
publication.

L'Astragale caused great controversy. According to Karin
Schwerdtner, this is because delinquency was still considered unfem-
inine behaviour, and criminal women were conceptualised as rebels
rather than heroes.[4] A positive and renewed interest in this work has
recently emerged. In the past decade alone, *L'Astragale* has inspired
a *bande dessinée* (BD) ('graphic novel') and film of the same name
(both in black and white, highlighting the retrospective representation), and a new edition of the English translation has been printed,
prefaced by punk poet Patti Smith.[5] This can be explained in part by
a desire to trace the legacy of contemporary writing by francophone
sex workers, that has risen exponentially since the millennium.
Indeed, women's writing scholar Isabelle Boisclair identifies Sarrazin
as one of the few precursors to this field.[6] It is also logical that at a
time of increasing political potency within feminist movements –
#balancetonporc ('out your pig') being a prime example – we
should turn to the wilful action of our rebellious forebears for inspiration. A transtemporal reading of Sarrazin's *L'Astragale* is therefore
valuable on two counts: as a way of certifying the literary value of
writing by a criminal woman, that was obfuscated by the initial critical backlash; and to identify essential lessons for contemporary
feminism. The structural inequalities and injustices contested in this
novel pre-empt feminist activism of the 1970s in France and beyond,
and generate dramatic irony given enduring inequalities and injustices. Many of the problems faced by Anne and other female
characters on the labour market continue to affect women in France
today. Anne's radical reactions to unfair impositions of labour, as a
convicted woman hiding from the law in 1950s France, thus provide
a paradigm for feminist resistance of the future. It is in this vein that
I explore Anne's experiences and evaluation of domestic and sex
work, with transmedial reference to two adaptations of *L'Astragale*:
Anne-Caroline Pandolfo and Terkel Risbjerg's 2013 BD and Brigitte
Sy's 2015 film. I consider, in particular, the intersectional and postcolonial lens that Sy brings to Sarrazin's narrative plot, which
accentuates the protagonist's and author's Algerian heritage, and
provides allusions to the Algerian War of Independence (1954–62)
that took place at the time this story is set. These contextual elements

are almost entirely glossed over in the novel itself, as well as the BD, whose monochromic palette actually exaggerates the heroine's whiteness. I therefore examine how Sy's racially conscious adaptation advances the depiction of domestic and sexual labour for a contemporary audience. I focus on the representation of labour across three key spatial episodes: Pierre and Nini's 'guinguette'; Annie and Nounouche's apartment; and Anne's hotel room, Parisian streets and Jean's flat.

Domestic Work

Anne's first long-term hiding place is a former hotel owned by Pierre and Nini, Julien's acquaintances whom he pays to accommodate Anne. Although Anne is granted a whole room to herself, she feels trapped in their 'guinguette' ('roadhouse'), as though she had escaped from one prison only to be imprisoned elsewhere.[7] The narrative voice comments drily that Anne can at least lock *herself* into this new jail (p. 80). Anne's unease stems partly from a sense of debt and dependence, aggravated by Pierre and Nini who imply that she should pay for her keep. Their expectations are unwarranted since Julien supplies sufficient funds to cover Anne's protection and care (pp. 70–1), and her injury indisposes Anne for housework. Anne-as-narrator also explains that she would have done the same for an escaped convict were she in Julien's position (p. 71), doubtless to justify any inconvenience posed to her guardians, and to reject the idea that she is a 'kept woman' dependent on a man. The work demanded of Anne here, therefore, is not based on clear-cut transactions of labour in exchange for capital, but on the subjective emotions, desires and values of the two embittered owners.

Nini barely bothers to disguise her disregard for Anne, and signs of courtesy are presented as a hangover from Nini's days in the hotel trade: 'elle claironnait un "Alors, elle a bien dormi?" commercialement amène, elle tournait le bouton de la radio, ouvrait la fenêtre' (p. 43) ('she rang out with a professionally cheery, "Well now, did you sleep well?" she turned on the radio, opened the window' (p. 40)). Signs of affection are thus directed at Anne in the same impersonal fashion as airing the room, reflecting the dehumanising effects of monetised domestic labour. It takes little time for Nini's customer service patter to abate and for her to delegate tasks to Anne, as Anne relays to Julien: 'Nini m'a dit que, puisque je me déclarais ta femme, je n'avais qu'à m'occuper de ton linge' (p. 81) ('Nini told me that, since I called myself your wife, it was up to me to take care of your laundry' (p. 80)). This remark underscores the duties automatically anticipated of a wife, at a time when house-wifery was heralded as *the 'job for women'* to quote historian Claire Duchen.[8] While Anne endures the judging gaze of Pierre and Nini, Pedro, another runaway, receives a warmer reception, and is granted drinks on tap for him and Anne. If 'le client est roi' (p. 91) ('the customer is king' (p. 89)) this role is masculine in more than name, and Pedro's sense of entitlement is even more plainly displayed when he sleeps with Nini (p. 86). Labour at the guinguette is there-fore divided in line with conjugal and gender norms of the time. These scenes are noticeably absent from Sy's film, while Pandolfo and Risbjerg's BD remains faithful to the novel's narrative content. The pictorial characterisation in this work likewise constructs a clear sense of the heroes and villains of this piece, with Pierre and Nini's features looming large in many frames, and Pierre visibly oozes sweat to haptically convey his unapproachability (pp. 60, 99). Risbjerg's monochromic palette similarly juxtaposes spaces of oppression (black) and freedom (white). This binary representation of charac-ters and atmosphere echoes Sarrazin's narrative, that pits Pierre and Nini unambiguously against the anti-heroine Anne, and which underscores Anne's sense of entrapment, aggravated by unjust demands for 'women's work'.

The narrative intimates that Nini is deeply resentful of her personal circumstances; of having lost her youth and beauty (she is tellingly scathing of Anne's ample bust (p. 90)) and of occupying consecutively submissive roles. As Anne explains, 'Pour passer de l'état de servante à celui de maîtresse, Nini a dû s'aider de ses dons culinaires' (p. 38) ('To rise from the status of servant to that of mistress, Nini least [*sic*] have made good use of her talents as a cook' (p. 36)). Advancing her status as mistress of the house therefore begets Nini more labour. The narrator alludes to this concept again when Pierre insists that his wife 'n'est pas la bonniche' ('isn't some kind of maid'), acknowledging parenthetically, 'C'est vrai, on ne peut pas être et avoir été' (p. 43) ('That's true, one can't be one and have been one') (p. 41)). Anne's narrative statement undermines the notion that Nini's servitude is a thing of the past, and the word-play recalls the real Anne's (Sarrazin's) literary feats, which distinguish her definitively from the role of maid typically allocated to women. Anne consciously disassociates herself from signs of domesticity: she criticises Nini's sticky eggs (p. 42), signifier of cis-womanhood *par excellence*, and prefers to drink and smoke with the male guests while Nini cleans aggressively around them (p. 81). The ashtray fills up like a 'sin' between them, in stark opposition to the feminine, wholesome and generative charge connoted by Nini's eggs (p. 90). When Anne cleans, she does so to irritate rather than appease Nini, as a minimal release in a stifling environment. For instance, she purposely stains her sheets while washing Julien's shirts (p. 81). In sum, whether or not Nini serves Anne breakfast in bed – the initial point of contention (p. 43) – it will do little to narrow the gap between their increasingly disparate lives as 'skivvy' and liberated *demoiselle*.

Anne's rejection of domestic ideals reflects the founding premise of *The Feminine Mystique*, a critical commentary on the housewife ideal in the United States during the 1950s. Betty Friedan argued that to consign women's duties to housework stoppers their broader intellectual potential and personal flourishing. The time had come, she affirmed, 'when the voices of the feminine mystique ... [could] no longer drown out the inner voice that ... [was] driving women on to become complete'.[9] Anne's rejection of housewifely duties is doubly transgressive for that time, moreover, in contravening the feminine 'mystique' while refusing to comply with the demands of her present protectors. Anne's precarious living situation reminds us that gendered impositions of housework often affect less privileged women, contrary to Friedan's study that was criticised for focusing almost exclusively on white, affluent, suburban housewives.[10] In his BD illustrations, Ribsjerg also provides a portrait of Anne at both ends of the spectrum: sunbathing with a cigarette, a book by her side to denote literary projects; a lady of leisure and intellectual labour (p. 94).

Disadvantages aside, housework is presented as an enjoyable and wholesome activity at Anne's second 'safehouse'. Shortly after her ankle operation, Julien transfers Anne to his friend Annie's, an ex-sex worker turned tie maker who lives in a two-room flat in Paris with her daughter Nounouche (p. 94). Anne is only granted privacy during Julien's visits and the girls' weekly trips to La Santé prison to see Nounouche's father (p. 95), and she is under strict orders not to venture out to the local boulevard (p. 99). Despite this claustrophobic setting, Anne, Annie and Nounouche coexist initially in a state of mutual contentment. Anne feels compassion for Annie and her daughter and resolves to sew ties to assist them throughout her stay (pp. 97–9). Annie and Anne forge a merry atelier, stitching, singing and smoking together (p. 102), showing that genuine enjoyment and companionship can be gained from legitimate forms of paid labour; granted, the sewing machine is 'found' for them by Julien (p. 98). This scene also combines activities deemed traditionally feminine and masculine, if we follow Sarrazin's depiction of smoking as a man's activity at the guinguette. This convivial scene is noticeably lacking from Sy's cinematic adaptation, which results in a disappointingly one-dimensional representation of Anne's days on the run and undermines Anne's later reference to Annie as a reconciled friend. The need to reflect Anne's growing frustration within two hours of running time might explain this omission, yet it underplays the pleasure and collaboration to be gained from domestic labour as presented in Sarrazin's novel.

The BD succeeds in demonstrating pleasurable domestic collaboration through a scene of Anne and Annie sewing together, and when Anne voluntarily cleans the house with enthusiastic thoroughness during Annie and Nounouche's trips to the prison visiting rooms. Such tasks are easier for Anne since leaving the roadhouse, once her leg is largely healed, and is a way to surprise and please her hosts. It is implied, however, that Anne reaps pleasure largely from being left alone, as emphasised a few frames later when Annie walks in on Anne and Julien in bed, reinforcing the couple's limited moments of intimacy (pp. 120–3). The novel likewise stresses the importance of 'me time', although it shows housework to be valuable in and of itself. Cleaning the flat is vital within a modest living space and with professedly messier roommates (p. 94) and is also genuinely enjoyable. For one, Anne likes cleaning and tidying Annie's flat because there is no obligation to do so. Annie refuses Anne's help in light of her injury (p. 101) and housework thenceforward becomes an occasional and guilty pleasure of Anne's whenever the girls leave. She relishes the chance to discover the hitherto hidden recesses of the apartment (p. 103), savouring rare time alone and establishing a sense of at-homeness. Housework is entertaining in this setting, moreover, as Anne is made to feel welcome. She ends her cleaning routine by buying treats for the girls to prepare them a reciprocal 'accueil' (p. 104), which Anne mentions during a conversation with Julien in the BD. These narrative descriptions of domestic

labour resonate with the view of Marxist-feminist theorist Martha E.
Giménez:

> Domestic labour can include activities and experiences of agency,
> self-realisation, caring, reciprocity, and cooperation, which are the
> material basis for the emergence of needs and values critical of the
> selfish, competitive, and dehumanising world of capitalist work
> and social relations.[11]

At Annie's, housework provides unparalleled opportunity for crucial
me time on the one hand and tighter interpersonal connections on
the other. Anne and Annie complete chores in a reciprocal, co-operative and caring fashion, of their own volition. This shared economy
of labour is reinforced by the nominal parallels between the two
women, separated only by one 'i'. It also allows instances of self-realisation, enabling Anne to claim ownership of the space and
appreciate her roommates (pp. 103–4). Household chores are thus
completed in a way that nurtures rather than drains these two
women.

Cleaning at Annie's additionally allows for critical reflection on
comparatively 'dehumanising' forms of 'capitalist work and social
relations', namely those witnessed at Pierre and Nini's. Housework
at their place constitutes part of a wider money-making project to
profit from guests, which culminates in a cruel and dysfunctional
attempt to extract free labour from the subterfuge visitors themselves. Further, the parallels between this scheme and the hotel
industry – as with Nini's aforementioned customer-service rhetoric
– highlight the exploitative nature of capitalist systems in general.
Anne and Annie's approach to housework has the opposite objective and outcome; they split the workload to maximise each other's
comfort and pleasure as opposed to seeking individual fulfilment or
capital. This conveys the positive potential of what Giménez calls
'cooperative solutions' to the problems inherent to domestic labour
and its capitalisation, including 'the creation of partial communities, like cohousing; sharing domestic tasks with friends, relatives,
and neighbours, etc'.[12]

These happier memories notwithstanding, this women-centred
utopia reaches breaking point owing to the exigencies of a capitalist
economy, which imply that a steady income is needed to sustain
interpersonal relationships within a capitalist system and to thereby
make labour worthwhile. This is in keeping with the arguments of

Marxist-feminist theorist Sue Ferguson, that forms of labour under capitalism are not necessarily alienating, but that for activities to operate in the interest of 'life not capital ... workers must ... organise their labour according to revolutionary principles of cooperation'.[13] With this in mind, it is unsurprising that Anne and Annie's harmonious division of labour is only temporary, and Pandolfo, Risbjerg and Sy are arguably right to limit scenes of domestic solidarity in their adaptations. Tensions eventually arise in Sarrazin's novel owing to disputes over money: Anne wheedles cigarettes from Annie and Annie bemoans the price of groceries (pp. 116–17 and 119–20). Anne grows keenly aware of her lack of resources to the extent that, in her words, 'je n'ai plus à leur proposer que moi, moi nue' (p. 114) ('I have nothing to give them but myself, myself naked' (p. 111)). This pre-empts an imminent return to sex work.

Sex Work

Several men proposition Anne as she walks the streets of Paris following this argument with Annie (pp. 118–19), and she unceremoniously accepts an offer: 'Je suis absente, docile, je ne pense à rien. ... Et je ne lorgnerai plus jamais les poches d'Annie' (p. 119) ('I am absent, submissive, I don't think about anything ... And my eyes will never be riveted to Annie's pockets again' (p. 117)). The syntactical accent on her 'submissive' status, and lulling rhythm, recreate her steeling process, steadying her nerves for the task at hand – the matter-of-fact ending indicates that the experience was quick if not completely painless. The structural isolation of the final sentence stresses that the cost involved was a small price to pay for regained financial independence. This economic efficiency is reflected through visual economy in Sy's film: the footage is restricted to a swift verbal exchange between Anne and a client, and to fragmentary shots in a non-descript room: of the client's face as he orgasms; Sarrazin's (notably clothed) upper body; and the transfer of banknotes. The event, or non-event, is depicted as an unpleasant but practical transaction.

Despite its shortcomings, Sarrazin portrays sex work as relatively lucrative compared to labour-intensive options such as Annie's tailoring venture. The narrator hypothesises that Annie would need to spend hours on her *cravates* to match ten minutes' earnings from sex work (p. 97). As the friction peaks and Anne decides to leave

Annie's for good, these competitive financial rewards are what cement Anne's reversion to sex work. Earning more money is vital for Anne to furnish a more comfortable living situation for her and Julien (p. 128) and to repay him a percentage of her recovery and protection expenses – this is not because she feels indebted *per se*, but so that Julien will recognise that she loves him freely, not 'pour l'en remercier' ('to thank him' (p. 128)). Crucially, Anne believes that this will enable her to deflect competition from Julien's 'other woman' (p. 136). Legitimate and illegitimate forms of labour undertaken by Anne leave a great deal to be desired then, but sex work presents itself as one of the least unfulfilling options available to her as a marginal subject. The joys of financial independence are clearly conveyed in the BD, which includes images of Anne beaming as she purchases groceries, flowers and clothes, enjoying a sense of 'normality'. The monochrome blocks are replaced by mixed tones, to bring an impression of 'colour' (if not actual colour) back into her life. This BD also hints at Anne and Sarrazin's experiences of sex work at the age of sixteen, expressed via a barmaid's direct speech: 'bonne retape, ma douce' ('welcome back to the job, sweetie' (p. 145)), a key parallel between the protagonist's trajectory and the author's biography.

This money-making scheme is not without significant sacrifice. Anne's discomfort in this role is indisputable – physically and symbolically accentuated by the daily rain (p. 128) – and she fears assimilation. Anne's movements and comments can be considered instinctive responses to abject entities that, as theorised by Julia Kristeva, push us to insist 'Not me. Not that' as a defence against annihilation.[14] She avoids streetwalking and follows random routes, for example, because, in her words, 'je ne suis pas plus pute qu'autre chose' (p. 131) ('I don't seem more a whore than anything else' (p. 129)), implying that once one is singled out as a sex worker one becomes defined solely by that role. This appears to be the case for friends of Anne:

> Dans les bars où s'agglutinent les prostituées, j'ai retrouvé quelques mineures de Fresnes, qui tapinent en clandé jusqu'à l'âge requis pour la carte ... [M]es petites sœurs gardaient le même masque, pâle, marbré ou congestionné, les cernes maquillant les yeux, et cet air fade, anonyme, uniforme. (pp. 129–30)

> In the bars where prostitutes gather, I've run into several minors from Fresnes again, who are hustling on the sly until they're old

> enough to get their identity card ... [M]y little sisters would always
> wear the same mask – pale, mottled or flushed, dark circles under
> the eyes, and that stale, anonymous, uniform air. (p. 128)

Anne's 'younger sisters' are indistinguishable in their common role
and don the same sickly uniform. Anne's previous associations with
these women and sex work in Paris make it highly probable that she
could be included in their fold, emphasised by the term 'aggluti-
nent' (Southgate's translation 'gather' loses the sense of 'stickiness'
inherent to the original verb). Her reluctance is clear when she
feigns a case of mistaken identity: 'Je réponds que je ne m'appelle
pas Anne, que je fais ma "nouveauté" à Paris' (p. 130) ('I answer that
my name isn't Anne, that I'm making my "debut" in Paris' (p. 128)).
The threat of abjection attached to prostitution therefore constitutes Anne's prime grievance against the industry. In Sy's film, Anne
finds it difficult to enter the market because of contextual contingencies rather than personal disinclination: Anne walks through an
area occupied by older sex workers, who claim there is no room for a
new and younger member, and when asked whether she did time at
Doullens, Anne responds in the affirmative. Anne heads to a hotel
recommended for younger workers but is greeted by a hostile
manager and leaves almost immediately. This version of events is far
less rosy than in Sarrazin's prose, with fewer savoury avenues open to
Anne, and a less jubilant reception from other sex workers. Sy
refuses to overplay Anne's agency. In this way, the film delivers an
arguably more realistic reflection of the difficulties faced by sex
workers in 1950s Paris and today.

As for the stratification of collective identity based on employment and skillsets – glaringly apparent among the 'minors from
Fresnes' described above – this is not unique to sex work. Anne and
her fellow inmates at Fresnes prison, for one, are assigned groups
'd'après ce qu'elles savent faire' (p. 25) ('according to what they
know how to do' (p. 22)). These sex workers and prisoners are then
likely to feel alienated from themselves and others as they adapt
their self-development to these roles.[15] The narrator similarly
conveys the tedium involved in regulated work, by comparing sex
work *in situ* and retail:

> Elles restent au bar: elles attendent que la comptée vienne à elles,
> elles n'ont rien d'autre à faire; elles attendent ... comme attendent
> les vendeurs à la porte des boutiques, les mains au dos, là-haut, au
> sortir du royaume des putains. (p. 130)

They stay at the bar: they wait for the customer to come to them, they have nothing else to do; they wait ... as shopkeepers wait at the doors of their shops, hands behind their backs, up there, at the exit from the kingdom of whores. (p. 128)

This literary image is aptly recreated in the BD, in which the illustrations of sex workers in bars or on the street resemble mannequins modelling clothes for sale, implying their status as alienated workers and objects of consumption (pp. 129, 144–5). Sy omits this picture from her film, with references to sex work appearing in more discrete places such as apartment blocks or rooms, emphasising Anne's loneliness. In each case, Anne clearly disapproves of regimented forms of labour, whether paid or unpaid, institutionalised or marginal (though the reference to an 'identity card' and minors working 'on the sly' in the preceding paragraph indicates that sex work was still fairly regulated in the 1950s, despite the closure of the *maisons closes* the previous decade). One of sex work's few attractions for Anne is the lack of a set schedule or training plan (p. 131). Working on her terms and unfixed turf, away from other employees, is also a shrewd business move: her aloofness and nonconformity to 'le genre' (p. 131) ('the type' (p. 129)) are attractive assets on the market. In sum, sex work does not *de facto* entail depersonalisation, discipline, boredom and minimal wages. Anne finds a more fulfilling version of the job by navigating free zones and distinguishing herself from the workforce.

There are, nonetheless, more worrying motives behind Anne's movements. Anne is obliged to work incognito lest she be recognised and recaptured (p. 131), and she is afraid of the police because she has no identification documents to show them (pp. 130–1). Anne also avoids sleeping with the same men twice (pp. 130–1) and she consistently leaves her hotel room in an immaculate condition since, as she explains, 'j'ai un peu le trac des femmes de ménage, ensuite parce que, peut-être, je n'y reviendrai plus jamais.' (p. 129) ('chambermaids scare me a little, secondly because, maybe, I'll never come back to it again' (p. 127)). We have seen how cleaning was refused as an oppressive imposition of labour at Pierre and Nini's and accepted as a form of self-realisation and relationship building at Annie's, while here it becomes a means of survival. One imagines Anne's fear of the cleaners stems from the possibility of them uncovering her identity and informing the authorities, and Anne's rationale thus reflects the intensity of her precarity: at risk of discovery in her place of rest as well as outside of it. The possibility of not returning also alludes to the danger of being harmed or killed at work. Clients have the unequivocal upper hand in this exchange. Even Jean who invites Anne to stay with him indefinitely and thus knowingly harbours a criminal – keeping photos and clothes of hers to boot – considers himself safe from the law as her client (p. 163).[16] Hence, while Anne insists on the benefits of working alone and anonymously as part of her pursuit for independence, one cannot help but interpret this approach to sex work as a dangerous by-product of her illegal status.

The extent of Anne's precarity is even more heavily accentuated in Sy's film. Anne dons a blonde wig and there are several references to her false identification documents, visual and verbal markers of being on the run – the incongruousness of Anne's wig reflects the transparency of her invented identity. Conversely, the contrast between Anne's dark skin and fair hair alludes to racist social perceptions of the time, as blondeness helps Anne to go unnoticed in Parisian society. In addition, sex-work scenes are darkly lit, to invoke the threat that they represent, and Anne's assertion that 'I'm at home everywhere' drips with irony. A sex worker, opium user and friend of Annie's also informs on Anne to the police to avoid incriminating her drug dealer and losing her daughter to social services. This exposes additional forms of social marginalisation affecting sex workers and emphasises Anne's vulnerability. In Sy's film Anne is actually stopped and interrogated by police too, after arousing suspicion for being at a night club with two Black men. During her interrogation, the sound of the men's screams is heard offscreen as they are 'dealt' with by prison guards, and Anne is dismissed so that the remaining guard can 'assist' his colleagues. The film thus draws attention to more dangerously marginalised subjects and Sy's transtemporal interpretation integrates a racial optic, a reminder, at the heart of the 'Justice pour Adama' ('Justice for Adama') movement, of the severe abuse experienced by racial minorities at the hands of French authorities. Sy likewise incorporates a postcolonial reading of social precarity by accentuating the protagonist's, and by extension Sarrazin's, Algerian heritage, and by alluding to the Algerian War of Independence, ongoing at this point of Sarrazin's autofictional story. When Anne and Julien witness a street police search, for instance, and promptly turn around, Anne reassures Julien that the police are too preoccupied with Algerians to bother anyone else, to which Julien replies, 'with your Swedish air, we'll be fine', a satirical reminder that Anne too could be stopped consequent to racist or nationalist prejudices. Both actors cast in these two roles are also French of Algerian descent, which lends additional and embodied irony to Julien's joke, as the line hints at a shared collective memory outside of the cinematic frame. Sy thus provides a racially conscious and postcolonial interpretation of Sarrazin's plot, to attest to past and present racial and national inequalities in France, and to provide an intersectional portrait of Anne's social precarity.

Despite this ongoing vulnerability, Anne ultimately finds relative stability and security in sex work in Sarrazin's novel courtesy of Jean, a mechanic who showers Anne with husbandly attentions (p. 140). He wines and dines her, tucks her into bed at night, provides a shoulder to cry on, takes her shopping and offers to buy a house for them, evolving a classic boyfriend-girlfriend experience into a full-scale *Pretty Woman* saga (pp. 127, 138–9 and 162–7). We observe Anne's inner turmoil as she assesses the upsides of this situation against her personal aversions. On the one hand, Anne finds Jean neither especially attractive nor unattractive, so that working for him is neither unbearable nor jeopardises her commitment to Julien (p. 167). Jean's flat is also conveniently located in a neighbourhood where 'il est normal de vivre en concubinage avec beaucoup plus vieux ou beaucoup plus jeune que soi' (p. 166) ('it's normal to live with someone much older or younger than yourself' (p. 164)) thereby sparing them from suspicion. Even so, Anne resents her renewed role as 'le colis' (p. 164) ('the package' (p. 162)), carried first by Julien and now by Jean. Jean's devotion and her performance of wifely duties make her equally uneasy, as demonstrated through the disgust she expresses when Jean relishes her cooking (p. 165). Prior to meeting Jean, she seldom stayed with clients overnight, opting for brief, impersonal transactions (pp. 129 and 139), and this semi-permanent and intimate alternative deprives Anne of newfound freedoms. She continues to earn money for Julien on the side and informs Jean with harsh honesty that 'je rentre ici tous les soirs, ou presque. Pourquoi? Parce que ça m'arrange' (p. 166) ('I come back here every evening, or almost. Why? Because it suits me' (p. 164)). These actions enable Anne to sustain a degree of independence and to diminish, I believe, a hypocrisy that she deplores in this monetised relationship. Sex work of this kind thus involves Anne compromising her convictions: she is uncomfortable with reneging on her independence and romantic 'authenticity', yet continuing to meet clients and to be frank with Jean vindicates her acceptance of the support that he proposes (p. 140). We are left in no doubt about the human cost, however, as Anne turns to drinking as a means of coping with the physical and emotional toll of this labour (p. 164).

These advantages and disadvantages of a more permanent clientele are neatly displayed through the antithetical depiction of Jean in the film and the BD. Jean in Sy's film – here named 'Roger' – makes only token appearances, and the emphasis is placed on Anne's scathing indifference. Sy's focus on Anne's subjective responses to Jean's attentions, amplified by the minimal representation of her male client's views or feelings, exemplifies film scholar Russell Campbell's observation about world cinema that '[i]f one of the projects of the patriarchal paradigm is to reduce the prostitute on screen to an object of male desire, a vital feminist response has been to insist on the representation of female subjectivity'.[17] In the BD, however, Jean is presented as a gentle giant with soft features, who comforts Anne in times of distress. Anne is portrayed as comparatively heartless, reinforced by the pictorial positioning: Jean occupies the bottom left-hand corner of the frames, while Anne looms over him from the top right, or via close-ups that fill entire frames. Contrariwise, the umbrella Jean carries is finished by a knife-like point indicative of his predatorial power, reinforced by his great girth (p. 163). This more nuanced representation, like the novel, reflects the demands of contemporary sex-worker theorists that we avoid categorising sex workers as either wholly victims or fully consenting agents.[18]

This period with Jean is succeeded by a series of trials and tribulations with Julien: Julien is arrested (p. 143); Anne burgles the office of a client to secure some funds for Julien (p. 147); and Annie steals the money (p. 157–9). In the end, Anne is still able to offer Julien a respectable token of reimbursement when they are reunited (p. 176), and her compromising labours are thus successfully recompensed. Julien initially wavers over his commitment to Anne because of the benefits that his other lover presents: a residence in Paris and an 'honest' job that wins his family's approval (pp. 187–8), yet he is moved by a collection of Anne's letters to commit himself wholly to her (pp. 185–8). With dramatic irony she is caught by the police the next day, and the frogmarched Anne is described as 'claudiquant à peine' (p. 192) ('hardly limping at all' (p. 190)). This suggests a prevailing form of freedom even while she returns to her status of confined criminal. The success of Anne's letters also pre-empts Sarrazin's eventual fame as a writer that is fictionally narrated in *La Traversière*, in which Albe secures work as a journalist and published author.[19] This presents itself as the most freeing form of labour for Albertine Sarrazin. It is highly appropriate, then, that the BD should end simply with words transcribed on a blank page (p. 221), and that Sy should include several scenes in her film that reflect Anne's literary ambitions: of Anne writing, of Julien reciting lines of her poetry by heart, and of Annie reading aloud from Anne's journal.

Conclusion

All forms of labour in *L'Astragale* are shown to entail a certain level of sacrifice, especially for Anne whose movements are limited as an injured female convict on the run. Ultimately, the only choice available to Anne is to decide what work and rules she is beholden to and to negotiate accordingly. And it is these mitigated choices that prove exemplary for feminist action then and now. At the *guinguette*, Anne refuses to comply with the gendered division of domestic labour, while she is physically incapacitated and legally restrained. This refusal demonstrates an impressive strength of conviction that we would do well to imitate today, at a time when women still undertake the majority of unpaid housework within heterosexual relationships.[20] Conversely, the narrator is unforgiving of Nini's begrudging acceptance of her 'lot', which encourages us to reflect on the types of labour that we accept and whether we are working in good faith. Pandolfo and Risbjerg's faithful reflection of these events through BD imagery, contrary to Sy's omissions, does justice to the value of domestic work and spaces in Sarrazin's *L'Astragale*, that reflects glaring gendered inequalities of the past and present. In both this BD and novel, Anne's time at Annie and Nounouche's reveals that domestic work can provide opportunity for community-building, and the female characters are able to share housework constructively in a way that allows for reciprocal self-advancement. Within a capitalist economy, however, sex work is shown to be the most financially viable and logistically freeing form of paid labour available to women in France, especially socially marginalised women, even though it involves palpable social abjection and severe demands of the body and mind. The BD for instance emulates the pleasures inherent in buying goods from money earned in sex work, in addition to associated pains. It is mostly the pitfalls of sex work that Sy brings to the fore in her cinematic interpretation of *L'Astragale*, which she enriches with an intersectional and postcolonial lens. Sy's adaptation stresses the level of racist attitudes at the time Anne's story is set, which continues to carry devastating consequences in France today. These contemporary interpretations by Pandolfo, Risbjerg and Sy thus reflect the lasting significance of the issues raised in Sarrazin's *L'Astragale* in relation to domestic and sex work, particularly from an intersectional feminist perspective, and we have seen that the revived zest for 'bad girls' of the 1960s is vindicated: many of the inequalities and injustices affecting Anne as a marginalised woman in 1950s France endure to this day, and Anne's radical resistance to and renegotiation of demands for labour teach us to be bolder in our own feminist strategies, as women of a later and arguably more privileged generation.

Works Cited

Albertine Sarrazin: Albertine en liberté, France Culture, *INA*, 29 March 1968.

Boisclair, Isabelle, 'L'agentivité sex/tex/tuelle de la travailleuse du sexe à travers le prisme de l'écriture au *Je*', *Erudit*, 32/1 (2019), 35–47.

Campbell, Russell, *Marked Women: Prostitutes and Prostitution in the Cinema* (Madison WI: University of Wisconsin Press, 2006).

Duchen, Claire, 'Occupation housewife: the domestic ideal in 1950s France', *French Cultural Studies*, 2/4 (1991), 1–11.

Ferguson, Sue, *Women and Work: Feminism, Labour, and Social Reproduction* (Toronto: Between the Lines, 2019).

Friedan, Betty, *The Feminine Mystique* (New York: W. W. Norton and Co., 1997 [1963]).

Gill, Jo, '"Quite the Opposite of a Feminist": Phyllis McGinley, Betty Friedan and Discourses of Gender in Mid-Century American Culture', *Women's History Review*, 22/3, 422–39.

Giménez, Martha E., *Marx, Women and Capitalist Social Reproduction: Marxist Feminist Essays* (Chicago IL: Haymarket, 2019).

Kristeva, Julia, *Pouvoirs de l'horreur: Essai sur l'abjection* (Paris: Seuil, 1980).

L'Astragale, dir. by Brigitte Sy (Alma Films, 2015).

Marx, Karl, 'Unalienated Labour', in Lawrence H. Simon (ed.), *Karl Marx: Selected Writings* (Indianapolis IN: Hackett, 1994), pp. 58–67.

Merteuil, Morgane, *Libérez le féminisme!* (Paris: L'Editeur, 2012).

Niget, David, 'David Niget – Mauvaises filles: incorrigibles et rebelles', *Librairie Mollat*, 14 December 2016, *www.youtube.com/watch?v=sMzgh_QxSjs* (accessed 23 November 2021).

Pandolfo, Anne-Carole, and Risbjerg, Terkel, *L'Astragale*, intro. by Jean-Jacques Pauvert (Paris: Sarbacane, 2013).

Pfefferkorn, Roland, 'Le Partage inégal des "tâches ménagères"', *Framespa*, 7 (2011).

Sarrazin, Albertine, *Astragal*, trans. by Patsy Southgate and intro. by Patti Smith (London: Serpent's Tail, 2014 [2013]).

Sarrazin, Albertine, *L'Astragale* (Paris: Pauvert, 1965).

Sarrazin, Albertine, *La Traversière* (Paris: Pauvert, 1966).

Schwerdtner, Karin, 'Errances interdites: La Criminalité au féminin dans *L'Astragale* d'Albertine Sarrazin', *Etudes françaises*, 40/3 (2004), 111–27.

Notes

1　From 1804 to 1958 in France, fathers could legally intern their children on the grounds of unruly behaviour. David Niget, 'David Niget – Mauvaises filles: Incorrigibles et rebelles', *Librairie Mollat*, 14 December 2016, *www.youtube.com/watch?v=sMzgh_QxSjs* (accessed 23 November 2021).

2　This is the version of events as presented in *Albertine Sarrazin: Albertine en liberté*, *France Culture, INA*, 29 March 1968.

3　The terms 'sex work' and 'sex worker' are preferred in this study, and the words 'prostitution' and 'prostitute' are used only where a pejorative connotation is implied in a referenced case.

4　Karin Schwerdtner, 'Errances interdites: La Criminalité au féminin dans *L'Astragale* d'Albertine Sarrazin', *Etudes françaises*, 40/3 (2004), 112–3, 118.

5　Anne-Caroline Pandolfo and Terkel Risbjerg, *L'Astragale*, intro. by Jean-Jacques Pauvert (Paris: Sarbacane, 2013); *L'Astragale*, dir. by Brigitte Sy (Alma Films, 2015); Albertine Sarrazin, *Astragal*, trans. by Patsy Southgate and intro. by Patti Smith (London: Serpent's Tail, 2014 [2013]).

6　Isabelle Boisclair, 'L'Agentivité sex/tex/tuelle de la travailleuse du sexe à travers le prisme de l'écriture au *Je*', *Erudit*, 32/1 (2019), 35.

7　Albertine Sarrazin, *L'Astragale* (Paris: Pauvert, 1965), p. 39; and Sarrazin, *Astragal*, p. 32. All translations are taken from this edition.

8　Claire Duchen, 'Occupation Housewife: The Domestic Ideal in 1950s France', *French Cultural Studies*, 2/4 (1991), 1. Emphasis in the original.

9　Betty Friedan, *The Feminine Mystique* (New York: W. W. Norton and Co., 1997 [1963]), p. 396.

10　Jo Gill, '"Quite the Opposite of a Feminist": Phyllis McGinley, Betty Friedan and Discourses of Gender in Mid-Century American Culture', *Women's History Review*, 22/3, 425. It should be noted though that Sarrazin received a bourgeois education, as explained in *Albertine Sarrazin: Albertine en liberté*.

11　Martha E. Giménez, 'Loving Alienation: The Contradictions of Domestic Work' (2006), in *Marx, Women and Capitalist Social Reproduction: Marxist Feminist Essays* (Chicago IL: Haymarket, 2019), p. 269.

12　Giménez, 'Loving Alienation: The Contradictions of Domestic Work', p. 272.

13   Sue Ferguson, *Women and Work: Feminism, Labour, and Social Reproduction* (Toronto: Between the Lines, 2019), e-book, loc. 2844.

14   Julia Kristeva, *Pouvoirs de l'horreur: Essai sur l'abjection* (Paris: Seuil, 1980), p. 10.

15   As per Karl Marx's thesis on 'Alienated Labor', in Lawrence H. Simon (ed.), *Karl Marx: Selected Writings* (Indianapolis IN: Hackett, 1994), pp. 58–67.

16   This is no longer the case since the implementation of the Loi n° 2016–444 penalising clients.

17   Russell Campbell, *Marked Women: Prostitutes and Prostitution in the Cinema* (Madison WI: University of Wisconsin Press, 2006), p. 386.

18   See, in particular, Morgane Merteuil, *Libérez le féminisme!* (Paris: L'Editeur, 2012), p. 106.

19   See Albertine Sarrazin, *La Traversière* (Paris: Pauvert, 1966).

20   As argued by Roland Pfefferkorn in 'Le Partage inégal des "tâches ménagères"', *Framespa*, 7 (2011), para. 1 and 3.

Chapter 2

Good Housekeeping: Domestic Noir and Domestic Work in Leïla Slimani's *Chanson douce*

CIARA GORMAN

Leïla Slimani's Prix Goncourt-winning *Chanson douce* ('*Lullaby*') has enjoyed both commercial and critical success since its publication in 2016, capturing the public imagination in spite of its harrowing subject matter.[1] The novel charts the relationship between a middle-class Parisian couple, Myriam and Paul Massé, and Louise, whom they hire as a nanny so that Myriam can take up paid employment outside the home. Glowing references testify to Louise's excellence, and she initially lives up to her reputation as 'the perfect nanny',[2] positively transforming the lives of the Massés by caring for their young children, Adam and Mila, and managing the majority of their housekeeping. However, a lifetime spent in service to others eventually takes its toll on Louise and cracks begin to appear in her perfect façade. Desperate to stay in the home that she has come to consider her own, Louise unsuccessfully attempts to entice Myriam into having a third baby. Ultimately, she comes to see Adam and Mila as obstacles to this goal, and her story ends where the novel begins: with the murder of the children that she cares for.

Louise's longing for stability and inclusion is, in large part, due to her existence on the fringes of life. Sarah Arens highlights Louise's spatial marginality, suggesting that the location of her home in a run-down Parisian suburb draws on well-recognised images of Paris as a city of 'social inequality, violence and poverty' to add to her characterisation as an isolated figure.[3] Expanding on this analysis of the connection between place and Louise's killer aesthetics, I focus in this chapter on the other significant space in the novel: the domestic space, which Slimani portrays as a dual place of threat and intimacy, terror and love. I suggest that Louise's emotional and economic marginality persists even in the heart of the home where she is a near-constant presence, and that this isolation amongst intimates is a key factor in her turn from carer to killer.

Given the interplay between the paradoxical and often violent nature of the home in *Chanson douce* and the novel's focus on the subjective experience of its complex female protagonists, I position it in the category of domestic noir. A contemporary and capacious subgenre of crime fiction, domestic noir is concerned with themes of family, betrayal, love and the ambiguity of people and places considered to be safe or even sacred.[4] Women's desires, labour and independence are among its other salient themes. Julie Rodgers has demonstrated how Slimani articulates these issues through the lens of mother-work and care work: Myriam and Louise are both held hostage by unrealistic standards of mothering, and the erasure of their sense of self leads them to depression and crime.[5] Drawing on this account of the consequences of reproductive labour on the labourer, I wish to examine the other part of Louise's nannying job: domestic work. More specifically, I explore how, through this work, Louise destroys the safe haven that she is hired to create. In doing so, I build on the analysis of Jessica Rushton, who similarly identifies domestic work as Louise's chosen outlet for violence and reads her as a new avatar of the nineteenth-century maidservant.[6] I suggest that Louise may alternatively be read as an innovative representation of the dangerous intimate in domestic noir – commonly portrayed as an abusive partner, relative or friend, and here reimagined by Slimani in the figure of the nanny, whose relationship to her employers is as delicate and personal as that of a lover. I will begin with a brief exposition of the domestic noir themes adopted and adapted by Slimani in *Chanson douce* and will then examine the cost of relying on Louise's 'good housekeeping' to create a happy home – and how the Massés ultimately pay for it with more than their money.

Reading *Chanson douce* as Domestic Noir

Julia Crouch coined the term 'domestic noir' in 2013 to describe the emerging trend of crime novels interrogating domesticity, violence, the subjective experiences of women and the complexities – and latent threat – of interpersonal relationships.[7] At the heart of the subgenre are female protagonists who wrestle with 'the complicated intersections between feminism, ambition, family, sex and desire', as exemplified by Myriam's struggles with postpartum depression and guilt over returning to paid employment.[8] They are often both the perpetrators and victims of violence; Louise, for instance, is unequivocally guilty of the murders of Adam and Mila and has also been subjected to physical and emotional abuse throughout her life. Like other domestic noir narratives, *Chanson douce* interrogates the 'tropes and mythologies' layered around women in fiction and in real life.[9] Rodgers details the extreme pressure that both Myriam and Louise are under to fulfil fantasies of perfection in mother-work, represented respectively by the illusory ideals of the self-sacrificing mother and the infallible 'Mary Poppins' nanny figure.[10] I further suggest that romanticised notions about domestic work are equally pernicious to both women. In keeping with the reality of domestic labour as a highly feminised sector where women's contributions go 'unrecognised and consequently unpaid',[11] women alone in *Chanson douce* seem responsible for 'keeping house' and their struggles to do so go largely ignored. The consequences of the emotional and financial precarity engendered by such gross dismissal of the fundamental work of sustaining human life are made clear, as Louise takes recourse in subtle and overt violence to deal with the pressure that she labours under.

Domestic noir is equally marked by a feminist approach to setting: like its antecedents, the Gothic novel and the marriage thriller, domestic noir disrupts the notion of the home as a 'sanctuary'.[12] Its female protagonists may spend a lot of time in the home, but they 'are not at home there', finding themselves trapped as often by violent ideologies around motherhood and femininity, success and productivity as by abusive partners and souring intimate relationships.[13] From the moment we open *Chanson douce* and find children lying dead and dying amongst their toys, we are called to engage with the home as a crime scene; the illusion of its safety is irreparably shattered, and the novel continues to emphasise this unsafety through the lens of reproductive and domestic labour, which fatigues and depresses both Myriam and Louise. Just as both mother and nanny are subject to the pressure of impossible standards in mother-work,[14] Louise is shown to be no less affected by the draining nature of running a home simply because she is paid to do it. The difficulty is in fact magnified for Louise by pressure to perform as a consistently flawless employee, and by the increasingly blurred boundaries between her work and private life – making the domestic (work)space in *Chanson douce* one of concentrated harms.

Bernice M. Murphy notes that domestic noir builds on a tradition of 'female-focused psychological suspense thrillers' where intimate relationships, 'be they marital, romantic or familial … represent the greatest source of threat'.[15] In *Chanson douce*, that intimate relationship is based on the transactional exchange of money for labour, but is no less susceptible to rancour, betrayal or unexpected violence. Louise might be a stranger whom the Massés pay to become part of the secret inner workings of their lives, but their relationship is as personal as that between partners; she and Myriam share a cup of tea in the morning, a glass of wine at night, and Myriam looks to her for advice and addresses 'mots doux' (p. 198) ('compliments' (p. 165)) to her. It also carries the same kind of threat: Louise's deep involvement in the Massés' lives means that she is ideally placed to manipulate and terrorise them. Illusion and duplicity are key concerns in domestic noir and in *Chanson douce*; neither the home nor its inmates are what they appear to be. Slimani's particular take on core domestic noir elements is thus mediated through the domestic worker, whose labour both makes and breaks the home she works in. I turn now to an examination of how this is done.

Creating the Cradle: Domestic Work and the Home

Louise is hired by the Massés primarily for childcare, so that Myriam can take up a position at her friend's law firm and alleviate her post-partum depression. Although childcare itself implies a certain amount of domestic labour – preparing meals for the children, cleaning up after them – from Myriam's guidance about the care of certain ornaments and garments when Louise arrives for her first day of work, we can extrapolate that she is also expected to take on a range of housekeeping duties. This is the case for many nannies, but the extent of Myriam's expectations is never made clear; neither is

Louise's pay, nor what the arrangements are for her overtime.[16] What is clear is that Louise approaches household tasks with a zeal that is perhaps unexpected. She mends clothes without being asked, washes the curtains of grime and keeps the kitchen spotless at all times. Gone are the piles of unopened envelopes and discarded toys; under the iron fist of Louise, the Massé home is transfigured into a 'parfait intérieur bourgeois' (p. 37) ('an ideal bourgeois interior' (p. 22)), full of light and space. With this new order comes harmony: the children are better behaved, the Massé parents are more relaxed, and even Myriam is now 'impatiente comme une amoureuse' (p. 63) ('impatient as a lover' (p. 45)) on the tram home from work, yearning to be back in the home that she once found carceral and stifling.

I suggest that this profound shift in the dynamic of the Massé home is due to more than Louise's evident efficiency in completing household tasks. Gaston Bachelard theorises a deep connection between the emotional wellbeing of a household and what he terms 'housewifely care': tasks such as polishing precious objects, mindfully decorating interiors and generally tending to the emotional needs of a house's inhabitants.[17] Such care, he argues, turns the house into a 'large cradle':[18] an idealised home that nourishes and shelters all who live there. Louise has extensive practice in this art of making a house a home, demonstrating her proficiency by hanging lavender sachets in the wardrobes and always having fresh flowers on display. Her sensitivity to the emotional dynamic of domestic work is most evident in the kitchen, where nourishing meals, appetising smells and handmade tablecloths cultivate an image of domestic bliss that spiritually, as well as physically, nourishes the Massé family. Her culinary marvels are devoured by the children and enchant the friends and colleagues whom Myriam and Paul begin to invite for dinner – allowing them to establish social connections, advance their careers, increase their income and generally rediscover a *joie de vivre* that is noticeably lacking in the life of the woman holding their lives together. As the Massés thrive, their employee slips further into emotional and financial precarity, widening the already significant class gap between them. Louise is cut off from a personal social life, spending so much time at the Massé apartment that she goes home merely to sleep and change, and no matter how vital her labour is to the Massés, her salary seems insufficient for her to pay her rent on time.[19] Her dreams – of beautiful clothes, running away to Greece, belonging to a family unit – are fulfilled only in a warped and demeaning way: she gets new clothes, but they are Myriam's cast-offs; she goes on holiday, but as their babysitter; she is part of their family, but only when they pay her to be so. The benefits of Louise's expertise in 'housewifely care' seem to run in one direction only.

The connection between the new paradigm governing the Massé home and their increased happiness, productivity and success testifies to the power of the 'affective dimension of the home' to shape its inhabitants' relationship to the outside world and to each other.[20] However, maintaining this positive atmosphere requires enormous effort, and *Chanson douce* makes clear that under the loving veneer of the Massé home hides a whirlpool of exhaustion, a void of burnout, particularly for the women to whom its upkeep is consigned. The physical exertion required by scrubbing, cooking and tidying, coupled with the ceaseless emotional burden of attending to the needs of its denizens, is presented as a threat to the health of both Myriam and Louise. The intimacy of the home – created not just by the relationships that it shelters, but by the presence of personal items, the homely call of soft furnishings, the private rooms – at once provides both women with a sense of shelter and belonging, and paradoxically turns them into automatons. Each experiences a period of depression, claustrophobia and indifference to the children that they love when their reserves are depleted by the strain of running a household. Like the home, housework itself is shown to have an affective dimension that can positively and negatively affect she who carries it out. Slimani's use of the lens of domestic work helps expand the domestic noir concept of the unsafe home beyond the notion that danger strikes when things go wrong; the effort of keeping things *right* appears equally threatening to the women who live there.

Chanson douce further undermines illusions of the home as a neutral or positive environment by exposing the power dynamics at play there. Many domestic noir narratives do this through the lens of romantic relationships; Slimani adds a new dimension to this interrogation by transposing the tensions of the employer-employee relationship to the home – notably the pressure of performance. Louise must shoulder the burden of domestic work that once crippled her employer and do it with a smile, suppressing any of the ambivalence or lassitude that people feel about housekeeping in the name of her performance as 'the perfect nanny'. Maintaining this persona is vital for Louise, as the Massés' delight in – and indeed their dependence on – her efficiency secures her a steady source of income and a place in their family unit. However, Louise is obliged to be constantly wary, as this position is always unstable: any conflict with her employers carries the potential consequences of dismissal, ruptured relationships with the children she cares for, and a stain on her reputation that may prevent her from securing another job.[21] Indeed, at several points in the novel the Massés' ideas of what is acceptable or not clash with Louise's, and the urge to dismiss her is momentarily very strong in their minds. Louise works hard to turn the apartment into a place where the Massés feel relaxed, protected and secure, but she cannot benefit herself from the tranquillity of the domestic haven that she has created, separated from the fruits of her labour by the contingency of her employment. However, in keeping with the domestic noir theme of illusion, it gradually becomes clear that the power dynamics between Louise and the Massés are not as clear-cut as that between the powerful employer and the precarious employee. The perfect nanny soon reveals a more sinister side, as Louise turns her domestic arts to her own dreadful, desperate designs.

The Cuckoo's Nest: Domestic Work as a Means of Control

The nature of in-home domestic work blurs the boundaries between public and private, between work and home for both employers and nannies, and Louise purposefully pushes this blurring even further. When not with the Massés, Louise exists in a world of loneliness and silence; she has no contact with her only daughter, her husband is dead, and she lives alone in a small studio on a rundown street. Even among the other nannies in the square at lunchtime she remains intensely private to the point of aloofness. Her most significant human connection is with her employers, with whom she spends most of her time and in whose home she stealthily makes the 'nid' (p.67) ('nest' (p. 48)) of security and belonging that she yearns for. When Paul, finding her waiting on the stairs outside their apartment on her first morning, encourages her to enter and to 'fai[re] comme chez vous' (p. 36) ('make yourself at home' (p. 21)), it is an invitation that she takes literally, carefully using the arts of 'housewifely care' to weave a web of dependence around the Massés that simultaneously secures her financial position and offsets her emotional precarity. It is arguable that by the end of the novel, she has succeeded in entirely taking over their home: neither Paul nor Myriam return to the apartment after the murders, and it remains forever marked by Louise's final, fatal actions.

Mere weeks after her arrival, Louise has established a dominance over the running of the household that goes beyond feeling at liberty to rearrange furniture and cupboards and extends to subtle control of the Massés themselves. She encourages Myriam and Paul to go to evening events, insisting she is happy to stay later and later, and then to stay overnight once or twice a week – literally taking up space in their rooms and in their family unit. Resistance to her authority is dangerous; when Myriam expresses a desire to cook, Louise refuses to give way, holding on to the handle of the casserole dish in an unexpected and alarming display of dominion, disguising it as an act of service in the name of Myriam's relationship with her children: 'Profitez de vos enfants ... vous ne me verrez même pas' (p. 65) ('Enjoy your children ... You won't even see me' (p. 47)). Our image of Louise, especially in the context of her crimes, thus becomes increasingly complicated as the novel progresses. Her remit is certainly large enough to overwork anyone, as the Massés give over much of the running of their household to her, but Louise deliberately encourages them to do so. The portrait of Myriam painted at Louise's trial – that of an absent mother who exploited her nanny – does not account for Louise encouraging her to *be* absent.

Although in her own home, Myriam eventually finds herself afraid to do anything to upset Louise, whose doll-like appearance conceals a violent temper. Mindful of Louise's strictures on preserving lefto-vers and wasting nothing, Myriam begins to take out the bins late at night, after Louise has gone home, testifying to her feeling of being surveilled and judged by Louise even when she is not there. Paul mocks his wife for her fear of being scolded by Louise, but his mental image of the apartment as an aquarium suggests that he too feels trapped and observed, like a fish in a bowl (p. 146). The rules that initially brought order to the chaos of the Massés' lives now seem to strangle and terrify them, and yet they cannot liberate themselves from Louise's grip. Myriam promises that she will re-establish some authority over Louise but never really does, too much in thrall to the 'fantasmes de famille idéale' (p. 38) ('fantasies of idyllic family life' (p. 23)) that Louise has made reality. The challenges of living with and leaving controlling partners is a familiar domestic noir trope that Slimani reimagines by making the manipulator in question an employee, who is remunerated for the time that she spends exercising her tyrannical grip on the family she works for.

Louise's cunning regulation of the Massés' lives through her work in their home adds to the sense of the sinister about her, already visible in the way she tells the children dark fairy tales and prolongs games of hide-and-seek past the point of pleasure to spy on their distress. Louise betrays her employers' trust in progressively disturbing ways, from minor but unnerving infractions such as using Myriam's cosmetics to secretly staying in the apartment while the Massés are on holiday, eating from reserves of food they know nothing about. The privacy of the master bedroom is consistently flouted by Louise, who moves in and out of it with as much ease as if she were part of Myriam and Paul's relationship. One morning, Myriam steps out of the shower to find herself face to face with Louise, whose unblinking, impassive presence carries a vague sense of threat, a foreshadowing of what is to come: in this moment, the stranger turned trusted intimate becomes strange again. Later, deep in her obsession with the idea of a third baby, Louise abuses her domestic services to invade their privacy even further. Under the cover of cleaning their room, she carefully inspects Paul and Myriam's bed for traces of their lovemaking and tracks drops of Myriam's menstrual blood on the floor of the bathroom. Where once the Massés could not do anything without Louise, they now cannot do anything without her knowing.

Sarah Weinman asserts that domestic noir narratives 'turn ordinary household chores into potential for terror',[22] and likewise in *Chanson douce* the domestic work that Louise carries out comes to represent violence and coercion, effectively reversing the initially positive dimension of her 'housewifely care' for the Massés. This is evident in possibly the most unnerving scene in the novel, where what was once comforting and delightful about Louise – her culinary skills, her devotion to nourishing the family, her insistence on cleanliness and preservation – is taken to horrifying extremes. Financially, Louise is in dire straits; her rent is so far overdue that her lease has been terminated, and her efforts to secure additional employment are unsuccessful. Things come to a head when the *Trésor public* ('Public Treasury') writes to the Massés, suggesting that they divert a portion of her salary directly to them to pay off the

debts of Louise's deceased husband. Louise has been steadfastly
ignoring their letters, unable to face yet another burden on her
already strained finances. Paul roundly scolds Louise for causing
them embarrassment; and although Myriam offers Louise assistance
to get her finances in order, she puts her employee's difficulties
down to personal negligence, rather than to a lifetime of underpay-
ment in the care industry. Louise retreats in fear and shame and
then lashes out: she retrieves a spoiled chicken from the bin, cooks
and feeds it to the children, and rewards their participation in her
act of reprisal with sweets and soft drinks. She then enlists their help
to clean and reassemble the bones on the kitchen table for Myriam
to find when she comes home. Standing in the kitchen – where
Louise's work in service of her employers has been most visible, a
place of laughter, nourishment and of shared moments between
nanny and mother – Myriam confronts the realisation that she has
sorely misjudged Louise, and that her home is not the safe haven she
believed it to be. It is to the kitchen that Louise will later return to
source the murder weapon – a final proof of the symbolic rotting of
what used to be the heart of the Massé home.

The Massés decide to let Louise go after the carcass incident, but
not until it suits them, until after the summer holidays – reflecting
both how indispensable Louise is to them and their apparent indifference to her mental wellbeing. Neither of them ever discusses the
event with Louise, even though Myriam senses it is a display of her
'appétit de vengeance' (p. 185) ('appetite for vengeance' (p. 154)).
She understands that both metaphorically and literally, Louise has
the keys to their castle. The knowledge of their routines and particu-
larities that made her such an excellent employee is precisely what
makes her a formidable enemy. Myriam fears that even if Louise is
ousted from their home, she will return to threaten them, 'comme
un amant blessé' (p. 191) ('like a wounded lover' (p. 159)), emphasising Slimani's innovative positioning of a paid stranger in a category
often reserved in domestic noir for threatening romantic interests.
Paul, meanwhile, seems unable to grasp the complexity of their relationship to Louise, patronisingly reminding Myriam that the woman
who holds their entire life together is 'notre employée, pas notre
amie' (p. 198) ('our employee, not our friend' (p. 165)). Myriam
alone recognises the danger that Louise poses, and paradoxically the
knowledge that is now so threatening to her is one she paid Louise to
gain. Fears about what domestic employees can do with the intimate

knowledge of their employers' lives, habits and possessions is long-standing; servants were suspected of everything from theft to murder to 'contamination' of the house's inhabitants, and such suspicion towards domestic workers persists today.[23] These fears draw not only on anxiety around protecting the dwelling from invasion or destruction, but on class and racial discrimination, as is evidenced by Paul's declaration at the beginning of the novel that he would hire neither Muslim women nor undocumented immigrants. As a white Frenchwoman, Louise seemed to allay the Massés' fears and satisfy their racist, classist standards of what a 'suitable' domestic worker looks like, but those characteristics ultimately prove meaningless; the aspects of Louise's character which should be most concerning to them remain hidden until it is too late. The Massés and Louise find themselves in the fight of their lives, for and against each other, and everybody loses. Intimate relationships in *Chanson douce*, in their rupture and disrepair, are the literal making and breaking of life.

As the novel marches inexorably towards its conclusion, we see the Massé home being undone by the very person who put it together. The rooms themselves betray Louise's unravelling as she buckles under the multiple strains in her personal and work life: the kitchen now serves up unpalatable rather than miraculous dishes, the living room is disorderly and doors are slammed as Louise and Myriam deliberately avoid each other. Knowing her time with the Massés is coming to an end, Louise finds herself facing a double eviction from both her studio and the workplace that she considers her 'real' home. The devastating reality of the nanny's position is once again made clear: despite her efforts and expertise, the products of Louise's labour in the domestic (work)space never truly belong to her. The familial harmony she has nourished and the orderly living space she has maintained will be withdrawn from her, as they have been every time she has concluded a term of employment with a family – leaving her with nowhere to feel at home, no way to sustain herself, and no family unit to be part of. Louise may have moved on that first morning from the liminal place of the stairwell – a place of coming and going, where one can simultaneously be noticed and not truly seen – into the heart of the Massé family unit, but her position of centrality is only temporary; she can never truly leave her outsider status behind.

Wrung out from years of this demanding cycle, unable to contemplate starting all over again with a new family, Louise slides into a depression. Her relationship to the apartment sours: the nest becomes a prison of anxiety and apathy. She eventually lights on the solution of inducing Myriam to have a third baby, knowing that the additional workload incurred by another child would make her indispensable once more. Again, Louise demonstrates a willingness to leverage the challenges and affective dimensions of domestic and reproductive labour to her advantage, as she has previously done to bind the Massés to her. Her culinary magic returns as she serves the oblivious Myriam dishes supposedly favourable to fertility; she washes undergarments by hand, reciting prayers over them; she makes the parents' bed with special care. However, the return of her enthusiasm for 'housewifely care' does not have the transformational effect that it had at the beginning of the novel. Detached from reality, Louise comes to see Adam and Mila's presence as the real obstacle to the success of her plan and finds herself prepared to do anything to protect the nest she has made for herself – and so it is that she calls the children to her in the bathroom one day in May, a sushi knife hidden in the palm of her hand. The intimacy of the Massé home – physically compact, composed of tight-knit relationships, lovingly created by 'housewifely care' – is no shield against harm; rather, Louise's violence is unleashed precisely to protect that intimacy from impending collapse.

Conclusion

Slimani's recasting of the domestic noir's 'dangerous intimate' as the nanny, whose presence in the home is based on a contractual rather than a romantic interest, demonstrates how flexible the subgenre can be in examining the power dynamics and latent threat of personal relationships in the domestic space. Louise's manipulation of the Massés through the domestic work that they pay her to provide attests to its power; indeed, its emotional and physical weight is so strong as to be a threat. Both nourishing and noxious, domestic work in *Chanson douce* therefore reflects the duality of the space it helps to create. It is also the lens through which Slimani asks us to consider how a home may be built and destroyed, forcing us to reckon with the consequences of romanticising and dismissing the effort, pain and struggle of the women who 'keep house' for us.

Works Cited

Arens, S., 'Killer Stories: "Globalizing" the Grotesque in Alain Mabanckou's *African Psycho* and Leïla Slimani's *Chanson douce*', *Irish Journal of French Studies*, 20 (2020), 143–72.

Bachelard, Gaston, *The Poetics of Space*, trans. by Maria Jolas (New York: The Orion Press, 1964; repr. New York: Penguin Books, 2014).

Crouch, J., 'Notes from a Genre Bender', in L. Joyce and H. Sutton (eds), *Domestic Noir: The New Face of 21st Century Crime Fiction* (Cham: Palgrave Macmillan, 2018), pp. v–viii.

Gillis, S., and J. Hollows, 'Introduction', in S. Gillis and J. Hollows, *Feminism, Domesticity and Popular Culture* (Oxford: Routledge, 2009), pp. 1–14.

Ibos, Caroline, *Qui gardera nos enfants?* (Paris: Flammarion, 2012).

Joyce, L., 'Introduction to *Domestic Noir*', in L. Joyce and H. Sutton (eds), *Domestic Noir: The New Face of 21st Century Crime Fiction* (Cham: Palgrave Macmillan, 2018), pp. 1–7.

Macdonald, Cameron Lynne, *Shadow Mothers: Nannies, Au Pairs and the Micropolitics of Mothering* (Berkeley CA: University of California Press, 2010).

Murphy, B. M., '"We Will Have A Happy Marriage If It Kills Him": Gillian Flynn and the Rise of Domestic Noir', in B. M. Murphy and S. Matterson (eds), *Twenty-First-Century Popular Fiction* (Edinburgh: Edinburgh University Press, 2018), pp. 158–69.

Nummelin, J., 'Q&A with Sarah Weinman on Domestic Suspense', *http://pulpetti.blogspot.com/2013/11/q-with-sarah-weinman-on-domestic.html* (accessed 12 July 2022).

Redhead, L., 'Teenage Kicks: Performance and Postfeminism in Domestic Noir', in L. Joyce and H. Sutton (eds), *Domestic Noir: The New Face of 21st Century Crime Fiction* (Cham: Palgrave Macmillan, 2018), pp. 115–35.

Rodgers, J., 'Deviant Care: *Chanson douce* and the Killer Nanny', *Australian Journal of French Studies*, 57/3 (2020), 380–94.

Rodríguez González, C., 'Geographies of Fear in the Domestic Noir: Paula Hawkins's *The Girl on the Train*', *Miscelána: A Journal of English and American Studies*, 56 (2017), 109–27.

Rushton, J., 'Destabilizing the Nineteenth-Century Maidservant Revolt Narrative: Leïla Slimani's *Chanson douce* (2016)', *MHRA Working Papers in the Humanities*, 15 (2020), 38–46.

Slimani, Leïla, *Chanson douce* (Paris: Éditions Gallimard, 2016).

—— *Lullaby*, trans. by Sam Taylor (London: Faber and Faber, 2018).

United Nations, *Policy Brief: The Impact of Covid-19 on Women* (New York: UN Women, UN Secretariat, 2020).

Waters, D., and H. Worthington, 'Domestic Noir and the US Cozy as Responses to the Threatened Home', in L. Joyce and H. Sutton (eds), *Domestic Noir: The New Face of 21st Century Crime Fiction* (Cham: Palgrave Macmillan, 2018), pp. 199–218.

Notes

1 Leïla Slimani, *Chanson douce* (Paris: Éditions Gallimard, 2016).
2 This is also the translation of the novel's title in the edition published in the United States. All English-language quotations included in this chapter are taken from the UK edition, *Lullaby*, trans. Sam Taylor (London: Faber and Faber, 2018).
3 S. Arens, 'Killer Stories: "Globalizing" the Grotesque in Alain Mabanckou's *African Psycho* and Leïla Slimani's *Chanson douce*', *Irish Journal of French Studies*, 20 (2020), 156.
4 J. Crouch, 'Notes from a Genre Bender', in L. Joyce and H. Sutton (eds), *Domestic Noir: The New Face of 21st Century Crime Fiction* (Cham: Palgrave Macmillan, 2018), p. viii.
5 J. Rodgers, 'Deviant Care: *Chanson douce* and the Killer Nanny', *Australian Journal of French Studies*, 57/3, (2020), 380–94.
6 J. Rushton, 'Destabilizing the Nineteenth-Century Maidservant Revolt Narrative: Leïla Slimani's *Chanson douce* (2016)', *MRHA Working Papers in the Humanities*, 15 (2020), 41.
7 Crouch, 'Notes from a Genre Bender', p. vii.
8 L. Redhead, 'Teenage Kicks: Performance and Postfeminism in Domestic Noir', in Joyce and Sutton, *Domestic Noir*, p. 117. See further Crouch, 'Notes from a Genre Bender', p. viii and L. Joyce, 'Introduction to *Domestic Noir*', in Joyce and Sutton, *Domestic Noir*, p. 5.
9 L. Joyce, 'Introduction to *Domestic Noir*', p. 2.
10 Rodgers, 'Deviant Care', 384–8.
11 S. Gillis and J. Hollows, 'Introduction', in S. Gillis and J. Hollows (eds), *Feminism, Domesticity and Popular Culture* (Oxford: Routledge, 2009), p. 6. A recent UN survey indicated that women carry out three times more unpaid reproductive and domestic labour than men. United Nations, *Policy Brief: The Impact of Covid-19 on Women* (New York: UN Women, UN Secretariat, 2020), p. 13.
12 Crouch, 'Notes from a Genre Bender', p. vii.
13 D. Waters and H. Worthington, 'Domestic Noir and the US Cozy as Responses to the Threatened Home', in Joyce and Sutton, *Domestic Noir*, p. 210.
14 Rodgers, 'Deviant Care', 385.
15 B. M. Murphy, '"We Will Have A Happy Marriage If It Kills Him": Gillian Flynn and the Rise of Domestic Noir', in B. M. Murphy and S. Matterson (eds), *Twenty-First-Century Popular Fiction* (Edinburgh: Edinburgh University Press, 2018), p. 160.
16 This omission highlights the potential for exploitation faced by nannies due to under-protection by French labour laws and clandestine, contractless arrangements. See further, Caroline Ibos, *Qui gardera nos enfants?* (Paris: Flammarion, 2012), pp. 30–1.
17 Gaston Bachelard, *The Poetics of Space*, trans. by Maria Jolas (New York: The Orion Press, 1964; repr. New York: Penguin Books, 2014), p. 88. Bachelard specifically exempts men from such tasks, as they 'know little or nothing of the "wax" civilisation' and apparently have no need to

learn of it (p. 88). This moves his philosophy away from its potentially radical appreciation of the emotional and physical efforts and results of 'home work' towards a tired reformulation of the Victorian 'separate spheres' doctrine, which not only consigned housekeeping and chil-drearing to women on account of their supposed superior morality and 'natural' affinity for domestic matters, but stopped just short of legally constraining women to remain at home and out of the 'masculine' public sphere.

18 Bachelard, *The Poetics of Space*, p. 29.
19 Arens suggests that sovereignty in *Chanson douce* is portrayed less as state power than as 'the individual's purchasing power' ('Killer Stories', 158). The wealthier Massés exercise and increase their independence by purchasing more of Louise's time, but this does not translate into increased personal sovereignty – be that financial or emotional – for her, as she becomes beholden to her job rather than empowered by it.
20 C. Rodríguez González, 'Geographies of Fear in the Domestic Noir: Paula Hawkins's *The Girl on the Train*', *Miscelána: A Journal of English and American Studies*, 56 (2017), 114.
21 Word-of-mouth references are vital to employment opportunities for nannies and indeed, Louise was hired in part on the positive testimony of her previous employer (Slimani, *Chanson douce*, p. 30).
22 Nummelin, J., 'Q&A with Sarah Weinman on Domestic Suspense', *http://pulpetti.blogspot.com/2013/11/q-with-sarah-weinman-on-domestic.html* (accessed 12 July 2022).
23 Rushton, 'Destabilizing the Nineteenth-Century Maidservant Revolt Narrative', 41.

Chapter 3
A Woman's *Huis clos*: Exhausted Feminism in Paule Constant's *Confidence pour confidence*

JENNIFER WILLGING

In Paule Constant's Goncourt Prize-winning novel *Confidence pour confidence* ('*Trading Secrets*') (1998), four middle-aged women spend the morning after an academic conference in 'Feminine Studies' at the home of the conference's organiser.[1] Two of them are distinguished academics of transcultural origins (Gloria, the organiser, is a Caribbean-African-American, and Babette is a repatriated Jewish *pied-noir* now living in the United States); a third, Aurore, is a French novelist who shares some biographical details with Constant herself, including having spent her childhood in colonial Africa; and the last, Lola, is a nomadic, formerly famous Norwegian actress brought to the conference to read passages from the writer's novels.[2] All four are experiencing mid-life crises in their personal or professional lives, or both. While ostensibly supporting one another in their common struggle to conserve a sense of value and dignity in the face of advancing age, none of them is honest or vulnerable, and each passes more or less silent judgement on the others. Not truly friends, none of them has managed to establish or maintain a fulfilling family life either. Babette has just been abandoned by her Anglo-Saxon American husband of twenty-five years and is on the verge of a breakdown. Like Estelle in Sartre's play *Huis clos* ('*No Exit*'), Lola feels increasingly invisible, to the point where she can no longer find herself in a mirror and must therefore not just play up but draw with make-up the missing features of her face.[3] The organiser, Gloria, the only one of the four to have a child, maintains the façade of a happy family life, but her husband and daughter resent coming in second to her work and so have distanced themselves from her both emotionally and physically. As a child, Aurore, the writer, suffered the loss of her family in a bush fire in colonial Africa and is therefore on a perennial and thus far fruitless search for a place to call home. At this point in their lives, the professional roles in which the four women have ostensibly succeeded no longer seem to provide them with the identity that they thought they had earned for good, as if these labels had begun to peel off their bodies with age.

This chapter will examine the often-antagonistic relationships between these characters' professional and personal lives, as well as among the four women as they play out in the closed, non-professional and paradigmatically feminine space of the home.[4] The novel appears to assert that the promise second-wave feminism made to women of the protagonists' generation – that a career and the independence it would provide could free and fulfil them – has rung hollow. At times it seems to confirm the claims of some contemporary anti-feminists, such as French writer Michel Houellebecq, that feminism has left both women and men exhausted and riddled with the 'sensation de s'être fait baiser quelque part' ('the feeling of having been screwed somehow'), and not in a good way.[5] Yet while acknowledging the novel's troubling representations of feminism and feminists, this chapter suggests that it is not only feminism but another, more pervasive contemporary ideology that is on trial in *Confidence pour confidence*. This ideology is neoliberalism, whose largely negative effects on individual identity formation are explored, as this chapter will show, through the complex portrayals of the novel's four protagonists.

Colonialism – a major theme and object of critique in the majority of Constant's novels – is evoked in *Confidence pour confidence* through the identities of three of the four protagonists, as is the bigotry that especially Gloria but also Babette have faced in their lives.[6] The novel focuses more directly, however, on the disproportionate burden of ageing on women in general, although the protagonists' geographical, racial and/or ethnic origins certainly inflect the nature of the problems that each confronts. The novel is in large part an interrogation of what it presents as the mixed legacy of second-wave feminism. While second-wave feminism has long been taken to task both by some of its adherents and later by so-called 'third-wave feminists' for its insufficient attention to race, among other inequalities, *Confidence pour confidence* does not address directly this particular shortcoming.[7] If, once again, many of Gloria and Babette's struggles are acknowledged to be consequences of their race or ethnicity, it is still a seemingly common 'womanhood' that bears the greatest scrutiny in the novel, further universalised by being exclusively heterosexual.

Constant has said that the novel is based on a real experience she had at a conference on women's writing in Kansas in the late 1980s.[8] It took her eight years to complete the novel, she says, because she knew it would not be received well by 'certain' readers, feminists among them.[9] Some reviewers were indeed struck by its rather unflattering representation of middle-aged women. 'Constant illuminates the dark side of feminism', one noted, 'where women pay lip service to ideals but at the same time ruthlessly manipulate one another in the name of sisterhood'.[10] Another neatly summed up the novel as the story of 'Quatre mégères, quatre sorcières, qui s'étripent puis s'étreignent' ('Four shrews, four witches, who are at each other's throats and then embrace').[11] A third reviewer found that there wasn't a single sympathetic female character in the entire novel and that it presented second-wave feminists as bitter and lonely workaholics, and yet another wondered if the novel wasn't reactionary in its apparent condemnation of second-wave feminism.[12]

While this Goncourt-winning novel obviously enjoyed critical favour overall, such reviews did prompt a female journalist to ask the author shortly after its publication if she was 'antifeminist'. Constant hedged that she 'didn't see it that way', and that, 'Si le roman est un brin féroce' ('if the novel is a bit ferocious') it was because she refused to hide the reality that ageing is hard, despite what women's magazines claim.[13] Elsewhere I have discussed Constant's scepticism about what she sees as American-style political correctness, including American feminism, on which she comments in this interview.[14] In the United States, she says, 'les femmes sont redoutables: elles traquent les hommes, les incendient et surtout instaurent un monde où les rapports de compétition font rage' ('women are formidable: they hound men, massacre them, and above all, establish a world where competition rages').[15] Given the reference to American feminism in particular, it is significant that in the novel the name of Gloria and Babette's academic discipline, and that of the conference, is given, always in English, as 'feminine studies' rather than 'women's studies'.[16] Considering the treatment of the discipline in the novel, 'feminine studies' surely reads as at least mildly derisive to those who consider the modifier 'feminine' prescriptive rather than descriptive. *Confidence pour confidence* might therefore be read as symptomatic of 1990s 'post-feminism' – yet like post-feminism itself, which can refer to a backlash against second-wave feminism or to a new, third-wave feminism, the novel, as noted, takes an ambivalent stance towards feminism in general.[17]

The four women in *Confidence* are defined largely by their professions, and the reader familiar with Constant's work is tempted to apply to them the capitalised, professional labels the author affixes to characters in some of her other novels, such as her first, *Ouregano* (1980), in which the Administrator, the Judge, the Doctor and the Teacher arrogantly play out their assigned role in a colonial African outpost.[18] In fact, most of the men referred to in *Confidence* are designated in this way rather than by their proper names, no matter how ostensibly important they are in these women's lives. Gloria's white working-class husband is the Machinist, and Babette's bourgeois husband, the Pilot. Aurore's ex-husband is the Civil Servant, and subsequent lovers include the Doctor and the Photographer. Such labelling has at least two implications in Constant's work. One is that it is above all one's profession that determines one's value and place in contemporary Western society, particularly for men but increasingly for women. Another, more particular to *Confidence*, is that these men are merely instrumental in the protagonists' lives, offering the security and respectability that marriage traditionally confers on women, as well as, in the cases of Babette and Aurore, higher socioeconomic status. The only men in the novel to have proper names, although only first names and rather fanciful ones at that, are the gay assistants of Babette and Gloria, Babilou and Horatio. That they have names at all suggests they play a more significant role in the women's lives than their husbands, despite secretly despising their bosses. The women's homophobic diatribes against them – which confirm the third wave's indictment of the second for its heteronormativity – make clear that the feeling is mutual. Babette and Gloria's disdain for their assistants, however, in no way reduces their professional and emotional dependence on them as conspicuous signs of their elevated professional status and as safe substitutes for romantic partners.

If there is much emphasis on professional roles in *Confidence*, the setting of the novel is nevertheless a home. Moreover, the various scenes taking place the morning after the conference do not unfold in formal reception spaces, such as the living room or dining room, but in the more clearly domestic and private spaces of the kitchen, bedrooms, bathroom and unfinished basement. Yet this home is not very homely; for one thing, it is ruled by a computer program that locks down the house at night without appeal, literally trapping the protagonists in the very space from which second-wave feminism attempted to free women. There is little family life in it, as Gloria's work has spread throughout the house like the mould caused by either a recent flood or the dousing of a fire set by a pre-programmed hair-straightening iron gone rogue (pp. 47–8; 13). Although Gloria has a dedicated home office, a disdainful Babette notes that the kitchen table is strewn with papers, precluding (perhaps purposefully?) any family dinners aside from those hosted by Gloria's in-laws across town. The kitchen walls are dotted with steam-discoloured photos of writers and post-it notes scrawled with red ink reminding Gloria of the always urgent professional tasks she must accomplish (pp. 130–1; 89). There are no inviting smells emanating from this kitchen, and the only breakfast offered to the guests is coffee from the computer-commanded pot (p. 45; 29). Ironically, while Babette considers with her customary snobbery what she sees as 'le foutoir crasseux' (p. 130) ('the grimy dump' (p. 89)) that is Gloria's home, at the same time Gloria reflects that the disadvantage of working at home is that the household chores she could avoid while on campus take precedence (p. 38; 24). The little housekeeping that Gloria appears to do and the little time she spends at home are thus still more than she would like.

Appropriately enough, having given up the master bedroom to the faded diva Lola, Gloria wakes up in her office on a sofa bed that she hasn't bothered to pull open, thinking still about the success of the conference and the additional professional cachet it will bring her, despite, like Babette, having already beaten the odds against women in academia, women of colour in particular, by having been promoted to full professor.[19] Her thoughts also turn eagerly to the novel she is composing, which will finally reveal, she believes, her true identity as a writer, as an 'African' writer at that. Gloria's novel, however, turns out to be an English translation of one of Aurore's novels, which she plans to publish as her own (pp. 38, 81; 24, 54). As

noted, Constant often thumbs her nose at what she considers to be
political correctness. She seems to be doing so in this novel, in which
Gloria appears to be using 'American' identity politics to rationalise
her plagiarism and reassure herself that those who have endured
past injustices should have license to commit their own to get even
(p. 188; 131). While Gloria, like the other protagonists, is a complex
character with both virtues and flaws, it must be acknowledged that
it is at her expense that misguided notions about the objectives of
reclaiming identities that have been marginalised historically are
expressed in the novel. It is in passages such as these that, despite
Constant's sustained critique of colonialism, a certain sympathy with
French universalism is revealed.

Meanwhile, the censorious Babette has had her comeuppance in
being relegated to a cot in the unfinished basement, where she
wakes to the churning of the washing machine, also pre-programmed
by the computer (p. 30; 19). Although it was Babette who had
begged Gloria to let her stay with her rather than in an impersonal
hotel, 'elle pensa que C'ÉTAIT DÉGUEULASSE de loger quelqu'un
dans une cave, dégueulasse et méprisant' (p. 31) ('she thought it
was DISGUSTING to put someone in a cellar, disgusting and contemp-
tuous' (p. 19)). Constant periodically uses small capital letters within
free indirect discourse, which she deploys liberally to give the reader
a taste of the characters' points of view and speech patterns, as well
as, as in this passage, to lay bare through irony their frequent bad
faith. The haughty Babette is always quick to assume a slight, and she
is clearly only comfortable in domestic spaces that exhibit the marks
of the upper middle-class milieu into which she has clawed her way
since 'repatriation' in an alien and hostile France, with nothing but
a couscous pot on her back (p. 196; 134). She now regularly dons a
mink coat and Dior glasses as a kind of body armour against a world
she perceives as constantly threatening to put her back in her 'place',
whatever the place of this doubly exiled woman might be.

A place in which Babette had managed to feel secure is the home
that she and the Pilot had had built twenty years earlier in the most
beautiful neighbourhood in Missing, the American town in which
they live and whose name suggests an absence, a key trope in
Constant's work (p. 132; 90). For Babette, it takes twenty years to
establish roots in a place, 'pour être de quelque part et ne plus
jamais vouloir s'en aller' (p. 123) ('to be from somewhere and not
ever want to leave it' (p. 84)). Those twenty years are pulverised in

an instant the day before the conference, however, when her husband returns home unexpectedly to retrieve forgotten papers. Dressed in an old bikini, her skin pale aside from splotches of sunburn, perched awkwardly on the edge of an expensive armchair so as not to smear it with sunscreen, a startled Babette has only the time to think that:

> Elle aurait dû se redresser, rentrer le ventre, croiser les jambes … [E]lle était gênée qu'il l'aperçût ainsi, bien moins jolie que vêtue et tellement plus moche que nue … avec ses cuisses ouvertes, son ventre qui rebondissait au-dessus du slip et sa poitrine qui débordait de son soutien-gorge sans armature. (pp. 124–5)

> she should have sat up straight, pulled in her belly and crossed her legs … She was embarrassed that he should see her this way, far less pretty than when she was dressed and much uglier than when she was naked … with her open thighs, her plump belly emerging from the briefs, and her bosom spilling unsupported out of the bra. (p. 85)

Caught like an intruder in her husband's gaze, not only is Babette tastelessly out of place in her elegant living room, with her excess flesh she is taking up too much of that place. Seeing her so stricken with humiliation, the Pilot assumes that she has learned about his affair and admits to everything (p. 125; 85–6). The irony is that Babette had known nothing about it; the humiliation that her dense husband misinterprets is not that of betrayal but that of the feminine crime of occupying space while unattractive. Upon her entreaty to tell her why he wants to marry the other woman, he responds, as if it were only logical, 'Parce qu'elle est si jeune … et que tu es si forte' (p. 125) ('Because she's so young … and you're so strong' (p. 86)). Intentional or not, the double meaning of the descriptor 'forte' ('strong' and 'heavy') faults Babette for both too much flesh and too much strength. Her narcissistic husband is wrong, however, when he assumes that the strength she displays in her professional life will carry over into her emotional life.

In a rare moment of vulnerability, Babette discusses the trauma of learning of her husband's affair with Gloria, whom she has known since their undergraduate days as rag-tag recipients of a scholarship sponsored by a tomato-sauce company (p. 32; 20). While they had had much in common (their poverty, their foreignness, their minority status, but also their intelligence and ambition), they have come to see each other as rivals. On this morning, however, they find a moment of complicity – if a singularly unfeminist one – when they agree that the party to blame is not the Pilot but his mistress. Ironically, the first stone these second-wavers cast at her and all such 'jeunes femmes arrogantes' (p. 126) ('arrogant young women' (p. 86)) is that nothing is sacred to them but their careers. Yet when it comes to men, Gloria and Babette complain, these so-called 'career women' regress to the state of animals in heat 'et brûlent nos théories [féministes] sur le bûcher des sorcières' (p. 126) ('and burn our [feminist] theories at the stake' (p. 87)).

A solid decade younger than the husband-stealing 'pétasses' ('sluts') Babette and Gloria berate is Gloria's thirteen-year-old daughter Chrystal. Rather than being torn between two seemingly contradictory impulses, like these young women, this Gen Xer appears to embrace the brand of post-feminism that decisively renounces rather than revises second-wave feminism. In a video the Machinist had made for Mother's Day the previous year, he asks Chrystal whom she would most and least like to resemble; the answer to the first is 'Marilyn Monroe', and that to the second is 'MA MÈRE' (p. 140) ('MY MOTHER' (p. 96)). Before fleeing to her grandparents' home at the start of the conference, Chrystal takes care to inform her mother and her guests – 'Vieilles et moches comme les salopes que vous êtes' ('Old and ugly like the bitches that you are') – that she would rather kill herself at the age of thirty-six like Marilyn than become, like them, 'PITOYABLES de S'ACCROCHER ainsi' (p. 21) ('PATHETIC for HANGING ON like this' (p. 12)). On the walls of Chrystal's bedroom, Disney stickers have recently been covered over by a life-size poster of Marilyn struggling with the iconic air vent (p. 13; 6). For Chrystal, the narrator notes with patent irony, the white and blonde Marilyn represents 'l'idéal de femme' (p. 13) ('an ideal of womanhood' (p. 6)), suggesting that this budding, mixed-race post-feminist has been unaffected by the third wave's recuperation of racial, sexual, socio-economic and other differences ignored by the second wave. During one of their many veiled duels, Babette in fact accuses Gloria of being 'Mama' ('Mammy') to Chrystal's Scarlet ('Ose dire qu'elle est noire!' (p. 44) ('I dare you to say she's black!' (p. 28)), Babette retorts to Gloria's rejection of her characterisation of Chrystal as white). The vexed question of race aside, Chrystal does appear unwittingly to read Marilyn as might a particular strand of third-wave feminism, that is, as having been unafraid of her sexuality and having chosen to use it to secure wealth, power and recognition. Yet for feminist scholar Angela McRobbie, this kind of 'feminism' is a wolf in sheep's clothing, a pseudo (or post) feminism that borrows and flaunts second-wave rhetoric, such as 'empowerment' and 'choice', 'to ensure that a new women's movement will not re-emerge'.[20]

While the youngest, Chrystal is not the only post-feminist in the house. Lola's success as a film star had been due not to acting skills but to her exceptional talent at being a blank screen on which directors and spectators could project their fantasies (p. 213; 148). In her films of the 1960s and 1970s, Lola, like Aurore, had reflected back to female fans the image of the young, dynamic, liberated woman, but she had never been a feminist in real life (p. 162; 112). For her, these conferences by and for women, where there is 'plus un homme debout, plus un homme qui ne soit déchiqueté, émasculé, exécuté' ('no man left standing, no man who hadn't been torn to bits, emasculated, executed'), are 'son cauchemar' (p. 108) ('her nightmare' p. 74)). Mimicking Lola's voice through free indirect discourse, the narrator also seems to echo Constant's own voice in her comments cited above about formidable American feminists. Aurore, too, appears to have little feminist sensibility. At Gloria's conference she feels as she once had while on a fellowship at a residence for international women intellectuals, all taking refuge from an unhappy love life, spending their time trying to convince one another that they were still young enough to find love and make a fresh start (p. 98; 66). Aurore, however, does not count herself among these women, not because she has a fulfilling relationship with a man, but because '[l]es histoires d'amour ne l'avaient jamais enchantée' (pp. 106–7) ('she had never been enchanted by love stories' (p .72)). Physically Aurore resembles Lola (although without the ravages of years of alcohol abuse) and, like her, she has trouble finding her reflection in mirrors (p. 154; 107). She is thus in many ways the mirror – that is, the inverted – image of the actress, who on the contrary is devastated by the lack of romantic love in her life.[21] The two women nevertheless share a total inability to feel at home, whether in the physical world or within their own bodies, despite their apparent success.[22]

What is the reader of the 2020s to make of this novel, which appears to catalogue the multiple failures of second-wave feminism? Can it be called post-feminist, and if so in which sense of the term? Is it an artefact of the backlash current of post-feminism, even if written by a woman who experienced the institutional and social misogyny of an earlier period? Or is it a constructive feminist critique of an earlier feminism that had its share of blind spots? Or is it yet something else?

In pondering these questions, it is essential to consider that if the four protagonists in *Confidence pour confidence* are targets of Constant's biting and darkly comic irony, so are the dozens of other characters in her novels, whatever their gender, age, colour, nationality or other distinction. A key aspect of Constant's universalism is that for her, human nature is quite universally rotten. Her female characters are therefore much like her male characters in that they are both deeply wounded and deeply flawed. Some of her characters are more sympathetic than others, but none is a model of self-actualisation.

Moreover, in depending largely on their professional status for their self-worth, the women in *Confidence* could be read as typical neoliberal subjects, male or female. Under neoliberalism – which ostensibly values individual freedom and autonomy above all else – identity is no longer founded on traditional institutions such as family, religion or community, which are now considered to be obstructions between individuals and the expression of their 'authentic' selves. Rather, identity must be derived from the two principal preoccupations of contemporary Western subjects: work and consumption.[23] Indeed, Babette explicitly cites these as the two foundations of her own identity when she considers that the value of both her material possessions and her professional titles is that they serve as 'des garanties de dignité' (p. 228) ('guarantees of dignity' (p. 158)). With her diamond ring, her fur coat and her elegant home, Babette illustrates most clearly in the novel the essential role of consumption in contemporary Western identity construction. Worse for her than losing her husband is the prospect of losing her home in the divorce, but both losses would knock her down a peg from her elevated position in the American socio-economic hierarchy – that of the white, married, upper-middle-class homeowner – and thus assail her dignity, 'auprès de laquelle', she admits, 'l'amour comptait si peu' (p. 228) ('next to which love hardly counted' (p. 158)).

As for their professions, if, as tenured professors, Babette and Gloria's jobs are (or at least were in the 1990s) more stable than most other kinds of work under neoliberalism, the two women nevertheless feel perpetually compelled to prove their worth despite past laurels. Lola and Aurore, on the other hand, are examples of the self-employed workers typical of the neoliberal age, whose precarity Lola embodies most clearly, as the demand for her work as an actor has borne an inverse relation to her age (p. 206).[24] Considered under such light, at least some of the mostly existential but also economic precarity of *Confidence*'s protagonists can be attributed to a pervasive Western neoliberalism that individualises, interpolates and commands the behaviour of men and women alike, unfastening them from any fixed institutions and impelling them to construct themselves piecemeal through their work and their consumption. It is in this way that they endeavour, many of them unsuccessfully, to make of themselves a commodity that will command a high price on the social, sexual and professional markets.

And yet, if the neoliberal mandate to cultivate and maintain an attractive and therefore marketable self increasingly looms over both sexes, Constant in no way ignores the fact that it persistently weighs more heavily on women.[25] McRobbie writes that as a feminist in the 1990s she had 'attributed too much hope in the capacity of the world of women's magazines, to take up and maintain a commitment to feminist issues, encapsulating a kind of popular feminism'.[26] But quite early on, she notes, 'the idea of feminist content disappeared and was replaced by aggressive individualism, by a hedonistic female phallicism in the field of sexuality, and by obsession with consumer culture', which she argues has contributed largely to 'the undoing of feminism' (p. 5). In the 1999 interview previously cited, Constant appears to concur regarding such an assessment, stating that she was determined that her novel reject 'l'image glorieuse et triomphante que la presse féminine, sous prétexte de libération, renvoie sans arrêt aux femmes' ('the glorious and triumphant image that women's magazines, on the pretext of liberation, constantly display to their readers').[27] In another interview at the time of the novel's publication, Constant reveals more second-wave sensibilities when she affirms that it is women over forty who have built a more just world, into which young women now settle so naturally that they are unable to understand what their foremothers had complained about.

Confidence pour confidence portrays four middle-aged, professional women who likely resemble many of the professional women that Constant has known throughout her career as an academic and a writer, and perhaps they also resemble, in some measure, herself. If these women are 'victims' of the 1970s women's movement, as Houellebecq might argue, for him that movement is in fact nothing more than the bastard child of his personal pet peeve, the cultural revolution of the 1960s, which, for Houellebecq, with its obsession with the self, unwittingly ushered in neoliberalism.[28] Writer and journalist Annette Brierre appears to support obliquely such an indictment of neoliberal society when she contends that in *Confidence*, Constant's 'lucid' gaze 'nous montre en miroir notre société, si individualiste qu'elle s'est atomisée' ('reflects back to us our society, so individualist that it has broken itself apart').[29] In a response to the kinds of feminist critiques that *Confidence* received (cited above), Gill Rye argues that:

> if Constant's four protagonists are caricatures of aging women – rivals, bitter, obsessed by their relationships with men (or the loss of them) – the novel also treats the way that, despite feminist advances, aging is still painfully implicated in many women's sense of self in our image-laden societies where youth and beauty rule.[30]

In *Confidence pour confidence*, the enclosed space in which the protagonists struggle as if for air can be figured through numerous metaphors, including that of the cage in which Chrystal's pet rat languishes before being put of out its misery by Gloria (p. 235; 163). Given the prevalence of the trope in Constant's work, another might be a hall of mirrors, those mirrors that sociologist Anthony Giddens describes as relentlessly surrounding us in contemporary Western society and in which we search constantly but vainly 'for the appearance of an unblemished, socially valued self'.[31] A third might be an echo chamber in which the rhetoric not just of post-feminism but of various other contemporary ideologies – individualism, careerism, consumerism, the cult of beauty, the cult of youth – resonates as the protagonists ponder their fractured and fragile selves, but which finally rings hollow.

Works Cited

Baudrillard, Jean, *La Société de consommation* (Paris: Denoël, 1970).

Bourdieu, Pierre, *Contre-feux: Propos pour servir à la résistance contre l'invasion néo-libérale* (Paris: Raisons d'agir, 1998).

Brierre, Annette, 'Juste quelqu'un de bien', *Sud Ouest* (6 December 1998), *Lexis-Nexis*.

'Characteristics of Postsecondary Faculty', National Center for Education Statistics (NCES) (May 2020), *https://nces.ed.gov/programs/coe/indicator_csc.asp* (accessed 7 December 2021).

Constant, Paule, *Balta* (Paris: Gallimard, 1983).

—— *Confidence pour confidence* (Paris: Gallimard, 1998).

—— *Des chauves-souris, des singes et des hommes* (Paris: Gallimard 2017).

—— 'Échos et miroirs dans une œuvre romanesque', in *Conferencias del curso academic 1999/2000* (Granada: University of Granada Press, 2000), pp. 37–42.

—— *Ouregano* (Paris: Gallimard, 1980).

—— 'Portrait. Paule Constant', interview with Catherine Argand, *L'Express* (1 April 1998), *www.lexpress.fr/culture/livre/paule-constant_802007.html* (accessed 7 December 2021).

—— *Trading Secrets*, trans. by Betsey Wing (Lincoln NE: University of Nebraska Press, 2001).

—— *White Spirit* (Paris: Gallimard, 1989).

Coppermann, Annie, 'Confidence pour confidence de Paule Constant–Femmes entre elles', *Les Échos* (22 June 1998), 56, *LexisNexis*.

'Fall Staff in Postsecondary Institutions, 1993', NCES (April 1996), *https://nces.ed.gov/pubs96/96323.pdf* (accessed 7 December 2021).

Featherstone, Mike, 'The Body in Consumer Culture,' *Theory, Culture and Society*, 1/2 (1982), 18–33.

Fevre, Ralph, *The New Sociology of Economic Behaviour* (New York: SAGE, 2003).

Giddens, Anthony, *Modernity and Self-identity: Self and Society in the Late Modern Age* (Stanford CA: Stanford University Press, 1991).

Gill, Rosalind, and Christina Scharff, 'Introduction,' in Gill and Scharff (eds), *New Femininities: Postfeminism, Neoliberalism and Subjectivity* (London: Palgrave MacMillan, 2011), pp. 1–15.

hooks, bell, *Ain't I a Woman? Black Women and Feminism*, 2nd edition (New York: Routledge, 2014 [1981]).

Houellebecq, Michel, *Extension du domaine de la lutte* (Paris: Nadeau, 1994).

—— *Les Particules élémentaires* (Paris: Flammarion, 1998). Translated as *Atomised* by Frank Wynne (New York: Vintage, 2001).

—— *Soumission* (Paris: Flammarion, 2015).

Johnston, Bonnie, 'Trading Secrets. (General Fiction)', *Booklist*, 98/4 (15 October 2001), 381, *Gale Literature: Book Review Index, https://link.gale.com/apps/doc/A79967375/BRIP?u=colu44332&sid=BRIP&xid=f28a92af* (accessed 7 December 2021).

Kinser, Amber E., 'Negotiating Space For/Through Third-Wave Feminism', *NWSA Journal*, 16/3 (2004), 124–53.

'Le Jury du Goncourt ému par le chagrin des femmes selon Paule Constant', *Le Temps* (10 November 1998), *LexisNexis*.

McDonald, Matthew, Stephen Wearing and Jess Ponting, 'Narcissism and Neo-Liberalism: Work, Leisure, and Alienation in an Era of Consumption', *Loisir et Société/Society and Leisure*, 30/2 (2007), 489–510.

McRobbie, Angela, *The Aftermath of Feminism: Gender, Culture and Social Change* (New York: Sage, 2009).

Miller, Margot, *In Search of Shelter: Subjectivity and Spaces of Loss in Paule Constant's Fiction* (Lanham MD: Lexington Books, 2003).

Rye, Gill, '*Confidence pour confidence: Une réponse*', *Women in French Newsletter*, 13/2, (1999), 10.

—— 'The (Im)Possible Ethics of Reading: Identity, Difference, Violence and Responsibility (Paule Constant's *White Spirit*)', *French Studies*, 54 (2000), 327–37.

Sartre, Jean-Paul, *Huis clos* (Paris: Gallimard, 2019 [1945]).

Trout, Colette, 'Les Françaises aujourd'hui: Quelques réflexions sur la condition feminine contemporaine à travers trois textes', *Women in French Newsletter*, 18 (Spring 1999), 17–18.

Willging, Jennifer, 'Existential Angst and Role-Playing Revisited in Paule Constant's Fiction', *French Forum*, 31 (2006), 75–97.

—— 'Strange Bedfellows: Paule Constant, Michel Houellebecq, and Political Correctness', *Australian Journal of French Studies*, 56/1 (2019), 75–90.

Yillah, Dauda, 'Colonial Black Africa in Retrospect: A Reading of Paule Constant's *Ouregano*', *Francophone Postcolonial Studies*, 4/1 (2006), 41–65.

—— 'The Predatory Economics of Imperialism and Neo-Imperialism: Some Postwar Metropolitan French Intellectual Perspectives', *Forum for Modern Language Studies*, 53/4 (2017), 483–507.

Notes

1 Paule Constant, *Confidence pour confidence* (Paris: Gallimard, 1998). Translations of quotes from the novel are taken from Betsy Wing's translation, *Trading Secrets* (Lincoln NE: University of Nebraska Press, 2001), except in rare instances when a more literal rendering is needed. All other translations are my own.

2 The term *pied-noir* (literally translated as 'black foot') referred to settlers of colonial Algeria of European origin. When Algeria won its independence from France in 1962, the vast majority of *pieds-noirs* were 'repatriated' to a France they had never seen.

3 Jean-Paul Sartre, *Huis clos* (Paris: Gallimard, 2019 [1945]). For an analysis of Constant's novel *Ouregano* (Paris: Gallimard, 1980) through a Sartrean lens, see Jennifer Willging, 'Existential Angst and Role-Playing Revisited in Paule Constant's Fiction', *French Forum*, 31 (2006), 75–97.

4 It should be noted, nevertheless, that a number of other, often hostile places are evoked in the characters' memories, such as the decidedly un-feminine space of the truck-stop bar from which the four are ejected for responding less than solicitously to a patron who had wanted them to pay a 'toll' before leaving (pp. 94–5; 64).

5 Michel Houellebecq, *Soumission* (Paris: Flammarion, 2015), p. 94. Incidentally, Houellebecq's *succès de scandale*, *Les Particules élémentaires* ('*Elementary Particles*'), lost the 1998 Goncourt to *Confidence pour confidence*, which provoked a scandal in its own right. For a discussion of the scandal see Jennifer Willging, 'Strange Bedfellows: Paule Constant,

Michel Houellebecq, and Political Correctness', *Australian Journal of French Studies*, 56/1 (2019), 75–7.

6 Constant's novels *Ouregano* (Paris: Gallimard, 1980), *Balta* (Paris: Gallimard, 1983); *White Spirit* (Paris: Gallimard, 1989); and *Des chauves-souris, des singes et des hommes* (*'Of Bats, Monkeys, and Men'*) (Paris: Gallimard, 2017), for example, all take place in West Africa either during or after the French colonial period and illustrate, through Constant's liberal use of biting irony, colonialism's tragic consequences. For studies on the damning portrayals of colonialism in Constant's work, see, for example, Dauda Yillah, 'Colonial Black Africa in Retrospect: A Reading of Paule Constant's *Ouregano*', *Francophone Postcolonial Studies*, 4/1 (2006), 41–65 and 'The Predatory Economics of Imperialism and Neo-Imperialism: Some Postwar Metropolitan French Intellectual Perspectives', *Forum for Modern Language Studies*, 53/4 (2017), 483–507; Gill Rye, 'The (Im)Possible Ethics of Reading: Identity, Difference, Violence and Responsibility (Paule Constant's *White Spirit*)', *French Studies*, 54 (2000), 327–37; and Willging, 'Existential Angst'.

7 For a concise sketch of the contested meanings of 'first-wave', 'second-wave' and 'third-wave' feminisms, see, for example, Amber E. Kinser, 'Negotiating Space For/Through Third-Wave Feminism', *NWSA Journal*, 16/3 (2004), 127–31. For a seminal critique of racism and classism in second-wave feminism, see bell hooks' *Ain't I a Woman? Black Women and Feminism*, 2nd edition (New York: Routledge, 2014 [1981]).

8 Paule Constant, 'Échos et miroirs dans une œuvre romanesque', *Conferencias del curso academic 1999/2000* (Granada: University of Granada Press, 2000), p. 37.

9 Constant, 'Échos et miroirs', p. 38.

10 Bonnie Johnston, 'Trading Secrets. (General Fiction)', *Booklist*, 98/4 (15 October 2001), 381.

11 Annie Coppermann, 'Confidence pour confidence de Paule Constant – Femmes entre elles', *Les Échos* (22 June 1998), 56.

12 Colette Trout, 'Les Françaises aujourd'hui', *Women in French Newsletter*, 18 (Spring 1999), 17; 'Le Jury du Goncourt ému par le chagrin des femmes selon Paule Constant', *Le Temps* (10 November 1998).

13 Paule Constant, 'Portrait', interview with Catherine Argand, *L'Express* (1 April 1998), 1.

14 See Willging, 'Strange Bedfellows'.

15 Constant, 'Portrait', 1.

16 Constant, *Confidence*, pp. 21. 'Feminine Studies' could simply be an overly literal translation of the French 'Études féminines', which first became an academic discipline in France with Hélène Cixous's founding of the Centre d'études féminines at Paris 8 in 1974, or it could be a misguided transplantation of British 'Feminine Studies' into an American context. Whatever the case, that the name is given only in English and always in italics makes it appear as if in quotation marks, as if the narrator were distancing herself from the term.

17 See Rosalind Gill and Christina Scharff, 'Introduction', in Gill and Scharff (eds), *New Femininities: Postfeminism, Neoliberalism and Subjectivity*

(London: Palgrave MacMillan, 2011), pp. 3–5, for a discussion of the multiple meanings of the term 'post-feminism'.

18   Constant, *Ouregano.*

19   In 1993 only 15 per cent of full professors in the United States were women ('Fall Staff in Postsecondary Institutions, 1993', National Center for Education Statistics (NCES) (April 1996), 31), and only 2.9 per cent of all full professors, male or female, were African-American, making Gloria's achievement truly exceptional ('Fall Staff', 32). By way of comparison, in 2018 the percentage of full professors in the United States who were women was 34.4 per cent, but African-American women made up only 2 per cent of all full professors ('Characteristics of Postsecondary Faculty', NCES (May 2020)).

20   Angela McRobbie, *The Aftermath of Feminism: Gender, Culture and Social Change* (New York: Sage, 2009), p. 1.

21   As Constant herself writes in her essay 'Échos et miroirs dans une œuvre romanesque' ('Echoes and Mirrors in My Work'), doubling is a pervasive motif in her work.

22   See Margot Miller's *In Search of Shelter: Subjectivity and Spaces of Loss in Paule Constant's Fiction* (Lanham MD: Lexington Books, 2003), for a thorough exploration of the themes of homelessness and loss in Constant's work.

23   Matthew McDonald, Stephen Wearing and Jess Ponting, 'Narcissism and Neo-Liberalism: Work, Leisure, and Alienation in an Era of Consumption', *Loisir et Société/Society and Leisure*, 30/2 (2007), 490. McDonald, Wearing and Ponting offer a concise discussion of theories of identity construction under neoliberalism by sociologists such as Jean Baudrillard (*La Société de consommation* (Paris: Denoël, 1970)), Anthony Giddens (*Modernity and Self-identity: Self and Society in the Late Modern Age* (Stanford CA: Stanford University Press, 1991)), and Ralph Fevre (*The New Sociology of Economic Behaviour* (New York: Sage, 2003)).

24   Pierre Bourdieu's *Contre-feux: Propos pour servir à la résistance contre l'invasion néo-libérale* (Paris: Raisons d'agir, 1998) was a seminal warning against increasing social and economic precarity.

25   Mike Featherstone, 'The Body in Consumer Culture', *Theory, Culture and Society*, 1/2 (1982), 22.

26   McRobbie, *The Aftermath of Feminism*, pp. 4–5.

27   Constant, 'Échos et miroirs', p. 2.

28   The 'hippie' zeitgeist of the 1960s comes under fire throughout Houellebecq's oeuvre, perhaps most notably in his first novel, *Extension du domaine de la lutte* (Paris: Nadeau, 1994) and in the novel that Constant's beat out for the Goncourt, *Les Particules élémentaires.*

29   Annette Brierre, 'Juste quelqu'un de bien', *Sud Ouest* (6 December 1998). Appropriately, the British have translated *Les Particules élémentaires* as *Atomised.*

30   Gill Rye, '*Confidence pour confidence: Une réponse*', *Women in French Newsletter*, 13/2, (1999), 10.

31   Giddens, *Modernity and Self-Identity*, p. 172.

Chapter 4
A Life's Work: Accounting for Birth in *Naissances*

AMALEENA DAMLÉ

In *A Life's Work*, Rachel Cusk writes that '[c]hildbirth and motherhood are the anvil upon which sexual inequality was forged', framing
her autobiographical writing as an attempt to describe the experiences of birth and mothering precisely as 'work, requisitioned from
a woman's life'.[1] There has been a swell of women's writing in French
over the past couple of decades that has reflected with fine-tuned
attention upon contemporary iterations of the work of mothers, the
institution of motherhood and the myriad routes embarked upon
towards experiences of mothering in the twenty-first century. Yet,
despite the often-expansive ways in which motherhood is fore-
grounded in narrative and poetic forms, the subject of birth itself
– in the sense of the embodied experience of labour – seems to
remain, curiously, a life's work that evades sustained literary
portrayal. Gill Rye, whose pioneering *Narratives of Mothering* has
ushered in a wave of scholarly analysis of depictions of mothering in
French, observes that there have historically been few women-
authored birth stories in literature: 'childbirth narratives tend to be
either male authors' accounts of their own birth, or "audience"-
based narratives, such as obstetrics manuals, or the accounts of a
by-stander or an omniscient narrator. Alternatively, birth in literary
texts simply happens behind closed doors, off-stage.'[2] This relative
paucity of cultural narratives of the birthing body is doubtless bound
up with, but also contributes to, the forging of sexual and gender
inequality to which Cusk alludes, continuing to make it difficult to
talk about birth in meaningful ways. Birth tends – still – to be
enshrined as an event that is somehow part of a secret and

mysterious body of knowledge, an enshrinement that corresponds to a complex, politicised and pernicious mythologisation of the birthing body.

Written over four decades ago, Adrienne Rich's trenchant analysis of the submission of women's birthing bodies to forms of medical knowledge that have historically been dominated, regulated and constrained by heteropatriarchal requirements still bears much relevance to thinking about how birth enters into contemporary knowledge. Rich contends that the majority of women, regardless of their social circumstances or education, have encountered childbirth as a charged and highly specific experience: 'mysterious, sometimes polluted, often magical, as torture rack or as "peak experience". Rarely has it been viewed as one way of knowing and coming to terms with our bodies, of discovering our physical and psychic resources.'[3] Since the publication of Rich's work, birthing women and people may arguably avail themselves of a wider and better-informed set of perspectives around birth-giving within an expanding field of manuals, blogs and online forums, but this is a relatively recent development and birth still occupies the margins of healthcare. That birth-giving continues to be occluded and mythologised appears in some ways to be bound up with a curious chasm between competing discourses of birth, often a polarisation of medical perspectives and 'natural' or 'positive' approaches, which arguably misses an opportunity to provide genuinely empowering ways to think about birth as an embodied experience and also as a form of knowing.[4] In this chapter, I argue that this tendency can also be explained by birth's stark and prolonged absence from philosophical and literary domains. Analysing narratives of birth in *Naissances* ('*Births*'), a collection of short stories and reflections written by some of France's leading authors, I first probe the discursive mythologisation of birth across the stories that leaves its traces in the representation of the birthing body as unspeakable, unthinkable, disavowed, at a remove.[5] Then, reading in turn Camille Laurens's reflective prose and Marie Darrieussecq's short story, I argue for a feminist understanding of birth as a relational and narrative epistemology, one that accounts for the embodied event of birth as a limit-experience *and* as a way of knowing, and that foregrounds the birthing body itself as a site of epistemic strain. Throughout, I pursue the relationship between birth and work in two interrelated ways, then, in the sense of birth itself as a form of inarticulable or invisible labour, and in the embodied, relational and narrative forms that respond to this particular life's work and that themselves may constitute a work of feminist embodied and epistemological labour.

A Delicate Empiricism: Towards a Negative Rule of Gynaecology?

Knowing oneself or others, seeing the ways that we are constituted, regarding our hidden insides, what makes us alive or dead – these are all, as Jessie Greengrass writes in her evocative novel *Sight*, funda-mental concerns of the digging in the dark of philosophical and narrative endeavour:

> How simple things would be if only I could know myself or others; if, stepping in between a light source and a screen, I could see the way that I was constituted, those hidden structures, the bones, the joints that give the rest its shape – and then I might know some-thing for certain, that I was alive or that I would be dead, these two differently slanted articulations of the same fundamental under-standing: but instead there is only this excavation, a digging in the dark: precarious, uncertain, impossible to complete.[6]

And yet, while death, our commonly defining finitude, has long been a structuring principle of continental philosophy, birth has yet to receive the same levels of critical scrutiny. Lily Gurton Wachter comments on the relative dearth of narratives of birth in compar-ison to the extensive literary portrayal of death in war, even though both testify to the experience of the body in battle: 'we don't have a familiar canon of nuanced literary or philosophical texts about the experience of having a child, even though having a child, too, is a profound, frightening, exhilarating, transformative experience at the boundary of life, an experience from which one comes back a different person.'[7] Far from being located as a limit-experience at the opposite end of the life spectrum to death, the body in birth is always entangled with death, brought to the absolute edge of exist-ence, whether the birth outcome itself is one of positive life-giving or not. As Maggie Nelson writes in her searing work of autotheory, *The Argonauts*: 'If all goes well, the baby will make it out alive, and so will you. Nonetheless. You will have touched death along the way. You will have realized that death will do you too, without fail and without mercy.'[8]

While philosophy could look at birth as an opportunity to open new perspectives on the distinction between self and other, the relation between body and mind, and the meaning of life itself, most philosophers have approached the topic in, as Gurton Wachter observes, 'tangential asides in which they try to control women's bodies rather than understand them'.[9] One recent philosophical exception is Luce Irigaray's *To Be Born*, though in accounting for natal experiences in the theorisation of the human subject, Irigaray (much like Hannah Arendt, or Adriana Cavarero) offers insight into birth from the perspective of being born, rather than giving birth.[10] While Julia Kristeva's theorisation of the semiotic or Bracha Ettinger's conceptualisation of relational subjectivity via what she terms the 'matrixial borderspace' attend to the psychoanalytical signification of primary object relations, birth as an embodied event in itself tends to be eclipsed.[11] As Nelson observes, one promising approach emerges in the perhaps unexpected location of Peter Sloterdijk's *Bubbles*. Debunking what he refers to as the 'confused narcissism concepts of psychoanalysis' as being misled by the object and imago concepts, Sloterdijk emphasises instead the pre-visual aspects of the foetal and peri-natal world, as being constituted in sensory, embodied flows, of 'blood, amniotic fluid, voice, sonic bubble and breath'.[12] In ways that resonate with Irigaray's infamous specular critique, Sloterdijk proposes a 'negative gynaecology', suggesting that in approaching birth 'one must reject the temptation to extricate oneself from the affair with outside views of the mother-child relationship; where the concern is insight into intimate connections, outside observation is already the fundamental mistake' (p. 321). Renegotiating tired metaphors of the exploration, excavation and specular capture of the reproductive body, Sloterdijk suggests instead a 'delicate empiricism' that might position knowledge of birth precisely as an epistemological conundrum, the outlines of which might begin to be traced but never objectively recorded from the outside: 'By observing incipient life with delicate empiricism, one can attempt to sketch outlines of its being-in-the-cave' (p. 321).

In her own reflections on philosophies of birth, Nelson applauds Sloterdijk's turn from objectivity and mastery towards the sensory, immersive bubble. But as she wryly comments, the material constraints of writing alongside caring for or birthing a baby are myriad: 'I feel no urge to extricate myself from this bubble. But here's the catch: *I cannot hold my baby at the same time as I write*' (p. 45). In what follows, I mobilise notions of delicate empiricism and negative gynaecology to foreground this dichotomy, suggesting a feminist approach that focalises birth as an embodied event, and as a limit-experience, that probes questions about how to think about birth, how to *think birth*, and, crucially, from whose perspective, while figuring the birthing body as a site of both epistemic strain and epistemological labour.

Writing (and) the Bubble

I cannot hold my baby at the same time as I write. This idea ripples through *Naissances*, and it carries a charge of layered meanings. From the patriarchal mythologisation of labour as an unspeakable event around which only clichés may be articulated, to the traumatic unavailability of birth, the practical impossibility of balancing a pen in hand at the same time as a baby, and the heteropatriarchal imperative that women are excluded from creative work by virtue of their participation in procreative labour – read as a collection the stories suggest that there is always a gap between birth and writing, that the articulation of birth as a life's work is always somehow alienated. The narrator of Marie Desplechin's 'Maya' shows how the absence of cultural and familial narratives of birth makes it difficult for her, as young woman, to contemplate birth as a prospect:

> Les femmes de ma famille, ma mère, mes tantes, ma grand-mère, parlaient peu de leurs accouchements. Entre elles, peut-être. Mais aux enfants, à qui pourtant on n'épargnait pas grand-chose, pas un mot. Quelques anecdotes, un peu de contexte, sur le ton de la blague, et c'était tout. À côté de mourir, qui faisait toute une histoire, naître se passait de mots. (p. 76)

> The women in my family, my mother, my aunts, my grandmother, spoke little about their birth experiences. Among themselves, perhaps. But to the children, for whom nothing much was otherwise spared, not a word. A few anecdotes, a bit of context, said in a jokey tone, and that was it. Compared to dying, which was always a big drama, birth went without remark.

While Maya alludes to the silence around birth, the speculative 'entre-elles' immediately designates birth as a taboo confined to those who have experienced it, but, importantly, not something about which knowledge might be passed down or shared, except in fragments and accompanied by the kind of self-deprecating humour that belittles its subject. Here too, it is stressed that death takes narrative precedence over birth, which is relegated to women's conversations. On the other side of the event, Maya is benignly informed that one simply forgets, and she herself finds after giving birth that forgetting is a phenomenon shared between child and mother. If the narrator professes to a certain personal pride in the different conditions under which she has gone on to give birth, Desplechin highlights her internalisation of the patriarchal undermining and silencing of birth, as she admits that she does not see in those myriad experiences anything that might be worth recounting to others, in this sense invisibilising her own physical and epistemological labour.

The lack of shared language around labour mingles with the experience of birth as at once intimate and remote, both part of oneself and not, accompanied by a feeling of having been traversed by something unaccountable and incommensurable:

> La mémoire, plutôt, un peu embuée, d'avoir été traversée par un mystère, dans le même temps possédée et dépossédée, et rendue à l'ignorance. Une ignorance débordée, faite de mémoires successives, d'images qui déboulent et s'agglutinent, font écran, et occultent à jamais le souvenir de l'instant. (p. 81–2)

> The memory, then, slightly blurry, of having been traversed by a mystery, at once possessed and dispossessed, and relegated to ignorance. An overflowing ignorance, made up of sequential memories, images which tumble and coalesce, form a screen, and occlude forever the memory of the moment.

The language of mystery, occlusion and disappearance proliferates alongside a series of snapshots that elude the narrator's recall. Birth is something glimpsed but never grasped, always at a remove, hidden, secret. The narrator of Michèle Fitoussi's 'Le Cordon' ('The Cord') similarly reiterates the post-partum 'forgetting' of birth, in the recognisable and well-circulated premise that 'j'ai oublié la souffrance' (p. 166) ('I've forgotten the pain'). So too is the reality for the narrator of Helena Villovitch's 'Mon lapin' ('My Bunny'), who exclaims 'J'ai tout oublié' ('I've forgotten everything'), while recounting medical terminology as an ineffective aide-mémoire, 'Non, de tout ça, je ne me souviens pas. Je suis nulle en histoires d'accouchement' (p. 33) ('No, none of that, I don't remember. I'm terrible at birth stories'). Villovitch's narrator disassociates herself from the clichés of television dramas, women on the brink of birth impossibly repeating the only words that have become culturally valent: 'c'est pas possible, mon Dieu, c'est pas possible'; 'je n'ai jamais autant souffert de ma vie'; 'arrêtez tout, je ne veux pas de bébé' (p. 34) ('I can't, oh god, I can't'; 'I've never been in so much pain in my life'; 'make it stop, I don't want a baby'). Arguably 'j'ai tout oublié' repeats a different kind of cliché, however, one that courses through these stories where the absence of empowering ways of talking about birth, and the lack of varied, complex cultural references is highlighted by an insistence that birth remains out of reach, irrecuperable, unrepresentable, even unthinkable. As Geneviève Brisac's narrator opines, 'Quoi de plus beau, c'est vrai, et de plus impensable' (p. 116) ('What could be more beautiful, it's true, and more unthinkable').

Nonetheless, the stories themselves do represent such a cultural intervention, emphasising in highly self-conscious ways the feminist narrative labour of circulating birth stories, and interrogating the heteropatriarchal exclusion of mothers from creative practice. They also seek out new ways of approaching birth's incommensurability through what we might, after Sloterdijk, term a delicate empiricism. Desplechin's narrator harbours hopes of being a writer, only to be told that only men can be writers, while women have children (p. 77). Enraged by this comment, the narrator later reflects back on it, recalling Nietzsche's phrase *aut liberi, aut libri*, and finding a way to reinterpret it as suggesting not a relationship of mutual exclusion between children and books, but rather one of resemblance (p. 88). For her, the idea of birth itself (*naissance*) draws together children and books, childbirth and writing, suggesting a creative rebirth of revelation, passage and new beginnings (p. 89). To birth and to write, and to write birth, then, constitutes a complex embodied and political act, a life's work that is set in motion by the reality of being 'traversé par le corps d'un autre' (p. 89) ('traversed by the body of another').[13] Dismantling long-held assumptions around the dichotomy of creation and procreation may not simply involve writing stories about birth, however. As Desplechin suggests, and as we shall see further in Laurens and Darrieussecq, approaching birth with delicate empiricism may involve attending to the relationality and provisionality of its life's work in embodied epistemological acts of feminist labour.

Naissance, Reconnaissance, Co-Naissance

Several stories in the collection linger on the language of birth, experimenting with variety and nuance to consider the plural ways that birth may occur: being born (*naissance*), giving birth (*accouchement*), delivering (*délivrance*) or extracting (*extraction*). In this regard, Laurens's searching prose provides a particularly sustained reflection on the language of birth and its incommensurability. In 'Abandon*nés*', Laurens revisits the traumatic circumstances of the birth of her son, who died two hours after he was born, an experience that she elaborates upon elsewhere in *Philippe*; here she reflects too upon the subsequent birth of her daughter.[14] Throughout, Laurens is concerned with the inadequacy of the words, knowledge and clichés that circulate around birth. 'On dit: avoir un enfant', she writes, 'Mais on n'a pas d'enfants, on n'a pas un enfant comme on a une voiture. On dit: voir le jour. Mais on voit aussi la nuit. La naissance, pour la mère comme pour le bébé, c'est perdre quelqu'un, c'est être perdu. La terre natale est toujours un exil' (p. 102) ('One says: to have a child. But one doesn't have children, one doesn't have a child like one has a car. One says: to see the light of day. But one also sees darkness. Birth, for the mother as for the baby, is to lose someone, it's to be lost. The territory of birth is always exile'). For Laurens, it is not just that these phrases are trite, but that in their focalisation of the joy of 'un heureux événement' (p. 97) ('a happy event'), they fail to account for what lies at the heart of birth's incommensurability: birth is always cut through with loss, absence and abandonment. In her own circumstances, the birth of Philippe is accompanied by silence, senselessness and the absence of life: 'Né sans sens. Aucun sens à rien. Né en silence. Pas vu le jour, pas pris le temps. Pas donné la vie' (p. 98) ('Born without sense. No sense at all. Born in silence. Not seeing the light of day, not seizing time. Not given life'). But in her description of giving birth for a second time, Laurens talks of being absent herself, or rather of having absented herself. Interpreting her presence as synonymous with Philippe's death, her absence becomes critical to her daughter's life, so much so that she feels she must appear dead in order to succeed in giving her daughter life (p. 99). It is for this reason that Laurens opens her text with the words, 'J'ai accouché de deux enfants, un garçon et une fille, mais je n'ai aucune expérience de la naissance' (p. 97) ('I have given birth to two children, a boy and a girl, but I have no experience of birth'). If birth, for Laurens, is always at a remove, this is not only because of the dislocations of memory, as for Desplechin; rather, absence lies at the heart of birth's bubble itself.

Laurens' opening words are a reminder that birth (*accouchement, naissance*) is also an experience shared between mother and baby, never to be claimed by just one person but touching plural lives. Yet, if birth is an event that cannot quite be experienced let alone expressed, she underscores that 'irrecuperability' and loss belong to both mother and child. Laurens reflects that birth stories are related to us by our mothers, or otherwise by our neuroses, but rarely put into our own words from the perspective of being born (p. 100). Birth is never simply one's own because its separation derives precisely from an entanglement with the other. In this, Laurens suggests, the sensations of birth always share a close proximity with grief: a sudden coldness, a physical anguish that grips the body, a desire to scream out, an extraordinary vulnerability, the extreme exposure of an unwanted separation. 'Naître', writes Laurens, 'c'est rompre un lien qu'on ne peut défaire, c'est un abandon paradoxal: on est abandonné à quelqu'un: on se sépare d'un être dont on ne peut pas se passer' (p. 101) ('to be born is to break a link that one cannot undo, it's a paradoxical abandonment: one is abandoned to someone: one separates from a being that one cannot leave behind'). Here, with marked ruptures in her evocation of birth, Laurens gives breathless form to the abandonment engendered in birth's story of two lives, spherically separated and entwined. In a sense, she speculates, all babies are foundlings, children lost then found, born through abandonment:

> Nous sommes nés abandonnés. La naissance est un lieu à haut risque, un danger qu'on essaie de passer sous silence, un état sauvage qu'on tente d'encadrer comme une photo de famille, le passé qui se déchaîne sur l'avenir, le commencement de la fin. Lieu de naissance: mortel. (p. 106)

> We are born abandoned. Birth is a place of high risk, a danger submitted to silence, a wildness one tries to frame like a family photo, the past that unchains into the future, the beginning of the end. Place of birth: mortal.

If birth, or the memory of birth, cannot be recorded or framed in this way, regarded with an empirical, external view, then, it is because it is tangled up with the grief of separation and abandonment, and with the unknowability of death.

That birth cannot be fully known arguably contributes to its mythologisation as a secret, hidden experience, for which birthing women and people are not afforded the epistemic tools to navigate. This unknowability gives rise to discourses of birth as a fundamentally primitive act that relegates birth-givers to their nature in less than empowering ways. Indeed, Laurens observes that the words birth and nature have a close etymological relationship in French: 'Le mot "naître" a la même origine que le mot "nature": la nativité est naturelle, la naissance est un acte spontané de notre mère nature' (p. 106) ('The verb "to be born" has the same origin as the word "nature": nativity is natural, birth is a spontaneous act of our mother nature'). But as Laurens's autobiographical writing makes plain, not all births proceed according to this simplistic dogma that binds birthing women and people in an ossifying relationship with the natural. As she continues, the Latin root *nativus* has also generated the adjective 'naïf', a notion that suggests a lack of knowledge, or ignorance, but that insinuates at the same time a coming-to-knowledge: 'Toute naissance devrait être naïve, ingénue, innocente comme l'enfant qui vient de naître, une connaissance innée, une reconnaissance immédiate et sans détours – la reconnaissance du ventre' (p. 107) ('Every birth should be naïve, innocent like the child being born, an innate understanding, a recognition, immediate and without detour – the recognition of the womb'). Birth is described here as a coming-to-knowledge, innate in the sense of being entangled in the sensory embodiment of the bubble, but also a reconnaissance, a *recognition* of the entangled other. If the word 'reconnaissance' carries undertones of a (military) survey of the landscape of the body, specifically the womb, Laurens renegotiates this idea in ways that resonate with Sloterdijk's negative rule of gynaecology as a way of approaching birth with delicate empiricism, and in provisional form, rather than with specular excavation. Reconnaissance allows the physicality of the birthing body to be recognised, rather than recorded, offering forms of knowledge that move from innocence and ignorance not to empirical regard but to the relational and the provisional. Playing on the French words *naissance* and *connaissance*, Laurens shows that birthing is always already caught up in relational webs of entangled knowledge: 'la naissance est une connaissance – une co-naissance. Il y a la mère qui met au monde, il y a l'enfant qui vient au monde. Ça va ensemble, ça se tient. Sinon, c'est n'être' (p. 98) ('birth is understanding – a co-understanding. There is the mother who brings life into the world, there is the child who comes into the world. They go together, they belong together. Otherwise, birth isn't (*n'être/ naître*)'). In emphasising entanglement and separation, Laurens's notion of co-naissance allows for ways of recognising the body, and here the womb, as the locus of birth, placing knowledge at the heart of birth while staging the possibility of that knowing in question. In the triadic naissance, co-naissance and reconnaissance, Laurens attends, then, to birth as a form of shared, liminal, irrecuperable experience, but also as a way of coming to – and labouring for – relational, provisional and ever-evolving forms of knowing.

Birth and (Embodied) Aporia

While Laurens scrutinises the irrecuperability of birth at the level of language, the formal aporia surrounding birth is particularly striking in Darrieussecq's 'Encore là'. Opening the collection, Darrieussecq's fictional story draws into relief the traumatic sense of alienation from her own birth-giving that the narrator experiences. This first-person narrative recounts the story of a woman who has recently undergone a C-section after being informed that her baby is positioned transversely. Put under a general anaesthetic for the procedure, the narrator is disappointed, bereft even, not to be able to witness the birth of her daughter, 'le voir sortir gluant et braillant' (p. 10) ('to see her coming out sticky and bawling'). The circumstances of the birth lead to the narrator becoming anaesthetised in more ways than one, resulting in increasing feelings of detachment, post-natal depression and anorexia: 'Je gardais l'impression d'être encore sous l'effet de l'anesthésie, comme si les résidus des produits ne voulaient pas s'évacuer' (p. 13) ('I still had the feeling of being under the effects of the anaesthetic, as if the retained products didn't want to evacuate'). The birth is figured as incomplete in the mind of the narrator, whose self-berating for not having been present is exacerbated by the vocabulary of 'extraction' (p. 9) used by medical professionals to connote the delivery of her baby since, in her telling and internalised understanding, '[o]n ne dit pas *accouchement* quand il y a a césarienne. On n'*accouche* que par voie basse' (p. 11) ('you don't say *give birth* when you have a C-section. You only *give birth* from down there'). That the narrator refers to what has been 'extracted' as 'les résidus des produits' evokes the medical terminology of an 'incomplete' miscarriage rather than acknowledging a newborn baby and underlines her own traumatic sense that the birth has not quite happened.

From the outset, the narrator's sense of guilt and trauma for not having been present to her labour come through starkly in not knowing, and not being able to testify to what has happened, and how:

> Mais il y a eu un petit problème, je n'ai pas bien saisi lequel, et il a fallu m'endormir, m'anesthésier entièrement. Je n'ai pas tout suivi parce que c'est allé très vite, et mon mari a été prié de quitter la salle. Un masque sur mon visage, quelque chose dans ma perfusion, et je n'étais plus là.' (p. 10)

> But there was a little problem, I don't know exactly what, and they had to put me to sleep, to put me under a general anaesthetic. I didn't follow everything because it all happened so quickly, and my husband was urged to leave the room. A mask on my face, something in my perfusion, and I was no longer there.

The repeated fragment 'je n'ai pas' reverberates through the opening pages, accentuating the narrator's feeling of not having been able to participate in the birth, and is amplified further by iterations of the phrase 'je ne sais pas' ('I don't know'), signalling her exclusion from knowledge about the birth. She contrasts this sense of self-absence with the birth of her son, during which she recalls the sensations of his passage brought on by the force of her contractions. With the aid of a controlled epidural, the narrator feels that she has been able to 'bring' her son into the world, a powerful sensation that she now lacks, but that is clearly exacerbated by an internalisation of birth discourses that insist upon the superiority of the 'natural': 'Est-ce que ça m'a manqué aussi de ne pas emmener ma fille au bout de moi, par les *voies naturelles*?' (p. 12) ('Did I also miss being able to bring my daughter to the edge of myself, through *natural passage?*'). The aporia surrounding the birth, around which she has no answers to her many questions (p. 11), is intensified by not having been able to hear the visceral confirmation of her baby's passage into life: her first cry. After she awakens, she feels incapable of asking about it, not knowing who might be able to relate to her the story of 'ce moment inestimable' (p. 11) ('that inestimable moment'), but which she assumes must be utterly unremarkable for the medical professionals present. In her insistence on the narrator's not knowing, Darrieussecq illuminates how her experience of birth precludes her desire to make contact with the embodied passage of knowledge that she remembers previously having experienced.

If the narrator senses that the birth is somehow not her story to tell, she reveals after the opening pages that birth is not in fact the subject she wishes to discuss. Instead, '[j]e voulais parler de mon régime' (p. 12) ('I wanted to talk about my diet') becomes the textual refrain of the story. Unable to connect with her daughter, the narrator instead focuses her energies on losing weight and recuperating a slender form, intending to evacuate herself, not only of the baby, placenta, amniotic fluid and blood, but also the three to four kilos of excess weight that she had gained during pregnancy. It is her stomach area in particular – her 'ventre', the French word also designating the uterus – which vexes her, the excess weight almost seeming to deny that the birth has indeed taken place, and she stares at her C-section scar instead to furnish that bodily evidence: 'Et la cicatrice attestait qu'elle était sortie de moi, qu'elle était bien sortie par là, qu'elle n'était plus du tout dans mon ventre. Je regardais ma cicatrice, et j'essayais de me persuader que mon ventre était vide' (p. 14) ('And the scar proved that she had come from me, that she had really come out through there, that she was no longer in my womb. I looked at my scar, and I tried to persuade myself that my womb was empty'). Noticing that breastfeeding helps her to lose weight, the narrator begins to regulate her own food intake to further empty out her insides, rapidly ridding herself of a couple of kilos per week. The narrator displays all the signs of an incipient anorexia from her singular focus on weight loss, to a willed lack of hunger that belies an unconscious ravenousness that makes itself known only in her dreams, to accentuated tiredness and weakness, and an extreme anguish and isolation that cannot be articulated except through her desperate bodily evacuation (p. 20–1). If the story begins by foregrounding her struggle with not knowing and not being able to tell the story of her daughter's birth, it ends with the narrator having lost contact with others, endeavouring to make herself heard as she embodies the absence enforced by the circumstances of her daughter's birth: 'Personne ne m'entendait. Je parlais, pourtant' (p. 29) ('Nobody could hear me. I was still talking, though').

In her analysis of anorexia and readerly empathy in this story, Kathryn Robson suggests that although the narrator is still speaking at the end, the point is that she is invisible and inaudible, and, like her family, the reader is placed in the position of struggling to make sense of her thoughts. This readerly impasse responds to the narrative fabric of Darrieussecq's story, full of the gaps and aporia already discussed, but also tending to digressions and detours, including frequent though under-developed fragments about the narrator's husband's job reconstructing railway tracks on the Eurostar, and allusions to the bodies of migrants found in the tunnel. For Robson, Darrieussecq creates an equivalence between these damaged bodies, hidden from sight underneath the trains, and the damaged subject of her story who cannot quite be seen and understood. As she writes:

> The point is not to try to look through to see the bodies that lie underneath (which would mean assuming that we can see them independently of the discourses that construct them), not to try to explain or render intelligible the suffering that they denote, but to register the limits of our own vision faced with the revelation of suffering bodies.[15]

Though Robson finds the text's focus on anorexia surprising in a collection devoted to birth stories, I would argue that the form of this story, both in the sense of the evacuated embodied form of the narrator, and in the sparse evacuated form of the text with its aporia and digressions, testify precisely to the traumatic alienation of the birth experience, as well as its invisibility and irrecuperability *as* a story. Just as the narrator cannot be bodily present, cannot *see* the birth of her daughter, so too are we as readers confronted by the impossibility of an empirical account of birth, and, as the narrator's perinatal body disappears before us, by the contingency of our sight.

Conclusion

In *Sight*, Greengrass opens a constellation of ideas and images about what we can and cannot see in ourselves and others. Travelling through the hidden, inscrutable elements of our fleshy, entangled relations, sight is figured as a coming-to-knowledge, the 'digging in the dark', as we saw earlier, of life's impossible quest. The novel follows the protagonist's internal monologue as she grapples with memories of the loss of her mother and narrates her own experiences of pregnancy and birth. Greengrass's prose is interspersed with historical accounts of figures in science, medicine, psychoanalysis and art, who are all in some way engaged in this 'digging in the dark', in the precarious projection of an inside that can never be fully known. Through x-rays, excavations of the mind, casts and imprints, there is a clasping of the body in literal and meta-phorical forms of imaging, though there is always something about the flesh that remains out of sight.

For the authors studied in this chapter, as for Greengrass, birth encapsulates these precarious, uncertain, impossible glimpses of knowledge of the other, the infant and the mother 'coextensive but not conjoined, so that they were like the maps of two mazes inter-leaved, path laid on path but uncrossable, each lending back only into itself'.[16] Reading stories from *Naissances* to mobilise Sloterdijk's negative gynaecology within feminist frames, this chapter has shown how the authors dismantle the dichotomy of creation and procrea-tion, and offer ways to rethink the incommensurability of birth. Just as they draw into relief popular clichés surrounding birth, including those of the unspeakable and the unspoken, so too do they offer relational and provisional narratives that attend to birth as an embodied, epistemic and epistemological event, in ways that allow for insight into what a feminist negative gynaecology might look like. In the end, though, it is not simply that approaching birth demands forms of delicate empiricism, a sensitivity to the embodied entanglement of the bubble that coexists with forms of coming-to-knowledge that will always slip away from an external regard, but, crucially, that the feminist labour of thinking birth itself offers an unparalleled narrative, philosophical – and political – opportunity to reflect upon the epistemological conundrum epitomised by Greengrass, of stepping between a light source and a screen in the impossible attempt of knowing oneself and others.

Works Cited

Arendt, Hannah, *The Human Condition* (Chicago IL: Chicago University Press, 1958).

Cavarero, Adriana, *In Spite of Plato: A Feminist Rewriting of Ancient Philosophy*, trans. by Serena Andalini-D'Onofrio and Aine O'Healy (Cambridge: Polity, 1995).

Cosslet, Tess, *Women Writing Childbirth: Modern Discourses of Motherhood* (Manchester: Manchester University Press, 1994).

Cusk, Rachel, *A Life's Work* (London: Faber and Faber, 2001).

Greengrass, Jessie, *Sight* (London: J. M. Originals, 2018).

Gurton Wachter, Lily, 'The Stranger Guest: The Literature of Motherhood and New Pregnancy', *Los Angeles Review of Books* (29 July 2016), *https://lareviewofbooks.org/article/stranger-guest-literature-pregnancy-new-motherhood/* (accessed 6 December 2021).

Hill, Milli, *Give Birth Like a Feminist* (London: HQ, 2019).

Irigaray, Luce, *To Be Born* (London: Palgrave MacMillan, 2017).

Kristeva, Julia, *Histoires d'amour* (Paris: Gallimard, 1985).

Laurens, Camille, *Philippe* (Paris: Gallimard, 1995).

Lortholary, Isabelle (ed.), *Naissances: récits* (Paris: L'Iconoclaste, 2005).

Martin, Alison, 'Report on "Natality" in Arendt, Cavarero and Irigaray', *Paragraph*, 25/1, 32–53.

Nelson, Maggie, *The Argonauts* (London: Melville House, 2016).

Oakley, Ann, *Women Confined: Towards a Sociology of Birth* (Oxford: Robertson, 1980).

Phipps, Alison, *The Politics of the Body: Gender in a Neoliberal and Neoconservative Age* (London: Polity Press, 2014).

Rich, Adrienne, *Of Woman Born: Motherhood as Experience and Institution* (New York: W. W. Norton Company, 1995 [1976]).

Robson, Kathryn, *I Suffer, Therefore I Am: Engaging with Empathy in Contemporary French Women's Writing* (Cambridge: Legenda, 2019).

Rodgers, Catherine, 'Création ou procréation? Mise en perspective de la réponse de Marie Darrieussecq dans *Le Bébé*, *Dalhousie French Studies*, 98 (2012), 89–99.

Rye, Gill, *Narratives of Mothering: Women's Writing in Contemporary France* (Newark DE: University of Delaware Press, 2009).

—— 'Registering Trauma: The Body in Childbirth in Contemporary French Women's Writing', *Nottingham French Studies*, 45/3 (Autumn 2006), 92–104.

Sloterdijk, Peter, *Spheres*, vol. 1, *Bubbles*, trans. Wieland Hoban (Los Angeles CA: Semiotext(e), 2011).

Tomlinson, Maria, *From Menstruation to the Menopause: The Female Fertility Cycle in Contemporary Women's Writing in French* (Liverpool: Liverpool University Press, 2021).

Worth-Stylianou, Valérie, 'Birthing Tales and Collective Memory in Recent French Fiction', in Gill Rye *et al.* (eds), *Motherhood in Literature and Cultures: Perspectives from Europe* (New York: Routledge, 2018), pp. 58–69.

Notes

1 Rachel Cusk, *A Life's Work* (London: Faber and Faber, 2001), pp. 14–15.

2 Gill Rye, 'Registering Trauma: The Body in Childbirth in Contemporary French Women's Writing', *Nottingham French Studies*, 45/3 (Autumn 2006), 92–104; *Narratives of Mothering: Women's Writing in Contemporary France* (Newark DE: University of Delaware Press, 2009). See also Tess Cosslet, *Women Writing Childbirth: Modern Discourses of Motherhood* (Manchester: Manchester University Press, 1994).

3 Adrienne Rich, *Of Woman Born: Motherhood as Experience and Institution* (New York: W. W. Norton Company, 1995 [1976]), p. 157.

4   On the medicalisation of birth see Rich or Ann Oakley, *Women Confined: Towards a Sociology of Birth* (Oxford: Robertson, 1980). On the (neoliberal) intensification of 'natural' birth discourse, see Alison Phipps, *The Politics of the Body: Gender in a Neoliberal and Neoconservative Age* (London: Polity Press, 2014). For a 'birth manual' that endeavours to negotiate medical and 'birth positive' discourses through a feminist frame, see Milli Hill, *Give Birth Like a Feminist* (London: HQ, 2019).

5   Isabelle Lortholary (ed.), *Naissances: récits* (Paris: L'Iconoclaste, 2005). Despite the contributions of these prominent authors, scholarship on this particular collection remains relatively limited. See Valérie Worth-Stylianou, 'Birthing Tales and Collective Memory in Recent French Fiction', in Gill Rye *et al.* (eds), *Motherhood in Literature and Cultures: Perspectives from Europe* (New York: Routledge, 2018), pp. 58–69 for an analysis of memory and the time of labour, and the baby as animal; Kathryn Robson, *I Suffer, Therefore I Am: Engaging with Empathy in Contemporary French Women's Writing* (Cambridge: Legenda, 2019), which contains a section on Darrieussecq's story; and Maria Tomlinson, *From Menstruation to the Menopause: The Female Fertility Cycle in Contemporary Women's Writing in French* (Liverpool: Liverpool University Press, 2021), which considers stories by Darrieussecq, Desarthe and Villovitch. Catherine Rodgers also refers to the collection in 'Création ou procréation: Mise en perspective de la réponse de Marie Darrieussecq dans *Le Bébé*, *Dalhousie French Studies*, 98 (2012), 89–99.

6   Jessie Greengrass, *Sight* (London: J. M. Originals, 2018), p. 190.

7   Lily Gurton Wachter, 'The Stranger Guest: The Literature of Motherhood and New Pregnancy', *Los Angeles Review of Books* (29 July 2016), *https://lareviewofbooks.org/article/stranger-guest-literature-pregnancy-new-motherhood/* (accessed 6 December 2021).

8   Maggie Nelson, *The Argonauts* (London: Melville House, 2016), p. 167.

9   Gurton Wachter, 'The Stranger Guest'.

10   Luce Irigaray, *To Be Born* (London: Palgrave Macmillan, 2017); Hannah Arendt, *The Human Condition* (Chicago IL: Chicago University Press, 1958); Adriana Cavarero, *In Spite of Plato: A Feminist Rewriting of Ancient Philosophy*, trans. by Serena Andalini-D'Onofrio and Aine O'Healy (Cambridge: Polity, 1995). On the three thinkers' approach to natality, see Alison Martin, 'Report on "Natality" in Arendt, Cavarero and Irigaray', *Paragraph*, 25/1, 32–53.

11   Julia Kristeva, *Histoires d'amour* (Paris: Gallimard, 1985); Bracha Ettinger, *The Matrixial Borderspace* (Minneapolis MN: University of Minnesota Press, 2005).

12   Peter Sloterdijk, *Spheres*, vol. 1, *Bubbles*, trans. Wieland Hoban (Los Angeles CA: Semiotext(e), 2011), p. 320.

13   See Rodgers, 'Création ou procréation?' for a discussion of this dichotomy in recent French women's writing.

14   Camille Laurens, *Philippe* (Paris: Gallimard, 1995).

15   Robson, *I Suffer, Therefore I Am*, p. 36.

16   Greengrass, *Sight*, p. 160.

Chapter 5

Sexual Identity as Work in Mireille Best's *Il n'y a pas d'hommes au paradis*

BLASE A. PROVITOLA

Two recent award-winning and autobiographically inflected books have featured the flight of gay youth from conservative, working-class upbringings to the progressivism and social possibility of 'Gay Paree': Didier Eribon's Bourdieusian *auto-analyse Retour à Reims* ('Returning to Reims', 2009 [2013]) and Édouard Louis's *En finir avec Eddy Bellegueule* ('The End of Eddy', 2014 [2017]).[1] Both narratives chart the emergence of an urban gay identity whose promise of fulfilment necessitates severing ties with home, regardless of how alienating that process may be. For these sociologists, both of whom have distanced themselves from their families (as Louis's title indicates, he even changed his last name), their status as *transfuges de classe* ('class defectors') enables the development of their sexual identity. This chapter nuances male-authored accounts of working-class homophobia by adding the perspective of one lesbian writer whose life and works complicate the association of same-sex desire with cultural capital and 'gay flight'.

Mireille Best (1943–2005) grew up in Normandy in a working-class family and was employed at a factory before joining the civil service. Though her works were published by the prestigious Gallimard press and she received favourable reviews in mainstream and lesbian media alike, she eschewed the Parisian literary scene, citing as her primary source of inspiration 'Albertine Best, an itinerant fishmonger, my grandmother who brought me up and made me read all the good books'.[2] Best is one of the only French lesbian authors to – as one critic in *Lesbia* magazine put it – foreground 'la vie des gens simples, les quotidiens aux matins difficiles et aux fins de mois à bout de ficelle' ('whose mornings are tough and ends of the month are on a shoestring'), thus putting an end to 'le scandale du lesbianisme des intellectuelles, d'une minorité privilégiée par l'argent ou par le métier' ('the scandal of the lesbianism of intellectuals, of a minority privileged by money or by trade').[3]

This comes into sharp focus in her final novel, *Il n'y a pas d'hommes au paradis* ('There are No Men in Heaven') (1995), which focuses on the protagonist's struggle to pursue a same-sex relationship without losing her family. Josèphe's first-person narrative alternates between her coming-of-age and first love in Normandy during the *Trente Glorieuses* ('Glorious Thirty') and her life as a single, middle-aged woman in the South of France in the early 1990s, contemplating the chilling resurgence of anti-Semitism and rise of the National Front. As Josèphe manages her complex relationships with her parents and former girlfriend, it becomes clear that social class and cultural capital impact her understanding of sexual identity and approach to disclosure. This not only complicates teleological narratives common in the genre of the gay and lesbian *bildungsroman*, but also stresses that the management of sexual subjectivity constitutes a form of labour that disproportionately burdens working-class women.[4]

The 'Happiness Script' of Gay Identity

'J'aurais dû dire non. Non non non. J'aurais dû écouter mon père, empêcher Rachel de rêver ma mère au lieu de la regarder bien en face…' ('I should have said no. No no no. I should have listened to my father, stopped Rachel from imagining my mother instead of taking a good hard look at her…').[5] Looking back, Josèphe wishes she had trusted herself. She had been content with having her girlfriend, Rachel, over for dinner under the complicit eye of her father, with the ambiguity of their status as 'copines' ('friends') allowing them to ward off her mother's suspicion. Amidst her financial precarity and the mounting pressure of Rachel's exasperation, Josèphe is unsure of which path might bring her happiness: 'Mais je ne parvenais plus à m'orienter dans mon brouillard' (p. 104) ('But I could no longer find my way in my fog').[6] When Josèphe finally gives in, her mother kicks her out. Her subsequent cohabitation with

Rachel, however, is less a new beginning than it is the beginning of the end; unemployed and isolated, Josèphe spirals into a depression. While her unhappiness could easily be chalked up to the sorts of working-class homophobia common in contemporary gay *bildungsromane*, it is above all the result of her strenuous negotiation of visibility not only with her family but also with her wealthier girlfriend.[7] What is at stake for Josèphe is not whether she should pursue a relationship with a woman, but whether she and this particular woman are able to speak that relationship in the same language.

Love and desire are shaped by and translated into recognisable sexual identities and cultural narratives. In *Réflexions sur la question gay* (*'Insult and the Making of the Gay Self'*, 1999 [2004]), Didier Eribon uses Sartre's Jewish subject to theorise the gay self: he moves from a state of 'being-in-itself' ('en-soi'), in which he is constituted through the regard of others, towards a state of 'being-for-itself' ('pour-soi'), in which he constitutes himself as a subject by reappropriating the minority identity assigned to him.[8] He must 'se *faire* gay' (*'make* himself gay') to resist the violence of a society that 'le fait *être* homosexuel' ('makes him *be* gay'), a multi-layered process of 'coming out' that entails adopting and reworking cultural scripts shaped by socio-economic context.[9] Drawing on John D'Emilio, Eribon suggests that capitalism relies upon the reproductive power of the family unit while also lending some individuals the capacity to sell their labour elsewhere and thus acquire the mobility necessary to leave home and seek out urban sexual subcultures.[10] If, as Eve Kosofsky Sedgwick has argued, the epistemology of the closet has persisted as an admittedly reductive and yet nonetheless dominant paradigm for understanding same-sex desire in a Western context, then it is crucial to understand how this spatial metaphor and its attendant promises of fulfilment are conditioned by social class.[11]

This model of gay subjectivity subscribes to what Sara Ahmed calls the 'promise of happiness'.[12] People are pushed to orientate themselves towards objects associated with joy; it is what gives 'forward direction' to their narratives, even – and perhaps especially – when that promise fails to deliver. These socially sanctioned cultural narratives, or 'happiness scripts', shape identity by acting as 'straightening devices, ways of aligning bodies with what is already lined up. The points that accumulate as lines can be performatives: a point on a line can be a demand to stay in line' (p. 91). Emergent subjectivities coalesce around existent modes of being.

The 'coming out' model of gay identity, which adheres to the (fundamentally heterosexual) epistemology of the closet, can be considered an emerging happiness script. It may not appear coercive when compared with the dominance of heterosexual society, yet it still persistently reorientates same-sex desire around recognisable trajectories, tantalising subjects with the possibility of belonging. In Foucauldian terms, such a script can be understood as both disciplinary and productive: all scripts have a hold on us through the truth regime of sexuality, but not all of them have an equal hold.[13] The LGBT *bildungsroman* disseminates such narratives, staging the negotiation between individual trajectories and social forces.[14] And sometimes even the most liberatory narratives must mourn that which is lost in the pursuit of self-fulfilment. In *Returning to Reims*, Eribon owns up to the fact that, for him, the making of the gay self was constituted as much through the disavowal of his working-class origins as it was through his escape from working-class homophobia.[15] Sexual identity formation is itself a form of work whose performance differs according to social origins and cultural capital.

Sociologist Natacha Chetcuti has suggested that the making of the lesbian self is impacted by women's overall lower levels of economic independence and disposable income.[16] Salima Amari in turn demonstrates that lesbians of North African descent, and in particular those from working-class families, innovate approaches to tacitly communicate their sexualities without compromising family support structures, which can lead to tensions with same-sex partners who want to be 'out' in all spheres of their lives.[17] Working-class women who desire women must thus negotiate pressure from multiple conflicting happiness scripts: one from their family, who wants them to marry a member of the opposite sex, and one from their same-sex partner, who wants to be fully integrated into their family's life.

If social class shapes the naming and disclosure of sexuality, then it may also exacerbate the gap between what working-class subjects think they *should be* feeling and what they actually *do* feel when following a particular happiness script. Ahmed uses the term 'affect alien' to refer to someone whose feelings are out of step with the world around them, and who thus reveals the illusory and compulsory nature of such scripts. This strenuous management of strategy and affect can also be considered a form of what Arlie Hochschild has called 'emotion work': the management of affective responses to produce an observable effect for others.[18] If, as feminist scholars have demonstrated, work conditions behaviour outside the workplace,[19] then it follows that social class impacts the 'emotion work' inherent in negotiating gender performance[20] and identity disclosure.[21]

Mireille Best's works are rich with the staging of such complex negotiations, which cannot be neatly encapsulated in identitarian terms. She rejected the term 'écriture lesbienne' ('lesbian writing'),[22] insisting that lesbianism in her texts presents itself 'sans se faire remarquer, sans provocation, mais sans masque' ('without drawing attention to itself, without being provocative, but without masking itself either').[23] Her characters' frequent ambivalence to lesbian identity lends complexity to prevalent narratives of gay selfhood.[24] By portraying family as the intimate locus where work, sex and cultural capital structure identity and communication, *Il n'y a pas d'hommes au paradis* disrupts not only 'the promise' of happy heterosexuality, but also the more recent promise of happy homosexuality. For Josèphe, adherence to such scripts becomes its own form of work – whether through the pursuit of financial independence that enables greater privacy, or through the effort to retain ties to her community of origin while pursuing a life with Rachel. Attempting to follow a bourgeois gay happiness script constitutes a form of 'emotion work' that proves especially taxing for working-class women.

Tacit Communication as 'Emotion Work'

As Josèphe looks back on the first time she met Rachel, her childhood best friend's older sister, she recalls her mother's warning that she would never fit in with that family: 'Oh, ces gens-là… Ces gens-là ne sont pas de notre monde, tu seras mal à l'aise, tu verras' (p. 21) ('Oh, those people… Those people don't live in the same world as us, you'll be uncomfortable, you'll see'). Rachel's universe will – with the inevitability of the future tense – remain closed to Josèphe. Her mother's pronouncement functions less as a warning than as a performative utterance; Josèphe, foreshadowing the circumstances of their subsequent break-up, bitterly notes that 'Les prophéties de ma mère se réalisaient toujours' (p. 21) ('My mother's prophecies always came true'). Ultimately, Josèphe's discomfort with Rachel's social circles is one cause of their separation.

Later in the novel, Josèphe recalls that first afternoon at Rachel's house in words that echo her mother's warning against crossing social boundaries. And yet the uneasiness that she initially feels exhilarates her as she begins to form a palpable, unspoken connection with Rachel:

> Dans le bus qui me ramenait vers notre impasse boueuse, j'avais le sentiment d'avoir franchi une frontière et changé de monde le temps d'une sieste ensoleillée... Là-bas, une lumière venue d'ailleurs miroitait au bec de la théière   Sourdait du regard de Rachel   Me balayait l'intérieur du crâne comme un éclat de soleil renvoyé par un cent de miroirs... (p. 77, lack of punctuation in the original)

> In the bus that led me back to our muddy cul-de-sac, I felt as if I had crossed a border into a new world for the duration of a sun-kissed nap... There, an otherworldly light gleamed off of the teapot's spout   Welled up from Rachel's gaze   Swept through the inside of my skull like a sparkle of light bouncing off of a hundred mirrors...

Best's use of multiple spaces in lieu of semicolons underscores the rush of thoughts and images that overwhelm the protagonist. These gaps tend to appear at moments of emotional intensity and become as expressive as the words themselves. This stresses that it is not Rachel's speech that first strikes Josèphe, but her gaze which, compared to light reflected in a mirror, recalls Josèphe's loving father, who works in a mirror factory. This comparison juxtaposes such luminosity with the dark dead end where Josèphe lives. Her desire for intimacy, which stems from Rachel's singularity rather than her gender, manifests itself in glances, silences and refracted light.

They soon develop a close bond based upon 'un avertissement tacite, catégorique bien qu'informulé' (p. 79) ('a tacit warning, categorical yet unspoken'). Their shared attention to the non-verbal is at the very core of their friendship. Josèphe senses that naming their relationship could threaten it, sometimes abruptly leaving Rachel's house 'de peur de ne pouvoir retenir quelque abandon irréparable ou quelque aveu prématuré qui aurait l'air d'une reddition...' (p. 83) ('for fear of being unable to hold back some irreparable abandon or premature confession that would seem like a surrender...'). The noun 'reddition', which can refer to either a military capitulation or the presentation of an account for examination, frames the direct expression of love as a form of defeat and potential exposure to unwanted scrutiny. Their shared appreciation of subtle cues is threatened, however, once others discover the nature of their relationship.

Josèphe quickly discovers that her peers are focused on labels that are of little importance to her. When she shares the excitement and anxiety of this first love with her neighbour and close friend, Enrique, he ignores her emotional disarray and demands that she translate it into a term that he can understand, since the only word he knows – 'pédé' ('faggot') – does not seem to apply to girls. Infuriated by his obsession with labels, she remains focused on her affective experience: 'Moi j'avais le cœur entre braise et cendres, de vraies nausées d'incertitude ... et lui, tout ce qu'il trouvait à dire, c'est "Comment ça s'appelle?"!' (pp. 79–80) ('My heart was smouldering, I was sick from uncertainty ... and all he could think to say was "What's that called?"!'). She defines her relationship in universal, non-identitarian terms: 'Ça s'appelle l'amour, espèce d'abruti!' (p. 81) ('It's called love, you moron!'). Aware that others may view her newfound love in a less positive light, she sees no reason to risk jeopardising their time together by telling her parents. Her laborious management of discretion and disclosure thus protects her relationship – that is, until Rachel dismisses her strategy as nothing more than shame.

When communicating their relationship to their families, Josèphe opts for discretion and tacit recognition, whereas Rachel prefers to directly reveal it to her mother, Rosa. When Josèphe asks about Rosa's reaction, Rachel nonchalantly responds, 'Trois fois rien, que voulais-tu qu'elle dise?... Elle a dit que je la ferais mourir, c'est tout' (p. 91) ('Next to nothing, what do you expect?... She said I would be the death of her, that's all'). Rachel tempers Josèphe's alarm by explaining that, for her Jewish mother, such hyperbolic language is a form of acceptance: 'Elles sont à deux doigts de mourir cinquante fois par jour, les mamas juives, te tracasse pas!' (p. 92) ('Jewish mums are on the brink of death fifty times a day, don't worry!'). Though these words would mean outright rejection coming from Josèphe's mother, in the context of Rachel's family they signal that she will not be cast out just because of a same-sex relationship.

Josèphe knows that such a declaration would garner a violent reaction from her mother, whose frequent abusive outbursts are exacerbated by her alcoholism. Josèphe's father, on the other hand, though usually absent due to long factory shifts, is much more affectionate, and the novel's title is a lyric from a song he sometimes sings Josèphe to comfort her following bouts of her mother's cruelty. Josèphe thus strategically turns to him first for recognition of her relationship, testing the waters by nervously repeating to him a phrase she heard from Rachel: 'toutes les femmes sont lesbiennes' (p. 93) ('all women are lesbians'). To avoid coming out individually, Josèphe comes out for *all* women, making her sexuality tacitly understood while also framing it as proof of her gender conformity.

However, when he demands to know the source of this theory, she blurts out that it doesn't matter, and the implications of this unexpected generalisation begin to dawn on him: 'Est-ce que je comprends bien ce que tu veux dire?... Ah, nom de Dieu!' (p. 94) ('Am I following what you're saying here?... Good Lord!'). The meaning of this telling ellipsis is clear, but just when he asks her to stop beating around the bush, they are interrupted by Maman's unexpected return. They both know better than to pursue the discussion in her company, and their shared silence confirms to Josèphe that, like Rachel's mother, he will be – if not encouraging – then at least accepting.

When Josèphe asks her parents if she can have Rachel over for dinner, she sees 'un éclair d'appréhension' (p. 96) ('a flash of apprehension') in her father's eyes, an expression of his concern for what might happen if Maman discovers the nature of their daughter's relationship. He quietly assents under the pretence that he would enjoy having the opportunity to play music with Rachel, who is training to become a professional violinist. When Josèphe's mother begins berating him for wanting to play his 'accordéon minable' (pp. 96–7) ('shabby accordion') in front of a formally trained musician, Josèphe detects in her father's face a 'petit sourire qui [lui] disait de ne pas [s']en faire, que tout cela, à force, s'arrangerait' ('small smile telling [her] not to fret, that all of this would work itself out eventually'). He wordlessly reassures her.

The meaningful glances and expressive ellipses exchanged between Josèphe and her father begin to slowly weave her same-sex relationship into the fabric of the family home. Such exchanges echo Michel Verret's analysis of working-class cultures, whose non-verbal communication is often rooted in shared codes and gestures, some of which reflect factory culture.[25] Such influence is one example of what Kathi Weeks describes when she states that 'work does not thus simply abandon us to non-work pursuits but is carried by subjects into the temporalities, subjectivities, and socialities of non-work'.[26] Yet such nuances are lost on Rachel, who dismisses anything short of directly coming out as cowardly (p. 104).

Not wanting to appear ashamed, Josèphe ends up telling her father that she loves Rachel. Unsurprised though clearly disgruntled, he urges her to resume their strategy of complicity: 'Mais tu n'as pas besoin d'aller tout raconter à ta mère… D'ailleurs, tu la connais, elle ne posera pas de question. Alors tu peux au moins la boucler?' (pp. 103–4) ('But you don't need go telling your mother all that… Besides, you know her, she won't ask any questions. So can you at least keep your mouth shut?'). This plea is a way to both manage his own discomfort and enable Josèphe's familial and romantic relationships to co-exist with minimal conflict. As the reader subsequently learns, his approach to managing familial disclosure is conditioned by his and his wife's contrasting class trajectories.

Josèphe's father comes from a family of factory workers, whereas his wife was originally bourgeois. When she chose to marry him over the engineer that her parents had arranged for her, they severed all ties with her. Though he worked hard to support her, she had to take a job at a factory to make ends meet when he was sent off to a German labour camp during the war. When he came home from the war, he explains, 'C'est un peu comme si on lui avait volé sa vie…' (p. 133) ('It's almost as if her life had been stolen from her…'). She had become the spiteful woman that she would remain throughout her daughter's life. Josèphe, taken aback by her father's cavalier attitude towards his own devastating hardships, asks him: 'Et à toi, on ne te l'a pas volée, ta vie?' ('What about you? Wasn't your life stolen from you too?'). For the first time in her life, she sees tears well up in his eyes as he hesitantly responds 'Je ne sais pas' ('I don't know'). He is so acclimatised to the drudgery of manual labour that he only just then stops to consider that his life could have been otherwise. Though at work he spends his days manufacturing mirrors, he has always been so busy providing for his family that he never once had the time to stop and look at himself.

His wife's resentment of her own loss of cultural and actual capital, on the other hand, has left her desperately distancing herself from any signifier of her failure to live out the bourgeois life that she could have had – whether it be her husband's accordion or her daughter's deviant sexuality. Thus, when Josèphe ultimately caves to Rachel's repeated demands to reveal their relationship to both parents, her mother reacts by instantly kicking her out of the house, inflicting upon her own daughter the familial exclusion to which she had been subjected for marrying a factory worker. And it is at the very moment that she must definitively leave home that her mother's prophecy – that she will never fit in with *those* people – begins to come true as she struggles to adhere to the same happiness script as her wealthier girlfriend.

The Cost of Disclosure

With nowhere else to turn after being thrown out by her mother, Josèphe has no choice but to move in with Rachel's family as she is confronted with the realities of the job search. However, she refuses to 'vivre aux crochets de Rosa – ni même de Rachel, qui prétendait avoir des économies grâce à ses petits concerts' (p. 108) ('leech off of Rosa – or even Rachel, who claimed to have savings thanks to her little concerts'). Josèphe is hyper-aware that Rachel's career as a concert violinist is made possible only by her mother's support. Josèphe has no such financial security and so must abandon her dreams of studying philosophy in order to hurriedly find a source of income. Whereas coming out has little bearing on Rachel's material circumstances, it compromises Josèphe's opportunities for social mobility. Her disclosure of her love for Rachel quite literally costs her.

This precarity, which results from her non-conformity to heterosexual norms, harkens back to the story behind Josèphe's name at the start of the novel. During her pregnancy, Josèphe's mother is convinced that she is pregnant with a baby boy and insists that her son be named after her grandfather. When, much to her chagrin, she ends up having a daughter, her decision to foreground her superior origins outweighs norms of femininity. Yet when her husband goes to register the birth, the civil service employee refuses to accept Joseph as a girl's name, explaining that the bullying he endured due to his own name, Napoléon, drove him out of school and to his current dead-end bureaucratic position. Since femininity appears crucial for a young woman's professional success, the disgruntled Napoléon compromises by listing the feminised form. Later in life, her gender and sexual non-conformity ends up limiting her employment prospects.

As she desperately searches for her first job, the 'emotion work' of managing disclosure now gives way to the affective labour required for a woman to sell herself during job interviews.[27] After endlessly scanning job postings and waiting in line, she is received by 'un costume trois pièces dédaigneux' ('a disdainful three-piece suit'), the sartorial metonym of corporatism whose gaze indicates that 'ni votre dossier ni votre mine éteinte n'ont de quoi l'enthousiasmer' (pp. 108–9) ('neither your dossier nor your lacklustre expression impresses him much'). She describes leaving each interview 'prête à flinguer son propre reflet dans les glaces' (p. 109) ('ready to shoot her own reflection in the mirrors'), with this recurrent mirror imagery recalling her father's own alienation as a factory worker. Yet her alienation hinges upon the post-Fordist rise of a service economy in which, as Jeremy Lane puts it, workers are pressured to 'feign their intense commitment and motivation in even the most menial of service-sector tasks'.[28] The gendered nature of this false enthusiasm is clear as she imagines her disapproving mother chastising her for failing to properly perform happy femininity for potential employers: 'C'est donc une torture d'avoir le sourire? De mettre un soupçon de rouge à lèvres?' (p. 109) ('Would it be torture for you to smile? Or put on a hint of lipstick?'). In an imagined retort, she likens all work to sex work to highlight that she must sell her affect and body no matter what the job: 'Oui, maman, c'est une torture Oui ou non ai-je à vendre le travail que je peux fournir, ou une apparence en vitrine comme les prostituées d'Amsterdam?' (p. 109) ('Yes mom it would be torture Tell me am I selling the labour I can supply, or a window display like the prostitutes in Amsterdam?'). Josèphe refuses the gendered scripts necessary for professional success and social mobility, which weigh heavily upon women like her with no access to higher education.

Only when Josèphe finally gets a job is she able to re-establish contact with her mother. When she tells her father that she has been hired by the city as a cultural events planner, she feels her 'cage thoracique qui se décoince' ('rib cage loosen') as if she might '[s']envoler d'allégresse' (p. 110) ('take flight with happiness'), her modest ascension of the social hierarchy making her feel as light as a songbird. This normative marker of success might just lead Maman to cave to her husband's persistent attempts to reconcile her with their daughter. Josèphe's father continually reframes the situation for his wife until he manages to extract, as Josèphe puts it, 'non pas un assentiment mais une forme de concession à l'évidence...' ('not an agreement but a form of concession to the obvious...'), in part by telling her that their daughter's arrangement is 'très courant chez les artistes' (p. 255) ('very common among artists'). Maman will never truly embrace her daughter's proclivities, but she might passively accept them if cloaked in glamorous artists' garb that plays into her respectability politics. Indeed, Josèphe realises that her mother's begrudging respect for social mobility has finally worked in her favour: 'Cassandre ma mère vient d'être battue dans un coin de son territoire' (p. 110) ('My mother Cassandra has just been defeated on her own territory'). Yet if her mother is the Cassandra in the tragedy of their relationship, then her prophecies will still be fulfilled no matter how much Josèphe tries to ignore them. And so they are, through Josèphe's gradual estrangement from Rachel.

After they move into their own apartment amidst the protests of May 1968, Rachel grows distant and impatient with Josèphe's depression and inability to psychologically distance herself from her mother. Preferring the company of Rosa, who calls the student protests a 'Révolution de pacotille' ('sham Revolution'), Josèphe feels worlds away from Rachel who is off leading 'sa Révolution à elle, dans un groupuscule parisien qui contestait la chefferie mâle' (p. 137) ('a Revolution all her own, in a Parisian groupuscule contesting male chiefdom'). She becomes increasingly jealous of this 'minuscule planète de la galaxie lesbienne' (p. 139) ('miniscule planet of the lesbian galaxy'), an insular, privileged elite whose comfort in shared identity feels foreign to her. She describes the seemingly exaggerated pleasure that her girlfriend derives from her newfound bond with these women in terms akin to infidelity: 'Et ça n'en revenait pas – au propre comme au figuré, car Rachel s'attardait vraiment! – de s'aimer tant et de si bien s'entre-comprendre...' (p. 140) ('And she couldn't seem to get enough – literally and figuratively, since Rachel never made it home on time! – of so much mutual love and understanding...').

Like her parents, Josèphe comes to associate lesbian *identity* (though not same-sex love and intimacy) with cultural capital. That attitude is echoed by local Communist Party leaders, who smirkingly refer to her and Rachel as 'intellectuelles' (p. 179) ('intellectuals') before excluding them due to the association between lesbianism and bourgeois decadence. When they later discover a comrade stuffing a membership form in their postbox, Rachel brusquely stops him by telling him they are 'lesbiennes' (p. 180) ('lesbians'), only to be informed that the party line has changed. It is the first time that this term is used to refer to Josèphe, and it is Rachel who pronounces it, belying her desire for Josèphe to feel at home in this identity.

After May 1968, which is ultimately as politically insignificant in Josèphe's life as it is meaningful in Rachel's, Josèphe finds a new target for her jealousy: the gaggle of admiring lesbians that cluster around her girlfriend after every concert. This final mention of lesbian sociality only serves to underscore Josèphe's self-loathing as she feels herself shrink next to the immensity of their light and heat:

> Mais les lesbiennes me faisaient peur: elles rivalisent beaucoup moins qu'elles ne communient, et il montait de leur attente admirative une si formidable chaleur qu'auprès de ce brasier je n'étais plus qu'un morceau de bougie achevant de charbonner dans le courant d'air. (p. 191)

> But the lesbians scared me: they aren't so much in competition as they are in communion, and such a formidable warmth rose from their awaiting admiration that next to that blaze I was nothing more than a candle stub steadily blackening amidst the draught.

Restricting her use of the L-word to this ethereal sect, Josèphe distances herself from their warmth by likening herself to a household object whose purpose – to produce light – will soon have run its course. That they are convivial rather than competitive only worsens her sense of isolation; in a space where Rachel burns bright at the hub of a community of loving women, Josèphe's malaise deepens as she can only conjure the darkness of her family home and her mother's icy stare.[29] If, as Sara Ahmed reminds us, 'comfort is the effect of bodies being able to "sink" into spaces that have already taken their shape', then discomfort is 'an effect of bodies inhabiting spaces that do not take or "extend" to their shape'.[30] Josèphe is not merely *jealous* of potential rivals; she is *envious* of Rachel's capacity to find fulfilment among other like-minded women.

Thus, when she discovers that Rachel is cheating on her with one of these women, it appears as nothing more than the inevitable result of her growing alienation from a community to which she never felt she belonged in the first place. During their final fight, Rachel all but shouts at Josèphe that she is becoming her mother. Rachel moves out, and Josèphe does not pursue her. Instead, she finds a job organising cultural events at a church in a village in the south. After a long and solitary period witnessing the rise of the same anti-Semitism that her mother endorsed, lightning strikes the town's belfry just outside of her window, ending a cycle that not even her elderly mother's death had been able to break. This inspires Josèphe to return to Le Havre, if not to find a future with Rachel then to at least envision the possibility of any future at all. As Josèphe packs her bags, she imagines telling Rachel that '[elle a échappé] cette fois, à l'œil de [sa] mère' (p. 284) ('this time she escaped her mother's watchful eye'). Far from the social pressures of her adolescence, she is at last able to find her way in her fog.

Il n'y a pas d'hommes au paradis stages the drama of two women who do not share the same emergent happiness script of lesbian identity and community. Josèphe, the 'affect alien', never quite feels how she should; she makes sacrifices to abandon one 'script' in favour of another, only to find out that both scripts were wrong for her all along. Her persistent malaise highlights the hidden costs of the 'emotion work' required to conform to ultimately dissatisfying models of individual fulfilment. Best's novel, void of a tempting optimism, quietly urges readers to consider how certain working-class women pursue relationships with women while resisting lesbian happiness scripts and labouring to forge their own complex paths.

Works Cited

Ahmed, Sara, *The Cultural Politics of Emotion*, 2nd edition (Edinburgh: Edinburgh University Press, 2014 [2004]).

—— *The Promise of Happiness* (Durham NC: Duke University Press, 2010).

Amari, Salima, *Lesbiennes de l'immigration: construction de soi et relations familiales* (Vulaines sur Seine: Éditions du Croquant, 2018).

Best, Mireille, *Il n'y a pas d'hommes au paradis* (Paris: Gallimard, 1995).

Cairns, Lucille, *Lesbian Desire in Post-1968 French Literature* (Lewiston NY: Edwin Mellen Press, 2002).

de Ceccatty, René, 'Ça s'appelle l'amour', *Le Monde*, 7 April 1995.

Chetcuti, Natacha, *Se dire lesbienne: vie de couple, sexualité, représentation de soi* (Paris: Payot, 2010).

D'Emilio, John, 'Capitalism and Gay Identity', in *Making Trouble: Essays on Gay History, Politics, and the University* (New York: Routledge, 1992), pp. 4–14.

Downward, Lisa, and Giovanna Summerfield, *New Perspectives on the European Bildungsroman* (New York: Continuum, 2012).

Eribon, Didier, *Insult and the Making of the Gay Self*, trans. Michael Lucey (Durham NC: Duke University Press, 2004).

—— *Réflexions sur la question gay*, 2nd edition (Paris: Flammarion, 2012 [1999]).

—— *Retour à Reims* (Paris: Fayard, 2009).

——— *Returning to Reims*, trans. Michael Lucey (Los Angeles CA: Semiotext(e), 2013).

Forcedange, Laurence, 'Celles qui ont des ailes', *Lesbia* (May 1986).

Foucault, Michel, *Histoire de la sexualité I: la volonté de savoir* (Paris: Gallimard, 1997).

Garréta, Anne F., 'A Questionnaire: French Lesbian Writers? Answers from Monique Wittig, Jocelyne François and Mireille Best', *Yale French Studies*, 90 (1996), 235–41.

Gonnard, Catherine, 'Au Cœur de *Vlasta*', *Lesbia* (October 1988).

——— 'Portraits entre parenthèses', *Lesbia* (November 1988).

Hardt, Michael, 'Affective Labor', *boundary 2*, 26/2 (Summer 1999), 89–100.

Hochschild, Arlie Russell, *The Managed Heart: Commercialization of Human Feeling*, 3rd edition (Berkeley CA: University of California Press, 2012 [1983]).

Lane, Jeremy F., *Republican Citizens, Precarious Subjects: Representations of Work in Post-Fordist France* (Liverpool: Liverpool University Press, 2020).

Louis, Édouard, *En finir avec Eddy Bellegueule* (Paris: Seuil, 2014).

——— *The End of Eddy*, trans. Michael Lucey (New York: Farrar, Straus and Giroux, 2017).

——— *Qui a tué mon père* (Paris: Éditions Points, 2019).

——— *Who Killed my Father*, trans. Lorin Stein (New York: New Directions Publishing Corporation, 2019).

Miller, Meredith, 'Lesbian, Gay and Trans Bildungsromane', in S. Graham (ed.), *A History of the Bildungsroman*, 1st edition (Cambridge: Cambridge University Press, 2019), pp. 239–66.

Page, Marion, 'Le coin bibliothèque: à propos de Mireille Best', *Lesbia* (April 2008).

Ricouart, Janine, 'Enfance magique ou infernale? Un regard socio-critique sur l'œuvre de Mireille Best', Special Issue of *Women in French Studies* (2003), 150–65.

Schechner, Stephanie, '"If only you were a boy …": Friendship and Sexual Identity in Mireille Best's *Hymne aux Murènes*', *Journal of Lesbian Studies*, 22/1 (2018), 31–42.

——— 'The Lesbian Body in Motion: Representations of Corporeality and Sexuality in the Novels of Mireille Best', in Renate Günther and Wendy Michallat (eds), *Lesbian Inscriptions in Francophone Society and Culture* (Durham: Durham University, 2007), pp. 123–42.

——— 'The Young Woman and the Sea: Lesbians Coming of Age in Coastal Communities in the Novels of Mireille Best', *Women in French Studies*, 11 (2003), 50–63.

Tweedy, Amy J., 'Laboring lesbians: Queering emotional labor', *Journal of Lesbian Studies*, 23/2 (2019), 169–95.

Verret, Michel, *La culture ouvrière* (Paris: L'Harmattan, 1996).

Weeks, Kathi, 'Life Within and Against Work: Affective Labor, Feminist Critique, and Post-Fordist Politics', *ephemera*, 7/1 (2007), 233–49.

Wells, Hallie, 'Between discretion and disclosure: Queer (e)labor(ations) in the work of Tove Jansson and Audre Lorde', *Journal of Lesbian Studies*, 23/2 (2019), 224–42.

Wesling, Meg, 'Queer value', *GLQ*, 18/1 (2011), 107–25.

Notes

1   Didier Eribon, *Retour à Reims* (Paris: Fayard, 2009) and *Returning to Reims*, trans. Michael Lucey (Los Angeles CA: Semiotext(e), 2013); Édouard Louis, *En finir avec Eddy Bellegueule* (Paris: Seuil, 2014) and *The End of Eddy*, trans. Michael Lucey (New York: Farrar, Straus and Giroux, 2017).

2   Anne F. Garréta, 'A Questionnaire: French Lesbian Writers? Answers from Monique Wittig, Jocelyne François and Mireille Best', *Yale French Studies*, 90 (1996), 240. Translation in original.

3   Catherine Gonnard, 'Au Cœur de *Vlasta*', *Lesbia* (October 1988), 23. *Lesbia* has praised Best's literary subtlety, her characters who 'vivent leur lesbianisme de manière naturelle' ('naturally live out their lesbianism') and her remarkable writing 'dont il est difficile de parler sans risque d'en trahir le ton' ('that is difficult to discuss without risking betraying its tone'). See, respectively, Marion Page, 'Le coin bibliothèque: à propos de Mireille Best', *Lesbia* (April 2008), 34; Laurence Forcedange, 'Celles qui ont des ailes', *Lesbia* (May 1986), 33. See also René de Ceccatty, 'Ça s'appelle l'amour', *Le Monde*, 7 April 1995. All translations are mine unless otherwise noted.

4   This is not to say that it weighs only on working-class subjects. Other scholars have analysed this novel's substantial engagement with French anti-Semitism, including that addressed against Jewish lesbians such as Rachel. See for example Lucille Cairns, *Lesbian Desire in Post-1968 French Literature* (Lewiston NY: Edwin Mellen Press, 2002), p. 297.

5   Mireille Best, *Il n'y a pas d'hommes au paradis* (Paris: Gallimard, 1995), p. 104.

6   I thank Stephanie Schechner for her insightful suggestions on my translation here and elsewhere.

7   Janine Ricouart has argued that, contrary to many works of LGBT fiction, Best's oeuvre counteracts the elitist tendency to represent working-class families as especially homophobic by centring social class as much as she does sexuality. See Ricouart, 'Enfance magique ou infernale? Un regard socio-critique sur l'œuvre de Mireille Best', Special Issue of *Women in French Studies* (2003), 150–65.

8   My use of he/him pronouns reflects Eribon's exclusion of women from his study. Didier Eribon, *Réflexions sur la question gay* (Paris: Flammarion, 2012 [1999]), p. 171; Eribon, *Insult and the Making of the Gay Self*, trans. Michael Lucey (Durham NC: Duke University Press, 2004), p. 111.

9   Eribon, *Réflexions sur la question gay*, p. 171; *Insult*, p. 113.

10   John D'Emilio, 'Capitalism and Gay Identity', in *Making Trouble: Essays on Gay History, Politics, and the University* (New York: Routledge, 1992), pp. 4–14.

11   Eve Kosofsky Sedgwick, *Epistemology of the Closet*, 2nd edition (Berkeley CA: University of California Press, 2008). See also Eribon, *Réflexions*, p. 175.

12   Sara Ahmed, *The Promise of Happiness* (Durham NC: Duke University Press, 2010).

13 Michel Foucault, *Histoire de la sexualité I: la volonté de savoir* (Paris: Gallimard, 1997).

14 Meredith Miller, 'Lesbian, Gay and Trans Bildungsromane', in Sarah Graham (ed.), *A History of the Bildungsroman*, 1st edition (Cambridge: Cambridge University Press, 2019), pp. 239–66. See also Part II of Lisa Downward and Giovanna Summerfield, *New Perspectives on the European Bildungsroman* (New York: Continuum, 2012), which suggests that definitions of this genre have stressed autonomy and self-actualisation over social constraints, consequently marginalising the experiences of gender and sexual minorities.

15 Eribon, *Retour à Reims*, p. 25. Louis also discusses the pressure he feels to disavow his father in Parisian milieus in *Qui a tué mon père* ('*Who Killed My Father*') (Paris: Éditions Points, 2019), pp. 63–4.

16 Natacha Chetcuti, *Se dire lesbienne: vie de couple, sexualité, représentation de soi* (Paris: Payot, 2010).

17 Salima Amari, *Lesbiennes de l'immigration: construction de soi et relations familiales* (Vulaines sur Seine: Éditions du Croquant, 2018), pp. 140–5.

18 Hochschild differentiates between 'emotional labor', which is exchanged for wages (in the public sphere), and 'emotion work', which fulfils a human need (in the private sphere). Arlie Russell Hochschild, *The Managed Heart: Commercialization of Human Feeling*, 3rd edition (Berkeley CA: University of California Press, 2012 [1983]), p. 7.

19 Kathi Weeks, 'Life Within and Against Work: Affective Labor, Feminist Critique, and Post-Fordist Politics', *ephemera*, 7/1 (2007), 233–49. Amy J. Tweedy, 'Laboring lesbians: Queering emotional labor', *Journal of Lesbian Studies*, 23/2 (2019), 169–95.

20 Meg Wesling, 'Queer value', *GLQ*, 18/1 (2011), 107–25.

21 Hallie Wells, 'Between discretion and disclosure: Queer (e)labor-(ations) in the work of Tove Jansson and Audre Lorde', *Journal of Lesbian Studies*, 23/2 (2019), 224–42.

22 Catherine Gonnard, 'Portraits entre parenthèses', *Lesbia* (November 1988), 22.

23 Cairns, *Lesbian Desire*, p. 250. Translation in the original. This quote is from Cairns's private correspondence with Best in June 1998.

24 For informative analyses of the resistance to rigid identity in Best's novels, see Stephanie Schechner's studies: 'The Lesbian Body in Motion: Representations of Corporeality and Sexuality in the Novels of Mireille Best', in *Lesbian Inscriptions in Francophone Society and Culture*, eds. Renate Günther and Wendy Michallat (Durham: Durham University, 2007), pp. 123–42; 'The Young Woman and the Sea: Lesbians Coming of Age in Coastal Communities in the Novels of Mireille Best', *Women in French Studies* 11 (2003), 50–63; '"If only you were a boy …": Friendship and Sexual Identity in Mireille Best's *Hymne aux Murènes*', *Journal of Lesbian Studies*, 22/1 (2018), 31–42.

25 Michel Verret, *La culture ouvrière* (Paris: L'Harmattan, 1996).

26 Weeks, 'Life Within and Against Work', 242–3.

27 Michael Hardt, 'Affective Labor', *boundary 2*, 26/2 (Summer 1999), 89–100.

28 Jeremy F. Lane, *Republican Citizens, Precarious Subjects: Representations of Work in Post-Fordist France* (Liverpool: Liverpool University Press, 2020), p. 52.
29 As Stephanie Schechner has demonstrated, Josèphe consistently associates her mother with cold and ice. See Schechner, 'The Young Woman and the Sea', 58–9.
30 Sara Ahmed, *The Cultural Politics of Emotion*, 2nd edition (Edinburgh: Edinburgh University Press, 2014 [2004]), p. 152.

Chapter 6

Psychoanalytical Work in Chahdortt Djavann's *Je ne suis pas celle que je suis*

REBECCA ROSENBERG

Chahdortt Djavann reminds us in her text *Je ne suis pas celle que je suis* (*'I am not who I am'*) (2011), '[q]uelqu'un qui fait une psychanalyse est un "analysant", et non pas un patient. C'est à lui qu'incombe le travail d'interprétation et c'est pour cela qu'une psychanalyse peut durer de longues années' ('Someone who undergoes psychoanalysis is an "analysand" and not a patient. The work of interpretation is incumbent on them and that is why psychoanalysis can last for many years').[1] While the analyst has the role of creating a space for the analysand's psychoanalytic work to take place – thus instigating a co-operative process[2] – the analysand is the main and active participant, and must be prepared to work through repressions and other obstacles posing difficulties.[3] In addition to the inherent, continued labour of psychoanalytic work, there can be additional challenges that equally inflect this work. This chapter will consider, through the (auto)fictional analysand of Djavann's *Je ne suis pas celle que je suis*, how linguistic barriers, ethnicity and financial precarity intersect with the already arduous psychoanalytic work. First, this chapter will argue that the work of analysis is already present in the autofictional nature of the text and its polyphonic narrative structure; then, it will focus on one of the text's voices, the analysand's, and the nature of their psychoanalytic work both with regard to past trauma and linguistic challenges.

Autofictional Work and Plural Selves

Je ne suis pas celle que je suis is long and complex in the sense that it is polyphonic and confusingly autofictional; the reader does not know whether the voices are all the same woman (including Djavann the author) and the text paints a generally slippery portrait of selfhood and subjectivity. It is composed of four voices. The first, 'la narratrice' ('the narrator'),[4] relates and signs the prologue in the first person. It seems that she also narrates the body of the text, comprising two interwoven narratives set in different places and times. The first is set in Paris in 1994 and focuses on an unnamed Iranian woman who is about to commence psychoanalytic treatment; known as 'the analysand', she is the subject of most of this chapter. The second is about Donya, a student living in Iran in 1990. The analysand and Donya could be the same woman but they are never confirmed as such. There is thus a gulf of time, place and name between them; this also signals a form of overarching (psycho) analytic work taking place, perhaps by the narrator, to gradually narrate these two women (the analysand and Donya) and bring them together. The fourth and final voice in the text is Djavann, the author, who pens and signs the epilogue. She also could be seen as the narrative self, conducting psychoanalytic work through writing the text as she brings together three similar yet discrete female selves (the narrator, the analysand and Donya) in an attempt to reconcile them.

The separation of the narratives gestures to the analysand's psychoanalytic work and emotional labour that will see her merge and reconcile herself with Donya, her past in Iran before coming to Paris. The reader waits to see how, when, why and if the analysand in Paris and Donya in Iran coalesce; the reader's satisfaction is thus potentially contingent upon the 'success' of the analytic work. It is telling that the narrative and formal structure of *Je ne suis pas celle que je suis* continues with *La Dernière Séance* ('*The Last Session*') (2013) as if the psychoanalytic – and autofictional psychoanalytic – work of (re) constructing the self is an extended (autofictional) project that spans the duology. The polyphonic nature of the text, the length of the text (and indeed of the duology) and the blurred boundaries between the seemingly distinct women (the narrator, the analysand, Donya and Djavann), all allude to a form of psychoanalytic work taking place in the very structure and form of the text.[5]

Despite the psychoanalytic readings of the polyphonic structure of the text, Djavann's autofictional writing is slippery in terms of narrator-character-author identification. As Cristina Álvares asserts: 'Il n'y a pas chez Djavann d'identité entre auteur, narrateur et personnage qui assure l'intégrité du récit d'un moi stable et solide qui se regarde rétrospectivement' ('For Djavann there is no identity between the author, narrator and character that ensures a complete narrative of a stable and solid self that observes itself retrospectively').[6] However, there are striking similarities between the women in Djavann's texts, thus indicating an autobiographical kernel to these selves. As Samia Spencer writes 'les personnages des romans sont généralement des déracinées du même âge que l'écrivaine, copies conformes de leur génitrice dont le parcours et les préoccupations parallèlent ceux de Djavann' ('the characters of the novels are generally uprooted women of the same age as the author, clear-cut copies of their creator whose trajectory and concerns parallel those of Djavann').[7]

While Djavann denies, in the epilogue, the autobiographical readings of *Je ne suis pas celle que je suis* (pp. 519–20), she also writes '[j]e suis mon personnage et je ne le suis pas' (p. 520) ('I am my character and I am not her'). This playful resistance and refusal to assert her characters as autobiographical attests to their autofictionality. She deliberately blends her own life with other fictional characters who do not share the same name as her, while also not revealing which elements in her autofictions are autobiographical: 'Je confesse cependant que certaines de ses expériences me sont familières, mais vous me reconnaîtrez le droit de ne pas dire lesquelles' (p. 520) ('I confess, however, that some of her experiences are familiar to me but you will allow me the right to not say which ones'). Djavann's biography and her perspectives on Iran, gleaned from interviews, reveal striking similarities to her female protagonists. We can thus call her works autofictions deliberately blending autobiography and fiction, while also being, to borrow from Isabelle Grell's work on autofictional narratives of loss and trauma, '[un] témoignage d'une obsession' ('a testimony of an obsession').[8] Specifically, Djavann's texts reveal her obsessions with gendered experiences of exile, language and loss.

Autofiction is similarly employed by other diasporic Iranian writers such as Négar Djavadi in *Désorientale* (2016); a hybrid text combining a contemporaneous narrative in Paris penned by the queer, soon-to-be mother Kimiâ (detailing her family's life as exiled others) combined with her memories of Iran and her family history. Kimiâ, Djavadi's partly autofictional self, notes poignantly 'mes parents se débattaient avec les djinns de la dépression (mot dont je compris enfin la signification à Paris)' ('my parents battled against the djinns of depression (a word I finally understood in Paris)').[9] The non-belonging and alienation of exile in Paris have psychological impacts, to which Djavann attests in her autofictional writing: *Comment peut-on être français?* ('How can you be French?') (2006), featuring Roxane, another young Iranian woman who has fled to Paris from Iran and fallen in love with the city. Her disillusionment and alienation from others are due to linguistic barriers, which she tries to bridge by writing letters to Montesquieu, like her very own *Lettres Persanes* ('*Persian Letters*'). Djavann's hybrid epistolary text, according to Jeanette den Toonder, 'demonstrates the anxiety to address the trauma that confronts the narrating I with her unresolved pain', which has been exacerbated by the psychological impact of exile: 'alienation and isolation reinforce the initial trauma.'[10] The work of writing and learning French does not lead to integration or help with unresolved pain as Roxane attempts suicide.

While Djavadi's Kimiâ recovers, to certain extents, and attempts to forge her own, new hybrid identities, Roxane represents the nadir of exilic experience in Paris. It is significant that the analysand of *Je ne suis pas celle que je suis* has survived a suicide attempt when we meet her before she resolves to undergo psychoanalysis and attempt to survive. The autofictional avatar of Roxane has morphed into the analysand of this psychoanalytically inflected text, showing Djavann's autofictional desire to return to similar themes of psychological suffering and suicide, but also to use autofiction to explore another path for her autofictional avatar: Roxane's end is fatalistic, while the analysand starts to work towards survival. Djavann also attempted suicide and underwent psychoanalysis as she confirms in a radio interview,[11] and *Je ne suis pas celle que je suis* (in addition to its sequel) can thus be seen as ways to explore autobiographical experiences, question psychoanalytic work and stage diegetically (in the analysand's narrative) and autofictionally (through the extra-textual voices in the paratexts) the possibility of a reconstitution of self. The work of this process is evident in the autofictional narrative and form of *Je ne suis pas celle que je suis*, thus providing evidence of a potential split subject attempting to piece together different narratives, memories and identities. There is an exploration of psychoanalytic work and its challenges in the analysand's narrative while the whole text itself is psychoanalytic in the ways that it structurally alludes to an autofictional self using writing to bring together different voices such as the analysand's and Donya's. The identity of this autofictional self is not important, it is the use of narrative structure, polyphony and slippery boundaries between selves that underscores the core objective of the text: to emphasise the time and labour necessary for psychoanalytic work while also showing a female self in constant becoming as the text unfolds.

The text's first voice, the unnamed narrator, is the first autofictional voice of the narrative and points to the emotional and narrative labour to attempt to divest herself of her memories and past. She seems to want to forget: 'Je voulais partir … Tout laisser. Devenir une femme sans passé. Sans mémoire' (p. 11) ('I wanted to leave … Leave everything. Become a woman without a past. Without memory'). Her desire alludes to potential trauma impacting on her, however, this desire to start completely anew may be impossible to realise, as shown by Shoshana Felman and Cathy Caruth's theories on the inevitable, uncontrollable resurgence of trauma (memories) in the survivor's life.[12] We can interpret the text that follows the narrator's prologue (composed of the interwoven narratives of the analysand and Donya) as her way of writing and working through her past. Alternatively, the text can be seen as evidence of the narrator's inability to leave behind her past and memory, later parroted by the analysand:

> Elle savait pourquoi elle voulait faire une psychanalyse: ôter les artifices, les apprêts; éviter les mensonges, les astuces, les stratagèmes … Se mettre nue devant un spécialiste de l'esprit. Se débarrasser de tout ce qui n'était pas elle, détecter le problème, l'éliminer et accéder enfin à la quintessence de son âme … se libérer de tout ce qui la tourmentait, la torturait. (pp. 13–14)

> She knew why she wanted to do psychoanalysis: remove artifice and embellishment; avoid lies, tricks, stratagems … To bare herself before a specialist of the mind. To get rid of everything that was not her, detect the problem, eliminate it and finally access the quintessence of her soul … to free herself of everything that tormented and tortured her.

Her desire to return to a supposed authentic, even naked, self mirrors the narrator's desire to leave everything behind, thus demonstrating a potential link between the two. Furthermore, the interwoven narratives of the analysand and Donya (both related in the third person), which make up the body of the narrative, are potentially ways for the narrator (and Djavann) to attempt to expel past and multiple selves through the narrative. The autofictional labour thus has a potential purpose and objective and serves as two bookends to frame the diegetic psychoanalytic labour of the analysand and the emotional, psychological labour of Donya. The autofictional labour of the narrator is also a form of staging, seemingly allowing the voices and selves inside her to speak:

> Au gré des années et au hasard des conjonctures, j'ai incarné des identités aux prénoms différents. J'ai vécu à travers elles, avec elles, malgré elles; j'étais elles. Je les laisserai se raconter, ou plutôt se mettre en scène; moi, je n'interviendrai qu'entre les pages, entre les lignes. (p. 11)

> Over the years and at random conjunctures, I incarnated identities with different names. I lived through them, with them, despite them; I was them. I will let them tell their stories, or rather take the stage. Me, I will only intervene between the pages, between the lines.

This idea of simultaneously being these women while also implying their distinctness from her, is similar to Djavann's epilogue as the author and the fourth voice in the autofiction: 'Pour l'amour du ciel, qu'on ne vienne pas me demander si cette histoire est la mienne … si le livre est, finalement, autobiographique' (p. 520) ('For the love of god, do not come ask me if this story is mine … if the book is, in the end, autobiographical'). Djavann seems to also deny the exercise of writing an autobiography and she states categorically: 'Je ne crois pas à l'autobiographie. Nul ne se voit comme il voit les autres et comme les autres le voient' (p. 520) ('I do not believe in autobiography. No one sees themselves as they see others and as others see them'). The criticism of autobiography seems to lie in the fact that it might claim to present an accurate, rounded, hermetic account of a self, while Djavann invokes the necessity of multiple perspectives of others to obtain a complete portrait of an individual self or subject. This interpretation goes some way to explain the multiple perspectives of the text and the two interwoven chronological narratives of the analysand and Donya.

Donya's narrative is distinct in style and form to the analysand's psychoanalysis sessions. Instead of the repeated space of the analyst's office (and few other locations) in the analysand's narrative, as well as the intense focus on analytical work, Donya's narrative is a standard third-person narration of a life. Her life in Iran, however, could be the analysand's past or an imaginable version of it. In this way, Donya's narrative provides the backstory to the analysand's life in Paris, allowing the reader to see her past (or a verisimilar version of it), which she does not reveal in great detail during her analysis. The structural presence of Donya's narrative can function as evidence of the distance between the analysand's narratives in analysis, while also signalling the extent of the analytic work that she must realise in order to reach back into the past to narrate her life in Iran. The repression of her past, and the narrative separation (and thus psychological disassociation) between the analysand and Donya is manifested by the physical challenges the latter faces when she tries to talk about herself and her past. During one session, she has difficulty breathing and speaking: 'Asphyxiée par sa gorge nouée ... Une digue barrait le flux des mots' (p. 251) ('Asphyxiated by the lump in her throat ... A dam blocked the flow of words'). Her body cannot bridge this gap, instead causing her pain when she speaks to potentially remind and warn her of the past.

An additional crucial way that the analysand attempts to repress her past, resist speaking and thus protect herself is through the creation of different personalities and voices that speak for her and talk about 'elle' ('her'). These voices and switches to third-person description are initially confusing, making both the reader and the analyst wonder whether she has a personality disorder.[13] This diagnosis is never assigned or explored; instead, the analyst and reader bear witness to the changes in dress, body language, tone of voice and behaviour towards the analyst. These different personalities can be interpreted as ways of avoiding talking about her past and her suicide attempts; one calm voice states clearly 'elle est née suicidaire' (p. 86) ('she was born suicidal'). The analysand thus does not have to tell her analyst about her suicidal behaviours – an abstracted self does it for her. The analysand is self-aware about why she had to create these other voices or women inside of her, and why she had to disassociate. She tells the analyst 'J'ai dû me diviser, inventer des subterfuges, fuir, nier, annuler. J'ai dû m'absenter de moi-même' (p. 181) ('I had to divide myself, invent subterfuges, flee, deny, annul. I had to leave myself'). Amputated from her country, family and language, the disassociation and creation of new voices and personalities is understandable. Regarding exile and its psychological effects, Jane Hiddleston describes 'the introspective melancholia of "exile"'.[14] The splitting of the self and disassociation attest to the analysand's introspective, psychic actions to attenuate this 'melancholia'.

The analysand works through the disassociation, the multiple voices and personalities slowly disappearing. Nevertheless, the process of speaking for herself with one voice – rather than a disassociation – is laborious and painful. In one session she states hopelessly: 'Je n'arriverai jamais à faire la paix avec les femmes que je suis' (p. 292) ('I will never manage to make peace with all the women who I am'). Despite this suffering and fatalism, the analysand keeps working in her sessions. She takes control of the voices and thus the analytical work: 'Je garderai la situation sous contrôle. Il faut que je "travaille" "sérieusement" … Il faut que, d'une façon suivie, étape par étape, l'analyse progresse, et quelqu'un doit veiller sur l'évolution positive du processus analytique' (p. 101) ('I will keep the situation under control. I must "work" "seriously"… The analysis must progress, in a continued way, step by step, and someone must watch over the positive unfolding of the analytical process'). This appropriation of the psychoanalytical work is evidence of the analysand's grit and her determination to conduct the work herself despite the linguistic difference and difficulty, the physical and psychic labour and pain of talking including the necessity to overcome inculcated and internalised trauma regarding speaking out about herself, and the obstacles of her own defence mechanisms.

Psychoanalytical Work, Language Barriers and Bridges

Psychoanalytical work is language-based, repetitive and arduous, as the analyst's definition of the analysand's work in *Je ne suis pas celle que je suis* testifies: 'L'analysant dit, redit, raconte, répète, ressasse, tourne autour du pot, élude, refuse de parler ou alors revient sur les mêmes sujets des dizaines et des dizaines de fois' (p. 152) ('The analysand says, says again, recounts, repeats, rehashes, beats around the bush, eludes, refuses to speak or they return to the same subjects dozens of dozens of times'). His enumeration of actions emphasise the seemingly endless labour of speech and thought required of the analysand. The analyst's palpable exhaustion listing these actions is matched only by the exhaustion of the analysand who must carry them out. As the analyst reveals, the analysand is the one responsible for the labour in the sessions: 'Ce ne sont pas mes séances, ce sont les vôtres' (p. 208) ('They are not my sessions, they are yours'). These sessions will be particularly difficult and laborious for the analysand due to her particular circumstances of having just left the psychiatric hospital, which we find out later in the narrative is due to a recent violent and second suicide attempt (p. 87). The analytical process of talking, and the linguistic labour that this implicates, is challenging and difficult for the narrator for additional reasons: she works long, poorly paid hours, lives in a 'chambre de bonne' ('former maid's room') and is alone and alienated in Paris.

The narrator writes of her: 'Elle menait une vie de recluse' (p. 29) ('She has been leading the life of a recluse'). She labours incessantly: looking after children as a nanny, learning French while she is also clearly working, emotionally and linguistically, in her analysis. Speaking and working through her memories, traumas and symptoms is a linguistic labour that leads to periods of heightened psychological suffering. For example, when her employers are away for the summer holidays 'elle quitta rarement sa chambre. Sans lire, sans travailler les mots, elle s'enferma dans un état semi-végétatif' (p. 172) ('she rarely left her room. With no reading and no working words, she shut herself in a semi-vegetative state'). This nadir of exhaustion sees her renounce her physical, paid and menial labour as well as, tellingly, her linguistic labour: reading, learning French and her analysis (as her analyst is away for the break in August).

This same exhaustion can be seen painted on the faces of the workers and refugees participating in Alice Diop's documentary *La Permanence* (2018), depicting the linguistic difficulties and the legal and economic precarities of refugees/workers seeking medical help.[15] The difficulty to describe pain and illness is shown to stem equally from linguistic challenges, both not being fluent in French and unable to accurately translate in French their wounds and traumatic difficulties in order to describe how they became injured, ill and scarred. Diop significantly comments on the violent intersection of trauma and language in the documentary *Mariannes Noires* (2017). She speaks of the violence of Nicolas Sarkozy's language regarding migrants and refugees, which she links to a period in which she herself suffered from aphasia and difficulties speaking French. She also describes this language loss as a 'rupture psychique' ('psychic rupture'), underscoring the retroactive erosion that trauma and shock can have on the French that she has learnt from having been born and educated in France, creating a sense of alienation and non-belonging in the language.[16] She undertook psychoanalysis following this rupture, underscoring its potentiality to encourage and rebuild self-expression, while also intersecting with Djavann's analysand who senses the slipperiness of French and feels like she must perform in her analytical work, not making mistakes and working hard outside her session so she can avoid them.

Learning French is thus an initial barrier to analytical work, while also providing extra labour for the analysand. However, it also becomes beneficial to the analysand: she can re-narrativise and reclaim her past in French, rather than in the language of her trauma and memories. The acts of translation and self-interpreting that she carries out in analysis are creative as well as psychoanalytic practices that eventually provide solace and distance from her traumatic memories and her psychological suffering.[17] Mildred Mortimer, in her afterword to *Exiles, Travellers and Vagabonds: Rethinking Mobility in Francophone Women's Writing* (2016), writes (in relation to Marjane Satrapi's *Persepolis*) of how hybrid and interdisciplinary approaches to self-expression challenge established literary categories.[18] Thus the analysand's creative, hybrid linguistic written work (as evidenced by her notebooks) and psychoanalytic work can be seen as potential forces to provide narrative agency for the analysand in the face of trauma.

The analysand initially prepares her sentences and words for her sessions. This advanced preparation is aimed to facilitate the analytical work of self-expression; however, it also serves to impede her ability to spontaneously speak and give voice to certain experiences.[19] The first session is demonstrative of this: the analysand internally berates herself for making grammatical errors of gender while the analyst's question regarding an idiom in French, which the analysand does not know, leads to an impasse (p. 17). The analysand feels hamstrung by her linguistic limitations and the fact that she is still learning and in the stage of carefully listening to and then parroting the language of others (p. 114). She has to learn and check new words in French to be able to speak in analysis, adding extra labour to her psychoanalytical work. She must '[t]ravailler les mots, tous les mots' (p. 29) ('Work the words, all the words'). This extra labour of trying to communicate her memories (in Persian) in French, in addition to the difficulty of speaking about them, creates additional suffering for her as she describes '[s]e sentir à ce point dépossédée engendre une souffrance supplémentaire. Je crois que jamais les mots français ne pourront dire l'enfance que j'ai vécue.' (p. 114) ('To feel dispossessed in this regard creates additional suffering. I believe that French words will never be able to speak of the childhood I had'). This comment is magnified by additional moments of frustration and anger as she evokes the incommunicability and incomprehensibility of her life in Iran for the French analyst. These linguistic and cultural barriers relate to the existence of Donya's narrative as a separate, third-person narrative throughout the text. Indeed, it can be argued that both the analysand's silences and Donya's narrative are evidence of a silence that will persist without acts of translation. As Ioanna Chatzidimitriou writes about Djavann's *La Muette* ('Mute') (2008), 'translation is presented as a condition of comprehensibility and readability'.[20]

The analysand alludes to additional work of researching words in her French dictionaries and writing in her notebooks after the sessions. This is a sign of the impact of the analytical work in the sessions that is inspiring her to continue to work on her thoughts and self-expression outside the analytical frame. However, the mention of writing is another potential link to Donya's narrative. It seems easier for the analysand and/or narrator to write their experiences, with extra labour and care, through the autofictional avatar of Donya due to cultural and linguistic barriers that cannot be overcome in the organic, spontaneous moments of analysis. The analysand comments tellingly on the potential benefit of not only writing her narrative but also doing so in another language: 'Peut-être que raconter mon passé avec les mots étrangers pourrait l'exorciser, le laisser passer.' (p. 117) ('Perhaps recounting my past with foreign words could exorcise it, let it go'). This implies that there is a benefit to the distancing that a foreign language provides. The new, different words can provide further separation from the past.

The analysand's realisation of the benefits of conducting analysis in French evolves throughout the narrative and the vignettes of sessions. There was an initial double bind: lacking the language and cultural specificity in French to communicate her past in Iran, while conducting analysis in Persian in Iran would be impossible for her, particularly with a man (pp. 112–3). The slow embrace of French as the language of psychoanalytical work is fraught, and perhaps her increasing affinity with this labour is due to her equally increasing linguistic ability as she learns. However, her affinity (as she states it) derives mainly from the fruitful distance that French offers: 'Parler en retourne le couteau dans la plaie ... Le persan m'oppresse, m'étrangle, il me fait souffrir jusqu'à l'os, il appartient à un passé trop douloureux' (p. 115) ('Speaking in Persian twists the knife in the wound ... Persian oppresses me, strangles me, it makes me suffer right down to my bones, it belongs to a too painful past'). The violence and oppression of her native language, Persian, comes to be a metonymy for the suffering she endured when living in Iran. Donya's narrative situated in Iran in 1990 is evidence of such oppression. French, thus, becomes a way to sever ties with her past:

> Avec l'analyse, les mots français se sont enracinés non seulement dans ma tête, mais aussi dans mon histoire et dans mon corps ... Ces mots étrangers ont pris part à mes souffrances. Ils ont pris part à mon passé qui s'est passé sans eux. (p. 515)

> With analysis, French words have become ingrained not only in my head but also in my history and body ... These foreign words have taken part in my suffering. They have taken part in my past that occurred without them.

In this way, the analytical work in French, while challenging for various reasons, has enabled the analysand to narrate her past and pain while also providing separation through its inherent difference. This redemptive, positive note comes at the end of 500 pages of work, which has required linguistic struggles and learning both in and out of the sessions.

Conclusion

Despite the optimistic tone of the end of this chapter regarding the analysand's psychoanalytical work,[21] there are still many gaps and spaces for a continuation of this labour. The text continues with a second volume, *La Dernière Séance*, with more sessions of psychoanalysis interspersed with Donya's narrative until these narratives eventually merge into one, finally confirming the link between the analysand and Donya. The text, through the narrator and/or Djavann, is a testament to the seemingly ceaseless as well as repetitive, painful and autonomous work of psychoanalysis. On the one hand, Djavann reveals the multifaceted and complex underbelly of psychoanalytical work. On the other hand, she uncovers the specific linguistic, cultural and sociopolitical differences that consistently challenge the analysand's labours to survive, take control of her memories and deconstruct the psychic apparatuses that she has built to protect herself. Donya's narrative, while not analysed fully in this chapter, serves as an autofictional origin narrative for the analysand. However, Djavann's resistance and refusal to fully align or merge these women (including the narrator) in *Je ne suis pas celle que je suis* creates a structural and narrative comment on the psychoanalytical work that remains to be undertaken by the women, as well as the labour of writing to eventually unite them in one self.

Works Cited

Álvares, Cristina, 'Ni française ni iranienne. Sur Chahdortt Djavann', *Mondesfrancophones. com, Revue mondiale des francophonies* (2017), http:// mondesfrancophones.com/espaces/frances/ni-francaise-ni-iranienne-sur-chah-dortt-djavann/ (accessed 15 December 2021).

Bion, Wilfred R, *Learning from Experience* (New York: Routledge, 1984).

Caruth, Cathy, *Trauma: Explorations in Memory* (Baltimore MD: Johns Hopkins University Press, 1995).

Chatzidimitriou, Ioanna, 'Speaking Silence: Translation in Chahdortt Djavann's *La Muette*', *MLN*, 127/5 (2011).

Delourmel, Christian, 'Preface', in *Illusions and Disillusions of Psychoanalytic Work* (Oxford: Taylor & Francis, 2018).

Den Toonder, Jeanette, 'Writing in the Feminine: Identity, Language, and Intercultural Dialogue in Chahdortt Djavann's Comment peut-on être français? (2006)', *DiGeSt Journal of Diversity and Gender Studies*, 5/2 (2018).

Diop, Alice (dir.), *La Permanence* [DVD] (Paris: Docks 66, 2018).

Djavadi, Négar, *Désorientale* (Paris: Éditions Liana Levi, 2016).

Djavann, Chahdortt, *Je ne suis pas celle que je suis* (Paris: Flammarion, 2011).

—— *La Dernière Séance* (Paris: Fayard, 2013).

Felman, Shoshana, *Testimony: Crises of Witnessing in Literature, Psychoanalysis and History* (New York: Routledge, 1992).

Freud, Sigmund, 'Analysis Terminable and Interminable', in *On Freud's "Analysis Terminable and Interminable"* (London: Karnac Books, 2013).

Fruchon-Toussaint, Catherine, 'L'exil: Invitée, Chahdortt Djavann', *Radio France Internationale*, 3 February 2006.

Green, André, *Illusions and Disillusions of Psychoanalytic Work* (Oxford: Taylor & Francis, 2018).

Grell, Isabelle, *Autofiction* (Paris: Armand Colin, 2014).

Hiddelston, Jane, 'Reappropriating "Exile"? Transculturality between Word and Image in Leïla Sebbar's *Mes Algéries en France*', in *Exiles, Travellers and Vagabonds: Rethinking Mobility in Francophone Women's Writing* (Cardiff: University of Wales Press, 2016).

Jordan, Shirley. 'État Présent, Autofiction in the Feminine', *French Studies*, 67/1 (2012), 76–84.

Mortimer, Mildred, *Exiles, Travellers and Vagabonds: Rethinking Mobility in Francophone Women's Writing* (Cardiff: University of Wales Press, 2016).

Niang, Mame-Fatou and Nielsen, Kaytie (dirs), *Mariannes Noires* (2017), *www.mariannesnoires.com* (accessed 15 December 2021).

Spencer, Samia I., 'Mais qui est donc Chahdortt Djavann?', in *Protean Selves: First-Person Voices in Twenty-First-Century French and Francophone Narratives* (Newcastle upon Tyne: Cambridge Scholars Publishing, 2014).

Winnicott, Donald D. W., *Playing and Reality* (London: Routledge Classics, 2005).

Notes

1 Chahdortt Djavann, *Je ne suis pas celle que je suis* (Paris, France: Flammarion, 2011), p. 152.

2 See Wilfred Bion's theory of the container (analyst) and contained (the analysand's projected bad feelings) in *Learning from Experience* (New York: Routledge, 1984). Also see Donald W. Winnicott's theory of holding and holding space in *Playing and Reality* (London: Routledge Classics, 2005).

3 For challenges and resistance to the effects of analytic work, see André Green, *Illusions and Disillusions of Psychoanalytic Work* (Oxford: Taylor & Francis, 2018).

4 All translations from works by Djavann are my own.

5 See Shirley Jordan on how contemporary female-authored autofictions foreground psychoanalytic processes in narratives of unresolved pain. S. Jordan, 'État Présent, Autofiction in the Feminine', *French Studies*, 67/1 (2012), 79.

6 Cristina Álvares, 'Ni française ni iranienne. Sur Chahdortt Djavann', *Mondesfrancophones. com, Revue mondiale des francophonies* (2017), *http:// mondesfrancophones.com/espaces/frances/ni-francaise-ni-iranienne-sur-chah-dortt-djavann* (accessed 15 December 2021).

7 Samia I. Spencer, 'Mais qui est donc Chahdortt Djavann?', in *Protean Selves: First-Person Voices in Twenty-First-Century French and Francophone Narratives* (Newcastle upon Tyne: Cambridge Scholars Publishing, 2014), p. 110.

8 Isabelle Grell, *L'Autofiction* (Paris: Armand Colin, 2014), pp. 50–1.

9 Négar Djavadi, *Désorientale* (Paris: Éditions Liana Levi, 2016), p. 271.

10 Jeanette den Toonder, 'Writing in the Feminine: Identity, Language, and Intercultural Dialogue in Chahdortt Djavann's *Comment peut-on être français?* (2006)', *DiGeSt Journal of Diversity and Gender Studies*, 5/2 (2018), 12.

11 Catherine Fruchon-Toussaint, 'L'exil: Invitée, Chahdortt Djavann', *Radio France Internationale*, 3 February 2006.

12 Shoshana Felman, *Testimony: Crises of Witnessing in Literature, Psychoanalysis and History* (New York: Routledge, 1992), p. 65. In

Trauma: Explorations of Memory (Baltimore MD: Johns Hopkins University Press, 1995), Cathy Caruth examines Freud's exploration of the returning traumatic dream as a frightening, uncontrollable possession of the self (p. 5).

13 Djavann, *Je ne suis pas celle que je suis*, p. 80.
14 Jane Hiddeslton, 'Reappropriating "Exile"? Transculturality between Word and Image in Leïla Sebbar's *Mes Algéries en France*', in Mildred Mortimer, *Exiles, Travellers and Vagabonds: Rethinking Mobility in Francophone Women's Writing* (Cardiff: University of Wales Press, 2016), p. 80.
15 Alice Diop (dir.), *La Permanence* [DVD] (Paris, France: Docks 66, 2018).
16 Mame-Fatou Niang and Kaytie Nielsen (dirs), *Mariannes Noires* (2017), *www.mariannesnoires.com* (accessed 15 December 2021).
17 Mildred Mortimer, *Exiles, Travellers and Vagabonds: Rethinking Mobility in Francophone Women's Writing* (Cardiff: University of Wales Press, 2016), pp. 170–1.
18 Mortimer, *Exiles, Travellers and Vagabonds*, pp. 170–1.
19 See Green, *Illusions and Disillusions of Psychoanalytic Work*, p. 134, regarding patients writing outside of sessions and how this constitutes repression.
20 Ioanna Chatzidimitriou, 'Speaking Silence: Translation in Chahdortt Djavann's *La Muette*', *MLN*, 127/5 (2011), 1215.
21 Djavann, *Je ne suis pas celle que je suis*, p. 516.

Part II
Revolving Doors: Liminal and Precarious Spaces

'Be proud of all the Fatimas': From Alienated Labour to Poetic Consciousness in Philippe Faucon's *Fatima*

SIHAM BOUAMER

In his film *Samia* (2000), Philippe Faucon focuses on an adolescent, the title character, who navigates the restrictions imposed by her family unit as well as the systemic oppressive structures she faces as the daughter of Maghrebi immigrants living in France. The 2000 film received scholarly attention because it marked a narrative shift in cinema *de banlieue*, hitherto centred mainly on the experiences of young men.[1] While in *Fatima* (2015) we find similar tropes focusing on daughters of immigrants, those issues do not take centre stage. However, the film, which received several awards, warrants as much consideration for the depiction of a topic too often rendered invisible, or at best placed in the background, in cinema: the experiences of first-generation Maghrebi migrant women. Based on Fatima Elayoubi's *Prière à la lune* ('*Prayer to the Moon*') (2006), the film depicts the experience of an Algerian divorced woman who accumulates several cleaning jobs to financially support her two daughters, Nesrine and Souad. Overworked, she reaches her limits physically and emotionally and is forced to go on sick leave, which then extends to therapy work mediated through her poetry writing.

In the first book-length study focusing on the cinematic representations of first-generation Maghrebi women, Leslie Kealhofer-Kemp notes that little public attention has been granted to that specific demographic. Examining a large corpus of films, she aims to challenge the idea that Muslim women are 'silenced under the weight of poverty, illiteracy, Islamic tradition, and majority ethnic Islamophobia'[2] and show how 'cinematic processes, influence the ways and extent to which the voices and experiences of first-generation women come through in the films' (p. 5). Specifically, Kealhofer-Kemp seeks to analyse how short films, documentaries, *téléfilms* and feature films accentuate Maghrebi women's voices – verbal and non-verbal – and allow for some of the stereotypical representations to be contested, including their responsibility as guardians of 'traditions' – understood as the keepers of the country of origin's culture – or their lack of agency.

In an interview, Philippe Faucon similarly insists on the necessity to challenge the invisibility and stereotypical depictions of immigrants in French cinema. On his work on *Fatima*, he explains:

> These [immigrants] are characters that are generally absent from the screen … This is disproportionate to their actual place in the functioning of French society and their value. Usually in film, when you look at immigrant characters, their stories take place in the projects and are about difficulties, failures, violence, drugs or terrorism. Those things do have a place in the reality of French society, but that is not the whole picture. There are many other dimensions that are just as real … These types of characters lack representation. They are the people that get up at five o'clock in the morning to pick up the trash or to clean houses. This film was an effort to bring this [*sic*] people out of the shadows and onto the screen.[3]

The question of labour at the end of this passage is of particular interest for the analysis of the film *Fatima* in this chapter. In *Women at Work in Twenty-First Century European Cinema*, Barbara Mennel notes that 'film studies scholarship has marginalized labor as a topic, [and] it has given [even] less attention to women's work'.[4] The consideration of labour becomes even more critical for the study of films depicting the lives of Maghrebi-French people in order to challenge discourses often framed around themes such as unemployment and criminality, as emphasised by Faucon in the interview, and for women, the oppressive patriarchal structures of the domestic space. Indeed, migrant women are often represented as wives and mothers behind closed doors, neglecting the social reality of their active roles outside the household.

Kealhofer-Kemp draws attention to a short film, Faïza Guène's *Réduction du Temps de Travail* ('Work Time Reduction') (2002), in which the struggle of navigating both responsibilities as a mother and working long hours to support the family is central to the narrative.[5] In this chapter, I aim to explore the same dynamic involved in the negotiation between domestic and paid labour in cinematic depiction of first-generation Maghrebi women. While oppressive structures are often defined within the domestic space (duties as mothers and wives), my aim is to shift the focus to highlight the repressive system that a migrant woman like Fatima faces outside the household, as a worker. More specifically, I propose to probe the question through the lens of Sara Ahmed's concept of the 'affect alien', a figure who disrupts narratives of happiness within the framework of the family or the nation.

Reviews of Faucon's film often refer to Fatima's role as a mother. While I will also often use the word 'mother' throughout the chapter, describing the title character mainly through her maternal role does not do justice to her portrayal in the film. She is indeed a mother, but Faucon centres the narrative on the negotiation of her labour inside and outside the home. We follow Fatima performing domestic duties and taking care of her daughters, but a good part of the film depicts her work as a cleaning lady in multiple locations (the city of Lyon's waste reception centre, a school cafeteria and a private home), going to and departing from her different workplaces, or discussing the struggles that she faces at her work.

Cécile Kovacshazy argues that there is a long French cinematic and literary tradition of cleaning-lady characters.[6] Before assessing their narrative roles as main characters, she reminds us of their social reality 'tout en bas de la hiérarchie sociale professionnelle et directement confrontées à la précarité' ('at the very bottom of the professional social hierarchy and directly confronted to precarity') (p. 39). For example, she refers to their social status, low salary and long working hours. Faucon's film does not fail to screen this experience throughout the film. Fatima accumulates several jobs to support her daughters and, as her youngest Souad notes, 'elle part (au travail), il fait nuit, elle rentre, il fait nuit' ('she leaves [for work], it's night-time, she returns, it's night-time') (00:51:14–00:51:16).[7] Most importantly, Kovacshazy insists on the isolation of cleaning ladies, 'isolée dans son travail, mais un travail qui lui prend son temps et ses forces, elle vit dans un monde de déliaison forcée' ('isolated in her work, but a work that takes all her time and strength, she lives in a world of forced disconnection') (p. 40). This specific aspect will be of particular interest for this section.

Kovacshazy discusses how cleaning ladies' social isolation extends to the narrative structures of the novels and films in which they are represented. Despite being the title character in some cases, they are often relegated to the background, without a voice.[8] I argue that with *Fatima*, Faucon breaks this pattern and, as Grégoire Leménager notes, 'invente un nouveau personnage dans le cinéma français' ('invents a new character in French cinema').[9] The film focuses mainly on Fatima – with several close-ups – and spends much time screening her work as a cleaner and the tedious tasks that it involves. I will focus on the way that the film unfolds her difficult experiences at work from her perspective. In particular, I will analyse the few dialogues between Fatima and her employers and highlight the importance of the poetry she shares – directly with others or through voice-overs – to understand the implications of her affective alienation.

Among the three types of 'affect alien' identified in Sara Ahmed's *The Promise of Happiness* – feminist killjoys, unhappy queers and melancholic migrants – the latter is here useful to engage with the portrayal of Fatima. The melancholic migrant is one who 'bear[s] witness to the emptiness of the promise of happiness' within the discourse of citizenship, one who feels a sense of estrangement because of social inequalities.[10] It is no surprise that Ahmed turns to the role of labour to understand the processes of alienation of the melancholic migrant, since productivity is often a parameter evoked in narratives of integration and citizenship when it comes to immigration.[11] Drawing on Marx's theory of alienation of labour, she explains:

> [T]he more the worker works, the more the worker produces, the more the worker suffers. Alienation is both an alienation from the products of one's labor – a kind of self-estrangement – and a feeling-structure, a form of suffering that shapes how the worker inhabits the world. Workers suffer from the loss of connection to themselves given that the world they have created is an extension of themselves, an extension that is appropriated.[12]

Sara Ahmed's affective reading, alongside Marx's definitions, can help us here address Fatima's alienation as a melancholic migrant worker. I will explore how the film showcases the title character's estrangement from labour and from the self, while at the same time examining the process through which she reaches a certain consciousness of her alienation.

If the word 'alienation' is preferred here, rather than 'isolation', it is because Fatima is not alone. She is surrounded by her daughters, especially her eldest Nesrine with whom she shares a strong bond. A few scenes also show the camaraderie between Fatima and other workers. For example, two scenes focus on moments of complicity between a group of Maghrebi women – among whom Fatima – waiting for the shuttle to go to work at a waste reception centre early in the morning. She also shares in Arabic her sorrows with her co-worker at the school cafeteria; she confides feeling helpless during a parent-teacher conference because, due to her lack of proficiency in French, she was unable to participate in the conversation like the other parents (00:24:30–00:25:24). It is in this conversation that Fatima confirms the nature of one source of her alienation: language.

While in the exchange she communicates directly her frustration for the issues it creates in her personal life, Fatima often bears the burden of this linguistic gap in the workplace. Starting a new cleaning job in at the waste reception centre, Fatima receives instructions from her supervisor:

> – Vous passez bien la serpillère dans les vestiaires et dans les sani-taires. Il faut que ça soit fini d'ici la pause. Vous avez bien compris?
> – Oui, oui, je comprends, Madame. Je comprends. Sauf moi je ne parle bien français.
> – Si, si, vous parlez très bien Fatima. (00:47:05–00:47:07)

> – You need to mop the cloakrooms and the toilets. It needs to be done before the break. Clearly understood?
> – Yes, yes, I do understand, ma'am. Only I don't speak French well.
> – Yes, yes, you do speak well, Fatima.

The supervisor's response to Fatima's apologies about her language proficiency, which could be seen as an encouraging state-ment, is in fact, we infer from her condescending and stern tone in film, a way to dismiss any possible excuses for the professional faults she might commit. In addition, her insistence on the fact that Fatima clearly understands the instructions, with little preoccupation with her speaking skills, signals her lack of interest in building a collabo-rative workspace for Fatima. Her role is only limited to mechanical gestures in the hidden and 'low' spaces of the company.

Fatima's linguistic barrier is also visible in her work in a private home. When the new employer shows her the tasks to accomplish, Fatima silently follows her through the house and confirms that she understands the instructions with a nod or a 'yes' (00:08:18–00:08:38). Returning home from her first day, she asks Souad to clarify the meaning of the word 'persuadée' ('convinced') (00:12:17–00:12:32). While Fatima focused on this specific verb, she in fact grasped the general context in which the word was used. After asking Fatima if she agreed to be declared for two hours of work, the new employer tells her 'je suis persuadée qu'on va bien s'entendre' ('I am convinced that we'll get along') (00:11:30–00:11:31). Later, Fatima reveals to Nesrine that she knows that the woman is lying about her work hours in order to receive benefits from the government. She points out the irony that, while the employer is cheating the system, she is the one who must prove that she is not a thief. She suspects her employer to have left a ten-dollar bill – which Fatima returns – in the laundry to test her integrity (00:39:20–00:39:45). Faucon confirms the intent of the specific scene: 'La scène dit aussi combien le personnage vit dans le sentiment qu'elle est systématiquement regardée avec suspicion' ('The scene says how much the character lives with the feeling that she is systematically seen with suspicion').[13]

The feeling of always having to justify and defend herself is another cause of her alienation: stereotypes. Fighting this perception requires, Sara Ahmed notes, 'a perpetual self-questioning; the emotional labour of asking yourself what to do when there is an idea of you that persists, no matter what you do'.[14] Drawing on her work from *Strange Encounters* (2013), Ahmed attributes this feeling to the emotional labour associated to confronting racism:

> The experience of being a stranger in the institutions of whiteness is an experience of being on perpetual guard: of having to defend yourself against those who perceive you as somebody to be defended against. Once a figure is charged, it appears not only outside but *before* the body it is assigned to. (p. 218)

Despite the fact that we see Fatima returning the money on screen, her conversation with Nesrine seeks to emphasise the necessity for Fatima to perpetually defend herself, not only to her employers, but also to the audience who might 'charge' her, '*before*' those scenes, with preconceived ideas about her honesty. Later in the film, Fatima undergoes a similar experience when, at the waste reception centre, the supervisor questions Fatima for leaving work early:

> – Fatima, vous êtes partie à quelle heure mercredi?
> – A midi moins le quart.
> – C'est à midi que vous finissez.
> – Oui je sais, mais j'ai un problème pour ma fille.
> – Dans ce cas, vous m'en parlez à l'avance.
> – Oui, pardon, mais vous n'êtes pas là.
> – Si je ne suis pas là, sans autorisation, vous partez à l'heure prévue.
> – Mais mon travail il est fait. Tu peux contrôler.
> – A l'avenir, vous ne quittez pas votre poste sans y être autorisée. Vous êtes payée quatre heures, vous devez rester quatre heures. D'accord Fatima?
> – D'accord. (00:53:41–00:54:05)

> – Fatima, at what time did you leave on Wednesday?
> – At eleven forty-five
> – You're done at noon.
> – Yes, I'm sorry, but I had an issue for my daughter.
> – In that case, you have to let me know in advance.
> – Yes, I am sorry, but you are not here.
> – If I'm not here, without authorisation, you leave at the scheduled time.
> – But my work is done. You can control.
> – In the future, you do not leave work without authorisation. You are paid for four hours, you have to stay four hours. Ok Fatima?
> – Ok.

The language used in the dialogue – in particular the words 'authorisation' and 'control' – prompts us to consider Michel Foucault's work in *Discipline and Punish* (1975). Reflecting on the mechanisms of power involved in controlling bodies in the social order, he notes: 'Discipline increases the forces of the body (in economic terms of utility) and diminishes these same forces (in political terms of obedience).'[15] Indeed, the supervisor disregards Fatima's humanity – her life as a mother who needs to attend to her daughter in case of an emergency – to focus on compliance, policies and productivity, echoing the first conversation between the two. By insisting on the obedience to the rules, the supervisor attempts to cast Fatima as, and to borrow Lauren Berlant's expression, an 'infantilized citizen'. While Berlant identifies this concept within the broader political discourse of the 'national culture industry',[16] an infantilised worker can here be similarly defined as 'anesthetized [and] complacent' (p. 199).

Defeated, Fatima gives up and ends the conversation, unwillingly agreeing with her supervisor. Her acquiescence, we understand, aims to avoid being seen as 'aggressive', another perception, Ahmed explains, that 'strangers' need to resist during their encounters with racism. Avoiding being seen as aggressive can be part of 'speech politics: you have to be careful what you say … in order to maximise the distance between you and their idea of you'.[17] The scene described previously is one of the rare moments during which we see Fatima directly confronting one of her employers. In general, she stays silent, as we noted previously, but several scenes, focusing on Fatima with a close-up, reveal Fatima's frustration. When not completely silent, she timidly nods or speaks with a soft voice in the face of professional tension, because of the language barrier, but also, we can infer, to avoid being seen as aggressive, if too assertive. This voice differs from her forceful voice as a mother, especially with her daughter Souad, with whom she often clashes on topics such as clothing or school results.

'The demand not to be aggressive', Ahmed adds, can also take the 'form of body-politics … you have to be careful … how you appear' (p. 218) by 'softening the very form of your appearance' (p. 217). It manifests itself physically with her headscarf. On the subject, Faucon reveals in an interview that it was not his intention to focus on the headscarf.[18] Nevertheless, the bias against Muslim women wearing a headscarf is highlighted at the beginning of the film. In the opening scene, to which I will return in the conclusion, Fatima and her daughter are victims of housing discrimination, because of Fatima's presence, but it does not take centre stage in the film. It is, however, worth noting that Fatima 'softens' her appearance in the workplace. Indeed, while the film shows Fatima meticulously wrapping her head with a hijab in her daily life, at work, she wears a half headscarf, as her own decision to appear less aggressive, or probably because she is asked to do so by her employers.

The emotional adversity she experiences at work foreshadows her physical breakdown. Pushed to her limits, Fatima falls in the stairs while carrying a bucket at the waste reception centre and is put on medical leave because of an injured shoulder. After five months, she consults the family doctor to extend her leave, but he maintains that, medically, he cannot justify it. Bearing in mind that Foucault's concept of the 'docile body' is deeply ingrained in the medical field, Fatima contests the diagnosis, once again defending her integrity: 'je suis pas menteuse, je suis pas voleuse' ('I am no liar, I am no thief') (00:56:59–00:57:02). However, the family doctor's office is not the same hostile environment as Fatima's workplaces. He reassures Fatima that he believes her and advises her to seek the help of occupational medicine. The new health professional concludes the visit with the same diagnosis but refers her to Dr Keltoum Mebarki who, he indicates, speaks Arabic (1:00:00–1:00:10). While the new doctor understands her linguistically, she is also able to help Fatima give meaning to her pain: the psychophysiological effect of trauma.

In the same interview cited above, Faucon explains that the scene was directly taken from Fatima Elayoubi's lived experience: 'Le médecin qui l'[Elayoubi] a rencontrée a été frappé par la façon dont elle a décrit, avec ses mots, un processus de substitution psychophysiologique par lequel le corps humain exprime une douleur psychique par une douleur physique' ('The doctor who met with her was struck by the way she described, with her words, a process of psychophysiologic substitution through which the human body express a psychic pain with a physical pain') (p. 106). Before the appointment, Dr Mebarki studies Fatima's X-rays, which display that her injury is healed. Instead of sharing the medical diagnosis, she opens a space for Fatima to 'tell [her] what it's like',[19] to explain her pain in her own words. Fatima proceeds:

> – After the fall, I had nightmares for two months. Every night, the pain came back. I would dream that I had another fall. I felt afraid. I'd wake in a panic. Then the fear stopped. And instead there was this pain in my arm. I've seen doctors. They all say "you're fine".
> – The causes of such pain are not always understood by doctors. They believe what they see
> – It's true, it's my fault. I did not want to see or hear. I did not listen to my heart. All I wanted was to find strength for work. I put my family and my life aside. (1:01:19–1:02:25)

In this exchange, the doctors' misdiagnosis is as central as her symptoms to grasp Fatima's pain. Asked about the possible influence of Frantz Fanon's 'North African syndrome' in this scene, Faucon responds that he doubts that Elayoubi has read him, but that we can find resemblances.[20] Indeed, parallels can here be drawn with Fanon's work on the prejudices faced by North African workers in the medical world: 'The North African's pain, for which we can find no lesional basis, is judged to have no consistency, no reality. Now the North African is a-man-who-doesn't-like work. So that whatever he does will be interpreted *a priori* on the basis of this.'[21] While the doctor offers a neutral interpretation of the misdiagnosis, Fatima's response reflects some of the biases she has encountered. Beyond her financial needs, she pushed herself to continue working in order to avoid being seen as the '[wo]man-who-doesn't-like work'.

Fatima blames herself for the predicament she found herself in. While this avowal is founded in the structures of her alienation, it also marks the beginning of Fatima's change of consciousness. Drawing on Fanon's work on colonial alienation, Sara Ahmed draws conclusions on the processes involved in the affect alien's revolutionary consciousness:

> Consciousness of alienation involves both recognition of suffering and recognition of what produces that suffering. To become conscious of alienation is to become conscious of how one's being has been stolen. It is not simply to become alienated from the world but to become conscious of how alienation is already, as it were, in the world.[22]

In her conversation with the doctor, Fatima apprehends her suffering. When declaring 'I did not want to see or hear. I did not listen to my heart', she does more than acknowledge her responsibility. The words 'see', 'hear' and 'heart' denote a process of self-reflection on her agency towards but also out of this alienation. She also recognised what 'has been stolen' from her, namely her family and her life. However, while her cognisant consciousness happens officially in the medical office, the process has long been under way. Through her poetry writing, within the walls of her home, Fatima shares her awareness of the 'alienation ... in the world'.

Before turning to the content of Fatima's poetry, let us first consider the cinematic technique through which it is shared. Most of the excerpts are shared visually, with a close-up on her handwriting in Arabic on the pages of a notebook, but also audibly since we hear Fatima reading them. In her study on the use of voice-overs in the cinematic representation of migrant women's labour, Mennel delineates the main narrative functions of this technique:

> Voice also functions in forms of immaterial labor, producing an affective dimension and emotional surplus. Presenting female

migratory characters with their own voice constitutes a political gesture ... Cinematic strategies range from seizing the migrant's own speech in order to ventriloquize the receiver country's fantasies to subverting sound conventions in order to open up a space for critical reflection on the prosaic social reality on the screen.[23]

The affective and the notions of 'affective' labour and 'fantasy' resonate here with Sara Ahmed's discussion of the promise of happiness. The melancholic migrant's voice-over, as a medium for political and social criticism, allows to disrupt the script of happiness of social 'integration', as we shall see, through a reflection on labour and precarity.

Fatima shares her poems on five occasions. Those scenes are introduced during key moments of the film, which I will consider in my analysis. Let us first observe the second poem shared on screen:

In the city, life is fast. Many don't put their hearts into their work. Many have nothing to say. One has to earn bread and rent. Sometimes I seem cold. The heart sighs one day, and is full of hatred the next. Everyday I yell against other women, against my daughter. (00:25:30–00:26:40)

Those lines are shared between two work shift changes. It follows the segment with Fatima cleaning the school cafeteria and precedes a sequence focusing on Fatima and other Maghrebi women waiting for the shuttle that will transport them to the waste reception centre. While a full afternoon, evening and night elapse, there is a quick change between the two scenes, with a clip of less than a minute screening Fatima writing in her bedroom. On the pace of the film, Grégoire Leménager comments: 'on ne s'ennuie pas une seconde' ('you don't get bored for a second').[24] Indeed, the fast shifts from one work scene to another convey the impression, or rather the reality, that Fatima has no time to rest.

In the passage, Fatima criticises how a life driven by productivity and preoccupations to pay bills, creates a sense of alienation for people – 'many have nothing to say' – and for herself – 'I seem cold' – creating distance with others. She highlights here the consequences of both material and mental alienations which, following the Fanonian thought that has guided part of my analysis, are two conditions that (should) lead to a revolution, an inevitable step to freedom. Bearing that in mind, some of her writing could be seen as manifestos. A manifesto is by definition 'a written statement

declaring publicly the intentions, motives, or views of its issuer'.[25]
The two poems that I identify as such are public declarations since
they are the only ones she shares with other people, among whom
Nesrine for this particular passage:

> Fear starts to recede. Confidence returns. I am alone with my
> responsibilities and with my girls. Alone with the souls I have borne
> that they may enjoy childhood and youth. Alone with a tumultuous
> generation bubbling with energy, intelligence, life and ambition.
> Alone with my girls to face the whole of all of that. It is a great
> responsibility. It is my intifada. (1:09:52–1:10:23)

The repetition of the word 'alone' here has several effects. It is simultaneously a confession of her alienation, but also an assertion of her
agency, reinforced by the first two lines of the poem. The word
'alone' also resonates as an individual battle cry, supported by the
term 'intifada' ('uprising') which confirms the revolutionary tone of
her statement, with her responsibility as a mother as 'intentions
[and] motives' for this manifesto.

  The longest piece shared on screen presents a similar tone. After
her first appointment with Dr Mebarki, Fatima shares a poem with
her:

> That day fear entered into me because I saw the respect I had
> instilled collapsed … That woman and others like her needed
> Fatima when Fatima was well. That woman couldn't go to work
> without some Fatima. She couldn't buy scent or fine clothes with-
> out some Fatima. She couldn't earn her living or have a future,
> have a fine pension, without some Fatima. Every day that woman
> entrusts her keys, her home, her kids, to some Fatima. She sees her
> friends, goes to the shop because there is some Fatima. She comes
> home at night to a house with five rooms, two bathrooms cleaned
> by Fatima between 8 a.m. and 6 p.m. The house is clean, tidy, ready.
> At night, Fatima goes home. Nothing is ready. Cleaning, cooking,
> daughters await. A second day begins. Which is why one day, Fatima
> collapses. Don't be angry. Where a parent is hurt, a child is angry.
> Only this time, be proud. Be proud of all the Fatimas who clean
> working women's homes. (1:06:03–1:08:17)

This poem is a response to two specific events in the film. The
sequence follows a scene at the supermarket where Fatima attempts
to have a conversation with the mother of one of Souad's classmates
who cuts the conversation short and snobs her (1:04:39–1:06:10). It
also specifically addresses a tense conversation with her youngest.

After a meeting at Souad's school to discuss her poor results, Fatima scolds her daughter, warning her that if she continues in this path, she 'will have no future ... [and] end up a cleaner like [her] mother'. Souad responds violently: 'Alors là tu rêves, je préfère voler que nettoyer la merde des autres comme toi ... va faire ta bonniche, va te faire exploiter. De toute façon tu sers qu'à ça. T'es une cave, t'es une ânesse, t'es une incapable' ('Well dream on, I'd rather steal than clean people's shit like you ... Go, go be a servant, go and be exploited. Anyway, that's your only use. You're stupid, You're a donkey, you're incapable') (00:49:48–00:50:12). While those two incidents are screened in the film, the statement '[b]e proud of all the Fatimas' serves as a reminder, for herself, as part of the process of recognising her alienation, as well as a rallying cry for all the migrant women working in invisible spaces, essential for the good functioning of society or other women's households, career and leisure, at the expense of their own private and family life.[26]

To conclude, I would like to come back to an idea introduced at the beginning of the chapter: the focus on first-generation women in opposition to their children. While I argued that the film centred the narrative on Fatima, the importance of Nesrine and Souad cannot be ignored. Şirin Fulya Erensoy argues that *Fatima* shows the 'daily struggles [of these three women] individually ... as well as the tensions that arise among them and their surroundings ... [and how they] are trying to find their place in society, where each of the worries that they have to deal with is born out of being an immigrant'.[27] I would like to nuance here the implications of existing 'tensions' between Fatima and her daughters. The dynamic between mother-daughter of Maghrebi descent in France is often examined through their generational divide and the dichotomy between the cultures of home/host cultures. The film makes similar commentaries, with Souad, for example, who defies her mother's views on her clothing or love interests. However, by moving those issues into the background, the film is successful in going beyond this limited interpretation of the tensions that arise between mother and daughter. Souad is first a young woman in the throes of adolescence. Above all, she suffers from her mother's absence due to the demands of her work. On that pain, Fatima recognises in the last poem I have analysed: 'where a parent is hurt, a child is angry'.

With her daughter Nesrine, the relationship is less conflictual, but creates a similar pain. The only friction is caused by a tense situation involving their encounter with racism in the opening of the film. In the scene, Fatima, Nesrine and two of her friends wait in front of an apartment where the three young women hope to find their new home to begin their studies at the university. The owner refuses to show the apartment and pretends not to have the key. Walking away from the building, the four women attempt to make sense of this rejection. Nesrine's friend identifies the problem: 'trois filles, dont deux maghrébines, ça passe pas' ('three girls, two of whom are North African, it doesn't fly'). Fatima adds that she understands that it was probably because of her headscarf. Nesrine does not attempt to ease her mother's guilt and interprets what happened as 'bad luck' caused by her mother instead of naming the true problem: Islamophobia (00:01:30–00:02:42).

Such a comment contradicts the symbolism carried through the name 'Fatima', found in the expression 'hand of Fatima'. While the daughter wears the symbol as a necklace, she fails to recognise the fact that the true good luck charm is indeed her mother who, while she failed to help her daughter open the door in this sequence, or even was the reason it stayed closed, Fatima constantly struggles to push doors open for her daughter, to ensure that she doesn't end up 'a cleaner like her mother'. For example, she provides financial assistance for her studies by working extra hours and selling her jewellery. She also provides care, bringing food to her new apart-ment and doing her laundry so that she can focus on her studies. Her emotional support also plays no small role in the success of her daughter, encouraging her through the intensity of her first year in medical school. In sum, and to quote from the last poem, 'without some Fatima', Nesrine would not benefit from this support system.

While the help of Fatima is invaluable and admirable, it is also a double-edged sword. As Sara Ahmed points out, '[t]o be encour-aging is often thought of as generous, as a way of energizing somebody ... But to encourage can also be forceful ... The gener-osity of encouragement can hide the force of being directed somewhere'.[28] Despite this help, Nesrine suffers through her first year, mainly because of her fear of failing and disappointing her mother who sacrifices a lot and spends much time 'directing' her towards success. In an interview, Faucon establishes a parallel between Fatima's 'relentlessness' and her oldest daughter's.[29] Fatima even describes her daughter as 'tak[ing] after her'. She did indeed transmit her work ethic and drive to her daughter, but sadly also, through the intergenerational trauma caused by social inequalities, her alienation towards that which she is socially forcefully 'directed'. For example, Nesrine refuses to associate with other students because she feels alienated from a milieu in which she fears, as the daughter of a cleaning lady, having no voice and credibility.

Ultimately, challenging the erasure of first-generation 'Fatimas', as I intended in this chapter, does not overshadow the study of their children's experiences, but instead helps understand their alienation, often hypermediatised around false, or at best incomplete, narratives of the 'promise of happiness' and access to social mobility and citizenship.

Works Cited

Aguilar, C., 'Losing Her Voice: In Philippe Faucon's Poignant *Fatima*, an Immigrant Faces Cultural Difference Even Within Family', *MovieMaker*, 16 September 2016, *www.moviemaker.com/philippe-faucon-cultural-difference-family-fatima/* (accessed 3 January 2022).

Ahmed, Sara, *The Cultural Politics of Emotions* (Edinburgh: Edinburgh University Press, 2014).

—— *The Promise of Happiness* (Durham NC: Duke University Press, 2010).

Berlant, Lauren, *The Queen of America Goes to Washington City: Essays on Sex and Citizenship* (Durham NC: Duke University Press, 2002).

Erensoy, Şirin Fulya, 'Approaches to Othered Identities and Spaces in French Cinema', in J. Harvey (eds), *Nationalism in Contemporary Western European Cinema* (Basingstoke: Palgrave Macmillan, 2018), pp. 63–84.

Faucon, Philippe (dir.), *Fatima*, Pyramide Distribution, 2015.

'Faut-il aller voir *Fatima*, César du meilleur film?', *Le Figaro*, 27 February 2016, *www.lefigaro.fr/cinema/ceremonie-cesar/2016/02/27/03020-20160227A RTFIG00098-faut-il-aller-voir-fatima-cesar-du-meilleur-film.php* (accessed 3 January 2022).

Fanon, Frantz, 'The "North African Syndrome"', in *Towards the African Revolution*, trans. Haakon Chevalier (New York: Grove Press, 1967 [1964]), pp. 3–16.

Foucault, Michel, *Discipline and Punish: The Birth of the Prison*, trans. Alan Sheridan (New York: Vintage Books, 1995 [1975]).

Kealhofer-Kemp, Leslie, *Muslim Women in French Cinema: Voices of Maghrebi Migrants in France* (Liverpool: Liverpool University Press, 2015).

Kovacshazy, C., 'Épousseter la précarité: narrer les femmes de ménage (littérature et cinéma)', in R. Böhm and C. Kovacshazy (eds), *Précarité: Littérature et cinéma de la crise au XXIe siècle* (Tübingen: Narr Francke Attempto Verlag, 2015), pp. 39–49.

'Manifesto', *Merriam Webster Dictionary*, *www.merriam-webster.com/dictionary/manifesto* (accessed 3 January 2022).

Mennel, Barbara, *Women at Work in Twenty-First-Century European Cinema* (Urbana IL: University of Illinois Press, 2019).

Stojanovic, S., 'Should the Subaltern Clean?', *Mosaic: an Interdisciplinary Critical Journal*, 53/1 (2020), 39–54.

Taïbi, N., 'De *La Désintégration* à *Fatima*: levons les voiles! Entretien avec Philippe Faucon', *Sens-Dessous*, 2/18 (2016), 103–6.

Tarr, C., 'Grrrls in the *banlieue*: *Samia* and La Squale', in *Reframing Difference: Beur and Banlieue Filmmaking in France* (Manchester and New York: Manchester University Press, 2005).

Vergès, Françoise, *Un féminisme décolonial* (Paris: La Fabrique éditions, 2019).

Notes

1   On *Samia*, see, for example, Carrie Tarr's chapter 'Grrrls in the *banlieue*: *Samia* and *La Squale*', in *Reframing Difference: Beur and Banlieue Filmmaking in France* (Manchester and New York: Manchester University Press, 2005), pp. 111–23.

2   Leslie Kealhofer-Kemp, *Muslim Women in French Cinema: Voices of Maghrebi Migrants in France* (Liverpool: Liverpool University Press, 2015), p. 1.

3   Carlos Aguilar, 'Losing Her Voice: In Philippe Faucon's Poignant *Fatima*, an Immigrant Faces Cultural Difference Even Within Family', *MovieMaker*, 16 September 2016, *www.moviemaker.com/philippe-faucon-cultural-difference-family-fatima/* (accessed 3 January 2022).

4   Barbara Mennel, *Women at Work in Twenty-First Century European Cinema* (Urbana IL: University of Illinois Press, 2019), p. 13.

5   Kealhofer-Kemp, *Muslim Women in French Cinema*, pp. 80–4.

6   C. Kovacshazy, 'Épousseter la précarité: narrer les femmes de ménage (littérature et cinéma)', in R. Böhm and C. Kovacshazy (eds), *Précarité. Littérature et cinéma de la crise au XXIe siècle* (Tübingen: Narr Francke Attempto Verlag, 2015), pp. 39–49; p. 40.

7   All the film quote translations in this chapter are modified versions of the English subtitles. All other translations are my own.

8   See also Sonja Stojanovic's study on the narrative hypervisibility and invisibility of cleaning ladies, 'Should the Subaltern Clean?', *Mosaic*, 53/1 (2020), pp. 39–54.

9   'Faut-il aller voir *Fatima*, César du meilleur film?', *Le Figaro*, 27 February 2016, *www.lefigaro.fr/cinema/ceremonie-cesar/2016/02/27/03 020-20160227ARTFIG00098-faut-il-aller-voir-fatima-cesar-du-meilleur-film.php* (accessed 3 January 2022).

10   Sara Ahmed, *The Promise of Happiness* (Durham NC: Duke University Press, 2010), p. 154.

11   See Sara Ahmed, *The Cultural Politics of Emotions* (Edinburgh: Edinburgh University Press, 2014), pp. 135–6. She notes on migrancy and labour: 'To love the other requires that the nation is already secured as an object of love, a security that demands that incoming others meet "our" conditions. Such conditions require that others "contribute" to the UK through labour.'

12   Ahmed, *The Promise of Happiness*, p. 167.

13 N. Taïbi, 'De *La Désintégration* à *Fatima*: levons les voiles! Entretien avec Philippe Faucon', *Sens-Dessous*, 2/18 (2016), 104.
14 Ahmed, *The Cultural Politics*, p. 217.
15 Michel Foucault, *Discipline and Punish: The Birth of the Prison*, trans. Alan Sheridan (New York: Vintage Books, 1995 [1975]), p. 138.
16 Lauren Berlant, *The Queen of America Goes to Washington City: Essays on Sex and Citizenship* (Durham NC: Duke University Press, 2002), p. 185.
17 Ahmed, *The Cultural Politics*, p. 218.
18 Taïbi, '*De La Désintégration* à *Fatima*', p. 105.
19 For quotes in Arabic in the film, I have included only the English translation.
20 Taïbi, '*De La Désintégration* à *Fatima*', p. 106.
21 Frantz Fanon, 'The "North African Syndrome"', *Towards the African Revolution*, trans. Haakon Chevalier (New York: Grove Press, 1967 [1964]), p. 6.
22 Ahmed, *The Promise of Happiness*, p. 167.
23 Mennel, *Women at Work*, p. 104.
24 'Faut-il aller voir *Fatima*, César du meilleur film?'.
25 'Manifesto', *Merriam Webster Dictionary*, *www.merriam-webster.com/dictionary/manifesto* (accessed 3 January 2022).
26 On the invisibility of racialised cleaning ladies, see Françoise Vergès, *Un féminisme décolonial* (Paris: La Fabrique éditions, 2019), p. 8.
27 S. F. Erensoy, 'Approaches to Othered Identities and Spaces in French Cinema', in J. Harvey (ed.), *Nationalism in Contemporary Western European Cinema* (Basingstoke: Palgrave Macmillan, 2018), p. 78.
28 Ahmed, *The Promise of Happiness*, p. 47.
29 Aguilar, 'Losing Her Voice'.

Chapter 8
Chimerical Cashiers: Exposure, Ableism and the Foreign Body in Marie-Hélène Lafon's *Gordana* and *Nos vies*

SONJA STOJANOVIC

A satirical cartoon by Olivier Ranson in the 15 April 2020 print edition of *Le Parisien* uses cashiers as a punchline in the context of the Covid-19 pandemic and the debate regarding the reopening of schools in France. The drawing features a reluctant child saying: 'Mais moi j'ai pas envie de retourner à l'école!' ('But I don't want to go back to school'), who is then told by her parents: 'Tu veux finir caissière au supermarché si tu ne fais pas d'études?!' ('You want to end up a cashier if you don't go to university?!').[1] A gendered comment, this statement is far from an innocuous joke levelled by many white middle-class French parents at their daughters to ensure that they comply and do their homework. This casting of cashiers as a cautionary tale and their conflation with (educational) failure can perhaps be tied to the technological advancements that automated many of the accounting tasks that were once part of the job description,[2] but it can also be linked to the general devaluation of women's labour; in France, women make up 90 per cent of the profession and only a decade ago that number was 95 per cent.[3]

While we cannot speak of cashiers in the same way that we do of women in other gendered professions – for instance, cleaning ladies or nannies, who often work in precarious conditions and can be dismissed overnight – if we consider how contemporary French cultural productions exaggerate cashiers' alleged lack of intellect, I would argue that they do occupy a precarious literary and, by extension, sociocultural space. In addition, what has been further exacerbated by cashiers' positions as essential workers during the pandemic is a notion that has long been, in many ways, the hallmark of the profession: namely, exposure. We are indeed now much more aware of what 'the condition of being subject to some effect or influence' or a virus might mean, but 'exposure' also signifies the 'disclosure of something secret', as well as 'the condition of being presented to view or made known',[4] that is, to be seen and thus potentially rendered vulnerable.[5] Being exposed can take on a range of meanings (which to some extent will all be explored here), but it becomes rapidly clear that the centrality of the body (affected or seen) is paramount. Focusing on Marie-Hélène Lafon's novel *Nos vies* ('*Our Lives*') (2017) and its precursor, the novella *Gordana* (2012), I want to consider how both the cashier's body and, in turn, the narrator's biases are exposed from the first sentences on. I contend that this intense focus on the body is a symptom of both the constraints of the job and the idea that cashiers have, as one says, 'rien dans la tête' ('nothing between their ears').[6]

Fact is that outward presentation *as* a cashier is one prominent requirement and emphasises the body from the start. Anna Sam, who wrote *Les Tribulations d'une caissière* ('*Checkout Girl: A Life Behind the Register*') (2008), a non-fiction book (based on her blog)[7] recounting in a humorous fashion observations made while working as a cashier, indeed notes: 'Je suis dans le regret de vous rappeler que la caissière, même derrière sa caisse, doit pouvoir être immédiatement identifiée par le client comme étant bien... une caissière'[8] ('I'm sorry to have to remind you then that even though cashiers stand behind registers, clients have to be able to immediately identify them as being... cashiers').[9] Sam goes on detailing the various uniforms that visually tell the client in what kind of store they are shopping; rather than being fully realised persons, cashiers are a sign. They are not only confined to a small space, working in difficult conditions, subjected to contempt from shoppers or literally exposed to viruses, they are also meant to be interchangeable: they embody a function, and it matters little to the shopper who sits behind the cash register or till. Like their more financially precarious counterparts (cleaning ladies, nannies), cashiers are convenient empty canvases onto which fantasies can be projected. This is emphatically the case for Lafon's texts, which centre on the narrator's obsession with a cashier working in a branch of the supermarket chain *Franprix* located in the twelfth arrondissement of Paris.

Both the novella *Gordana* and the novel *Nos vies* are written from the perspective of Jeanne Santoire, the narrator, a retiree and frequent shopper. In fact, save for a few words, the novella and the novel are identical – the only difference is that the novel continues where the novella leaves off – and I will come back to the ending of both texts shortly. The book flap for the novella, which bears the cashier's name, praises Lafon for her choice of setting and notes that 'elle transforme ce lieu le moins propice à la littérature en théâtre même de la fiction' ('she transforms this place which is least favourable to literature into the very theatre of fiction').[10] One may certainly wonder what makes the supermarket an unfavourable literary space, Émile Zola's *Au Bonheur des Dames* ('*Ladies' Paradise*') (1883) set in the universe of *le grand magasin* ('department store') – an avatar of its future competitor *la grande distribution* ('mass-market retailers') – has shown precisely how a location in which the private is put on public display can be ripe for fiction. But what is perhaps deemed to be unfavourable for literary attention is the very figure of the cashier – someone who is generally understood as lacking intellect and perhaps even interiority. Indeed, all the promotional materials for the novella show a focus on the cashier's body and the cashier *as* (merely) a body. This same book flap begins with excerpts from the text: 'Gordana n'a pas trente ans. Son corps sue l'adversité et la fatigue ancienne ... Le corps de Gordana, sa voix, son accent, son prénom, son maintien, viennent de loin' ('Gordana is not yet thirty. Her body oozes adversity and old fatigue ... Gordana's body, her voice, her accent, her first name, her demeanour come from afar').[11] On the publisher's site for the novella, we read: 'Caissière, elle n'est aussi qu'un corps, mais quel corps ...' ('A cashier, she is also just a body, but what a body ...').[12] Everything about Gordana is meant to put her both on display and at a distance, as some*thing* to be considered as a foreign, quasi-monstrous entity and scrutinised for her otherness.

Everything about this cashier is unusual: she is assumed to be an immigrant and thus marked as an alien, intrusive and expansive body – even her first name, 'ce prénom rugueux, inusité, hirsute' ('this rough, unusual, unkempt first name'),[13] that is to say, a name decidedly not French, has been engulfed in this 'too-much-ness' of the foreign.[14] It thus does not come as a surprise that her accent is described as an accent 'qui ne chante pas du tout, qui écorche et racle et crisse' (p. 21) ('which doesn't sing at all, which scrapes and drags and screeches'). This enumeration of audibly unpleasant verbs is highlighted by the superfluous repetition of 'et' ('and'), which signifies an accumulation of uncomfortable proportions. What matters is only how foreign she is: 'On ne sait pas où Gordana fut petite fille. Je suppose la fin des années quatre-vingt, l'est de l'Est, et les ultimes convulsions de républiques très moribondes' (p. 14). ('We do not know where Gordana was as a little girl. I guess the end of the eighties, the east of the East and the final convulsions of very moribund republics'). From that point on, in an ever-escalating fashion, the narrator will imagine the horrid childhood that the cashier must have had based on the supposed place she is from and on two photos that have fallen out of Gordana's wallet: 'Les photos de Gordana ont été avalées, radiographiées, englouties, deux sur les trois' (p. 20) ('Gordana's photos were swallowed, x-rayed, engulfed, two out of the three'). The narrator's fabulating of Gordana's childhood based on these digested bits of picture, can then be understood as excretion, as waste. Yet, this tragic invented backstory generates more fiction, for it is, in fact, an excuse for the narrator to reminisce about her own childhood and her family's history, drawing a sharp contrast to the cashier's supposed poor upbringing.

At first, the narrator seems to understand the power differential between the two of them. While she, as the shopper, is able to manage her time as she pleases and to observe the cashier, she realises that this possibility is a luxury of sorts. But rather than delving into this topic herself, she lends her own thoughts to Gordana and imagines that the cashier would share her opinion and would cast herself as the 'other', the 'foreigner', the 'illegitimate one':

> Elle [Gordana] n'en a pas les moyens, ce serait un luxe insensé, c'est bon pour les autres, les natifs, les légitimes qui n'ont pas à se battre pour tout et habitent chaque seconde de leur pays, de leur langue, sans même y penser. (p. 21)

> She [Gordana] does not have the means, it would be an insane luxury, it is good for the others, the native-born, the legitimate ones who do not have to fight for everything and who inhabit every second of their country, of their language, without even thinking about it.

Throughout *Nos vies*, there is an underlying narrative about 'Frenchness', constructed in opposition to all those who are not. Lafon is known for writing about rural France, and although *Nos vies* takes place in Paris, Jeanne Santoire is a transplant and spends pages recalling her discussions with her grandmother about her family's history in rural France; making these lives, oft neglected by (contemporary) authors, visible has been lauded by critics. Writing about Lafon's first collection of short stories *Liturgie* (2002) – featuring a protagonist similar to our narrator also named Jeanne – Alexandre Salas qualifies the author's style as follows: 'une écriture qui a une saveur crue et un tranchant intact pour autopsier des vies perdues'[15] ('a writing that has a raw flavour and an intact edge to autopsy lost lives'). One could certainly say that the same impetus is found in *Gordana* and *Nos vies*, yet this 'autopsy' of 'lost lives' takes on a different meaning when you talk about fantasised immigrant lives – the narrator is not actually telling readers of Gordana's life, she is telling readers about her own fantasies – and fears – of the 'foreign'.

While the narrator's friends and neighbours are French and white, several other characters are explicitly singled out as having a foreign background. For instance, although their appearances are beyond the scope of this chapter, the characters of Horatio Fortunato, a fellow shopper of Portuguese origin, and Karim, the narrator's ex who is Algerian, bear mentioning. However, the most revolting portrayals of 'foreigners' in this novel are the racist caricatures of a number of other cashiers in the local *Franprix* who are not even given a name but are rather described as an indistinct group. Of these fellow cashiers, we know only that they are women of colour, that they are presumed to be migrant workers and that their individuality is erased. They appear only in the following quote and serve no other purpose in the text than to prop up Gordana's story and to reproduce what Mireille Rosello in *Declining the Stereotype* has described as 'the familiar "All the [insert ethnic group ...] are [insert adjective]"'.[16] In the midst of a detailed description of their physical attributes that hinges on the racist trope of 'sameness' – 'mêmes dents éclatantes' ('same dazzling teeth'), 'mêmes peaux sombres et lisses' ('same dark and smooth skins') – we find out the following:

> les autres qui se ressemblent toutes, ont l'air de venir du même endroit du monde, ni l'Afrique noire, ni le Maghreb, ni l'Asie, je dirais l'Indonésie, ou l'Inde, ou les Philippines ... on ne comprend

pas ce qu'elles se disent entre elles, d'une caisse à l'autre ... elles prononcent avec soin en français les formules apprises et nécessaires, leur accent est impénétrable, ni chantant ni rugueux, leurs blouses sont fermées, elles sont très disponibles pour la clientèle, elles se mettent en quatre, mon père aurait dit ça, ces femmes se mettent en quatre, elles aident, elles se penchent se tournent sur leur siège pivotent s'appliquent et Gordana est au milieu d'elles comme un grand corps blanc, jaune, rêche, raide et étranger. (pp. 57–8)

The others who all look alike seem to come from the same spot, not sub-Saharan Africa, nor the Maghreb, nor from Asia, I would say Indonesia, or India or the Philippines ... one does not understand what they say to each other, from one register to the next ... they carefully pronounce in French the necessary formulas they learned, their accent is impenetrable, neither singsong nor rough, their blouses are closed, they are very receptive to the clients, they bend over backwards, my father would have said that, these women they bend over backwards, they help, they bend over they turn in their seats they swivel and they make every effort and Gordana, in their midst, is like a big body, white, yellow, rough, stiff and foreign.

As we read here the narrator's litany of ethnic stereotypes,[17] the mention of her father is also telling: this is something that has been repeated and transmitted. Describing certain women as available and helpful based on their ethnicity or race is the opposite of a compliment, as Rosello points out, so-called 'positive' stereotypes still use 'the same type of racist language structures' and ideology.[18]

Moreover, the racist portrayal of these fellow cashiers also speaks to what Françoise Vergès has described as 'l'économie d'*usure* de corps racialisés, d'épuisement des forces, dans laquelle des individus sont désignés par le capital et par l'État comme étant propres à être usés' ('the economy that *wears out* racialised bodies, depletes the strength of certain individuals designated by capital and by the state as fit to be used up').[19] Taking this notion of 'being used' in the context of narrative economy, I want to focus on why these women are instrumentalised and used by the narrator in her description of Gordana. One has noticed throughout the text the narrator's desire to 'other' the cashier. In this description, everything is meant to highlight how peculiar and unfit for her position Gordana is: starting with a reminder of her rough accent and unruly body, she is notably portrayed as 'stiff', while her nameless colleagues, in 'bending over backwards', are qualified by the narrator as belonging at the top of a hierarchy – based on racist stereotypes – of (great to under par) migrant workers; they have no other role in the novel.[20] Gordana, who is white and seemingly does not fit the narrator's preconceived ideas based on race, has to be, then, further qualified as an excessive and 'deviating'[21] body; she undergoes, in the narrator's descriptions, a process of 'othering' and 'racialisation'.

As Sara Ahmed has argued in a discussion of 'moments when the body appears "out of place"', 'even bodies that "appear" with a white surface … still have to pass in order to pass into white space: the white body must also be a respectable and clean body'.[22] While for Ahmed, who approaches this question through a focus on queer bodies, this body is 'therefore also middle class and straight',[23] we can extend her argument to include certain conceptions of disability that cast a disabled person's body as deviating from a 'respectable' and 'clean' norm and therefore it is being understood as 'out of place'.[24] In what follows, I want to argue that the hyperbolic descriptions of Gordana's body and this scrutiny of her as a 'foreign body' is meant to culminate in the revelation that she is a disabled woman. The narrator's entirely ableist approach 'positions the other in terms of corporeal difference, and the inherent power dynamics in such illicit looking often serve to dehumanize or devalue the disabled individual as in the medical model of disability'.[25] In fact, the inquisitiveness of the narrator when it comes to the cashier's body (and her imagined life) is relentless up until the exposure of Gordana's supposedly shameful secret. From that moment on, the narrator is even more resolved in painting the cashier as a specifically 'foreign' body inching ever closer to a grotesque and chimerical animal.[26]

Starting from the very first sentences of both texts, the cashier is described in a knowingly intrusive way: 'le regard se détourne du crâne de Gordana, comme s'il avait surpris et arraché d'elle, à son insu, une part très intime' (p. 11) ('the gaze turns away from Gordana's cranium as if it had, without her knowledge, surprised and ripped away from her, a very intimate part'). Every part of this sentence highlights the violence of this stolen gaze: 'surpris' ('surprised'), 'arraché' ('ripped away'), 'à son insu' ('without her knowledge') – from the start one is made to witness something that is intentionally described as relating to private matters. But the intimacy is not welcomed, and it is not even accurately portrayed. It is in fact all fantasised. These descriptions, then, reveal more than intended: while the narrator is exposing in great detail the appearance (and supposed behaviour) of the cashier, all her invented details, in turn, tell us about the ideologies and biases that underpin her (the narrator's) remarks.

Every minute aspect of Gordana's body, down to the sounds emitted by her throat, is exaggerated and made hyperbolic. It is only after two pages of overly detailed description that open the novel that we are tangentially introduced to Gordana's occupation and to the reason that she is in full view of the narrator's gaze: 'On se tient devant eux, on voudrait penser aux produits, faire les gestes dans l'ordre, sortir déposer ranger, vider remplir, la carte le code' (p. 13) ('We stand in front of them, we would like to think about the products, do the actions in order, go out and put away, empty and fill in, the card the code'). Here, the narrator (whose collection of verbs, barely separated by commas, associated with putting items on a belt and checking out, is meant to hint at Gordana's occupation) is beside herself, not because of the encounter with the cashier but because of her body parts; she is not standing in front of a person, but rather standing in front of breasts – 'eux' ('them').

Every description we come across is given through an intrusive stare meant to portray an unruly and even monstrous body. In the narrator's redoubled focus on Gordana's breasts, she uses verbs and expressions often heard when speaking critically of migrants who are viewed as inherently transgressive (of boundaries, of proper manners and customs). Indeed, the entire passage is teeming with negations that show supposed disrespect, 'ni, pas, rien, personne, aucun' ('neither, not, nothing, no one, no'):

> Et que dire des seins ... Ils abondent, ils échappent à l'entendement; ni chastes ni turgescents; on ne saurait ni les quali-fier, ni les contenir, ni les résumer. Les seins de Gordana ne pardonnent pas, ils dépassent la mesure, franchissent les limites, ne nous épargnent pas, ne nous épargnent rien, ne ménagent personne, heurtent les sensibilités des spectateurs, sèment la ziza-nie, n'ont aucun respect ni aucune éducation. (pp. 12–13)

> And what about the breasts ... They abound, they escape compre-hension; neither chaste nor turgid. They cannot be qualified, contained or summarised. Gordana's breasts do not forgive, they go beyond measure, cross boundaries, do not spare us, spare us nothing, spare no one, offend the sensibilities of the spectators, sow discord, have no respect nor education.

We could easily compare the description of Gordana's body in Lafon's texts to Marie Darrieussecq's *Truismes* ('*Pig Tales*') (1996): the narrator, who is famously oscillating between a woman and a sow, is described by Shirley Jordan as an expression of the 'abject … protean and uncontainable'[27] body. Not only are Gordana's breasts (and other singled out body parts like her neck or her thighs) described in a way that makes her seem like a chimera, a 'grotesque monster, formed of the parts of various animals',[28] the fact that they are portrayed as lacking education is also alluding to the idea that cashiers are uneducated and vacuous, that they are nothing more than a physical body there to serve. Furthermore, this portrayal, at the same time, reveals the discomfort that the narrator feels towards immigrants who are always 'too much'. The fact that Gordana, as we have read, is explicitly not French, adds to the notion that her unruly, disabled and 'foreign' body – or even body parts in this specific case – is, to borrow from Sara Ahmed, 'tak[ing] up [too much] space'.[29]

Artist Nihâl Martli echoes this visually in her illustrations for the novella *Gordana* by cutting up and zooming in on the cashier's body parts, as if she were too vast to fit on one single page. On the cover (which is repeated as the first illustration inside the book), we see a white woman with short reddish hair, from the back, while in the centre of the painting figures her bare neck. The second illustration of presumably this same woman centres once again on the neck, this time from the front; the painting does not go above her mouth and stops underneath the collarbones. The third illustration is a lone disembodied hand resting on a knee or a black chair – reminding us of the cashier's profession – while the fourth shows her hands handling merchandise.[30] It is noteworthy that this marks something of a departure from Martli's usual focus: her paintings, which for the great majority are full-length portraits of women, draw attention to the materiality of the body without cutting it up.[31] We thus become even more aware, in the context of the novella, that this zooming in on individual body parts takes away from the person as a whole, we cannot actually make out who Gordana is: she is a chimeric assembly of parts.

After spending a further page on Gordana's breasts, we eventually find out exactly where we are: 'rien ne lui fut donné, ni à elle ni à celles et ceux qui l'ont précédée, l'ont fabriquée et jetée là, en caisse quatre' (p. 14) ('nothing was given to her, neither to her nor to those who came before her, made her and threw her here, in register four'). What is of note in this description is that it accurately reminds us of the realities of this occupation and the high turnover rate: Gordana, preceded by others, is here, and she is followed at the end of the novel by another woman whose body is also made to be a distinguishing attribute, 'la caissière ronde et brune désormais vissée en caisse huit' (p. 183) ('the plump, brown-haired cashier henceforth glued to register eight'). But the question of who 'made' her, who 'threw' her here is interesting; the cashier in this novel is constructed by a shopper with an obsession (and by an author who found a convenient figure as a plausible empty canvas). This is not a story in which the cashier is self-fashioning an identity while calling out the difficulties of the job, in the vein of Sam's *Les Tribulations d'une caissière* in which the cashier herself addresses a potential newcomer. In Lafon's texts, to the contrary, we have a supposedly all-knowing narrator, often hiding behind the indeterminate 'on', dissecting the body and imagining Gordana's dreadful life, which will culminate in the discovery that she is a disabled woman – a marker of ultimate difference in the narrator's ableist mindset.

While *Gordana* does not entirely follow the type of ending of a *nouvelle à chute* ('novella with a surprising ending'), where the entire story must be re-evaluated according to new and unexpected information, I want to propose that, nevertheless, the revelation of Gordana's disability at the very end functions as a way to highlight her otherness and diminish her humanity. As the narrator sees Gordana getting up from her seat to help a colleague, she notices her gait and describes it in a way that is increasingly dehumanising:

> Quelque chose, très vite, alerte, accroche dans sa démarche, écorche, m'écorche, nous écorche. Gordana se propulse plus qu'elle ne marche, elle ahane à la sauvage, tout son corps ploie, plonge, à chaque pas semble chercher, inventer un équilibre impossible à affermir ... En deux bonds d'araignée affolée Gordana est devant l'armoire vitrée. (p. 46)

> Something, very quickly, alerts, lags in her gait, grates, grates me, grates us. Gordana propels herself more than she walks, she pants like a wild one, her whole body bends, dives, with each step seems to seek, to invent a balance that is impossible to reach ... In two panicked spider leaps Gordana is in front of the glass cabinet.

For the narrator seeing this gait is so bothersome that the verb 'écorcher' ('grating') is repeated in three variations – this same verb

has been used to describe Gordana's foreign accent – and she immediately assumes that her walk is a shameful matter for the cashier;
the comparison to a spider further emphasises the perceived
monstrosity and excessiveness of her leg. This is the final scene of
the novella *Gordana* and as the cashier walks back to her register, the
narrator pretends to be looking inside her bag, while she notes that
for Gordana this signifies not only something to be ashamed of, but
also something from which she needs to be rescued: 'Je n'ai rien vu,
rien surpris, Gordana pourrait le croire quand, écrasée, mâchoires
verrouillées, elle regagne enfin le providentiel habitacle de la caisse
quatre' (p. 47) ('I saw nothing, I caught nothing, Gordana might
believe it when, crushed, jaws locked, she finally returns to the safe
space of register four'). The last sentence of the novella paints the
register as a safe haven for Gordana (even though the intrusiveness
of the narrator-shopper proves that it is anything but), a shelter from
the gaze of the narrator whose pointed pretence that she has not
seen anything only reinforces the idea that disability is something to
be hidden. Once the narrator has observed this, the novella is over,
the mystery of this excessive woman is wrapped up and the cashier
has been exposed.

When Lafon expands on this story in *Nos vies*, the narrator explicitly jumps to the conclusion that she has discovered Gordana's
closely guarded secret: 'Gordana sait que j'ai vu … il y a quelque
chose de vaincu en elle, elle a été humiliée' (p. 55) ('Gordana knows
that I saw … there is something defeated in her, she was humiliated'). I have already mentioned that Lafon's texts operate from a
'deficit' model of disability, and in the novel her discovery will lead
to more fabulation that immediately prompts the narrator to
imagine a hypothetical child for Gordana. However, in doing so, she
emphasises the way that she, the narrator, views disability – as something that makes one 'monstrous' and animal-like:

> Gordana aurait eu peur que l'enfant naisse comme elle, comme
> ça, affublée, infirme, handicapée, mal formée, mal fichue, mal
> foutue, de traviole, avec une patte folle un pied pas fini bouffi
> impossible à regarder un pied de bête un sabot rose. Elle aurait
> voulu ne pas garder l'enfant, surtout s'il était comme elle. (p. 63)

> Gordana would have been afraid that the child be born like her,
> like that, badly made, crippled, handicapped, badly formed, badly
> put together, badly assembled, with a crazy paw a foot not finished

puffy impossible to look at the foot of an animal a pink hoof. She would have wanted to not keep the child, especially if he was like her.

As the narrator revels in ableist imagery and vocabulary – again using the conditional mood as a disavowal of her own responsibility in imagining such a life – she continues with her musings and goes back to considering what Gordana's own childhood might have been like. Rather than hearing from Gordana herself, we have an interpretation of her life offered by the narrator who cannot imagine that disability can be apprehended other than through a 'deficit' prism; while to the contrary, as Céline Roussel and Soline Vennetier have argued, 'ce que nous nommons handicap peut être une source de plaisir et de créativité esthétiques, partant, le moteur d'une réflexion nouvelle sur le corps et sa signification' ('what we call disability can be a source of aesthetic pleasure and creativity, hence the means for a new reflection on the body and its meaning').[32] Throughout Lafon's texts, the intense focus on Gordana, her body, her disability is also meant to further emphasise her as a 'foreigner'. The narrator links these by ascribing to Gordana the regret of having been born outside of Western Europe (revealing her own ideologies in the process), even suggesting that her ableist views are the cashier's own:

> En cherchant sur Internet Gordana aurait compris qu'elle aurait pu être soignée, il aurait fallu commencer très tôt … Si elle était née en France, en Allemagne, ou en Angleterre, en Italie même, si elle était née du bon côté, elle aurait été réparée; elle se le disait comme ça, avec ce verbe, réparer, et cette expression, du bon côté, mais elle n'en parlait pas. (pp. 135–6)

> By searching the Internet Gordana would have understood that she could have been treated, it would have had to start very early … If she had been born in France, in Germany, or in England, even in Italy, if she had been born on the right side, she would have been repaired; she said it to herself like that, with this verb, to repair, and this expression, on the right side, but she does not speak about it.

Of course, once again, everything is written in the conditional mood. This is just a thought exercise for the narrator – she can imagine the lives of others without it having to be true – she can even ascribe thoughts and words to the cashier and explain it away while hiding behind this grammatical sleight of hand. Though Gordana as a character is actually never given agency over the narration of her past, her childhood and her body – the narrator's thoughts are the ones being centred and the 'minuscule life' that is graced with this attention can simply be grateful.

As we have read, the discovery of Gordana's disability is the final point in the novella – the *chute* (literally, 'the fall') – and when we turn to the ending of the novel, the narrator lists this realisation as something that is world-shattering:

> Il y a comme ça des périodes où les plaques tectoniques de nos vies se mettent en mouvement ... où l'ordinaire sort de ses gonds; ensuite le décor se recompose et on continue ... rien ne pourra faire que ça n'ait pas existé, que Madame Jaladis ne soit pas morte, que Gordana n'ait pas un pied-bot, que ma mère n'ait pas élégamment déserté le jour des attentats du 11 septembre, que Karim ne soit pas revenu d'Algérie. (p. 58)

> There are times like this when the tectonic plates of our lives are set in motion ... when the ordinary is unhinged; then the decor is recomposed and we continue ... Nothing will be able to make it so that it did not happen, that Madame Jaladis is not dead, that Gordana did not have a club foot, that my mother did not elegantly leave like a deserter on the day of the September 11 attacks, that Karim did not come back from Algeria.

This discovery, this stolen intimate knowledge becomes a temporal marker in the narrator's own life: 'un an et quatre mois presque jour pour jour que je suis à la retraite, et huit mois que nous savons pour le pied de Gordana' (p. 182) ('one year and four months almost to the day that I'm retired, and eight months since we have known about Gordana's foot'). This marker established, it becomes Gordana's final disembodied textual appearance in the novel. The narrator evokes this because it has been two weeks since she has last seen her. While she immediately jumps to the conclusion that the cashier is on vacation 'au pays' (p. 180) ('in her country') – stereotypically assumed to be bringing gifts and money to her family to make up for working far away – she finds out that Gordana has actually gone.

When it comes to the ending of the novel, it echoes recent depictions of cashiers in which 'getting out' is often the end goal. By quitting extra-diegetically, Gordana has disappeared without making a fuss, but in doing so she has also put an end to the narrator's fantasies and indirectly corrected at least one assumption (that she was coming back). While the narrator had assumed throughout the novel that she has understood Gordana's life, that she knows exactly who the cashier is, she is proven wrong, at least on that one count. This is perhaps why the cashier who replaces Gordana answers the question about her whereabouts 'sur un ton quasiment triomphal' (p. 183) ('in an almost triumphant tone'). The last sentence of the novel – 'elle reviendra pas Gordana elle a quitté elle est partie' (p. 183) ('She will not come back Gordana she quit she left') – is in fact also Gordana's triumph and not necessarily or merely because she made it out. As she was used as an excuse to read about the narrator's own life and fantasies, Gordana's exit is the end of the narrative. For more than two weeks – all the while, the cashier had long been gone – the narrator continued to make wrong assumptions about Gordana's whereabouts and revealed her utter lack of understanding of migrant workers' lives. It is perhaps only as such, in subtracting her body from the view of both narrator and reader, that Gordana finally gained – even if ever so tenuously – the upper hand.

Works Cited

Ahmed, Sara, *Queer Phenomenology: Orientations, Objects, Others* (Durham NC: Duke University Press, 2006).

Berberi, Tammy, and Jennifer Row (eds), 'Disability's Worldmaking: Pasts and Futures', special issue of *L'Esprit Créateur*, 61/4 (Winter 2021).

Chabert, A.-L., 'De la nécessité de changer notre manière de regarder le handicap', in C. Roussel and S. Vennetier (eds), *Discours et représentations du handicap: Perspectives culturelles* (Paris: Classiques Garnier, 2019), pp. 305–18.

Diome, Fatou, 'La Préférence nationale', in *La Préférence nationale et autres nouvelles* (Paris: Présence africaine, 2001), pp. 83–94.

Dula, A., 'B(e)aring the Beast: Deformity, Animality, and the Ableist Gaze in French Literary Variants of "Beauty and the Beast"', *Marvels & Tales*, 34/2 (2020), 197–220.

Haigh, S., 'Personal or Political?: Representations of Disability in Contemporary French Fiction', *Journal of Literary & Cultural Disability Studies*, 6/3 (2012), 307–25.

Institut national de la statistique et des études économiques, 'Les métiers du commerce et de l'artisanat commercial: de la diversité mais peu de mixité', 17 October 2019, *www.insee.fr/fr/statistiques/4232605* (accessed 29 December 2021).

Jordan, S., 'Saying the unsayable: identities in crisis in the early novels of Marie Darrieussecq', in G. Rye and M. Worton (eds), *Women's Writing in Contemporary France: New Writers, New Literatures in the 1990s* (Manchester: Manchester University Press, 2002), pp. 142–53.

Lafon, Marie-Hélène, *Gordana* (Paris: Les Éditions du Chemin de Fer, 2012).

—— *Nos vies* (Paris: Buchet Chastel, 2017).

Martli, Nihâl, [personal website], *https://nihalmartli.com/* (accessed 29 December 2021).

'Que faire de nos fils et de nos filles? Caissière', *Le Petit Écho de la Mode*, 1 August 1926, p. 12.

Ranson, Olivier, 'untitled' [drawing], *Le Parisien*, 15 April 2020, p. 2.

Rosello, Mireille, *Declining the Stereotype: Ethnicity and Representation in French Cultures* (Hanover NH: University Press of New England, 1998).

Roussel, C., and S. Vennetier (eds), 'Introduction', in *Discours et représentations du handicap: Perspectives culturelles* (Paris: Classiques Garnier, 2019), pp. 11–34.

Salas, A., 'Voix de province: individu et communauté dans la France des "pays perdus"', in D. Rabaté (ed.), *En quel nom parler?* (Pessac: Presses Universitaires de Bordeaux, 2010), pp. 347–61.

Sam, Anna, 'Caissière no futur' [blog], *http://caissierenofutur.over-blog.com/* (accessed 29 December 2021).

—— *Checkout Girl: A Life Behind the Register*, trans. Morag Young [Kindle edition] (New York: Sterling Publishing, 2011).

—— *Les tribulations d'une caissière* (Paris: Stock, 2008).

Stojanovic, S., 'Should the Subaltern Clean?', *Mosaic: An Interdisciplinary Critical Journal*, 53/1 (2020), 39–54.

Thompson, H., 'French and Francophone Disability Studies', *French Studies*, 71/2 (April 2017), 243–51.

Vergès, Françoise, *A Decolonial Feminism*, translated by Ashley J. Bohrer with the author (London: Pluto Press, 2021).

—— *Un féminisme décolonial* (Paris: La Fabrique éditions, 2019).

Zola, Émile, *Au Bonheur des Dames* (Paris: Gallimard, Folio, 2002).

Notes

1 *Le Parisien*, 15 April 2020, p. 2. All translations unless otherwise noted are my own.

2 In the early twentieth century, women's weeklies advertise the profession as a suitable career choice for young women, emphasising the need for accounting skills and noting that '[o]n ne confie guère d'emploi de caissière à des personnes âgées de moins de vingt ans') ('one does not entrust the position of cashier to those who are not yet twenty years old'). 'Que faire de nos fils et de nos filles? Caissière', *Le Petit Écho de la Mode*, 1 August 1926, p. 12.

3 *Institut national de la statistique et des études économiques*, 'Les métiers du commerce et de l'artisanat commercial: de la diversité mais peu de mixité', 17 October 2019, *www.insee.fr/fr/statistiques/4232605* (accessed 29 December 2021).

4   See 'exposure', *Merriam Webster Dictionary*, *www.merriam-webster.com/
    dictionary/exposure* (accessed 29 December 2021).

5   The question of exposure is not one-sided: cashiers are privy to people's
    most intimate purchases and shoppers can thus also feel exposed.

6   See Fatou Diome's 'La Préférence nationale' ('National Preference')
    (2001), in which the narrator quips: 'Si vous aviez ce que j'ai dans la
    tête, vous ne seriez pas caissière au supermarché' ('If you had my brain,
    you wouldn't be a cashier in the supermarket'). Fatou Diome, 'La
    Préférence nationale', in *La Préférence nationale et autres nouvelles* (Paris:
    Présence africaine, 2001), p. 91.

7   While the blog is no longer updated, it is still available to read: *http://
    caissierenofutur.over-blog.com/* (accessed 29 December 2021).

8   Anna Sam, *Les tribulations d'une caissière* (Paris: Stock, 2008), p. 21.

9   Anna Sam, *Checkout Girl: A Life Behind the Register*, trans. Morag Young
    [Kindle edition] (New York: Sterling Publishing, 2011), chapter 3.
    Translation modified.

10 Marie-Hélène Lafon, *Gordana* (Paris: Les Éditions du Chemin de Fer,
    2012), back flap.

11 Lafon, *Gordana*, back flap.

12 Les Éditions du chemin de fer, 'Gordana – Marie-Hélène Lafon'
    [publisher's website], *www.chemindefer.org/catalogue/Gordana/l-auteur-
    marie-helene-lafon/l-auteur-marie-helene-lafon.html* (accessed 29 December
    2021).

13 Marie-Hélène Lafon, *Nos vies* (Paris: Buchet Chastel, 2017), p. 38. All
    quotations are from *Nos vies* though they are almost identical in
    Gordana.

14 For a discussion of the politics of 'foreign' names in contemporary
    French fiction, see S. Stojanovic, 'Should the Subaltern Clean?', *Mosaic:
    An Interdisciplinary Critical Journal*, 53/1 (2020), 39–54.

15 A. Salas, 'Voix de province: individu et communauté dans la France des
    "pays perdus"', in D. Rabaté (ed), *En quel nom parler?* (Pessac: Presses
    Universitaires de Bordeaux, 2010), pp. 347–61.

16 Mireille Rosello, *Declining the Stereotype: Ethnicity and Representation in
    French Cultures* (Hanover NH: University Press of New England, 1998),
    p. 107.

17 These are similar to the stereotypes discussed in Rosello, *Declining the
    Stereotype*, pp. 111–12.

18 Rosello, *Declining the Stereotype*, p. 112.

19 Françoise Vergès, *Un féminisme décolonial* (Paris: La Fabrique éditions,
    2019), p. 115. Emphasis in the original. Françoise Vergès, *A Decolonial
    Feminism*, translated by Ashley J. Bohrer with the author (London: Pluto
    Press, 2021), p. 76. Emphasis in the original.

20 I thank Siham Bouamer for suggesting considering this hierarchy.

21 I borrow this term from Sara Ahmed, *Queer Phenomenology: Orientations,
    Objects, Others* (Durham NC: Duke University Press, 2006), p. 137.

22 Ahmed, *Queer Phenomenology*, pp. 135, 136.

23 Ahmed, *Queer Phenomenology*, p. 136. Although Ahmed stresses that
    'bodies that pass as white, even if they are queer or have other points of

deviation, still have access to what follows from certain lines ... mak[ing] some things reachable that would not be reachable for those of us who are of color' (pp. 136–7).

24   The only explicit mention of disability by Ahmed is in a footnote in relation to Merleau-Ponty's phenomenology, although her larger discussion of 'motility' and 'points of deviation' suggests that disability could figure in this line of argumentation. For a discussion of 'deviant bodies', see also Samantha Haigh, 'Personal or Political?: Representations of Disability in Contemporary French Fiction', *Journal of Literary & Cultural Disability Studies*, 6/3 (2012), 307–25.

25   A. Dula, 'B(e)aring the Beast: Deformity, Animality, and the Ableist Gaze in French Literary Variants of "Beauty and the Beast"', *Marvels & Tales*, 34/2 (2020), 204. This has also been termed 'a "pathology" or "deficit" model of disability' as opposed to a '"social model" of disability, that is the belief that disability is a socially constructed entity rather than a medicalized pathology'. H. Thompson, 'French and Francophone Disability Studies', *French Studies*, 71/2 (April 2017), 245, 248. Both models have been extensively critiqued, see A.-L. Chabert, 'De la nécessité de changer notre manière de regarder le handicap', in C. Roussel and S. Vennetier (eds), *Discours et représentations du handicap: Perspectives culturelles* (Paris: Classiques Garnier, 2019), pp. 305–18; and Haigh, 'Personal or Political?', 307–25.

26   On disability as a '"monstrous" spectacle', see Dula, 'B(e)aring the Beast', 197–220.

27   S. Jordan, 'Saying the unsayable: identities in crisis in the early novels of Marie Darrieussecq', in G. Rye and M. Worton (eds), *Women's Writing in Contemporary France: New Writers, New Literatures in the 1990s* (Manchester: Manchester University Press, 2002), p. 144.

28   See 'chimera', *Oxford English Dictionary Online*, *https://oed.com/* (accessed 29 December 2021).

29   Ahmed, *Queer Phenomenology*, p. 24.

30   There are a total of fifteen illustrations, these four focus explicitly on Gordana.

31   Nihâl Martli, [personal website], *https://nihalmartli.com/* (accessed 29 December 2021).

32   C. Roussel and S. Vennetier (eds), 'Introduction', in *Discours et représentations du handicap: Perspectives culturelles* (Paris: Classiques Garnier), p. 19. See also Tammy Berberi and Jennifer Row (eds), 'Disability's Worldmaking: Pasts and Futures', special issue of *L'Esprit Créateur*, 61/4 (Winter 2021).

Chapter 9

Subterranean Space and Subjugation: 'Being Below' in Delphine de Vigan's *Les Heures souterraines*

DORTHEA FRONSMAN-CECIL

The growing corpus of contemporary French workplace fiction, a literary 'subgenre' that often critiques the vicissitudes of the French economy and working life, draws from a deep well of varied signifiers of the 'human condition'. Several critics attribute contemporary writers' interest in penning stories of harassed, oppressed workers to a sociological interest in chronicling the effects of neoliberal ideology and economics on modern French people.[1] However, while contemporary workplace fiction may echo and even cite sociological theories, its artistic purpose is to represent individual human emotional, social and biological processes (and breakdowns) in the face of material realities of work. Scholars of French workplace fiction have noted such novels' common use of fragmented narratives, minimal character development and obstacles to bodily movement through post-industrial cityscapes. Diana Marcela Patiño Rojas, for example, designates these features of recent French workplace novels such as Delphine de Vigan's *Les Heures souterraines* ('*Underground Time*') (2009) and Nathalie Kuperman's *Nous étions des êtres vivants* (2010) as a shared poetics of contemporary realism.[2] While I agree that these novels' detailed portraits of everyday life echo French realism in certain respects, I maintain that their metaphors of space and motion are distinctly postmodern.

By moving between individual emotions or physical sensations and a grander scale of societal issues, workplace fiction informally theorises a biopolitics of neoliberal work culture while gesturing to and often questioning the metanarrative or *grand récit* (grand narrative) that legitimates the ideology of our society and historical era. Although realist fiction of the nineteenth century portrayed people from disparate social strata within a cohesive metanarrative that linked them as participants in the same society, contemporary French workplace fiction suggests that modern people share a sense of alienation rather than social bonds. Jean-François Lyotard contends that while the metanarrative of modern political and social philosophy envisions the movement of History as progress towards universal liberty, the dehumanising results of technological and economic 'progress' in the postmodern era belie these ideas.[3] The postmodern era that Lyotard describes – one marked by increased but fragmented access to information and new narratives of social atomisation and stalled progress – coincides with the end of the economic boom following the Second World War, which economist Jean Fourastié dubbed 'Les Trente Glorieuses' ('The Glorious Thirty'). I contend that contemporary novels of working life after the *Trente Glorieuses* underscore this gap between the metanarrative of progress and actual social realities through a poetics of *décalage* ('discrepancy' or 'lag') between the passage of time and obstructions to physical movement, including efforts to be among other people.

If contemporary workplace fiction commonly represents subjects whose progress towards liberation and fulfilment is fettered, then it is remarkable that novels of women in the workplace – who have seen even less 'progress' in economic equality than men – employ a poetics not only of immobility, but of being cast downward and aside. This chapter addresses the use of spatial metaphors of 'being below' in Delphine de Vigan's workplace novel *Les Heures souterraines* as allegories for the subjugation of women in contemporary workplaces. Analyses of metaphors of embodiment and space have been central to previous scholarship on Vigan and *Les Heures souterraines*. Elise Hugueny-Léger argues that Vigan's use of metalepsis – the intrusion of one narrative within another – questions the limits between self and other.[4] Similarly, Kathryn Robson maintains that Vigan's novels examine the possibilities (and limits) of empathy, or of imagining oneself in someone else's place.[5] Agnès Vandevelde-

Rougale contends that *Les Heures souterraines* reflects the power of workplace harassment to engender uncertainty about the relationship between words and (physical) reality.[6] Finally, Anne Mulhall considers the novel's metaphors of movement and obstruction as a form of bodily refusal against the exploitative paradigms of working life in France.[7] Surveying this scholarship spurs me to ask which forces – social, physical or otherwise – ordain these barriers, insufficiencies of language and failures of empathy in Vigan's work.

By analysing the uses of subterranean spaces and downward or backward movement in *Les Heures souterraines*, I consider how the novel uses what narrative theorist Lily Alexander calls the 'chronotope of rise and fall' to illustrate women losing the progress gained by feminism within neoliberalism. A chronotope, or 'artistic time-space continuum', describes the physical dimensions or 'topography' of the fictional world in conjunction with the 'chronology' of the narrative. Alexander identifies the chronotope of rise and fall as 'a variation of the chronotope of ordeal proposed by Bakhtin', which is 'associated with a journey'. 'A radically shaped spatial landscape affects the drama of the characters – their ordeals, physical/psychological movement, the meaning of their journey and spiritual survival.'[8] Although Alexander theorises that considering this chronotope is most useful for analysing films and visual storytelling, I contend that examining this chronotope is also helpful for appraising fiction with narratives plotted on a nexus of movements (both forced and voluntary) upward and downward. Notably, using this chronotope in workplace fiction opposes the 'errance' ('wandering') that Georg Lukács described as a characteristic narrative (and physical) movement of classical *Bildungsromane* – novels of (often itinerant) vocational, social and emotional apprenticeships that were some of the first novels of working life.[9] In this chapter, I examine the novel's use of isolated and low spaces as metonymic representations of Mathilde's social and professional existence, noting her movements within and occupation of such spaces as she works and commutes. Finally, I ask what implications the literary representation of women 'being below' has for narrative art forms and discourses of feminist progress in late capitalism.

Subaltern Subjects, Subterranean Spaces

What relationship does 'being below' have with being subaltern? In Antonio Gramsci's coinage, people excluded from the socio-economic institutions of their society by a hegemonic class are *subaltern* groups. Women who do not cede to male bosses' and colleagues' demands for subordinate behaviour frequently lose their toehold in the key socio-economic institutions of clan, circle, market, corporation, (social) movements and associations. Economist Sven-Erik Sjöstrand contends that these six institutions exist to 'reduce fundamental uncertainty and facilitate the effective and legitimate coordination of human action'.[10] Indeed, when the protagonist of *Les Heures souterraines*, Mathilde, faces exclusion from these institutions, her life is plunged into uncertainty. Her boss Jacques cuts Mathilde from his circle of favoured employees after she contradicts him in a meeting; quickly, she is left out of communication with the clan of her colleagues; Mathilde is demoralised and loses time, energy and space to be with the literal clan of her family. Eventually, Mathilde is pressured into leaving the corporation, forced into unemployment and potentially out of the (economic and labour) market(s) into a 'lower' socio-economic status.

In France, real-life stories of working women facing gender discrimination are not unusual. In 2008, a year before *Les Heures souterraines* was published, French women had earned only 75 per cent of what French men had earned since 1995, while the employment gap between genders had shrunk to only 10 percentage points.[11] French women executives comprise only 42 per cent of corporate employees and only 26 per cent of high-level executives; their median salary is 16 per cent less than male executives and 8 per cent less than men in the same roles.[12] Corporate employees over the age of forty fear the all-too-common *mise au placard* ('putting into the closet'), when companies who cannot fire employees with seniority deprive them of responsibilities and communication to force them to quit. Although the two alternating omniscient narratives of *Les Heures souterraines* recount parallels between two middle-aged professionals' impossible commutes, days in unfriendly workspaces and thwarted attempts at social connections, the two protagonists' professional frustrations are quite different. Travelling physician Thibaut's unhappiness is inherent to his job, while Mathilde's misery stems from her boss Jacques' bullying. Jacques frequently targets her on issues that are common motifs of gender harassment, such as her appearance and time spent on domestic and parenting tasks.[13] Mathilde is emblematic of women of her generation struggling to find a way forward (and upward) despite myriad social and economic obstacles.

Integration and Rejection: Women Workers' Bodies in/as Corporate Mechanisms

Les Heures souterraines illustrates how being pushed down and around in physical space and socio-economic status causes working women to lose their sense of humanity and bodily autonomy. Mathilde has already survived other instances of loss, disorientation and reorientation during her life's trajectory. After giving birth to twins, she lost her husband in a car accident; their car tumbling off the hard shoulder and crashing is a clear metaphorical disruption of the chronotope of the road. Mathilde re-entered the workforce as the 'adjointe' (the 'assistant' who is 'connected') to Jacques Pelletier, the Director of Marketing of the Nutrition and Health branch of a multinational food company.

The novel uses the language of bodily integration to reflect Jacques and Mathilde's lack of boundaries and 'adjoined' roles: 'Il avait fait de Mathilde sa plus proche collaboratrice, son *bras droit* ... Parce que d'emblée ils se sont accordés'[14] ('He had made Mathilde his closest collaborator, his *right hand* ... because from the start he and she agreed'[15]) on everything. The term *accorder* comes from ad- ('to', 'of') and cor- ('heart', 'soul'); an agreement is joining one's heart or soul to another. As Jacques' extended 'body part', Mathilde works without credit; words flow from her mind to her hands, then Jacques' mouth: 'Peu à peu, elle s'était mise à écrire ses discours pour lui et à prendre en charge la gestion directe d'une équipe de sept personnes' (p. 29) ('Gradually, she began to write his speeches and take control of the management of a team of seven' (p. 20)). As a single mother, 'situation qui, jusque-là, lui avait valu plusieurs refus' (p. 28) ('a situation which up until then had brought her only rejections' (p. 20)). Mathilde senses that she must ignore sexism (such as illegal hiring discrimination) and *faire corps* ('become one (body)') with powerful men to find her place in the professional world.

Mathilde does not complain about the evening she spends at home finishing her (and Jacques') reports and presentations (p. 29;

21). This obliging quality spares Mathilde from Jacques' characteristic rages and cutting sarcasm, which often 'provoquaient les
sanglots des dames' (pp. 166–7) ('reduced women to tears'
(pp. 168–9)). Their closeness has never been sexual, but Jacques
controls Mathilde's body by dictating what she wears: 'Jacques lui
avait demandé si elle pouvait porter des chaussures plates, tout au
moins aux jours où ils devaient se déplacer ensemble à l'extérieur'
(p. 89) ('Jacques had asked her if she could wear flat shoes, at least
on days when they had to go out together' (p. 85)). As long as
Jacques can subjugate Mathilde to his whims, keep her physically
below him and claim credit for her work, he gives her no trouble.

However, after she contradicts him in a meeting, he begins
policing Mathilde's body in a more destructive way by criticising her
appearance, her presence, her absence and the products of her
physical touch. In a sarcastically solicitous tone, Jacques proclaims
that she has a 'sale tête' (she 'looks dreadful') then a 'sale gueule'
(p. 45) ('look(s) like crap' (p. 39)); the word 'gueule', literally an
animal's maw, underscores Jacques' desire to dehumanise and
'lower' Mathilde. She tries to ignore 'ses attaques – réflexions
ironiques sur ses chaussures ou son nouveau manteau, remarques
désobligeantes sur la date de ses congés de Noël ou l'illisibilité
soudaine de son écriture' (p. 32) ('his attacks ... ironic comments
about her shoes or her new coat, the mean remarks about the dates
of her Christmas holidays or the sudden illegibility of her handwriting' (p. 24)). Soon, Jacques excludes her from meetings and
refuses to accept any strategies that Mathilde has helped her team
develop. Although Mathilde's children become concerned by her
fatigue and distractibility, she is unsure how to explain what is
lowering her morale. After being rejected from its symbiosis with
Jacques, her body is stuck in 'une autre mécanique ... qui n'aurait
de cesse de la faire plier' – a 'mechanism' that will make her fold and
bring her down (pp. 28; 21).

After months of harassment, Jacques informs Mathilde of 'une
nouvelle affectation de l'espace, afin de faciliter la circulation
d'information au sein de notre groupe' (p. 89) ('a new organisation
of space in order to facilitate the information flow within our team'
(p. 86)) – 'au sein de' meaning literally ('at the breast/heart of').
Namely, Jacques has hired a replacement; a much younger woman is
sitting in Mathilde's office when she arrives. Information can circulate in the office space, but Mathilde cannot; she is 'loin de Jacques,

loin de tout, à l'autre bout,' ('far away from Jacques … from every-thing, at the other end') in an office 'privé de fenêtre … (qui) jouxte les toilettes Hommes de l'étage, séparé par un mur en contreplaqué' (p. 96) (that 'has no window, shares a wall with the men's toilets, from which it is separated by a plywood wall' (p. 97)). Mathilde feels humiliated by her literal 'mise au placard' (casting out, 'putting in the closet') in a dusty furniture storage room that elicits jokes within the office. 'Dans l'entreprise, on appelle le bureau 500–9 "le cagibi" ou "les chiottes". Parce qu'on y perçoit très distinctement le parfum Fraîcheur des glaciers du spray désodorisant pour sanitaires, ainsi que le roulement du distributeur de papier hygiénique' (p. 97) ('In the company, room 500–9 is known as "the storeroom" or else "the shit-hole". Because you can very clearly detect the smell of Glacier Freshness air freshener as well as the sound of the toilet-paper dispenser' (p. 94)). On the same day that Jacques relegates her to a spatially distant, socially lowly space, Mathilde also loses access to the departmental intranet server – the abstract professional space in which information circulates.

Mathilde's average workday has long included a series of spatial rises and falls; each day, she takes the lift to her workplace on the fifth floor of the company's office tower. 'La tour scintillante … (aux) parois vitrées' (p. 86) ('glittering tower (with) glass sides' (p. 82)) is a symbol of hopes for a bright future of corporate ladder-climbing. Nevertheless, its deceptive, reflective façades are impenetrable despite their putative transparency; the high-rise's panels evoke the 'glass ceiling' that keeps working women down. As Alexander writes, towers have become topoi of social (as well as professional, economic and other) rises and falls in modern narra-tives. 'In the civilized space of the Western city culture, there were no more limitless paths and spatiality free from control … the heroes, pursuing freedom and the possibility of a journey, had nowhere to go but up' (p. 30). Alexander argues that cinematic narratives stopped representing these spatial ascents as routes to social and economic success in the early 1950s, when 'stories associated with … towers, lighthouses, (and) mountain slopes inevitably began to carry a tragic tone'. Mathilde's story takes place far past that first moment of narrative acrophobia in the 1950s, but the French cultural tradi-tion has its own tragic towers. For instance, the Eiffel Tower symbolises national military force and loss in Guillaume Apollinaire's *calligramme*. Victor Hugo's Quasimodo plummeted from

Notre-Dame's bell tower into a shared grave. Louis Malle's businessman protagonist in *Ascenseur pour l'échafaud* ('*Lift to the Scaffold*') fails to exit the scene after murdering his boss when he gets trapped in his office building's lift. The skyscrapers of La Défense – the business district named after a now-removed statue commemorating the defence of Paris during the Franco-Prussian war and the reintegration of Paris within national territory after the fall of the Paris Commune – are monuments to the triumph of capital. The existence of these skyscrapers brings pride to some and dread to others; Mathilde's office building, which is likely to be in La Défense, also inspires her ambivalence.

Following Mathilde's reassignment to the distant 'cagibi' ('cupboard'), she daydreams of the building's possibilities for physical and metaphorical journeying, discovery and progress – all traits of the chronotope of the road that will allow her to regain her freedom. She longs to:

> (s)ortir de son bureau ... traverser l'étage ... faire irruption ... sans frapper ... déclarer la fin des hostilités, l'avènement de la créativité individuelle, l'abolition des marges brutes ... elle va errer dans les couloirs, pieds nus, elle ira au hasard, caressera les murs ... Elle prendra l'ascenseur, appuiera sur n'importe quel bouton. (p. 180)

> Leave the office ... hurry across the floor, burst in ... without knocking ... declare an end to hostilities, a new era of individual creativity, she'll abolish gross margins ... she'll wander the corridors barefoot ... stroke the walls ... she'll take the lift, press buttons at random. (pp. 185–6)

In Mathilde's fantasy, fulfilling work and a turn from profit to human interest spring from visions of joyous *errance* ('wandering') up, down and through the office, her feet unleashed from her high heels – symbols of women's professional attire and restrictive beauty standards – and her hands healing the hostile workspace with nurturing motions. After her human resources director suggests an internal transfer to a new position, Mathilde takes a break outside, where she meets a newly hired young woman who engages her in friendly conversation. Her optimism renewed, Mathilde then soars back up to her office in the lift (pp. 192–3). Unfortunately, Jacques also blocks this path to happiness. When Mathilde sees him waiting for the lift and asks to talk, Jacques evades her, rushing into the lift and descending. Shortly thereafter, during a phone call where the other employees hear only him, he 'stoops even lower' by behaving as though Mathilde is insulting him when she is not speaking (pp. 208–9).

Les entrailles de l'économie ('the Entrails of the Economy'): Disintegration, Dissolution, Displacement and (In)digestion

Mathilde's struggles with work and bodily freedom extend beyond the office building's boundaries. While commuting to work on the day that she is 'exiled', Mathilde misses her connecting train due to an obstruction in the underground. Later, Mathilde breaks from an unsympathetic crowd of commuters and gets off the train again to help a woman whose claustrophobia and anxiety about her precarious temp job have precipitated a panic attack. Despite this moment of solidarity between women workers in the hostile, unnavigable subterranean space, the other woman cannot recover and get to work (pp. 58–65). The metaphors of obstacles preventing women from working and keeping them underground reverse the chronotope of the road or journey of adult professional life, instead privileging the chronotope of rise and fall. Her body alternately moved and immobilised against her will, Mathilde imagines the underground as a refuge: 'Elle se demande au fond s'il ne serait pas plus doux de rester là, toute la journée dans les *entrailles* du monde ... s'extraire du flot, du mouvement. Capituler' (p. 72, my italics) ('She wonders deep down whether it wouldn't be better to spend the whole day in the *bowels* of the earth ... remove herself from the flow, the movement. Give in' (p. 68)). The word *entrailles* is intriguingly ambiguous – in literary French, it can also refer to a womb, a place of comfort and growth. At other times, Mathilde sees the underground as a place of disintegration: 'Elle serait victime d'un attentat ... une bombe exploserait, puissante ... elle serait éparpillée dans l'air saturé des matins d'affluence ... dispersée aux quatre coins de la gare ...' (p. 13) ('[S]he would be the victim of an attack ... a powerful bomb would explode ... she would be scattered in the stifling air of the morning rush hour, blown to the four corners of the train station' (p. 3)). Mathilde, whose occupational illness nauseates her, imagines the underground as the city's digestive system, ready to dissolve and excrete her.

The stomach – the 'lower' part of the body, socially and culturally, as well as physically – and its emanations and excretions figure in

French psychoanalyst and literary critic Julia Kristeva's theories of
abjection to symbolise the loss of distinction between subject and
object, or between self and other.[16] By reading Vigan's text through a
Kristevian lens, we can see that Mathilde's sense of embodied selfhood, rejected from its integration with Jacques, is disintegrating;
therefore, she conceptualises her feelings of abjection through ideas
of dissolution. Her body is 'vidé de sa matière' (p. 40), ('emptied of
its substance' (p. 33)); 'chaque jour elle entame sa substance' (p. 14)
('with every passing day she is eating into her substance' (p. 4)).
Several times, Mathilde remarks that the air is heavier and more
resilient than she is, possessing 'quelque chose qui résiste à la ville,
son empressement, qui fait opposition' (p. 111) ('something which
resists the city, its eagerness, which opposes it' (p. 109)). When
Jacques moves her to the room beside the men's toilets – a uniquely
abject locale – 'il lui a semblé qu'elle allait se dissoudre, disparaître'
(p. 90) ('It seemed to her as though she was going to dissolve, disappear' (p. 86)). In the dismal office space, Mathilde feels that 'ses
gestes n'existent plus' (p. 206) ('her gestures no longer exist'
(p. 213)) and that she will spill and stream out like 'une flaque'
(p. 208) ('a puddle' (p. 215)) when she sees Jacques. A distressed
Mathilde also imagines a violent end for Jacques, his body and office
destroyed. She would prefer that her young replacement 'se désin-
tègre, là, devant ses yeux, qu'elle se dégonfle ou parte en poussière'
(p. 211) (would 'disintegrate before her eyes, or deflate or dissolve
into dust' p. 218)), pulverised by the weight of the workplace's
cruelty towards women.

Eventually, Mathilde seeks support from her human resources
director, Patricia Lethu, who advises Mathilde to remain 'adaptable';
Lethu only realises that Jacques is scapegoating Mathilde when he
moves Mathilde to the 'cagibi'. Although Lethu then tries to help,
her efforts come too late. Mathilde also visits her union supervisor,
Paul Vernon: 'Dans le récit de Mathilde, rien ne semble l'étonner.
Ni la situation dans laquelle elle se trouve, ni le temps qu'il lui a fallu
pour appeler. Il a dit: dans ces cas-là, on attend toujours trop
longtemps. On cherche à lutter et on s'épuise' (p. 154) ('Nothing in
Mathilde's account seems to surprise him. Neither the situation in
which she found herself, nor the time it had taken her to call. He
said: In cases like this, people always wait too long. They try to fight
and run out of steam' (p. 156)). Her loyal colleague Laetitia has
urged her to seek Vernon's help – 'Il faut que tu aies un syndicat

derrière toi. Seule, tu ne peux pas y arrive … Il faut que tu te fasses aider, Mathilde' (p. 153) ('You need to have the union behind you. You won't manage it on your own … You need to get help, Mathilde' (p. 155)). Nevertheless, 'Elle a voulu se battre. Seule. Maintenant elle sait qu'elle s'est trompée' (p. 147) ('She has wanted to fight. Alone. Now she knows that she was wrong' (p. 149)). Mathilde finally realises her errors in deciding to 'faire corps' ('become one (body)') with the boss instead of her union; one isolated, weary body is not enough to fight back against Jacques.

Laetitia wryly observes spatial and social dynamics in the company, noting that disloyal colleagues are most likely to advance in their careers: they 'sont prêts à tout pour gravir un échelon ou un coefficient de classification' (pp. 134–5) ('are ready to do anything to climb the ladder or move up a grade' (p. 136)). Unlike Mathilde, Laetitia draws firm boundaries between her work and her personal life. 'Elle pointe à dix-huit heures trente tous les soirs et sa vie est ailleurs' (p. 135) ('She clocks out at six thirty every evening. Her life is elsewhere' (p. 135)). Mathilde had found Laetitia's ethics and boundaries overly idealistic until Jacques closed off the office's space to her.

Subsumption, Subjugation and Subterfuge

To conclude this chapter, I would like to examine the book's portrayal of the 'always-on' culture of the corporate sector as a force that invades Mathilde's leisure time and domestic space. In Alexander's theory of the chronotope of rise and fall, the home is a constant high point, a refuge that is the 'shielding frame' of the hero(ine)'s story. 'It contains vertical lines, but it is also connected to the earth through horizontal lines that emphasize balance and protection. For this reason, the House is the ultimate way of holding one's ground, of surviving above the ground level of life' (p. 38). In *Les Heures souterraines*, Mathilde is proud of having made her home a joyful refuge for herself and her children. Her sons even give her a protective symbol, a World of Warcraft trading and game card called the 'Défenseur de l'Aube d'Argent' ('Defender of the Silver Tunic'). Its name promises the start of auspicious, abundant futures: in French, 'aube', meaning 'dawn' as well as a priest's vestment, derives from the Latin *alba* ('white'), a colour that evokes the new beginning of a blank page; 'argent' means not only 'silver' but also

'money'. Nevertheless, Mathilde's need to work overtime troubles
the protective frame of the home and her family life. After months
of bullying, Jacques unexpectedly asks Mathilde to write an article
for the company newsletter over her weekend. Although she has
planned a family vacation, Mathilde consents, hoping to appease
Jacques. 'Elle se débrouillerait. Elle était partie à la campagne avec
son portable, avait travaillé une bonne partie de la nuit du samedi au
dimanche. Le reste du temps, elle avait ri, joué aux cartes, participé
à la préparation des repas' (pp. 100–1) ('She'd cope somehow. She
took her laptop to the countryside and worked through most of the
night from Saturday to Sunday. The rest of the time she laughed,
played cards, helped prepare meals' (p. 98)). Even outside the
office, Mathilde's work subsumes her time and space, leaving her to
fish out moments of domestic leisure from amidst an unending
stream of responsibilities; ultimately, Jacques claims not to receive
the article that she sends him.

Vigan's novel illustrates the need for human social connection
within families, social groups and cities by showing Mathilde with-
ering as her work cuts her off from these ties. Yet Mathilde has a
stalwart friend and advocate in her colleague Laetitia, who models
how women workers can continue to claim space for themselves by
serving their own emotional and social interests and allying with
colleagues and unions rather than indifferent bosses. Therefore, I
would like to underscore how both women's workplace fiction and
feminist political theories illustrate the importance of caring for
families, friends and society and demonstrate that work (and other
everyday occupations) must accommodate human (and women's)
needs. Feminist political theorist Anna Jónasdóttir's theories of the
significance of shared 'women's interests' draws on Marxist critiques
of the notion of separation between public and private interests. In
Jónasdóttir's account, political agency derives from having needs
and demands met across our existence as 'private' social subjects as
well as 'public' economic and political subjects. Asking whether 'we
can differentiate between general (human) interests ... and interests derived from the historically defined gendered reality of human
existence', Jónasdóttir proposes that we consider not only the historically gendered division of labour, but the historically gendered
'division of love'.[17] Jónasdóttir cites this as a central reason that
women's political activity (both activism and policymaking) has
focused more than (and differently from) men's political activity on

providing for reproduction, health and other biological needs and social cohesion through frameworks of care. To secure meaningful work, equal treatment and time-space for friends, family and ourselves, women workers must seek this 'being-among' in the world and in workplaces by pursuing 'common interests' through political and social actions of class and gender solidarity. However, in the Marxist framework from which Jónasdóttir and I both draw, the situation of women workers in one country, such as France, can only improve when we serve the political, social and economic interests of labourers throughout the world.

The conclusions that we can draw from this study of 'being below' in Vigan's novel indicate that contemporary French fiction is determined to show which forces keep women workers down. We might ask, however, to what end such contemporary fiction commonly shows the 'career path' – the chronotope of the road in professional form – and the 'career ladder' as impassable and thus obsolete conceptions of women's expectations for work in the twenty-first century. Literature's power to envision better outcomes for oppressed people makes it a potential tool of social theory. Yet contemporary French literature does not tell stories of victorious white-collar or blue-collar workers (although we do find an occasional narrative of plucky women in service professions).[18] Among the rare examples of workplace narratives in which women succeed, the American film *9 to 5* (1980) shows three businesswomen outwitting a sexist boss, winning promotions and introducing work-sharing programmes and an on-site day-care centre. However, this narrative took place at a more prosperous, hopeful historical moment (and in a country more optimistic about economic matters) and focused on women of a higher socio-economic status. This is even more reason for working women everywhere to write, read and demand more stories where we may 'be among' each other in solidarity and 'rise' together.

Works Cited

Alexander, L., 'Storytelling in Time and Space: Studies in the Chronotope and Narrative Logic on Screen', *Journal of Narrative Theory*, 37/1 (Winter 2007), 27–64.

APEC (Association Pour l'Emploi des Cadres), 'Les écarts de salaires femmes-hommes chez les cadres', 27 February 2020, *https://corporate.apec. fr/home/nos-etudes/toutes-nos-etudes/les-ecarts-de-salaire-femmes-ho.html* (accessed 18 August 2020).

Beinstingel, Thierry, *La représentation du travail dans les récits français depuis la fin des Trente Glorieuses* (Besançon: Littératures. Université Bourgogne Franche-Comté, 2017).

Engélibert, J. P., '"Ressources inhumaines": Le nouvel esprit du travail dans quatre romans français contemporains (François Bon, François Emmanuel, Aurélie Filipetti, Lydie Salvayre)', *TRANS-* 4 (2007). *http:// journals.openedition.org/trans/192* (accessed 20 October 2016).

Fourastié, Jean, *Les Trente Glorieuses, ou la révolution invisible de 1946 à 1975* (Paris: Fayard, 1979).

Higgins, Colin (dir.), *9 to 5*. IPC Films, 1980.

Lukács, Georg, *The Theory of the Novel: A Historico-philosophical Essay on the Forms of Great Epic Literature* (Cambridge MA: MIT Press, 1971).

Hugueny-Léger, É. S. M., 'D'après des histoires vraies: l'écriture à la lisière de Delphine de Vigan', in K. Averis, E. Kackute and C. Mao (eds), *Transgression(s) in Twenty-First-Century Women's Writing in French* (Leiden: Faux Titre, Brill, 2020), pp. 131–47.

INSEE, '*Tableaux de l'économie française, Édition 2018: Femmes et hommes*', 27 February 2018, *www.insee.fr/fr/statistiques/3303378?sommaire=3353488* (accessed 29 August 2020).

Jónasdóttir, A. G., 'On the Concept of Interest, Women's Interests, and the Limitations of Interest Theory', in A. G. Jónasdóttir and K. Jones (eds), *The Political Interests of Gender Revisited: Redoing Theory and Research with a Feminist Face* (London: SAGE Publications, 1988), pp. 40–2.

Kristeva, Julia, *Pouvoirs de l'horreur: Essai sur l'abjection* (Paris: Seuil, 1980).

Labadie, Aurore, *Le roman d'entreprise au XXIe siècle* (Paris: Presses Sorbonne Nouvelle, 2016).

Lescurieux, M., 'La représentation syndicale des femmes, de l'adhésion à la prise de Responsabilités: une inclusion socialement sélective', *La Revue de l'Ires*, 2/98 (2019), 59–82.

Lyotard, Jean-François, *Le Postmoderne expliqué aux enfants: correspondance 1982–1985* (Paris: Editions Galilée, 1988).

Mercier, E, 'Trois salariés sur dix sont victimes de harcèlement moral au travail', IPSOS.fr. *www.ipsos.com/fr-fr/trois-salaries-sur-dix-sont-victimes-de-harcelement-moral-au-travail#:~:text=Le%20ph%C3%A9nom%C3%A8ne%20est%20susceptible%20de,ou%20les%20ouvriers%20(32%25* (accessed 5 April 2020).

Milewski, F, 'Les femmes sur le marché du travail en France: les progrès marquent le pas', *Santé, Société et Solidarité* 1, *De l'égalité de droit à l'égalité de fait: Françaises et Québécoises entre législation et réalité* (2008), 67–74.

Ministère du Travail, de l'Emploi, et de l'Insertion, 'Dares Analyses. Femmes et hommes sur le marché de travail', March 2015. *https://travail-emploi.gouv.fr/IMG/pdf/2015–017.pdf* (accessed 5 April 2020).

Moret-Courtel, Catherine, *La Caissière* (Paris: Belfond, 2008).

Mulhall, A. M., 'Bodies in crisis in the French literature of the office: Lydie Salvayre's *La Vie commune* and Delphine de Vigan's *Les Heures souterraines*', *Modern & Contemporary France* 26/3: Work in Crisis (2018), 291–306.

Patiño Rojas, D. M., 'El mundo del trabajo en la novela francesa contemporánea: por una estética de lo real', *Escritos*, 26 (2018), 167–90, *10.18566/escr.v26n56.a08* (accessed 8 April 2020).

Robson, K., 'The Limits of Empathy and Compassion in Delphine de Vigan's *No et moi* and *Les Heures souterraines*', *Modern Language Review*, 110/3 (2015), 677–93, 925.

Servoise, S, 'Le Travail sans fin: Discours et représentations à l'œuvre', *Raison Publique*, 15 (November 2011), 7–202.

Sjöstrand, S.-E., 'On the Rationale behind "Irrational" Institutions', *Journal of Economic Issues*, 25/4 (December 1992), 1007–40.

Vandevelde-Rougale, A., 'Saisir les violences invisibles', in F. de Geuser and A. M. Guénette (eds), *Littérature et management: Le management comme roman et le manager comme romancier?* (Paris: L'Harmattan, collection Conception et dynamique des organisations, 2018), pp. 97–110.

Viart, D., 'Écrire le travail. Vers une sociologisation du roman contemporain?', in G. Rubino and D. Viart (eds), *Écrire le présent* (Paris: Collection Recherches, Armand Colin, 2013), pp. 133–56.

Vigan, Delphine de, *Les Heures souterraines* (Paris: Editions JC Lattès, 2009).

—— *Rien ne s'oppose à la nuit* (Paris: Editions JC Lattès, 2011).

—— *Underground Time*, trans. George Miller, George (New York: Bloomsbury, 2011).

Notes

1   See Aurore Labadie, *Le roman d'entreprise au XXIe siècle* (Paris: Presses Sorbonne Nouvelle, 2016). Thierry Beinstingel, *La représentation du travail dans les récits français depuis la fin des Trente Glorieuses* (Besançon: Littératures Presses Universitaires Bourgogne Franche-Comté, 2017). D. Viart, 'Écrire le travail. Vers une sociologisation du roman contemporain?', G. Rubino and D. Viart (eds), *Écrire le présent* (Paris: Collection Recherches, Armand Colin, 2013), pp. 133–56. S. Servoise, 'Le Travail sans fin: Discours et représentations à l'œuvre', *Raison Publique* 15 (November 2011), 7–202. J.-P. Engélibert, '"Ressources inhumaines": Le nouvel esprit du travail dans quatre romans français contemporains (François Bon, François Emmanuel, Aurélie Filipetti, Lydie Salvayre)', *TRANS* (online), 4 (2007), http://journals.openedition.org/trans/192 (accessed 20 October 2016).

2   D. M. Patiño Rojas, 'El mundo del trabajo en la novela francesa contemporánea: por una estética de lo real', *Escritos* 26 (2018), 167–90, *10.18566/escr.v26n56.a08* (accessed 8 April 2020).

3   Jean-François Lyotard, *Le Postmoderne expliqué aux enfants: correspondance 1982–1985* (Paris: Editions Galilée, 1988), pp. 45, 117.

4   E. S. M. Hugueny-Léger, 'D'après des histoires vraies: l'écriture à la lisière de Delphine de Vigan', in K. Averis, E. Kackute and C. Mao (eds), *Transgression(s) in Twenty-First-Century Women's Writing in French* (Leiden: Faux Titre, Brill, 2020) pp. 131–47.

5   K. Robson, 'The Limits of Empathy and Compassion in Delphine de Vigan's *No et moi* and *Les Heures souterraines*', *Modern Language Review*, 110/3 (2015), 677–93, 925.

6   A. Vandevelde-Rougale, 'Saisir les violences invisibles', in F. de Geuser and A. M. Guénette (eds), *Littérature et management: Le management*

comme roman et le manager comme romancier? (Paris: L'Harmattan, collection Conception et dynamique des organisations, 2018), pp. 97–110.

7   A. M. Mulhall, 'Bodies in crisis in the French literature of the office: Lydie Salvayre's *La Vie commune* and Delphine de Vigan's *Les Heures souterraines*', *Modern & Contemporary France*, 26/3, Work in Crisis (2018), 291–306.

8   L. Alexander, 'Storytelling in Time and Space: Studies in the Chronotope and Narrative Logic on Screen', *Journal of Narrative Theory*, 37/1 (Winter 2007), 28.

9   Georg Lukács, *The Theory of the Novel: A Historico-philosophical Essay on the Forms of Great Epic Literature* (Cambridge MA: MIT Press, 1971).

10 S.-E. Sjöstrand, 'On the Rationale behind "Irrational" Institutions', *Journal of Economic Issues*, 25/4 (December 1992), 1008.

11 F. Milewski, 'Les femmes sur le marché du travail en France: les progrès marquent le pas', *Santé, Société et Solidarité* 1, *De l'égalité de droit à l'égalité de fait: Françaises et Québécoises entre législation et réalité* (2008), 67–74.

12 APEC (Association Pour l'Emploi des Cadres), 'Les écarts de salaires femmes-hommes chez les cadres', 27 February 2020, *https://corporate. apec.fr/home/nos-etudes/toutes-nos-etudes/les-ecarts-de-salaire-femmes-ho.html* (accessed 18 August 2020). See also Ministère du Travail, de l'Emploi, et de l'Insertion, 'Dares Analyses. Femmes et hommes sur le marché de travail', March 2015, *https://travail-emploi.gouv.fr/IMG/pdf/2015–017.pdf* (accessed 5 April 2020).

13 Vigan indicates in her subsequent novel *Rien ne s'oppose à la nuit* (2011) that *Les Heures souterraines* draws from her own experiences without explaining to what extent Mathilde's story is invented.

14 Delphine de Vigan, *Les Heures souterraines* (Paris: Editions JC Lattès, 2009), p. 165; italics in the original.

15 Delphine de Vigan, *Underground Time*, trans. George Miller, (New York: Bloomsbury), p. 167.

16 Julia Kristeva, *Pouvoirs de l'horreur: Essai sur l'abjection* (Paris: Seuil, 1980).

17 A. G. Jónasdóttir, 'On the Concept of Interest, Women's Interests, and the Limitations of Interest Theory', in A. G. Jónasdóttir and K. Jones (eds), *The Political Interests of Gender Revisited: Redoing Theory and Research with a Feminist Face* (London: SAGE Publications, 1988), pp. 40–2.

18 See Catherine Moret-Courtel, *La Caissière* (Paris: Belfond, 2008).

Chapter 10
In Concrete Terms: Gendering Labour in Anne Garréta's *Dans l'béton*

JENNIFER CARR

For the child narrator of Anne Garréta's *Dans l'béton* ('*In Concrete*') (2017), the aptly nicknamed Fignole (an echo of *fignoler*, meaning 'to perfect' or 'to tinker'), family life is a series of home-improvement projects, undertaken with a hapless father, a kid sister, Angélique, and a well-worn concrete-mixer. Early in *Dans l'béton* – Garréta's first single-authored novel since *Pas un jour* ('*Not One Day*') earned her the Prix Médicis in 2002 – Fignole and Angélique's mother inherits a dilapidated house in the countryside from an uncle with no progeny of his own. Her husband and children promptly set about 'modernising' the place, triggering a succession of mishaps that culminate with Angélique buried alive in concrete. As the father embarks on a frantic search for help, Fignole, tasked with keeping Angélique company, passes the time recounting shared childhood exploits whose winding progression unfolds in an orthographically malleable, riotously vulgar and resolutely vernacular French.[1]

Dans l'béton's digressions are nonetheless anchored by the family at its centre. Fignole and Angélique, their mother and father, a grandmother and a grandfather form a nucleus whose nominally heteropatriarchal structure reveals itself to be another malfunctioning machine: a faulty perpetuator of normative logics whose flaws surface, notably, in representations of labour. Fignole and Angélique inherit distinct parental models of labour that are conditioned by gender norms even as they unwittingly highlight their inadequacies. The ways in which gender is constituted through work transpire, moreover, in the novel's very language, which enacts a laborious suspension of its first-person narrator's gender identity. *Dans l'béton* thus foregrounds French as a worksite, a terrain where identity is constructed – situating this process against the backdrop of a 'modern' France whose changing economic realities have occasioned their own gender reconfigurations, at work and at home. By troubling a constitutive nexus of the (re)productive family unit: the gendered division of labour – whose injunctions, like a defective concrete-mixer, exert forces by turns centripetal and centrifugal – the novel locates the elaboration of gendered subjectivity at the intersection of language and embodied work.

Although little scholarship has been published on *Dans l'béton* as yet, this chapter builds on a recent article by Annabel Kim that delineates the novel's political project, its coordinated attack on the oft-naturalised foundations of heteropatriarchy and race.[2] What follows also responds to reviews of *Dans l'béton* that appeared in the French press subsequent to its publication, by shifting focus towards the novel's targeted erasure of gender – a refrain in Garréta's literary corpus that passes, in this instance, through the relationship between gender and labour. Whether via the mother's largely invisible work or the father, Angélique and Fignole's highly visible manual labour, *Dans l'béton* demonstrates the contingency of efforts to map gender onto the work bodies do. Meanwhile, the novel's ambiguous temporality, its nebulous suggestion of a post-war, 'modernising' France, functions as a poignant framework for exploring disrupted legacies and the space they afford non-normative subjectivity – embodied or linguistic, gendered or otherwise.

Family Matter: Concretising Gendered Labour

Dans l'béton's interrogation of gendered labour coalesces perhaps most conspicuously around the family 'patriarch', who, at a glance, embodies a stereotyped working-class masculinity. Fignole and Angélique's father is stoic, defined by his relationship to manual labour, shaped by homosocial settings (notably a youth spent in military service) and invested in an aggressive performance of heterosexuality premised on homophobic views parroted – if not wholly uncritically – by his two children.[3] Yet in his masculine excesses, the father is not so much tyrannical as caricatural, his blink-ered pursuit of 'modernisation' through manual labour literalised to particularly caustic effect in an early chapter, 'Boulesaille': As Fignole, Angélique and their father clean the mother's inherited house, preparing to lay the floors with concrete, the father tosses debris from a window at an inopportune moment and a gust of wind blows the collected filth back into his eyes, temporarily depriving him of sight. In agony, in a house with no running water, he implores his children to spit on him. The siblings dutifully take up posts before their kneeling father and, conjuring images of culinary deli-cacies, are able to make themselves salivate, eventually rinsing his eyes in a rapid-fire volley of spittle. The chapter ends on a moralistic note, delivered with Garrétian irony: 'Des aventures de chantier ... on en a eu plein ... Mais celle-là, d'aventure, et ce jour-là, y sont exceptionnels. Parsske c'est quand même le jour où j'ai appris kya des fois où cracher à la gueule de ses ascendants, c'est un devoir filial. Et même un devoir d'humanité'[4] ('Our worksite escapades ... were plentiful ... This particular escapade, though, and this particular day, were exceptional. After all, this was the day I learned that sometimes, spitting in the face of your forebears is a filial duty. A duty to humanity, even'). Far from embodying unassailable authority, then, Fignole and Angélique's father is the target of an unhinged subversion of it. He is spat on in 'Boulesaille,' hypotheti-cally cannibalised in a later chapter and, though he may helm the family's construction projects, his legacy is an entropic one, his chil-dren perpetually left to clean up his mess.

By contrast, it is the mother who works a steady job, who inherits the property that is the site of her husband's accident, and later Angélique's. She supports the family financially, heading to work as her husband and children clean house: 'On l'a remise dans le train pour Paris. Fallait qu'elle retourne travailler. Qui sans ça nous offrirait nos bétonneuses, nos machines à laver, nos générateurs' (p. 30) ('We put her on the train back to Paris. She had to return to work. Otherwise, who would supply our concrete-mixers, our washing machines, our generators'). Though the mother (who remains nameless) is a diffident figure – attempting, in vain, to keep her children clean as they return home caked in concrete – through her, the family is able to maintain something of a 'respectable' middle-class existence. Unlike her husband, who has kept the habits of a childhood spent in poverty – exhausting family appliances before stripping them for parts – Fignole and Angélique's mother invests in the clean and the new, values she tries, unsuccessfully, to instil in her children. And though the nature of her employment is never specified, we know she works 'en ville, [où] tout est déjà si moderne' (p. 118) ('in the city, [where] everything is already so modern'), earning enough to support her husband's insatiable desire for the raw materials and machinery of 'modernisation', a term used repeatedly to both describe and justify the family's construction projects.

It is notable that the mother's remunerated labour, indispensable to the family's economic stability, also happens to be invisible. If, historically, domestic labour has been performed away from public view, and women's work has been unpaid or undervalued, *Dans l'béton* unsettles this dynamic, too, by obscuring the work that the mother does outside the home. Meanwhile, within its confines, she frets over cleanliness in ways laden with their own gendered baggage, her concern with the appearance of her children suggesting linkages between propriety and femininity, but also class status and property. As Fignole notes, 'Nos grands-parents sont très méticuleux. Donc je pense que c'est sous l'influence de notre père que notre mère a perdu son sens de l'ordre. Ou alors, elle y a renoncé, et elle est devenue bordélique par amour' (pp. 78–9) ('Our grandparents are very meticulous. So I think it was under our father's influence that our mother lost her sense of order. Or else renounced it, becoming slovenly out of love'). The mother's surviving sense of propriety would, in other words, appear to be inherited by obscuring the work that the mother does outside the home. Fignole and Angélique are aware, in any case, of their mother's suffering and attempt to sensitise their father to his role in it, in terms that, moreover, conflate their mother with the appliances that have ironically made her domestic life more difficult: 'la bétonneuse souffrait, la machine à laver souffrait, notre mère souffrait. Ma ptite sœur en a fait l'observation, avec beaucoup de tact et de sang-froid, à notre père' (p. 17) ('the concrete-mixer was suffering, the washing machine was suffering, our mother was suffering. My kid sister indicated as much to our father, with a good deal of tact and sang-froid'). Ultimately, although the mother works outside the home, she is largely confined to her place within it, her labour visible only in the domestic sphere, her character ultimately mired in heteropatriarchy.

Still, between a breadwinning, self-effacing mother and an evidently unemployed, farcically virile father, Fignole and Angélique inherit models of labour that do not quite map onto gender norms, a discrepancy further heightened by the father's role as a caretaker (of his children, with whom he spends his days, but also of various animals, notably a bull he cared for in its infancy and with which he is later improbably reunited). And though the father, in particular, is enmeshed in narrow notions of gender identity, in practice, the rigidity of these notions cedes to slippages in familial divisions of labour as financial and practical considerations take precedence over norms. Moreover, to the extent that the heteropatriarchal family replicates binary gender and reproductive heterosexuality – to the extent that its viability is premised on these things – these slippages register as foundational threats, even as they manifest variously in Angélique and Fignole, who would seem to perform, respectively, an inverted exaggeration and an eclipsing of gendered labour.

Angélique's devotion to construction work bears her father's distinct imprint. In fact, she proves more adept at manual labour than he: the ideal heir in all respects but two, since she is not her father's son but his daughter, as well as his younger child. Angélique performs the exaggerated masculinity that her father seems determined to transmit, irrespective of his children's gender – her identification with paternal models extending even further up the family line: 'Angélique, en tout elle veut ressembler à notre grand-père' (p. 79) ('Angélique wants to resemble our grandfather in all respects'), Fignole notes. It is thus fitting that the grandfather should be the one to free Angélique from her concrete casing in the novel's final chapter. Yet while he meticulously chips away at her shell with various domestic implements (a toothbrush, a pair of tweezers), Garréta does not allow readers to forget that Angélique's proximity to masculine hubris is what precipitated her accident. In the novel's final pages, we learn that the father, ever eager to fast-track his construction projects, had used a quick-setting cement, inadvertently imperilling his children even further.

Still, though Angélique seems to perform – indeed outperform – her father's understanding of masculinity, she does so in ways that are ultimately not as stultifying as her accident might suggest (she is, after all, quite literally immobilised by the very stuff of her father's 'modernisation' projects). The reader is never granted meaningful access to Angélique's interiority, to how she understands her familial allegiances and identity. Yet for her apparent attachments to masculinity, Angélique is 'une femme d'action' (p. 12) ('a woman of action'),[5] her character aligned with femininity in ways that tacitly interrogate manual labour's relationship to the masculine (and, by extension, domestic work's ties to the feminine). Moreover, though Angélique and Fignole occasionally parrot their father's bigoted lexicon, at school they valiantly defend a boy who is the target of their male classmates' homophobia, mobilising the strength they have gained through manual labour against the type of hyper-virile, heteronormative masculinity enacted by their father through construction work.

While Angélique eagerly assists her father in this work, Fignole claims a more passive role, asserting 'Moi, j'ai jamais eu voix au chapitre' (p. 10) ('As for me, I never had a say in the matter'). This denial of agency can, of course, register as deeply ironic given that *Dans l'béton* is narrated in Fignole's voice, which structures its eighteen *chapitres*,[6] remaining stylistically coherent even as it embarks on digressions that threaten to derail the frame narrative, ever deferring Angélique's fate. Moreover, the stylistic coherence of *Dans l'béton*'s narrative voice belies the project of identity construction that subtends it, and the malleability of language on which this project relies. The novel, whose incipit reads, with biting irony, 'Le béton, c'est pas un métier de pédés' (p. 9) ('Concrete isn't a job for sissies'), traces Fignole's nascent sense of non-normative desire, of queer subjectivity[7] – initially presented to the reader as a source of anxiety: hidden from family and contemplated at night, a time when construction work cedes to work of a cerebral sort, and when the day's construction projects are concatenated with the act of constructing stories, of writing.

Writing is, of course, manual labour in a strict sense: it is work done with the hands. And, like other forms of manual labour, it is saddled with gendered connotations. Though their class associations may differ, the writer, like the worker, has, throughout French history, reliably defaulted to the masculine. Yet Garréta's fiction mounts a concerted challenge to assumptions about what it means to write from a gendered subject position – a challenge at once thematised and enacted in *Dans l'béton*, whose depictions of construction work also foreground language as a site of excavation where gender can be inscribed or occluded. At school, Fignole 'creuse des trous dans la grammaire et … concocte des évasions' (p. 118) ('digs holes in grammar and … concocts escape plans'),[8] language work that, furthermore, erodes a system where 'le vocabulaire, les bourges, y croient ksa leur appartient' (p. 123) ('the bourgeoisie think vocabulary belongs to them'). Language, then, is another inheritance – a class signifier like the mother's modern appliances, but also a system through which social categories are transmitted. The stakes of this transmission are particularly acute when it comes to gender's inscription in language, as it gradually transpires that the novel's radically malleable French not only subverts 'proper' language (and by extension bourgeois property and propriety), but also enacts a near-complete erasure of its narrator's gender.[9]

Dans l'béton systematically avoids linguistic constructions that would reveal Fignole's gender, which is left largely as indeterminate as the narrative's disjointed timeline. This deliberate occlusion, which Garréta has undertaken with enough laborious care to obscure the obscuring, as it were, should nevertheless come as no surprise to readers familiar with her work. After all, her debut novel, *Sphinx* (1986) managed, through a series of grammatical omissions and narrative ambiguities, to render unknowable the gender of its two protagonists. In the process, Garréta elaborated a French freed, at least in part, from the imprint of gender (no small feat, given the multiple ways French grammar interpellates subjects as masculine or feminine). The novel received considerable critical attention, much of it attributable to its textual manipulations of gender, and was quickly followed by *Pour en finir avec le genre humain* (1987), a book-length fictional dialogue whose interlocutors, as the title's polysemic play on the word *genre* suggests, are also ambiguously gendered, addressing one another in epicene terms.

The targeted, systematic excision of gendered language in these texts is an example of constrained writing: writing whose parameters are dictated by predetermined rules. Garréta's penchant for linguistic experimentation of this kind helps account for her membership in the Oulipo, or *Ouvroir de littérature potentielle*, a collective of mostly French writers and mathematicians with which she has been affiliated for more than two decades. Dedicated to mining the literary potential of constrained writing techniques, the Oulipo – as its name suggests – was conceived as an *ouvroir*, or 'workroom', a term that, moreover, conjures traditionally feminine workspaces (an irony surely not lost on Garréta, who has commented publicly on the group's overwhelmingly male membership). And though the Oulipo writ large has never been particularly invested in interrogating gender, its understanding of language as raw material to be shaped through constraints does dovetail with Garréta's corpus in one crucial respect: For Garréta, 'La littérature potentielle, c'est un art et une érotique queer du langage' ('Potential literature is a queer art and erotics of language'), attuned to the fact that 'Se déprendre de l'emprise normative, en littérature comme dans la vie suppose non pas la transgression, mais le jeu, l'invention' ('Loosening normative holds, in literature as in life, does not assume transgression but play, invention').[10] *Dans l'béton* applies this understanding of Oulipian constraints to binary gender, as Fignole reinvests the 'masculine' realms of writing and manual labour with a narratorial *je* largely freed of gender's marks and embedded in the realm of *jeux*, of childhood play.

Still, early reviewers of *Dans l'béton* often assumed, without much preamble, that Fignole and Angélique were both girls. The novel was thus variously packaged in French media outlets as 'une aventure familiale ... imposée par le père à ses deux filles, la narratrice, dont on ignore le prénom, et sa sœur' ('a family adventure ... imposed by the father on his two daughters, the narrator, whose name we never learn, and her sister')[11] and 'L'été de deux moufflettes, filles d'un bétonneur compulsif' ('The summer of two young girls, daughters of a compulsive concrete maker').[12] Other reviewers, such as Eric Loret, writing for *Le Monde*, were more nuanced: 'l'on apprend au bout d'un moment que l'enfant qui parle est une fille, surnommée Fignole' ('at a certain point, we learn that the child who is speaking is a girl, nicknamed Fignole').[13] Yet, in contrast to *Sphinx*'s reception, and perhaps recognising a Garrétian topos they deemed unworthy of renewed critical scrutiny, these reviewers devoted relatively little attention to how or why Garréta largely denies the reader access to her narrator's gender.

In fact, it is not clear that *Dans l'béton* offers any stable ground on which to ascertain Fignole's gender, even if a grammatical 'tell' does occur in the novel's penultimate chapter. At dawn on the day following Angélique's accident, the siblings are rescued by their grandmother, whose appearance on the horizon compels Fignole to break into song: 'Je chante que la rivière est profonde ... et qu'on serait heureuses jusqu'à la fin du monde' (p. 153) ('I sing that the river is deep ... and we could be happy forevermore'). This moment, as Kim has argued, can be viewed as both 'gendering and matriarchal alignment, [as] the narrator joins her sister and grandmother in the feminine *on* described as *heureuses* [and] repudiates the patriarchal model of family'.[14] Fignole's 'heureuses' does indeed signal another subversion of patrilineal transmission – an alliance with the grammatical (and familial) feminine. Yet surely the prolonged suspension of gender (to borrow a term Garréta has applied to *Sphinx*'s deft manipulation of French)[15] that precedes this moment merits consideration, too, given the space that it opens for rethinking gendered labour and language.

Moreover, in this scene, as elsewhere, Fignole's voice is shot through with intertextual allusions – in this instance, to a version of the children's song, *Aux marches du palais*, whose lyric 'Nous y serions heureux jusqu'à la fin du monde' Garréta feminises. Fignole's belated identification with the feminine, in other words, is filtered through an intertext and placed under the sign of the conditional (*serait*), so that, though striking, it hardly registers as conclusive. Rather, its deferred placement in the novel suggests that gender is a process mediated by social scripts. Hardening, perhaps, yet still malleable, Fignole's identity is analogised to the labour of writing, and of mixing and casting concrete. *Dans l'béton* is not utopian – its world is shaped by hierarchies and reductive binaries that, as Fignole and Angélique's many war games suggest, would require considerable, even violent effort to eradicate. Still, the text's idiosyncratic French, largely freed from the marks of its narrator's gender, suggests a capacious understanding of subjectivity whose investment in futurity exceeds the countervailing models of progress associated with the father and mother: 'modernisation' by brute force and a nebulously bourgeois concern with propriety, respectively – both fatally enmeshed in what Lauren Berlant terms the 'cruel optimism' of post-war precarity, an attachment to illusory stability and opportunity.

Filial Trouble: Disrupted Legacies in Post-War France

For its insistence on 'progress', *Dans l'béton* is noticeably devoid of spatial and temporal markers. The narrative unfolds in principally rural, anonymous settings whose rhythms would appear incompatible with Fignole's adamant refrain: 'On smodernisait' ('We were modernising'). The novel's temporal signposts, when they materialise, alternate between pre-industrial and resolutely contemporary. References to 'Gitmo' or 'cette chose mystérieuse et moderne qu'on appelle le ouèbe' (p. 160) ('that mysterious, modern thing they call the oueb') are interspersed with allusions to the 'primordial' countryside. *Dans l'béton*'s ambiguous temporality can nonetheless be sited somewhere within post-war France, just as Fignole's family and their 'modernisation' projects can be understood through the post-war period's attendant shift from the agricultural and rural towards the industrial and urban (and, later, the increasingly atomised economies of neoliberalism) – transitions that, incidentally, had profound implications for gendered forms of labour.[16]

Legacies of war loom large in *Dans l'béton*, whose titular material, concrete, is explicitly associated with German fortifications, with martial engineering. Prior to Angélique's accident, Fignole imagines building 'un sarcophage en béton ... un blockhaus boche blindé comme j'en ai vu quand nous fumes en famille au bord de l'océan' (p. 129) ('a concrete sarcophagus ... a reinforced Boche blockhouse like the ones I saw when our family went out to the coast'). A later chapter is entitled 'Blickskrieg' and Fignole evokes an adopted family surname, Oberkampf, that bears the dual imprint of industrialism and war: 'Le vrai [nom], il s'est perdu ... dans l'épouvante industrielle, dans la panique des foules chassées, pourchassées ... à travers champs, camps, fronts, frontières, tranchées et retranchements ... Ensuite de quoi, logiquement, notre père avait échoué dans un bagne où la patrie élevait de la chair à canon' (pp. 138–9) ('The real [name] is lost ... to the horrors of industrialism, to the panic of crowds chased, hounded ... across fields, camps, fronts, borders, trenches and entrenchments ... After which, logically, our father wound up in one of those labour camps the homeland uses to raise cannon fodder'). War, in other words, has indelibly shaped Fignole's family, rendering the origins of its patriarch unknowable even as it governs the legacy he leaves his children – a legacy that passes through concrete and the stability it seems to promise, but also through the violence enacted in Angélique and Fignole's own war games, detailed in the novel's later chapters.[17]

Yet concrete is not just a signifier of war, but also the material of French post-war reconstruction, emblematic of a national project whose architectures promised social mobility, material comfort and unfettered access to the modern in the wake of the Second World

War, during *les Trente Glorieuses* ('the Glorious Thirty'). Le Corbusier's architectural odes to concrete, alongside the many housing complexes built in twentieth-century French urban centres to accommodate an ever-growing industrial workforce – composed in significant part of immigrants from former French colonies – would appear, at a glance, far removed from the industrial horrors that shaped Fignole's family. Still, these architectures, much like wartime fortifications, are regimented by *patriarcat* and *patrie*, their scale a reflection of mid-century Fordism and the masculinised industrial labour that subtended it, their eventual decay a testament to the illusiveness of industrialism's promises, from which families like Fignole's – whose whiteness, though unnamed, is strongly implied – stood most to benefit.

Les Trente Glorieuses and its aftermath provide a useful temporal frame through which to read *Dans l'béton*, whose focus on the family car and appliances evokes a post-war rise in middle-class consumerism, echoing, notably, Kristin Ross's framing of automobiles and appliance-enabled hygiene as gendered pillars of the post-war consolidation of (white, bourgeois) 'Frenchness' around the nuclear family.[18] The decades following the Second World War were a period, as Jackie Clarke explains, 'when cars and domestic appliances became available to the mass market', their production regulated by the factory assembly line, their history 'inseparable from ... the post-war "fantasy of the good life", [a link] perhaps particularly strong in France, where this period saw rapid urbanisation and industrialisation associated with a major transformation in living conditions'.[19] This transformation did not, however, continue apace, as Fordist models of production and accumulation yielded to economic precarity. Clarke, Dominique Viart, Corinne Grenouillet and others have highlighted the ways in which this failed transmission of economic stability manifests in late twentieth and early twenty-first-century French literature. Viart, in particular, locates the phenomenon in a post-*Trente Glorieuses*, post-Cold War France grappling with the failures of totalising narratives, including those of Western humanism.[20] Refining the contours of a genre that he has termed the *récit de filiation*, or 'filiation narrative', and citing authors like Annie Ernaux, Leïla Sebbar and Patrick Modiano, he foregrounds contemporary literature's preoccupation with *ascendance*, particularly as it relates to a 'défaut de transmission dont les écrivains présents, ou leurs narrateurs, s'éprouvent comme les victimes' ('failure of transmission, of which these writers, or their narrators, understand themselves to be victims').[21]

Among the *récits de filiation* that proliferated in France at the turn of the twenty-first century, there emerged a strand that Clarke and Viart understand as *récits de filiation ouvrière* – narratives of working-class identity and intergenerational displacement that attest to historical discontinuity, as 'the possibility of infinite growth ... the temporal horizon of productivist ideology'[22] ceded to deindustriali-sation and contingent forms of employment. Clarke and Viart tie these *récits* to the figure of the father, who, even when silent or absent, haunts narratives, embodying manual labour as well as forms of transmission – wealth, values, genetic material – threatened by shifts in the political and economic order. For Viart, in particular, fathers' silences are laden with the weight of discursive authority, of 'la Parole qui s'est tue, le Discours qui n'est plus en mesure d'être tenu' ('Speech fallen silent, Discourse no longer tenable').[23] It follows, then, that interrupted transmission should also manifest in the structure of these *récits* and in their authors' examinations of their own relationships to language. In *Usines en textes, écritures au travail*, for instance, Grenouillet highlights the predilection, among texts written by and about the working classes during this period, for 'des formes caractérisées par un certain éclatement et une grande souplesse' ('forms characterised by a certain splintering and a great suppleness'), their aesthetics reflective of postmodernity's disinvest-ment in legitimising narratives.[24]

Though it was published well into the second decade of the twenty-first century (and, unlike many of the texts discussed by Clarke, Grenouillet and Viart, is decidedly fictional), *Dans l'béton*'s digressive structure, too, seems purpose-built to subvert the narra-tives of productivity and progress that guided post-war France. Moreover, the novel's foregrounding of family and labour as contested sites of transmission suggest that it may fruitfully be read in conjunction with certain *récits de filiation* and *écritures au travail*, whose categorical bounds are defined more by historically situated preoccupations than generic or stylistic coherence. Rather than dwell on the father as a site of silence and failed transmission,[25] however, *Dans l'béton* posits heteropatriarchy and its gendered divi-sions of labour as at once constitutionally unstable and obstinately driven to (re)produce. In Garréta's novel, patriarchal order is *dis*or-derly, attempts at modernisation prove entropic and manual labour is loosed from its associations with masculinity. Filiation is, in short, deeply unsettled by the text's portrayal of a family whose *ascendance* – and capacity for social ascension – are manifestly tenuous. The family surname, Oberkampf, is attributed to the Paris metro station of the same name, Fignole and Angélique's grandparents view the mother's marriage as a *déclassement*, or social downgrading, and the mother and father's respective investments in 'modernisation' prove fruitless, if not categorically destructive. This precarity is heightened by the novel's post-war temporality, which offers a wide historical frame through which to understand the contingency of gendered labour, whose divisions shifted across the twentieth century – reinforced by the masculine factory line, tested as more women entered the workforce, and sedimented in the public and domestic spheres' continued perpetuation of gender norms.

After Angélique's accident, her family resolves 'à plus rien moderniser' (p. 172) ('to no longer modernise anything'), apparently now content with the more sustainable enterprise of upkeep. Still, the novel concludes with a description of the *bétonneuse*, refurbished with a washing machine's motor so that it spins even more quickly, producing concrete at a prodigious rate. It would seem, then, that the family's 'modernisation' efforts are primed to continue apace. And yet, in a world where 'on s'meurt de vestiges comme de vitesse' (p. 141) ('both the residual and the rapid are deadly'), *Dans l'béton* gestures at the possibility of decoupling subjectivity from narratives of capitalist production, heteropatriarchal reproduction and the social categories they engender. These adult logics seep through the narrative, threatening to set like so much concrete. Nonetheless, *Dans l'béton* remains committed to language as both labour and laboratory, unsettling the gendered connotations of the work its characters do, while insisting on the creative labour involved in undoing gendered language – a sustained commitment to generative play that Garréta foregrounds one last time, as she concludes her novel with the dates of its composition: *12 août 2009 – 16 août 2016.* Seven years, or the time of a childhood.

Works Cited

Berlant, Lauren, *Cruel Optimism* (Durham NC: Duke University Press, 2011).
Billot, Léonard, '*Dans l'béton* d'Anne F. Garréta: Une chronique foutraque de l'âge tendre', *Les Inrockuptibles*, 22 September 2017, *www.lesinrocks*.

com/2017/09/22/livres/livres/anne-f-garreta/ (accessed 14 December 2021).

Clarke, Jackie, 'The récit de filiation ouvrière and the unfinished business of Fordism in twenty-first-century France', *Modern & Contemporary France*, 26/3 (2018), 261–73.

Garréta, Anne, *Dans l'béton* (Paris: Grasset, 2017).

—— 'Écrire demande d'être absolument sauvage', interview by Marie Richeux, *Par les temps qui courent*, Radio France, 2 October 2017, *www.franceculture.fr/emissions/par-les-temps-qui-courent/anne-garreta-ecrire-demande-detre-absolument-sauvage* (accessed 14 December 2021).

—— 'Éros mélancolique', interview by Gildas le Dem, *Têtu*, 18 March 2009, *www.univers-l.com/eros_melancolique_interview_anne_garreta.html* (accessed 21 December 2021).

—— 'Wittig, la langue-le-politique', in B. Auclerc and Y. Chevalier (eds), *Lire Monique Wittig aujourd'hui* (Lyon: Presses universitaires de Lyon, 2012), pp. 25–34.

Grenouillet, Corinne, *Usines en texte, écritures au travail: Témoigner du travail au tournant du XXIᵉ siècle* (Paris: Classiques Garnier, 2014).

Kim, Annabel, '*Dans l'béton, dans la merde*: Anne Garréta's Intractable Materiality', *Revue critique de fixxion française contemporaine*, 21 (2020), 121–30.

Loret, Eric, 'Anne F. Garréta, tambour béton', *Le Monde*, 23 November 2017, *www.lemonde.fr/livres/article/2017/11/23/anne-f-garreta-tambour-beton_5218988_3260.html* (accessed 14 December 2021).

Pachet, Yaël, 'Casser les murs avec une masse', *En attendant Nadeau*, 5 December 2017, *www.en-attendant-nadeau.fr/2017/12/05/murs-masse-garreta/* (accessed 14 December 2021).

Ross, Kristin, *Fast Cars, Clean Bodies: Decolonization and the Reordering of French Culture* (Cambridge MA: The MIT Press, 1995).

Tilly, Louise and Joan Scott, *Women, Work, and Family* (New York: Routledge, 1989).

Viart, Dominique, 'Le silence des pères au principe du "récit de filiation"', *Études françaises*, 45/3 (2009), 95–112.

Wittig, Monique, *Le chantier littéraire* (Lyon: Presses universitaires de Lyon, 2010).

Notes

1   The novel's language, which has been compared to the *néofrançais* of Raymond Queneau's *Zazie dans le métro* (1959), is supple, with phonetically rendered contractions (*yahvait, parsske*, etc.) conveying an unmistakable sense of orality, of a French that, in Garréta's words, 's'écrit à l'oreille' ('is written by ear'). See Anne Garréta, 'Écrire demande d'être absolument sauvage', interview by Marie Richeux, *Par les temps qui courent*, Radio France, 2 October 2017, *www.franceculture.fr/emissions/par-les-temps-qui-courent/anne-garreta-ecrire-demande-detre-absolument-sauvage* (accessed 14 December 2021).

2 Annabel Kim, '*Dans l'béton, dans la merde*: Anne Garréta's Intractable Materiality', *Revue critique de fixxion française contemporaine*, 21 (2020), 126–9.

3 In one of the narrative's many improbable turns, the father, too, inherits a dilapidated house in the countryside from a deceased man with no progeny of his own: a gay former army buddy whom the father disavows with a violence that throws his own professed heterosexuality into question.

4 Anne Garréta, *Dans l'béton* (Paris: Grasset, 2017), p. 39. All translations are my own.

5 This description can be interpreted as an ironic nod to the archetypal *femme d'action* of analytical psychology, a supposed embodiment of man's 'feminine' side. Incidentally, psychoanalytic traditions' investment in gender binaries and the heteropatriarchal family would seem a fecund target for *Dans l'béton*'s subversive project.

6 A number that corresponds to the age of majority in France.

7 Fignole's nickname is described, among other things, as a concatenation of 'feignant' ('lazy') and 'tafiole', a derogatory designation for gay men whose first three letters, *taf*, also happen to be a term for 'work'.

8 This approach to language as raw material is indebted, notably, to Monique Wittig's notion of the *chantier littéraire*, which posits literature as a privileged worksite where discursive fixity can be unsettled through 'la brutification du langage' ('the brutification of language'). See Monique Wittig, *Le chantier littéraire* (Lyon: Presses universitaires de Lyon, 2010), p. 26. For a detailed analysis of Wittig's influence on *Dans l'béton*'s poetics, see Kim, '*Dans l'béton, dans la merde*'.

9 On the polysemic play of *Dans l'béton*, Garréta has stated: 'Prendre la langue au pied de la lettre, c'est faire apparaître un peu de sa radicalité' ('to take language literally is to let something of its radicalism show through'). Garréta, 'Écrire demande d'être absolument sauvage'.

10 Anne Garréta, 'Éros mélancolique', interview by Gildas Le Dem, *Têtu*, 18 March 2009, *www.univers-l.com/eros_melancolique_interview_anne_garreta.html* (accessed 21 December 2021).

11 Yaël Pachet, 'Casser les murs avec une masse', *En attendant Nadeau*, 5 December 2017, *www.en-attendant-nadeau.fr/2017/12/05/murs-masse-garreta/* (accessed 14 December 2021).

12 Léonard Billot, '*Dans l'béton* d'Anne F. Garréta: Une chronique foutraque de l'âge tendre', *Les Inrockuptibles*, 22 September 2017, *www.lesinrocks.com/2017/09/22/livres/livres/anne-f-garreta/* (accessed 14 December 2021).

13 Eric Loret, 'Anne F. Garréta, tambour béton', *Le Monde*, 23 November 2017, *www.lemonde.fr/livres/article/2017/11/23/anne-f-garreta-tambour-beton_5218988_3260.html* (accessed 14 December 2021).

14 Kim, '*Dans l'béton, dans la merde*', 125.

15 According to Garréta, this suspension highlights at once the fragility and obstinacy of gender and sexual identity, which readers will tend to project onto characters, even ungendered ones. See Garréta, 'Écrire demande d'être absolument sauvage'.

184 'Taking Up Space'

16   As Louise Tilly and Joan Scott note in *Women, Work, and Family*, the
      Second World War initially led to a decrease in French women's partici-
      pation in the labour force, attributable to the rapid disappearance of
      small-scale agricultural operations, particularly family farms, as indus-
      trialisation and urbanisation, abetted by post-war reconstruction,
      helped spur *les Trente Glorieuses*. See Louise Tilly and Joan Scott, *Women,
      Work, and Family* (New York: Routledge, 1989), p. 216.

17   The novel also hints at a less-than-savoury wartime family history, the
      father's vaguely German lineage possibly obscuring complicity with the
      Nazi regime.

18   Kristin Ross, *Fast Cars, Clean Bodies: Decolonization and the Reordering of
      French Culture* (Cambridge MA: The MIT Press, 1995), pp. 71–105.

19   Jackie Clarke, 'The *récit de filiation ouvrière* and the unfinished business
      of Fordism in twenty-first-century France', *Modern & Contemporary
      France*, 26/3 (2018), 268.

20   Dominique Viart, 'Le silence des pères au principe du "récit de filia-
      tion"', *Études françaises*, 45/3 (2009), 97.

21   Viart, 'Le silence des pères', 97.

22   Clarke, '*Récit de filiation ouvrière*', 269.

23   Viart, 'Le silence des pères', 103.

24   Corinne Grenouillet, *Usines en texte, écritures au travail: Témoigner du
      travail au tournant du XXIe siècle* (Paris: Classiques Garnier, 2014), p. 188.

25   While Viart's 'récits de filiation' are often characterised by 'le grief du
      silence des pères' ('the reproach of paternal silence') (see Viart, 'Le
      silence des pères', p. 99), *Dans l'béton*'s father is rather gregarious, even
      if his speech is marked by certain 'zones obscures' ('zones of obscu-
      rity') (p. 142), notably around his experiences in the military.

Chapter 11

Woman at Sea? Space and Work in Catherine Poulain's *Le grand marin*

AMY WIGELSWORTH

Le grand marin (*'Woman at Sea'*), Catherine Poulain's debut novel, was published to great acclaim in 2016, receiving effusive media attention and garnering a clutch of literary prizes. The prestigious prix Joseph Kessel and a place on the shortlist for the Goncourt du premier roman were, among other achievements, in recognition of the literary quality of Poulain's novel, while accolades such as the prix de la Compagnie des Pêches and the prix du roman d'entreprise et du travail acknowledged her accomplished depiction of life and work at sea. The fictional account of French runaway Lili and her incursion into the male-dominated world of Alaskan fishing, based on Poulain's own experiences, brings the relationship between space and work as experienced by women into sharp focus. As Sara Ahmed points out, notions of space and work are etymologically linked: 'The word "occupy" allows us to link the question of inhabiting or residing within space ... to work, or even to having an identity through work (an occupation).'[1] This link is reinforced by the effort required if we are to succeed in occupying spaces in which we are considered interlopers: 'for bodies to arrive in spaces where they are not already at home, where they are not "in place," involves hard work; indeed, it involves painstaking labor for bodies to inhabit spaces that do not extend their shape' (p. 62).

The phenomenological lens proposed by Ahmed seems an especially apt one through which to analyse *Le grand marin*, given the emphasis that Poulain herself has placed on experience rather than ideological or literary pretensions when discussing the elaboration of her novel. When asked whether she was inspired by the great adventure novels of the likes of Scott, Verne and Conrad, for example, Poulain has said that, while she has read and enjoyed such works, they were not a driving force: 'Je pense que c'est un désir plus physique, le besoin d'aller voir, de sentir ce monde, de le prendre à bras-le-corps'[2] ('I think it's more of a physical desire, the need to go and see, to feel the world, to embrace it'). The novel in and of itself seems rather less important than the experiences it recounts. The phenomenologically informed approach also seems fitting given that the notion of orientation so central to Ahmed's thesis resonates as much within the diegesis as it does at the theoretical level: 'Il faudrait toujours être en route pour l'Alaska' ('You should always be heading to Alaska')[3] declares the narrative voice at the start of the novel, pointing to Lili's geographical orientation, while her oft-repeated desire to reach 'le bout' ('the end'), in echo of the opening sentence, also points to a dogged determination to push ideological boundaries (pp. 15, 97, 162, 231 and 332).

Taking Ahmed's study as a starting point, and using a close reading method, I propose to analyse Lili's engagement with the boat space as a whole and with the table – an object central to Ahmed's *Queer Phenomenology* – in particular, demonstrating how descriptions of these are used to evoke the character's experiences in her new working environment. The table also brings us to the question of space as it relates to the work of Poulain herself. Given the novel's strong autobiographical thrust, it seems reasonable to consider writer and character as one when discussing the occupation of writing.[4] Poulain's orientation as a first-time novelist with a distinctly non-literary background clearly echoes Lili's status as outsider, and the extra-diegetic narrative of the nomadic labourer-cum-author is arguably just as compelling as that of her protagonist.

Boats: Dis/orientation

Lili's default position when she embarks on her first fishing expedition, on board the *Rebel*, is one of disorientation. She is not only the sole female crewmember, but also a novice or *greenhorn*, and an undocumented immigrant. Unsurprisingly, given these multiple layers of disorientation, Lili is acutely aware of being 'out of place' and so makes a conscious effort to shrink into the background; verbs such as *s'écarter* ('to move aside') and *se serrer* ('to squeeze up') are used frequently, and when she is first introduced to Jude, the eponymous *grand marin* ('great sailor'), the narrative voice is distinctly apologetic: 'Je me fais toute petite. Il est à sa place ici. Pas moi' (pp. 35 and 125) ('[I make] myself small, unobtrusive. He belongs here. I don't' (p. 22)). She fantasises about being recruited for a winter trip, casting herself as a reverent, self-effacing spectator rather than an active participant, observing Jude go about his day-to-day existence 'sans jamais me mettre sur son chemin surtout' (p. 50) ('without ever, ever getting in his way' (p. 31)). As Lili sets to work, her main objective is to stay out of the way of her colleagues: 'Surtout ne pas être sur leur passage. Je me fais petite et finis d'arrimer les baquets sur le pont' (p. 39) ('Whatever happens don't get in the way. I make myself scarce and finish lining up tubs on the deck' (p. 24)).

Despite her efforts to play down her disorientation by blending in, Lili finds it compounded by the confined workspace and the unpredictable movements of the boat. The cabin, wheelhouse and galley are all described as *exigu* or *étroit* ('cramped') (pp. 32, 93, 118 and 192) and a number of episodes underline the lack of space: Lili is doused with water as she attempts to pull in a buoy – to cries of 'Fous le camp d'ici, Lili! C'est pas ta place' (p. 125) ('Get the hell out of there, Lili! It's not your place' (p. 72)) – is unable to get out of the way in time when Jude starts up the water pump (p. 138) and is overlooked by the skipper as he hoses down the deck (p. 172). Verbs such as *bousculer* ('to jostle') (pp. 40, 44, 150 and 171), *buter* and *se cogner* ('to bump' or 'bang into or against') (pp. 122 and 164; pp. 118, 123 and 192), and *s'écraser* ('to crash into') (p. 47) pepper the text, describing repeated knocks, collisions, pushing and shoving, while also pointing to ideological clashes, conflicts and antagonisms between those on board. Such scenes are in stark contrast to an early description of the men at work on the *Rebel* that evokes the control and coordination of their movements and interactions: 'Il y a une cadence et un rythme intangibles dans le ballet obscur et silencieux, presque fluide. Car les hommes dansent sur ce pont battu par les vagues. Chacun connaît sa place et son rôle' (p. 27) ('There's an intangible cadence and rhythm to this dark, silent, almost flowing choreography. Yes, that's it, the men are dancing on the wave-pummelled deck. Each knows his place and the part he plays' (p. 18)).

And yet Lili's physical knocks are arguably as much a reaction to her disorientation as they are a symptom of it. We see this most clearly when she begins to assert her physical presence, for example when working with a fellow *greenhorn*: 'Simon guette. Je le devance et le bouscule s'il se met sur mon passage ... C'est mon travail, ma tâche à moi. Je dois me défendre si je veux conserver ma place à bord' (p. 48) ('Simon's watching ... I move before him and push past him if he stands in my way ... It's my work, my job, mine. I need to fight my corner if I want to keep my place on board' (p. 30)). This is the 'hard work' referred to by Ahmed: rather than being at the mercy of her environment, Lili is working to clear space for herself, this physical displacement of her rival one of an accumulation of similar movements required to reshape a space that is not yet 'home'.

Later, after an upsetting altercation during which Ryan compares her to a promiscuous, thrill-seeking tourist – an accusation redolent with class implications as well as negative gender stereotyping – Lili's disorientation is evident again, as she staggers back from the bar to the boat:

> Je me suis levée. Mon tabouret s'est renversé ... J'ai marché d'un pas hésitant vers la sortie. On aurait cru que j'étais saoule ... J'ai longé les quais en rasant les façades des entrepôts. Je n'irai plus jamais au bar, j'ai pensé. Je suis rentrée précipitamment sur le *Lively June*, manquant glisser sur le ponton détrempé. (pp. 306–7)

> I stood up, knocking my stool over ... I walked hesitantly to the door. I must have looked drunk ... I walked along the quayside clinging to the sides of the warehouses. I won't ever go to their bars again, I thought. I hurried back to the *Lively June*, almost slipping on the soaking pontoon. (p. 177)

Lili's use of her body and her heightened awareness of it is typical of disorientation narratives according to Ahmed, who explains that '[o]rientations ... are about the intimacy of bodies and their dwelling places' and that the body is 'affected and shaped by its surroundings'.[5] Lili sustains a series of injuries – to her hand, her ribs and her leg – in her attempts to achieve this intimacy with her new environment. The emphasis given to proximity and 'reachability' in phenomenology means that hands in particular 'emerge as crucial sites in stories of disorientation, and indeed as crucial to phenomenology in general' (p. 165). Hands are a striking motif from the earliest pages of the novel, when Lili rejects the advances of a fisherman friend she has met up with in Seattle who wonders aloud whether he should strangle her. Lili watches 'ses deux grosses mains' ('his big hands') as well as her own 'dont je caresse les contours, indéfiniment' (p. 12) ('I look ... at my own hands as I rub them together, again and again' (p. 9)). There are multiple references to Lili's red, swollen hands while she is fishing, and a symbolic injury when a fish's tailbone becomes lodged in her thumb: a foreign body *en abyme*, causing a debilitating infection. In a key scene, she is thrown from the *Rebel* to another boat, so that she can be delivered to hospital: 'les hommes m'ont lancé vers le *Venturous* comme si le bateau me rejetait' (p. 76) ('the men threw me towards the *Venturous* as if the boat was rejecting me' (pp. 44–5)). Somewhat ironically, given that her resilience in the face of the injury has inspired the respect of her crewmates, the throwing scene represents a literal and emphatic loss of her space among them.[6]

Lili is increasingly self-conscious about her mannish hands, for example in the presence of a prim female bakery assistant: 'Mes mains d'homme démesurément grandes pèsent lourd à mes bras soudain' (p.145)[7] ('My disproportionately large man's hands suddenly weigh down my arms' (p. 84)). She notes, in contrast, '[l]es mains ... fines et translucides' of a male taxi driver: 'on les croirait en verre' (p. 262) ('His hands are slender, translucent; they could almost be made of glass' (p. 152)). Again, there is an intersection between gender and class here; masculinity is synonymous with gruelling manual work, hence the surprise implicit in the description of the taxi driver's ethereal hands and Lili's embarrassment at the condition of her own. The association is a crude one, however, and indicative of Lili's own outdated ideas about femininity. She remarks 'les poignets délicats, les mains fines et soignées' (p. 95) ('the delicate wrists, the slender manicured hands' (p. 55)) of a female ex-captain who gives her a lift to the hospital, but appears to misread their significance; rather than being a mark of femininity, they point to an occupation, like that of the taxi driver, rather less manual than Lili's. Her unease is exacerbated by Jude's prejudices, which become evident when he subjects her to a scornful attack, highlighting two apparently contradictory orientations and their relative importance. Lili cannot be both prodigious *marin* and desirable lover, or so he would have her believe:

Je baisse les yeux. Longtemps je malaxe et caresse mes mains
abîmées. Les yeux du grand marin flamboient. Il me regarde. Il se
moque. Il dit à Murphy en lui montrant mes mains gonflées, plus
larges que celles de beaucoup d'hommes, mes pognes rares:
   – Quel homme voudrait être caressé par ça, tu veux me dire?
(p. 244)

I turn away, rubbing and kneading my damaged hands. The great
sailor's eyes blaze. He's watching me, laughing at my expense. He
points at my swollen hands, my strange paw-like mitts, bigger than
many men's.
   'What sort of man would want to be touched by hands like that, I
ask you?' (p. 142)

In fact, the descriptions of other women working on the boats would
suggest otherwise; our attention is drawn, for example, to 'les doigts
fins et blancs' (p. 78) ('[the] slender white fingers' (p. 46)) of a
female crewmember on the *Venturous*. It is clear that while Lili
certainly feels self-conscious and disorientated, she is also disorientating her colleagues by upsetting their expectations of gender
orientation, as Jude's uncharacteristic cruelty attests.

   In the final pages of the novel, Lili's tumefied hands are described
as a badge of honour, and a passport into the male-dominated space
of the bar, an extension of the boat space that she has frequented,
but not convincingly 'taken up' thus far. Lili's new-found pride in
her hands is significant: 'Le bar hurlant est plein à craquer. Je
marche vers le comptoir tête haute. Je pose devant moi mes belles
mains de pêcheur, les paluches informes que je ne peux même plus
plier. Je n'aurai plus peur de personne et je bois comme un vrai
pêcheur' (pp. 353–4) ('The place is screaming noisy and full to
bursting. I go up to the bar, head held high, and put my beautiful
fisherman's hands onto the counter, shapeless paws I can't even
bend any more. I'm not afraid of anyone now, and I drink like a real
fisherman' (p. 205)).

   As Ahmed tells us, 'To be comfortable is to be so at ease with one's
environment that it is hard to distinguish where one's body ends and
the world begins. One fits, and in the act of fitting, the surfaces of
bodies disappear from view'.[8] This coalescence of space and body
clearly does not occur in Lili's case, but this is not to say that the
workspace fails to 'extend her shape'. The very prominence of Lili's
hands is what puts her in a powerful position, as she realises in her
final triumphant approach to the bar; the disorientation

engendered in her male colleagues is what enables her to take up the space that they had hitherto assumed their own.

Lili's disorientation is also increasingly offset by her colleagues' struggles to cope with the extreme, physically demanding working environment. On a subsequent *Rebel* expedition, when an otherwise formidable female colleague is incapacitated by chronic seasickness, Lili is shown the boat's controls (p. 291).[9] Elsewhere, the disorientation of Lili's colleagues is self-imposed, with episodes of inebriation punctuating the narrative. Jude is a frequent offender but perhaps the most notable opportunity for Lili is when she battles to pacify a floundering John on board the *Morgan*. She becomes increasingly self-assured, taking charge of the boat as he spirals into drunkenness (p. 342). Jude's *mal de terre* ('land-sickness') is also a recurrent theme, and arguably a disorientation even more acute than that of Lili, in that it remains unassuaged: 'il avait perdu sa belle fureur d'homme qui pêche ... Il allait d'un pas mal assuré comme en terre étrangère, incertain de sa marche et de sa direction' (p. 234) ('he'd lost the handsome rage of a fishing man ... His footsteps had no self-assurance, as if he were in a foreign country, unsure how to walk or which way to go' (p. 135)). Disorientation, far from being unique to Lili, emerges as something of a universal affliction. Just as she finds her sea legs, so Lili learns to recognise this ebb and flow, and quietly to capitalise on the disorientation of others to assert and clear space for herself. Having considered Lili's interactions with the boat space in general, I will now turn my attention to tables in particular. These emerge as privileged sites around which space is negotiated and transacted in the novel, as well as pointing to the narrative's extra-diegetic resonance.

Tables: Eating and Writing

Ahmed describes tables as 'kinship objects' that point to a shared orientation[10] and we see Lili's assimilation by the fishing community via her symbolic taking up of a space at the table in a scene towards the end of the novel where she is welcomed to dinner at the fishermen's shelter: 'Il y a du monde autour de la table ... Les gars ... se poussent pour me faire une place. Je retrouve une famille, mes frères' (p. 328) ('There's quite a crowd sitting at a table ... The men ... move up to make room for me. I'm back home with my family, among my brothers' (p. 190)). But rather than considering the table retrospectively, as evidence of successfully claimed space, I intend to focus here on the table as a site on and around which Lili's 'space clearing' is enacted, in other words emphasising the process of orientation rather than the result. My discussions will centre on the cutting table as well as the writing table.

The table, like the boat as a whole, often underlines Lili's disorientation, as in scenes where she is not strong enough to lift huge, thrashing halibut onto the cutting table:

> J'empoigne un flétan. Je serre les dents, cheveux dégoulinants de mer et de pluie. Je l'ai saisi à bras-le-corps et je tente de le soulever jusqu'à la table de découpe, une planche clouée en travers de la lisse et du rebord de cale. Il est bien trop grand, il glisse entre mes bras, la houle me fait perdre l'équilibre et la masse mouvante des corps qui couvrent le pont, sur lesquels je bute, nous tombons ensemble. (p. 344)[11]

> I grab hold of a halibut and grit my teeth, my hair dripping with seawater and rain. I take hold of it bodily and try to lift it onto the cutting table, which is just a plank nailed between the handrail and the edge of the hold. The fish is far too big and starts to slip from my grip, the swell makes me lose my balance and swills around the mass of bodies covering the deck, tripping me up: we fall together. (p. 199)

Ahmed would describe this as a subject/object mismatch and, more specifically, the failure of the table to extend Lili's body.[12] The fact that what is obviously a makeshift piece of furniture is not adapted to enable Lili to use it successfully, and that the mismatch is not even acknowledged – she is castigated by the drunken John for cleaning the fish kneeling on the deck and sent back to the table – points to the unwillingness of those around her to facilitate her orientation.

The table becomes something of a reorientation device, however, when it comes to Lili's eating activities. When she devours her meals around the table with her colleagues, the blurring of night and day suggests a blurring of the activities associated with the bed and the table; Lili's voracious hunger, and the men's ribald commentary on it, hint at a sexual appetite traditionally associated with the male rather than the female:

> Un petit déjeuner à quatre heures de l'après-midi, un déjeuner à onze heures du soir. Je dévore. Les saucisses qui baignent dans leur

huile, les haricots rouges trop sucrés, le riz collant, je pense que chaque bouchée va me sauver la vie. Les hommes rient.
– Mais qu'est-ce qu'elle avale! (p. 46)

Breakfast at four in the afternoon, lunch at eleven in the evening. I gobble it down. Sausages swimming in fat, baked beans with too much sugar, claggy rice, I feel every mouthful could save my life. The men laugh.
'She can really put it away!'[13] (p. 29)

The implied assimilation of the oral and the sexual, the mouth and the vagina, and of gluttony and lust, draws on a long literary history that we can trace back, for example, to Decadent fiction.[14] The bloody set pieces around the cutting table inevitably call to mind menstrual blood. The theme is again typical of Decadent fiction, and yet the scenes communicate rather more than a hackneyed dread of the menstrual cycle, and the female as 'la somme de ses sucs et de ses sécrétions' ('the sum of her juices and secretions'), which is Jean de Palacio's reading of the Decadent thematic.[15] A pivotal scene in this regard is one in which we see the men mock Lili when they see blood around her mouth:[16] 'C'est donc ça un *French kiss*? Tu me fais peur ... Tous riaient de ce sang autour de ma bouche. Pas moi' (p. 173) ('"So that's what you call a French kiss? ... You're scary!" And they all laughed about the blood around my mouth. Not me' (p. 100)). The men's mockery has its basis in the menstrual and sexual connotations of the bloodied mouth, but Lili is, in fact, breaking new ground rather than retreading familiar gender lines: the blood comes from her zealous work on the messy deck and also, significantly, from the fact that, on more than one occasion, she feels compelled to eat live fish hearts at the cutting table:

Un petit cœur pourpre continue de battre sur la planche de découpe, palpite sous le halo imperturbable de la lune dansante, nu et seul dans les tripes et le sang ... je l'attrape et l'avale – au chaud dans moi ce cœur qui bat, dans ma vie à moi la vie du grand poisson que je viens d'embrasser pour mieux éventrer ...
Je finis de vider les plus gros flétans agenouillée sur le pont ... Là, là... je murmure en faisant glisser ma main sur le corps lisse, je pleure encore un peu, je mange le cœur du beau gisant. (p. 347)[17]

A small dark red heart carries on beating on the cutting board, palpitating in the imperturbable halo of the dancing moon, naked and alone amid the blood and intestines ... I grab the heart and swallow – now I can feel this beating heart warm inside me, and

within my own life I can feel the life of the great fish I've just
hugged to me to make it easier to disembowel ...

    I gut the biggest of the halibut kneeling on deck ... There,
there, I murmur as I run my hand over each smooth body, still
crying a little, eating each beautiful dying creature's heart. (p. 201)

According to Palacio, erotic gestures, via prandial metaphors such as
ingestion, point to an appropriation of the masculine by the feminine.[18] Lili's act could therefore be said to point to a desire for sexual
agency, especially if read alongside a reference to Jude's 'baiser
carnassier' ('carnivorous kiss'): 'Sa bouche plongeait dans mon cou
... lui le lion moi la proie, lui le pêcheur moi le poisson au ventre
blanc' (p. 361) ('His mouth dived at my neck ... him as the lion and
me the prey, him the fisherman and me the white-bellied fish'
(p. 208)). But the bold and somewhat aberrant act has occupational
as well as sexual import; it serves to reconcile her to the table, and to
her work(space) more generally: 'Puis je ne tombe plus, je ne
sanglote plus. Je fais mon travail' (p. 347) ('And then I stop falling
over, and stop crying, and just do my job' (p. 201)).

Ahmed elucidates her phenomenological take on ingestion,
which she terms 'othering', in her discussion of Orientalism: 'The
"not me" is incorporated into the body, extending its reach.'[19]
Ahmed's 'othering' has the 'other' as object rather than subject of
the incorporation,[20] but it seems entirely conceivable that the 'other'
might take on the role of consumer and that this might be a deliberate means of turning the tables – quite literally, in the present
context – so as to extend an otherwise stifled reach.[21] Lili copies the
barbaric gestures of the men – 'J'ai pris un couteau, je le plonge
dans l'ouïe, je répète le geste des hommes' (p. 171) ('I pick up a
knife, I stab it into the gills and copy what I've seen the men do'
(p. 99)) – but also goes beyond mere mimicry; by consuming the
fish hearts, Lili creates her own, idiosyncratic gesture, which appals
the men as much as their brutality has revolted her, thereby symbolically assimilating the masculine role and appropriating the
masculine space. Or perhaps, even more radically, she could be said
to be rejecting the masculine/feminine dichotomy altogether: this is
an atavistic, animalistic gesture that transcends contemporary
gender mores, and in so doing promises a redefinition of 'space' in
which Lili's defining characteristic is not her gender specifically, but
her status as 'other' more generally.

The writing table, as the object nearest the body of the philosopher, has been a source of particular fascination for

phenomenologists such as Husserl;[22] for the same reason, I will
assume that the (writing) table in this novel is an object of similar
significance for the writer of fiction. Although there is no explicit
mention of the writing table in *Le grand marin*, references to other
tables point to the relationship of Lili (and, by extension, that of
Poulain) to the writing occupation. The 'comptoir' ('bar'), for
example, is the site of much extravagant storytelling by the male
crewmembers:

> Les hommes braillent et se saoulent, leurs mains écorchées posées
> sur le bois des comptoirs ... Ils racontent tous la même chose.
> Qu'ils ont été bons et qu'ils ont rempli la cale ... On parle d'un
> bateau qui serait parti au fond parce que le poisson mordait trop
> bien ... Jason raconte fiévreusement sa nuit ... il parle très vite, les
> mots se bousculent. (pp. 175–6)

> [R]aucous men [are] getting drunk, their scratched hands resting
> on the wooden counters ... They're all describing the same thing,
> how well they did and how they filled the hold. ... There's talk of a
> boat that sank because there were too many fish ... Jason gives a
> feverish account of his night ... He talks quickly, his words collid-
> ing with each other. (p. 101)

It is also a table to which Lili struggles to gain access: 'Des hommes
nous tournent le dos, accoudés au comptoir de bois, le cou rentré
dans les épaules' (p. 22) ('Men are sitting with their backs to us,
elbows on the wooden bar, heads slouched between their shoulders'
(p. 15)). After Lili rejects the advances of Ian, her skipper, he treats
the crew to an embellished version of his disappointing encounter
with 'Lili-la-très-sauvage' ('Lili-the-wildcat') as they clean longlines
and splice ropes around a table (pp. 193–5); although present at the
table, as the subject of the anecdote Lili is again excluded from the
storytelling.

There are a number of other occasions where we might equate
the table at which tangled fishing lines are cleaned and recondi-
tioned to the writing table, an area of semantic overlap between the
narratological and nautical fields facilitating the comparison: 'La
cuisse repliée contre sa poitrine, le pied droit sur la table pour
soulager ses reins, [Jude] s'acharne patiemment à démêler une
palangre que la mer nous a rendue en un amas de nœuds' (p. 70)[23]
('[H]is thigh bent against his chest, his right foot on the table to ease
his lower back [Jude is] stubbornly, patiently unravelling a longline
that the sea sent back tangled with knots' (p. 41)). The numerous

references to caught, tangled, broken or lost lines (pp. 54, 60, 179 and 223), the untying of mooring ropes (pp. 337 and 338) and the untangling of fishing lines (p. 72), as well as to the tension of those lines (pp. 43–4, 45 and 55), inevitably call to mind the Aristotelian metaphor of the knot, whose 'Complication' and 'Unravelling' were held to be crucial to a well-crafted tragic plot, and which endures in the French term *dénouement.*

Jude's foot resting nonchalantly on the table points to his mastery of the object and is in stark contrast to Lili's disquiet in the same position, which we see in a description of her tying gangions: 'Je m'assieds à la table. Je soupire. En face de moi, un tas de brins de cordelette blanche. Je me mets à nouer les anpecs, il n'y a rien d'autre à faire ... la fatigue s'abat sur moi et me cloue sur la banquette' (p. 220) ('I ... sit at the table in the galley, and sigh. In front of me, a pile of wispy ends of white cord. I start tying gangions, there's nothing else to do ... [T]iredness crashes down on me and nails me to the seat' (pp. 127–8)). Her despondency at having to sit to complete the task is especially striking; later, she expresses a similar frustration at being obliged to sit for most of the day when visiting Jude's friends in Anchorage (p. 252). Her aversion appears to be to the inertia necessitated by the writing process, rather than to the activity *per se.* Referring to the work of Charlotte Perkins Gilman, who shows how habitual bodily positions shape the body and what it is able to do, Ahmed explains that gender is an effect of what bodies 'do do', which in turn affects what they 'can do';[24] Lili's reluctance to sit suggests that she is not merely looking to 'take up [a predefined] space', but rather to delimit a space of her own and to shape her body in such a way as to optimise the elaboration and use of that space. There are implications for Poulain's work as well: 'J'ai toujours été tiraillée entre l'écriture et la vie, le besoin de créer et le besoin de sentir physiquement les choses' ('I've always been torn between writing and life, the need to create and the need to feel things physically'), she states in one interview,[25] while asserting elsewhere that, 'la vie est dans le mouvement'[26] ('life is to be found in movement'). Just as Lili endeavours to shape her own workspace, so Poulain seeks her own, inimitable space as writer, rather than one dictated by the orthodoxy of the writing table.[27] Her non-conventional writing persona, as we shall see, eschews the inertia that so frustrates her protagonist in favour of the 'mouvement' she deems fundamental to the depiction of life in all its vibrancy.

Jude's ease in the role of raconteur, and Lili's equivalent unease, is an ongoing theme. Despite his repeated appeals to Lili – '*Tell me a story* ... il murmure ... Raconte-moi une histoire' (p. 239)[28] – Jude is the one who, time and again, shares his memories and anecdotes, recounting childhood exploits with his brother, time spent working with his father (pp. 272–4) and a family legend as to why all the men in his family are named Jude (p. 283). The more expansive he becomes, the more conscious Lili seems of her own unease and inadequacy as a storyteller. Later, she states, 'Des histoires à lui dire je n'en connaissais pas' (p. 360) ('I had no stories to tell [him]' (p. 208)), but Lili's relationship to storytelling is probably rather more complex than she claims, mirroring Poulain's own attitudes towards writing. In a *France Culture* interview, the writer is defensive when quizzed about her enigmatic background and the motivations for her Alaskan adventure:

> Est-ce que c'est très important de dire pourquoi? Donc je parle de ['Manosque-les-Couteaux'][29] donc là-dedans il y a quand même l'idée de danger, qui est peut-être physique, mais il y a en tout cas une histoire de survie. Et je n'ai pas voulu en dire plus parce que ... il faut laisser un mystère.[30]

> Is it so important to say why? I talk about ['Manosque-les-Couteaux'], so there is certainly the idea of danger in there, perhaps physical danger, but there is in any case a story of survival. And I didn't want to say any more than that because ... you have to leave some mystery.

Lili's reluctance as storyteller must be seen as a deliberate stance: mystery is integral to her status as outsider and arguably it is in this role, rather than as a woman, that she is guaranteed a space in her new environment. As Ahmed puts it: 'the stranger is already "at home" and is familiar in its "strangerness." The stranger has a place by being "out of place" at home.'[31]

Adler's determined conflation of Poulain and her protagonist, though slightly acerbic, is nonetheless perceptive. In an interview promoting her second novel, in which Poulain acknowledges that she struggled to deal with the media hype surrounding *Le grand marin*, the language of disorientation invites a direct comparison between writer and character:

> Ça a été quelque chose d'un peu ... désorientant ... cet accueil magnifique qui a été fait au *Grand marin*?

– Oui, mais bien sûr, c'était extrêmement désorientant. C'était
mon premier roman, je ne m'attendais à rien du tout. J'étais
bergère et tout d'un coup voilà je suis dans pas mal de journaux et
je passe ...
– La bergère s'est retrouvée dans le troupeau?!
– Oui, oui, oui. C'était différent.[32]

Was it a little ... disorientating ... this magnificent reception
received by *Le grand marin*?
– Yes, of course, it was extremely disorientating. It was my first
novel; I wasn't expecting anything at all. I was a shepherdess and
suddenly there I was in quite a few newspapers and I'm on...
– The shepherdess found herself thrown into the flock?!
– Yes, yes, yes. It was different.

Poulain's disorientation is offset by moments where she is apparently comfortable in her role, again much like Lili, as in a *Madame
Figaro* joint interview with actress Isabelle Carré in which the two
women discuss *Le grand marin*, compare experiences and pose for a
studiedly casual photo shoot.[33] These glimpses of a mediagenic
Poulain, though undoubtedly facilitated by the marketing and
publicity team of her publisher, do invite us to reconsider instances
of apparent disorientation. Though Poulain's unease is undoubtedly genuine, it is also, clearly, the defining feature of an engaging
media persona. The novel's biographical front matter is an impressive and wide-ranging list of non-literary endeavours: previously
employed in an Icelandic fish cannery and on US shipyards, as an
agricultural worker in Canada and a barmaid in Hong Kong, the
novelist is now a shepherdess and a wine worker. Poulain is as
unlikely a writer as Lili is a sailor, and therein lies the crux of her
appeal: implicit in her portrayal as a writer in spite of herself is the
thrilling prospect that any one of us, irrespective of our occupation
and location, might enjoy similar literary success.

Conclusion

The boat space highlights Lili's disorientation within the context of
her chosen occupation. Her hands in particular bear testament to
her efforts to achieve intimacy with her environment. Their prominence is a source of embarrassment to her for much of the novel
but, more importantly, is instrumental in unsettling her colleagues;
their disorientation allows her to relativise her predicament and

extend her reach. The cutting table provides her with the opportunity to appropriate masculine space and disturb the subject/object dynamic. Arguably, she could be said to cut across the masculine/feminine dichotomy altogether, embracing an 'otherness' defined in much broader terms. Lili's distrust of the inertia implied by the writing table points to her desire for agency in her work and, beyond the diegesis, to Poulain's desire to shape a distinctive space as a writer, do justice to the vitality of her subject matter and engage and foster affinities with her readers. In this way, 'le grand marin' is a trope that transcends the boundaries of the text: Lili herself is a 'great sailor', negotiating with equal tenacity the turbulent Alaskan waters and the inaccessible spaces of her adopted profession, and her skills mirror those of Poulain, who emerges as an unlikely yet adept navigator of the French literary landscape. For both women, the status of 'other', far from hindering access to their field, is rather the passport to a customised and uncontested space within it.

Works Cited

Ahmed, Sara, *Queer Phenomenology: Orientations, Objects, Others* (Durham NC and London: Duke University Press, 2006).

Aristotle, *Poetics*, trans. S. H. Butcher (Project Gutenberg, 2013), *www.gutenberg.org/files/1974/1974-h/1974-h.htm* (accessed 28 September 2020).

'Catherine Poulain et Isabelle Carré, deux passionnées de l'océan', *Madame Figaro*, https://madame.lefigaro.fr/celebrites/catherine-poulain-et-isabelle-carre-deux-passionnees-de-locean-301216-128846 (accessed 28 September 2020).

Derrida, Jacques, '"Eating Well", or the calculation of the subject: An interview with Jacques Derrida', in E. Cadava, P. Connor and J.-L. Nancy (eds), *Who Comes After the Subject* (New York: Routledge, 1991), pp. 96–119.

—— *Of Hospitality: Anne Dufourmantelle Invites Jacques Derrida to Respond*, trans. Rachel Bowlby (Stanford CA: Stanford University Press, 2000).

Gilman, Charlotte Perkins, *The Home: Its Work and Influence* (Walnut Creek CA: AltaMira, 2002.)

hooks, bell, 'Eating the Other', in *Black Looks: Race and Representation* (London: Turnaround, 1992).

'Hors-Champs: Catherine Poulain: exploratrice en Alaska', *France Culture*, *www.franceculture.fr/emissions/hors-champs/catherine-poulain-exploratrice-en-alaska* (accessed 28 September 2020).

Husserl, Edmund, *Ideas: General Introduction to Pure Phenomenology*, trans. W. R. Boyce Gibson (London: George Allen and Unwin, 1969).

'Le temps des écrivains: Aventure avec Christian Garcin, Catherine Poulain et Jean-Paul Kauffmann', *France Culture*, *www.franceculture.fr/emissions/le-temps-des-ecrivains/aventure-avec-christian-garcin-catherine-poulain-et-jean-paul* (accessed 28 September 2020).

'Le temps des écrivains: Catherine Poulain et Makenzy Orcel', *France Culture*, *www.franceculture.fr/emissions/le-temps-des-ecrivains/catherine-poulain-et-makenzy-orcel* (accessed 28 September 2020).

Palacio, Jean de, *Figures et formes de la décadence* (Paris: Séguier, 1994).

Poulain, Catherine, *Le grand marin* (Paris: Éditions de l'Olivier, 2016).

—— *Woman at Sea*, trans. Adriana Hunter (London: Vintage Digital, 2018).

Rolland, Jacques, 'Getting Out of Being by a New Path', in E. Levinas, *On Escape*, trans. Bettina Bergo (Stanford CA: Stanford University Press, 2003), pp. 3–48.

Young, Iris Marion, *Throwing Like a Girl and Other Essays* (Bloomington IN: Indiana University Press, 1990).

Notes

1   Sara Ahmed, *Queer Phenomenology: Orientations, Objects, Others* (Durham NC and London: Duke University Press, 2006), p. 44.

2   'Le temps des écrivains: Aventure avec Christian Garcin, Catherine Poulain et Jean-Paul Kauffmann' (12:00–13:02), *France Culture*, *www.franceculture.fr/emissions/le-temps-des-ecrivains/aventure-avec-christian-garcin-catherine-poulain-et-jean-paul* (accessed 28 September 2020).

3   Catherine Poulain, *Le grand marin* (Paris: Éditions de l'Olivier, 2016), p. 9; Catherine Poulain, *Woman at Sea*, trans. Adriana Hunter (London: Vintage Digital, 2018), p. 8. All translations of the novel used here are from this edition; translations of other texts are my own.

4   I draw here on Laure Adler's discussion of Poulain's novel and her personal experiences as one and the same, an assumption unchallenged by Poulain, who herself refers to Lili as 'mon petit personnage qui ... oui ... est plus ou moins moi' ('my little character who ... yes ... is more or less me'). Adler refers thereafter to 'Lili-Catherine'. 'Hors-Champs: Catherine Poulain: exploratrice en Alaska' (06:14, 07:01, 10:08 and 10:27), *France Culture*, *www.franceculture.fr/emissions/hors-champs/catherine-poulain-exploratrice-en-alaska* (accessed 28 September 2020).

5   Ahmed, *Queer Phenomenology*, pp. 8, 9.

6   Drawing on Iris Marion Young's argument that orientations do not merely reflect differences between the sexes, but also reproduce them, Ahmed explains that lack of space becomes a self-fulfilling prophecy: 'Women may throw objects, and are thrown by objects, in such a way that they take up less space ... [W]e acquire the shape of how we throw' (*Queer Phenomenology*, p. 60).

7   See also pp. 68, 197 and 211–2.

8   Ahmed, *Queer Phenomenology*, p. 134. The comment is one made in relation to race, but seems equally pertinent in the given context.

9   On seasickness as a disorientation, see Jacques Rolland, 'Getting Out of Being by a New Path', in E. Levinas, *On Escape*, trans. Bettina Bergo (Stanford CA: Stanford University Press, 2003), p. 17. See also Levinas, *On Escape*, pp. 66–8.

10 Ahmed, *Queer Phenomenology*, pp. 26, 81.

11 See also pp. 171, 346.

12 Ahmed, *Queer Phenomenology*, pp. 49–50.

13 The sexual connotation of the original, conveyed by the verb *avaler* ('to swallow'), is lost in Adriana Hunter's translation.

14 See Jean de Palacio, *Figures et formes de la décadence* (Paris: Séguier, 1994), pp. 53–4.

15 Palacio, *Figures et formes*, p. 62.

16 Again, the motif is one commonly found in Decadent fiction: 'La femme de la Décadence porte ... comme une lésion ... une bouche gorgée de sang qu'elle ne demande qu'à dégorger, une bouche qui saigne comme une plaie' (Palacio, *Figures et formes*, p. 61) ('The Decadent woman carries, like a lesion ... a mouth full of blood that she seeks only to disgorge, a mouth that bleeds like a wound').

17 See also p. 171.

18 Palacio, *Figures et formes*, p. 57.

19 Ahmed, *Queer Phenomenology*, p. 115. See also p. 131.

20 As in bell hooks's article on cultural appropriation, 'Eating the Other'.

21 This echoes Jacques Derrida's 'Eating Well', which considers eating in relation to power dynamics and subject/object (or self/other) relations. The idea that the eater can become the eaten is revisited in *Of Hospitality*, which considers the fluidity of host/guest relations (the French *hôte* encompassing both concepts).

22 Ahmed, *Queer Phenomenology*, pp. 3, 30, 52 and 57–9.

23 See also p. 89. *Le grand marin* thereby inscribes itself into an existing body of sea-related novels with a metafictional bent, such as Annie Proulx's Pulitzer-Prize winning *The Shipping News* (translated into French as *Nœuds et Dénouement*).

24 Ahmed, *Queer Phenomenology*, pp. 59–60.

25 'Catherine Poulain et Isabelle Carré, deux passionnées de l'océan', *Madame Figaro*, *https://madame.lefigaro.fr/celebrites/catherine-poulain-et-isa belle-carre-deux-passionnees-de-locean-301216-128846* (accessed 28 September 2020).

26 'Hors-Champs' (28:07).

27 On furniture as a restrictive, prescriptive 'orientation device', see Ahmed, *Queer Phenomenology*, p. 168.

28 See also pp. 246, 277 and 360.

29 The reference is to Manosque(-les-Plateaux), the hometown of both Poulain and her protagonist, also referred to, enigmatically, as Manosque-les-Couteaux (*couteaux* meaning knives) in the novel.

30 'Hors-Champs' (02:46–03:16).

31 Ahmed, *Queer Phenomenology*, p. 141.

32 'Le temps des écrivains: Catherine Poulain et Makenzy Orcel' (03:43–04:12), *France Culture*, *www.franceculture.fr/emissions/le-temps-des-ecrivains/ catherine-poulain-et-makenzy-orcel* (accessed 28 September 2020).

33 'Catherine Poulain et Isabelle Carré, deux passionnées de l'océan'.

Chapter 12

From Cabaret to the Classroom: Bambi's Professional Transition

MAXIME FOERSTER

In Paris 1968, the cabaret artist Bambi (stage name for Marie-Pierre Pruvot), a thirty-two-year-old trans woman who had been performing at the *Carrousel* since October 1954, had an epiphany: 'Je sentais l'urgence de me préparer un avenir' ('I felt an urgency to prepare for my future').[1] Based on a combination of personal reflections and social oppressive structures, this sudden awareness led her to make a big decision: she registered to take correspondence courses in order to be ready to take the French Baccalaureate exam by June 1969. For seven months, while she kept on singing and stripping on stage almost every night, she came back home only to resume her lessons in French, English, German, Italian, mathematics, history and philosophy in order to be ready for the *Bac*, the exam every student must pass in France in order to graduate from high school.

Taking the *Bac* was an ambitious challenge, but Bambi felt that this was her window of opportunity to pursue a professional reinvention of herself: going back to school in order to find a decent day job, contribute to a retirement plan and prove to herself along the way that she deserved to enjoy the comfort of an ordinary and anonymous life. Little did she know, when she decided to take the *Bac*, that she would end up graduating from the Sorbonne with a CAPES (teaching diploma) and a master's in French Literature, thereby starting a twenty-nine-year career as a teacher of French in the public school system, the *Éducation Nationale*.

This chapter focuses on the professional transition of Bambi from 1968 to her retirement in 2000, from the spotlight of the *Carrousel* cabaret to the classrooms of the Pablo Picasso Middle School in Garges-lès-Gonesse, a city in the suburbs of Paris. The study of this pioneering case relies on three sources: the fourth volume of Marie-Pierre Pruvot's memoirs, *La Chanson du Bac* (2014), Sébastien Lifshitz's documentary *Bambi* (2013), and an interview with Bambi conducted on 20 February 2021, specifically focused on her professional transition and career as a teacher. Although Bambi's trajectory is rather unique, this chapter intends to articulate some of the characteristics of challenges facing trans women at work in contemporary France, with a focus on the rights of equality, dignity and privacy, which are threatened for them by discrimination in professional life and transphobia in the French context.

While the first part of this essay will offer a sociological synthesis of what is currently known about the experiences of transphobia at work for French trans women, the second part will establish the main reasons why, in 1968, Bambi made the decision to prepare for a stable future by going back to school. The third section will highlight the pressure, conditions and expectations associated with the years spent studying, from the *Bac* to the Sorbonne, with a new goal in mind: becoming a teacher and starting a career as a *fonctionnaire* ('civil servant'). The last part will focus on the stakes of navigating the career of a middle school teacher as a passing trans woman and a former famous cabaret performer.

Transphobia at Work in France: A Sociological Perspective

It took a long time for French authorities to recognise the concept of transphobia and the relevance of discrimination against transgender citizens in domains such as the family, education, healthcare and employment. In 1992, the European Court of Human Rights ruled that France, by refusing civil recognition of a sex change for an operated transsexual (the word transgender was already coined back then, but did not start replacing the transsexual terminology before the 2000s in France), violated Article 8 of the European Convention on Human Rights.[2] Consequently, France had to compensate the plaintiff and the *Cour de Cassation* (the highest court in France) was forced to issue a legal precedent granting civil gender recognition to French transsexual citizens who request it.

It is puzzling that the French authorities needed a condemnation from the European Court of Human Rights to realise that a transgender citizen looking for a job is likely to be discriminated against if his/her civil status contradicts his/her gender and exposes his/her transgenderism. In her autobiography *Un Sujet de conversation* ('*A Topic of conversation*'), Sophie Simon recounts the painful and humiliating job interviews she endured because of the number 1 on her social security number (meaning of the first number of the social security number in France: 1 for man, 2 for woman). Although she was qualified, motivated and available, she was never offered a job.[3]

It took many more years for the French state to update laws against discrimination in order to protect transgender citizens. In 2012, Article 225–1 of the Penal Code finally included *identité sexuelle* ('sexual identity') as a source of discrimination.[4] The *HALDE* (French Equal Opportunity and Anti-Discrimination Commission, created in 2004) and the *CNCDH* (French National Consultative Commission on Human Rights) both criticised the choice of the expression *identité sexuelle* and pleaded for the use of *identité de genre* ('gender identity') instead.

Due to the reluctance of French authorities to promote and fund research on transphobia, only one study to this day is available on this topic. Conducted by Arnaud Alessandrin and Karine Espineira from May to June 2014, the investigation collected data from 309 transgender people living in France. Almost 60 per cent of the respondents were between eighteen and thirty-nine years old (pp. 133–6). The results from this investigation establish a clear pattern of systemic discrimination of transgender citizens through life, from family to school, work and access to public services. A few statistics when it comes to transgender people and professional life: 85 per cent of the respondents experienced transphobia on the job, and trans women experienced more physical violence than trans men. A total of 28 per cent of respondents say they lost work because of transphobia, and one-third of the respondents suffered transphobic discrimination at work. Overall, 17.5 per cent of respondents were either unemployed or recipients of welfare, highlighting the precariousness that results from such discrimination (pp. 144–8). Also, 26 per cent of respondents declared they declined to enrol in an educational or professional training programme for fear of experiencing more transphobia.[5]

Another investigation was conducted by the European Union Agency for Fundamental Rights in 2014, collecting data from 6,579 transgender respondents living in France and other EU nations. The results from this investigation confirm the vast experience of precariousness and discrimination lived by transgender people at work:

> Trans respondents were more likely to say they had felt discriminated against because of being trans in the year preceding the survey in employment – particularly when looking for a job – than in any other area of social life covered by the survey. One in three trans respondents felt discriminated against because of being trans when looking for a job (37 %) or at work (27 %) in the 12 months before the survey, which is more than twice the equivalent percentage of lesbian, gay and bisexual respondents. Trans women – the term used for a transsexual person, or a woman with a transsexual past who was assigned a male sex at birth – are the most likely to have felt discriminated against, followed by trans men – the term used for a transsexual person, or a man with a transsexual past who was assigned a female sex at birth – and other trans categories.[6]

This investigation emphasises that transgender citizens face a higher level of discrimination at work than other sexual minorities (gays, lesbians and bisexuals) and also that, within the transgender spectrum, trans women face more discrimination than trans men. Given the high level of discrimination in employment for trans women in France today, it seems almost miraculous that Bambi was able to become a teacher in the 1970s and maintain a quiet and successful career for twenty-nine years until she retired in 2000, when she received the prestigious *Palmes Académiques* (French award for distinguished teachers). There is a lot to learn from her professional transition.

A Change of Mindset: The Show Mustn't Go On

Ida, the main character of the eponymous novella by Irène Némirovsky, is a prominent dancer and entertainer in a Parisian cabaret, but she is getting older and will not be able to maintain her crown for long. Instead of exiting with dignity at the height of her glory, she keeps postponing the moment of her farewell out of vanity and denial. In the end, she slips on stage and this embarrassing fall entails her brutal demise in the eyes of the audience and her younger rivals.

Bambi, who started working at *Madame Arthur* in December 1953 when she was eighteen, is thirty-two at the beginning of 1968. Upon

Coccinelle's departure from France to pursue a career abroad (Coccinelle was the French equivalent of Christine Jorgensen: the first trans woman to be widely represented in the media in France), Bambi became the leading star of the *Carrousel*, the most renowned transgender cabaret in Paris since the Second World War.[7] Unlike Ida and many of her previous colleagues, Bambi accepted that the show cannot go on forever and that she needed to plan a reinvention of herself behind the scenes in order to retire with grace in a timely manner. Being thirty-two in a cabaret where you have been performing for almost fifteen years put you in the embarrassing position of a trailblazer turned into an ancestor. Bambi realised that the peak of her fame could not be extended indefinitely:

> Car les années s'accumulaient. Et depuis que j'avais passé vingt-cinq ans, je voyais mon âge avancer. Serait-il alors raisonnable de poursuivre ma vie de cabaret, de continuer à chanter, à danser, à me montrer nue, à prétendre encore être la plus belle, la tête d'affiche, alors qu'affluait sans cesse une concurrence belle, jeune, tourbillonnante, capable, ambitieuse? … Je ne tenais plus à mes titres de cabaret, mais j'aurais été blessée qu'on me conteste, qu'on me ravisse ma place. Il fallait partir avant. Rien ne pressait, mais il était urgent de poser les bases d'une autre vie.[8]

> Because the years were piling up. And since I had passed twenty-five, I saw my age advancing. Would it then be reasonable to continue my cabaret life, to continue to sing, to dance, to display myself naked, to pretend to still be the prettiest, the headliner, while they flocked without end, beautiful, young, whirling, capable, and ambitious competitors? I wasn't clinging to my cabaret titles anymore, but I would have been hurt to be challenged for them, to have my spot stolen from me. I had to leave before. There was no rush, but it was urgent to build the foundation of another life.

Instead of focusing on the present, Bambi anticipated the future and understood that she could control her exit from the cabaret if she took up the challenge to leave it and start a new career. Ageism is a structural part of the cabaret culture, and Bambi became brutally aware of this sword of Damocles when, at twenty-five, a regular client started calling her *la vieille gloire* ('the old glory').[9] Her father died when she was still a child, but her mother was still alive. Bambi left Algeria in late 1953, just before the beginning of the War of Independence (1954–62), and then lived with her mother in Paris.

She felt a responsibility to look after her mother and knew that having a day job would be necessary at some point. Finally, during all these years working hard on the stages of *Madame Arthur* and the *Carrousel*, she made a decent amount of money, but was paid under the table by Monsieur Marcel, her manager and owner of the cabarets. Bambi realised that an official, regular day job would allow her to contribute to her retirement plan. Although these reasons were good enough to trigger a pressing need to lay out her future, Bambi was also driven to resume her studies (she dramatically left Algeria for Paris before she could take the *Bac*) for two more reasons.

Bambi owned her flamboyant career on stage due to her mesmerising beauty as a trans woman. She was admired and applauded, the centre of attention almost every night, but the price of stardom was to be objectified by the voyeuristic gaze of the audience. A lot of clients were transphobic and only came to see 'freaks', using their money to make vulgar and offensive jokes about the transgender artists. Harassment from the police was also a constant threat to the safety of these trans women, especially those engaging in sex work outside cabaret.[10]

Throughout the 1950s and 1960s, there were very few professional options for the first wave of trans women who were transitioning in France. Making a spectacle of the transgender body on stage was an opportunity only for a few of the youngest and most beautiful trans women, and this opportunity (which allowed Bambi to live comfortably, independently and to fund her sex change surgery in Casablanca, Morocco) came with many restrictions: 'Ma situation me parut dans toute son absurdité. Pour la centième fois, je faisais le point. Je reprenais mes études pour sortir de mon ghetto. Bien. Il était vivant, mon ghetto, attachant, drôle, familial, mais borné, et il ne fallait pas y vieillir' (p. 73) ('I saw my situation in all of its absurdity. For the hundredth time, I took stock of things. I would take up my studies again to get out of my ghetto. Well. It was lively, my ghetto, endearing, funny, familial, but limited, and it was necessary not to grow old there'). Although Bambi loved her work and established strong friendships with her trans sisters while at the cabaret, she also felt the burden of living in a 'ghetto' for trans women who had to work together at night, satisfy the voyeuristic male gaze, face police abuse and be paid clandestinely because their job could not be registered and recognised by the French authorities. In this restrictive and oppressive context, Bambi dared to dream of the possibility of stepping out of the trans ghetto and having a safe, regular job that French cis women were occupying during the post-war boom. She felt ready to exercise this new kind of freedom.

The last driving force explaining Bambi's disposition to go back to school was the uproar of History with a capital H:

> Et puis, il y avait autre chose. Mai 68 (cinq mois s'étaient écoulés depuis) avait exhibé le foyer d'agitation qu'était la Sorbonne. D'un coup, moi qui avais jusque-là considéré le Carrousel, mon cabaret, mon monde, comme le centre de l'univers, je m'étais sentie excentrée, dépassée. Je plaçais maintenant la Sorbonne plus haut que le Carrousel et je me demandais si, tout en passant mes nuits au cabaret, je ne pourrais pas, une fois le bac passé, hanter l'université le jour. (p. 10)

> And then, there was another matter. May 68 (five months had passed since) had exposed the hotbed of agitation that was the Sorbonne. All of the sudden, I who had considered until then the *Carrousel*, my cabaret, my world, the centre of the universe, I felt decentred, surpassed. Now I placed the Sorbonne higher than the *Carrousel* and I wondered if, while spending my nights in the cabaret, I couldn't, once I had passed the *Bac*, haunt the university during the day.

Shaken by the mediatic and political impacts of the May '68 uprising in France, Bambi became aware that France was going through a massive change and that the epicentre of this cultural earthquake was the Sorbonne, where students expressed the need for France to shed its authoritative, traditional values and implement a sexual and political revolution. Bambi had already carried out her personal sexual revolution before May 1968 (years of taking hormones, sex change surgery in 1961 by Doctor Georges Burou, and change of gender on her birth certificate in Algiers in February 1968), but she felt like she had lived these past years in a tunnel and had lost touch with her own, evolving country. The events of May 1968 made her feel ready to escape her golden, hidden cage and coordinate her emancipation with the radical politics associated with the Sorbonne.

Studying for the *Bac* was the beginning of an intellectual trajectory leading to a professional transition, but how magical would it be for Bambi to start a DEUG (first two years at the University after the *Bac*) and become a student herself at the Sorbonne, the tumultuous temple of knowledge and the barricades in Paris? In the end, preparing for the *Bac* and then going to the Sorbonne was fantasised about as an act of intellectual rejuvenation and a reunion with a country willing to embrace its future. Paradoxically, Bambi was getting too old to keep working at the *Carrousel* but felt much younger when she made the decision to go back to school.

Back to School

La Chanson du bac focuses on the seven months between late October 1968 and early June 1969 that Bambi spent preparing to take the *Bac* via a correspondence course. The title of the book refers to the recurring fantasy, like the chorus of a song, of taking the *Bac* and then becoming a student at the Sorbonne (p. 28). Although the *Carrousel* is based in Paris, the owner of the cabaret, Monsieur Marcel, used to send the artists (the most famous and professional ones) touring abroad, mostly in North Africa, Japan, Australia and other European countries. The tours in the Maghreb were very popular and this is how Jean-Pierre (as she was called then), a high-school student in Algiers, first heard of Coccinelle and other scandalous women from the Carrousel who came to perform in Algeria in the early 1950s.[11]

Bambi took a residency at the *Terrasse*, a cabaret in Zurich, Switzerland, and began working on her lessons and homework there when she finished performing at night. Instead of going to bed when she returned home around 2:00 a.m. she would sit in her bedroom and work for two to three hours on the disciplines required for the exam: French literature, English, German and a third foreign language (Italian in Bambi's case, a tribute to her father's Italian origins), history and geography, mathematics and philosophy. At the beginning of this process, the Sorbonne remained a secret fantasy and Bambi struggled with her self-confidence. A psychosomatic expression of the stress, Bambi developed a serious case of psoriasis during the months preparing for the *Bac* (p. 83). At the same time, she remembered how much she used to like to study when she was a student in high school in Algiers, and she was elated to again experience the joy of learning and the feeling of intellectual growth. Going back to school was both a projection towards the future and a nostalgic revival of her Algerian years. When she received the first round of feedback from the remote teachers who graded her homework, she opened the envelope with anxiety:

L'espoir pouvait durer aussi longtemps que l'enveloppe serait
fermée, mais aussi l'anxiété … j'ouvris … je découvris les notes et
les commentaires. Ils étaient assez bons, elles tournaient autour de
douze. Je le pris comme un immense succès. Le ressort, tendu
jusque-là, céda d'un coup. Je ne pus me retenir d'exploser d'un
bonheur qui me transporta dans un élan vers ma mère … Maman
chérie, nous sommes sauvées … maintenant je peux te le dire, oui,
aujourd'hui, je te fais une promesse. Devant Dieu qui nous voit, je
te fais la promesse que je vais travailler sans cesse et que tu me
verras sortir du cabaret et mener une vie de jour. (pp. 81–8)

Hope could last as long as the envelope remained closed, but also
the anxiety … I opened it … I found the grades and the comments.
They were rather good, they averaged about twelve out of twenty. I
took it as an immense success. The spring, tightly wound until that
point, relaxed all of the sudden. I couldn't contain myself from
bursting with happiness that transported me in a rush to my
mother … Mother dear, we are saved … now I can tell you, yes,
today, I make you a promise. Before God who sees us, I promise
you that I will work without stopping and you will see me get out of
the cabaret and lead a 9 to 5 life.

The expression 'get out of the cabaret' almost sounds like 'get out of
jail', but the reader will recall that in spite of her stardom, friends
and financial autonomy, the cabaret felt like a ghetto for young trans
women. Bambi's mother had tried to oppose everything (her child's
transition, escape from Algeria and artistic career at the cabaret),
but as a widow and mother of an only, determined child, she ended
up accepting Bambi's trajectory and was very supportive of her
daughter returning to school. Relieved and reassured by these
promising results (an average of 12/20 meant that she could pass
the *Bac* with distinction), Bambi knew then that her hard work
would open the doors of the Sorbonne for her, where she determined to keep on working hard until graduation with the CAPES
(secondary-school teaching diploma) and to begin her career as a
teacher. After spending all these years working on stage and living by
night, Bambi's new ambition (and a pledge to her ageing mother)
was to get off her pedestal and live the simple and discreet life of an
ordinary woman. Ironically, when so many women aspired to their
fifteen minutes of fame (following Andy Warhol's aphorism),
Bambi's dream was to pass as an average cisgender woman, dedicated to her work and happy to live a conventional existence.

Once the residency in Zurich was over, Bambi and her mother returned to Paris and the pressure increased as the *Bac* exam was getting closer, so Bambi used her savings to start paying tutors for private lessons in Italian and mathematics (pp. 135–6). When it became clear that passing the *Bac* was an absolute priority, Bambi made the decision to suspend her work at the *Carrousel* for a few weeks, concentrating her time and energy on revising before taking the exams:

> La décision s'imposa à moi plus que je ne la pris. De cette nuit-là commencerait mon nouveau rythme: dormir la nuit, et étudier le jour, jusqu'au bac. Je ne retournerais au Carrousel qu'après mon succès. Les bonnes résolutions s'imposaient: ne plus me laisser aller à des périodes d'exaltation suivies d'apathie, mais s'armer d'une détermination froide, du courage du quotidien. Moi, au plus bas de l'échelle sociale, je devais plus que personne travailler, travailler à occuper dignement la petite place que je me ferais dans la société. (p. 185)

> The decision imposed itself on me more than I made it. From that night on my new rhythm would begin: sleep at night and study during the day, right until the *Bac*. I would not return to the *Carrousel* until after my success. The good resolutions asserted themselves: no longer letting myself go through excited periods followed by apathy, but to arm myself with a cold determination, with everyday fortitude. Me, at the bottom rung of the social ladder, I had to work harder than anyone, work to occupy the little place that I would make for myself in society with dignity.

It is interesting that Bambi saw herself at the very bottom of society when she had been the headliner of the *Carrousel* for many years, and so many of her trans sisters had been struggling with precariousness. But this sentence depicts how much the stigma of being a trans woman leads one to experience vulnerability and self-loathing. Before she finally passed the *Bac* successfully, Bambi, growing more confident in the results of her hard work, had coffee with her mother on the terrace of a café close to the Sorbonne. While her mother was waiting for her outside, Bambi walked up the stairs and ventured into the building of the oldest and most famous university in Paris.

She walked quietly through the *Galerie Richelieu*, took a peek in the *Amphithéâtre Descartes*, and saw the spectacle of students listening to a professor: *c'était un enchantement* (p. 193) ('it was an enchantment').

The artist from the cabaret recognised that professors are also performers, and she aspired to become a student in the short term with the goal of ending up on stage again as a teacher in the long term. The book ends with the dreamful prospect of returning to the Sorbonne in a few months, this time as an enrolled student.

In autumn 1969, while the Sorbonne was still recovering from the marches, riots and revolutionary assemblies of May '68, Bambi, now a *bachelière*, was an undergrad majoring in French literature. She thrived on living a double life: while she performed at night as Bambi at the *Carrousel*, in the neighbourhood of Montparnasse (p. 169), during the day she was Marie-Pierre Pruvot, a student about ten years older than her peers (she made long-lasting friendships with some of them) who took her classes seriously and graduated with the *DEUG* (two years after *Bac*), the *licence* (Bachelor's degree, three years after the *Bac*), and passed the first part of the CAPES in 1973.

While the first part of the CAPES is a series of written exams, the second part requires each candidate to observe teachers and teach under their mentorship for one year. Alongside this year of internship, Bambi graduated from the Sorbonne with a master's in French literature, having defended a thesis on the topic of sexual inversion in Proust's oeuvre *À la recherche du temps perdu* ('*In Search of Lost Time*'). By the end of spring 1974, five years after taking the *Bac*, she received her first work assignment (randomly chosen by the Ministry of Education): she was going to teach French in a middle school in Querqueville, a little village on the coast of Normandy. Madame Pruvot's new career was about to start.

Teaching French in the *Éducation Nationale*

Directed by Sébastien Lifshitz, *Bambi* documents the journey of a *pied noir* (literally 'black foot', meaning people of European origins born in Algeria during French colonialism) trans woman who comes back to Algeria after forty-two years of absence. Bambi's ultimate wish was to return to Algeria and visit her family's graves one last time (her father, sister and grandmother are buried in the same cemetery). Towards the end of the documentary, Bambi recounts going back to school and starting her career as Madame Pruvot, a teacher and *fonctionnaire* of the French state. Growing up in a poor family in rural Algeria, Bambi and her mother considered civil servants to be people with a higher and prestigious status. It was a noble career to become a teacher, and that is what happened at last in 1974.

The documentary includes archival footage of Marie-Pierre Pruvot with her students from her first middle school in Querqueville. Especially at the beginning of her new career in the suburbs of Paris (her next and last posting after Querqueville), Marie-Pierre learned to live with the fear of being *démasquée* ('unmasked'), not so much by her students, who were too young, but by a colleague or one of her students' parents. If the connection was ever made between Madame Pruvot and Bambi, she would be the source of intense gossip and media coverage about her past, her reputation would be tarnished and she would probably end up resigning under the pressure. As a result, she was extremely careful not to disclose anything to anyone at school about her life and trajectory. She made very good friends among her colleagues and got along well with the principal, but she could not share an essential part of her life with them. In spite of this constant fear, Marie-Pierre was also aware that she was protected by a simple fact:

> J'ai laissé pousser davantage les cheveux et j'ai mis ces bandeaux d'indienne. Je ne voulais pas que quelque chose me trahisse … Personne, personne n'aurait imaginé qu'on pouvait sortir du Carrousel et entrer aussitôt dans *l'Éducation Nationale*. C'était inimaginable pour les gens. (00:54:00–00:56:00)

> I let my hair grow longer and I wore these Indian headbands. I did not want something to betray me … Nobody, nobody could have imagined that one could leave the *Carrousel* and immediately enter the national education system. It was unimaginable for people.

By growing her hair and wearing one of these 'Indian' headbands that were trendy in the 1970s, she adopted a new style that differed completely from the sexy, *femme fatale* touch that characterised her as Bambi at the *Carrousel*. However, the real shield came from the fact that nobody was psychologically ready to imagine that a trans woman performing in a cabaret could transition into a 'normal', respectable teacher in charge of the education of (potentially) anyone's children. It was not a threat because it was unthinkable.

Most of Marie-Pierre's career was spent in a middle school in Garges-lès-Gonesse, a city in the northern part of the Parisian region, Île-de-France. Instead of living in Paris and commuting, Marie-Pierre lived in the suburbs (Montreuil and then Presles) until she retired. A lot of project buildings were built in the city of Garges-lès-Gonesse during the baby boom of the post-war years and a high percentage of its population were immigrants or French citizens born from mostly sub-Saharan, north African and Asian immigrants. The city, just like Aulnay-sous-Bois and Tremblay-en-France nearby, became an illustration of what French people called the *banlieues* in a racist and pejorative way. Another characteristic of Garges-lès-Gonesses is that the French communist party (PCF) ruled the city from 1944 until 1995, through the election and subsequent re-elections of communist mayors.

The interview conducted with Bambi confirmed and detailed the happiness that she felt as a teacher. One piece of evidence testifying to her satisfaction is that she never requested to be transferred to another school or another region. She served happily at the Pablo Picasso Middle School until she retired in 2000, and she would have liked to work there for a few more years if French law did not force civil servants to retire at sixty-five.

She knew she was not going to make as much money as she did as a performer, but the most beautiful and rewarding part of her job was to feel useful to her students and to contribute to their intellectual itinerary. As a significant portion of her students grew up in homes where French was not spoken, she was passionate in her fight against illiteracy and in the transmission of her love for the French language and literature. She enjoyed giving dictations and recitations and some of her favourite texts to teach were *Les Contes du chat perché*, *Tristan and Iseult*, and a few classical plays by Molière and Racine. Also, the first year that she taught at Garges-lès-Gonesses, she gave free Arabic lessons (on top of her regular teaching load and without compensation) to the students who were fluent in Arabic but needed to improve their writing skills.

Working by day allowed Marie-Pierre to come back home every afternoon and take care of her mother, spending more time with her in the evenings. After her mother passed away in 1977, Marie-Pierre dedicated most of her time to French literature. Little by little, she started nurturing a new ambitious project: finding the time and energy to write about her life. This project became a reality after 2000 when Marie-Pierre retired, sold her house in Presles, and relocated closer to Paris in the city of Pantin. This marked the beginning of her last reinvention from teacher to writer.

Bambi's successful transition as a teacher in the 1970s is commendable, as she was the first among her sisters from the first wave of trans women to navigate a professional transition from the cabaret to the classroom. She was a pioneer, and today, in France, many students have transgender teachers from the *maternelle* ('kindergarten') to the university. However, a recent study on the situation of transgender teachers in the national education system illustrates the significant impact of transphobia in and around the classroom. A book chapter ('Le bricolage identitaire des enseignant.e.s trans') from *Actualité des Trans Studies* (2019), by Arnaud Alessandrin, makes the first assessment of the situation of these transgender teachers at work in France. Different trends emerge from the results of this investigation:

> Il convient alors de remarquer deux types de transition, qui ne mobilisent pas tout à fait les mêmes ressorts: les enseignant.e.s qui décident de faire leur transition en situation d'emploi et les personnes trans qui décident, une fois la transition effectuée, de passer un des concours de l'enseignement ... Aussi, les rares témoignages d'hommes trans tendent à faire penser que les transitions professionnelles sont légèrement moins éprouvantes que pour les femmes trans en contexte professoral. (pp. 70–1)

> It is suitable to note two types of transition, that do not exactly mobilise the same mechanisms: the teachers who decide to perform their transition while working and trans people who decide, once their transition is carried out, to apply for their teaching certification ... Also, the rare testimony of trans men tends to suggest that their professional transitions are slightly less punishing than for trans women in a teaching context.

The situation is, indeed, very different according to whether the transgender teacher is going to start transitioning while teaching in the *Éducation Nationale* or has already transitioned before becoming a teacher. Alessandrin notices the same persistent fear among transgender teachers who (like Bambi) have already transitioned, of being outed or, to use terminology found in Janet Mock's autobiography *Redefining Realness* or in the series *Pose*, of being *clocked* and exposed as a transgender person. Also, and this is probably due to the joint operation of transphobia with sexism, trans women teachers are exposed to more pressure, discrimination and violence than their trans men peers. In comparison with the hardship suffered by trans women teachers today in France, Bambi's fortunate and fulfilling career as a teacher in the 1970s remains all the more impressive and inspiring. Her professional transition offers a lesson of hope and resilience, shows the benefits of audacity and self-determination and illustrates the playful reversibility between the statuses of student and teacher.

Works Cited

Alessandrin, Arnaud, and Karine Espineira, *Sociologie de la transphobie* (Pessac: Maison des Sciences de L'Homme d'Aquitaine, 2015).

Alessandrin, Arnaud, *Actualité des Trans Studies* (Paris: Éditions des archives contemporaines, 2019).

——*Sociologie des transidentités* (Paris: Le Cavalier bleu, 2018).

FRA (European Union Agency for Fundamental Rights), 'Being Trans in the EU: Comparative Analysis of the EU LGBT Data', *https://fra.europa.eu/en/publication/2014/being-trans-eu-comparative-analysis-eu-lgbt-survey-data* (accessed 24 November 2021).

Foerster, Maxime, *Elle ou lui? Une Histoire des transsexuels en France* (Paris: La Musardine, 2012).

Lifshitz, Sébastien (dir.), *Bambi* (Paris: Epicentre films, 2013).

Mock, Janet, *Redefining Realness: My Path to Womanhood, Identity, Love & So Much More* (New York City: Atria Books, 2014).

Némirovsky, Irène, *Ida* (Paris: Gallimard Folio, 2007).

Proust, Marcel, *À la recherche du temps perdu* (Paris: Gallimard Quarto, 2019).

Pruvot, Marie-Pierre (Bambi), *J'inventais ma vie* (Plombières les bains: éditions Ex Aequo, 2013).

—— *La Chanson du Bac* (Plombières les bains: éditions Ex Aequo, 2014).

Simon, Sophie, *Un Sujet de conversation* (Paris: Stock, 2004).

Notes

1   Marie-Pierre (Bambi) Pruvot, *La Chanson du Bac* (Plombières les bains: éditions Ex Aequo, 2014), p. 174.

2   Maxime Foerster, *Elle ou lui? Une Histoire des transsexuels en France* (Paris: La Musardine, 2012), p. 175.

3   Sophie Simon, *Un Sujet de conversation* (Paris: Stock, 2004), pp. 141–5.

4   Arnaud Alessandrin and Karine Espineira, *Sociologie de la transphobie* (Pessac: Maison des Sciences de L'Homme d'Aquitaine, 2015), p. 60.

5   Arnaud Alessandrin, *Sociologie des transidentités* (Paris: Le Cavalier bleu, 2018), p. 79.

6   FRA (European Union Agency for Fundamental Rights), 'Being Trans in the EU: Comparative Analysis of the EU LGBT Data', *https://fra.europa.eu/en/publication/2014/being-trans-eu-comparative-analysis-eu-lgbt-survey-data* (accessed 24 November 2021), 9.

7   Foerster, *Elle ou lui?*, pp. 99–131.

8   Pruvot, *La Chanson du Bac*, p. 9.
9   Sébastien Lifshitz (dir.), *Bambi* (Paris: Epicentre films, 2013). 00:51:00–00:53:00.
10 Foerster, *Elle ou lui?*, pp. 149–53.
11 See Marie-Pierre Pruvot, *J'inventais ma vie* (Plombières les bains: éditions Ex Aequo, 2013).

Part III
From Opening a Few Doors to Blowing the Doors Off

Chapter 13

Women's *bénévolat militant* at the Beginning of the MLF

SANDRA DAROCZI

These past few years have seen an increased interest in and a return to second-wave feminism, manifested both in the form of popular culture productions,[1] as well as theoretical and research works.[2] We can clearly identify sociopolitical events that have directly contributed to putting girls' and women's issues centre stage around the globe: the 2014 Nobel Peace Prize awarded to Malala Yousafzai; the 2016 election of Donald Trump and the Women's March that followed his inauguration in January 2017; the numerous accusations against Harvey Weinstein and the global #MeToo movement that followed (with its multiple variations); the legalisation of abortion in the Republic of Ireland following the May 2018 referendum; and the November 2020 protests against the extremely restrictive abortion laws in Poland. The return to the 1970s is not just fuelled by historic and historiographic interests, but also by thematic ones: abortion, sexual harassment, violence against women and girls' education were also key themes during the second wave of feminism.[3] The current chapter will bring about such a return to the first half of the 1970s, more specifically to the period between 1971 and 1973, to focus on the scarcely explored area of women's *bénévolat militant*[4] as presented in the pages of the French feminist journal *Le Torchon brûle* (*Tb*) (*'The Burning Rag'*).[5]

French second-wave feminism is most often identified with *le Mouvement de Libération des Femmes* (MLF) (Women's Liberation Movement),[6] a non-hierarchical, loosely organised movement that brought under its umbrella numerous groups and tendencies, from feminist revolutionaries, Marxists, Trotskyists and labour-union members, to legal and medical specialists, university researchers, women artists and writers, proponents of *écriture féminine* and those that took a psychoanalytic approach to theorising women's condition, to name just a few. Scholars consider *Tb* to be the journal of the MLF,[7] as it was the first publication produced entirely by the movement. Marie-Jo Bonnet opens her recently published memoirs of the MLF years with her encounter with issue 0 of *Tb*, crediting it to be the spark that pushed her towards the MLF.[8] *Tb* was published irregularly[9] from the spring of 1971 to 1973; a total of six issues[10] with the last one amassing a circulation of 35,000 copies.[11] *Tb* mirrored well the spirit of the movement, as each issue was prepared by a different editorial team, with no one member taking the position of editor-in-chief or director of the publication. Moreover, the topics discussed were as diverse as the groups and tendencies of the MLF, while the modes of expression (essays, poems, short-stories, songs, drawings, collages, etc.) reflected the immensely creative currents that fuelled much of the 1970s.

The expression *bénévolat militant* used earlier is not without its own challenges. When I initially started collecting materials for this chapter, I loosely used terms such as 'volunteer work' or 'unpaid (activist) work'. However, I quickly became aware of the inadequacy of these terms, especially after speaking with former MLF activists[12] who did not see their involvement in the MLF as work – the unpaid element of it did not carry as much significance as I had initially estimated.[13] They spoke of militancy, of the sense of belonging to a movement that would enact change for generations to come. Therefore, the terminology 'unpaid work' was dismissed early on. The word *bénévole* is very close to the English 'volunteer' – someone who freely offers their time to the benefit of others, without remuneration.[14] When assessing French people's involvement with various non-governmental organisations, Prouteau and Wolff noticed a difference in the value assigned to the terms *bénévole* and *militant*, with the latter carrying more legitimacy in certain volunteering *milieux*.[15] These definitional issues were also raised by Archambault in an earlier study. For the purposes of her investigation, a *bénévole* was someone whose work could be carried out by an employee.[16] However, she clearly mentions *militantisme* ('militancy') as an area where the distinction is not as clear (p. 14). As such, the expression *bénévolat militant*[17] seemed best suited to account for activities that were simultaneously unpaid and militant. The unpaid element allows us to shed light on what becomes women's triple burden,[18] as they must simultaneously work, look after a family and be actively involved in the movement. The militant element helps us to stay as close as possible to the spirit and aims of the MLF.

Three standalone activities were chosen as the focus of this chapter: the publication of *Tb* itself, the organisation of *groupes de quartier* ('neighbourhood groups'), and the creation of *crèches sauvages*.[19] In every issue of *Tb* (except for issue 0), the editorial team wrote texts of various lengths discussing the challenges of working on such a publication. An in-depth look at these texts will shed new light on the successes and challenges of publishing a feminist journal. The *groupes de quartier* were very quickly identified as an opportunity to engage women in grassroots projects that could enact change at the local level. And yet, the debates that eventually led to the conflicts within the MLF itself were visible in the early days of these groups as well. However, the groups also displayed tremendous ability for self-reflexivity, as shown in the articles that they wrote for *Tb*. Finally, the topic of the *crèches sauvages* was chosen due to its close links to the *groupes de quartier*, but also because they were mixed activities, with both women and men volunteers. The chapter analyses how these three types of activity are represented in various issues of *Tb*, highlighting the difficulties encountered by women when juggling the responsibilities of the triple burden. The chapter does not offer an exhaustive analysis of all the instances in which work and its variations were mentioned in *Tb*; nonetheless, it aims to provide further opportunities for researching the little explored field of women's *bénévolat militant*. This research can also help us to understand the challenges facing current feminist social movements, while not losing sight of the debt that we owe to the MLF.

Le Torchon brûle – From Creative Fires to Burnout

In their reviews of the developments characterising the 1970s, both Kandel and Lasserre observe that the feminist press went through a process of professionalisation 'qui s'inscrit dans un véritable phénomène éditorial'[20] ('which was part of a real editorial phenomenon'). However, *Tb*, as a precursor to this phenomenon, remains characterised by a system of volunteering and do-it-yourself militancy. Nonetheless, these features can encourage creativity and a rapid response to societal changes, while also raising issues about financing, distribution and long-term sustainability:

> Il reste que, *sans ressource matérielle aucune, cette presse vit exclusivement du travail gratuit et anonyme des femmes qui y collaborent, que celles-ci sont plus ou moins nombreuses suivant les moments, que la gratuité n'a qu'un temps (celui des études ou du chômage,* souvent) et que le militantisme est en crise.[21]

> Without any material resources, the only thing keeping this press alive is the anonymous, unpaid work of the women who contribute to it; their numbers vary all the time, and the ability to work for free is time-bound (often during studies or unemployment); therefore, militancy is in crisis.

Kandel highlights that the position of *bénévole militant(e)*, working on a publication such as *Tb*, is only truly available to women who have the time resources: either students (or researchers), unemployed women (which could include stay-at-home and well-off women), or those working part-time (where it would be sufficient to support daily expenses). However, these positions being time-bound and transitory, they do not allow for consistency and sustainability. The issue of time availability is clearly underlined in *Tb* 3, where the editorial team recognised the fact that working women were excluded from their meetings organised during the day. Moreover, the team 'didn't feel the need to move the meetings to the evening because very few of the women busy during the day indicated their desire to work with us' (*Tb* 3, p. 24). Time pressures also affected group dynamics, especially when linked to the urgency of publication, which was acutely felt, even though the journal had irregular issue dates and self-imposed deadlines. The latter were necessary to avoid a lack of publication, but they also had a direct and significant effect on the team's 'état de tension' (*Tb* 3, p. 24) ('pent-up tension'). This in turn affected the composition of the editorial team, as it disincentivised others from joining once the editorial work was underway. A further consequence was the need to reassert the fact that the editorial team was not assuming leadership functions of either the journal or the movement (e.g., *Tb* 2, p. 16). Due to time pressures, the need for efficiency could be confused with a desire to take over: 'Les quelques "efficaces" ne tardent pas à être accusées de prises de pouvoir idéologique sur le contenu du journal' (*Tb* 3, p. 24) ('The few "efficient" ones among us were soon accused of an ideological takeover of the contents of the issue'). Nonetheless, the schedule described is not always conducive to a balance with other daily activities that women might be engaged in. Reflections about the urgency of writing punctuate the issue that was put together in 'une hâte quasi-fébrile' (*Tb* 3, p. 24) ('an almost feverish haste'). This urgency reflects the effervescence and creative energies of the movement. Simultaneously, it is conducive to extreme tiredness, a loss of 'qualités d'accueil' (*Tb* 3, p. 24) ('welcoming abilities'), and even marginalisation of certain groups who cannot adapt to the schedule due to work and family commitments. The extreme tiredness is best exemplified by the note written by the team of the third issue: 'Chères lectrices, l'équipe du no. 3 s'excuse de n'avoir pas écrit d'éditorial, elle est tout bonnement EXTÉNUÉE' (*Tb* 3, p. 24, capitals in the original) ('Dear sisters and readers, the team of issue no. 3 apologises for not having written an editorial, but we are simply EXHAUSTED'). The small note is the very last section of the journal, simultaneously emphasising a sense of accomplishment and an intense and unsustainable rhythm of work. The handwritten nature makes us think of a margin comment or an addition, while the emphasis on EXTÉNUÉE ('EXHAUSTED') is already indicative of some of the early problems of *bénévolat militant*.

These problems reappear in subsequent editorial notes (especially issue 5), but some also carry a ludic and optimistic note. The editorial note of issue 4 is a particular example of this playfulness (*Tb* 4, p. 24). First, the reader needs to turn the page ninety degrees anti-clockwise to be able to read the handwritten note. It appears on a green background, and at times it reads almost like a poem, with stream of consciousness insertions:

> Torchonner, ah oui! mais, l'édito? torchonner... lire les articles, le choix des articles, la prémaquette, le choix des caractères, parler de nous au milieu de tout ça, l'encre mauve ou rouge, on mange
> Comment que ça doit être un torchon?
> on boit, les tendances, les signatures, j'aime ce poème (*Tb* 4, p. 24)[22]

> Working on this rag, oh yes! but the editorial? working on the rag... reading the articles, choosing the articles, the pre-paste-up, the choice of fonts, talking about ourselves in the middle of all this, purple or red ink, we eat
> What do you mean this has to be a rag?
> we drink, the tendencies, the signatures, I love this poem.

While the note gives a sense of the editing work involved (from selecting the articles to formatting), it also mirrors the conviviality of the work and the excitement that it generated. There is a recognition of the difficulties of the process – 'Tout n'est pas chouette' (*Tb* 4, p. 24) ('Not everything is smashing') – but the final sentence leaves the reader with a note of optimism (as opposed to the sense of burnout we got from the note in the previous issue): 'Ah ce qu'on a bien torchonné quant à l'édito' (*Tb* 4, p. 24) ('Oh, but how much we enjoyed working on the editorial for this rag'). The creation of the journal is no longer presented just as an intense period of work, but also as an opportunity to continue meeting, spending time with and talking to other women; it becomes a *groupe de parole* ('discussion group') in itself.

Combining editorial work with the benefits of a *groupe de parole* were also the intentions of the team behind issue 5: 'Nous voulions que les réunions soit *un lieu de travail et de parole* à partir des problèmes posés par les articles' (*Tb* 5, p. 24, italics mine) ('We wanted the meetings to be a *space for working and talking* starting with the problems raised by the articles'). However, ideological and political differences led to disagreements and a difficult working environment. Nonetheless, it is through discussions that the members of the editorial team were able to reach a consensus:

> Cette discussion n'a pas modifié les problèmes que nous avions avant; mais *elle a débloqué certaines d'entre nous, au niveau du travail en commun au journal*, en changeant le climat des réunions et en réduisant l'agressivité entre nous. (*Tb* 5, p. 24, italics mine)[23]

> This chat didn't change the issues we had before; but *it did loosen things up for some of us, with regards to the work on the journal*, changing the atmosphere of the meetings and diminishing the aggressiveness between us.

Work on *Tb* was not just an opportunity to create a feminist journal, but also an opportunity to understand and accommodate the divergences within the movement, without necessarily solving or erasing them. The quotation above and the publication of issue 5 itself clearly indicate that common work is possible even when little common ground can be found between ideological and political projects. Creative outcomes can be the result of disagreements, if the disagreements are acknowledged and discussed rather than ignored or dismissed as irrelevant. Unfortunately, we do not have much evidence to assess to what extent this strategy was successful, as there is only one other available issue of *Tb*. The uniqueness of issue 6 is the fact that it was produced entirely by a group from Rouen.[24] Since there are no further issues of *Tb*, the following section will turn towards *groupes de quartier* ('neighbourhood groups'), which often acted as *groupes de parole* ('discussion groups') as well.

The *groupes de quartier* – Grassroots Challenges

In addition to the general meetings organised at the Beaux-Arts every two weeks, the MLF was made of a plethora of interest groups, many of them functioning at the level of the neighbourhoods and the *arrondissements*. The proximity of the meetings and the more manageable time commitments (regular meetings as well as larger, one-off events) would encourage more women to attend. To support the proliferation of such groups, women wrote articles in *Tb* about the successes, difficulties and lessons drawn from their own experiences of *groupes de quartier*. The group based in the twelfth *arrondissement* is a compelling case study, since there are articles about it both in issues 3 and 5, covering the period from February–March 1971 to July 1972. In almost eighteen months, the group goes from optimism and excitement (*Tb* 3, p. 7) to serious concerns about the future of the group (*Tb* 5, p. 15). These concerns are brought about by issues of leadership and difficulties in identifying the aims and objectives of the group, which would subsequently dictate the organisation of activities. We also observe that the debates played out at the level of the larger MLF (between theory and action, and between Psych et Po and the other tendencies) are reflected at the grassroots level as well, preventing the group from expanding its membership and activities.

Early on, there is an awareness that the women who started the *groupe du 12e* are not representative of all the women from the *arrondissement*: 'Nous souhaitions connaître de nouvelles femmes, ne pas rester entre nous, *intellectuelles, étudiantes, petites bourgeoises*' (*Tb* 3, p. 7, italics mine) ('We wanted to meet new women, so that we didn't just gather among ourselves, *intellectuals, students, petites bourgeoises*'). The main activity of the group – *les marchés* ('the markets') – aimed to both discuss women's issues and expand the membership base. Every week, the members of the group would go to the markets with various visual props (placards, posters, texts, collages, etc.) to start discussions about the pressing subjects of the time: contraception and abortion, family life, education (see *Tb* 3, p. 7). It is worth noting that the largest support was given by older women (*Tb* 3, p. 7).[25] The presence at the markets was successful in attracting women to the group. However, there were difficulties in retaining their involvement (*Tb* 3, p. 7), which meant that the pool of experiences and perspectives was still reduced, affecting the reach of the group. This is in addition to the fact that women of colour appear to be absent from the group. This absence and even exclusion, analysed by both Vergès and Bard,[26] characterised the MLF as a whole and will be touched upon again in the conclusion to this chapter.

Organisational problems are mentioned in issue 5 as one of the main sources of conflict, centred around an unnamed member of the group:

> Le fait que X. semblât détenir un certain pouvoir fut une des sources du conflit qui alla jusqu'au point *où X. a pu être accusée d'être un chef et à la fois de ne l'être pas assez* ... En effet, la présence d'un « chef » apparent ... faisait adopter aux autres une attitude de passivité: *on attendait que X. propose des objectifs et les mène à bien.* (*Tb* 5, p. 15, italics mine)

> The fact that X. seemed to hold a certain amount of power was one of the sources of conflict which went *as far as accusing X. of being a boss while also not being a strong enough one* ... The presence of a so-called 'boss' ... meant that the other women became passive: *we were waiting for X to set the objectives and to accomplish them as well.*

The lack of clarity surrounding the purpose and the activities of the group created an organisational vacuum filled by the presence of X. (who was part of a group working with Psych et Po (*Tb* 5, p. 15)). While this lack of clarity can have positive effects, being an opportunity to explore new ideas, to propose innovative initiatives and to attract a variety of members, it also prevents the group from asserting itself on the public scene and enabling change. Similarly, the emergence of a leader can provide focus and guidance. However, the ideological background of this leader can cause further debates and disagreements, as was the case with the *groupe du 12e*, as not all its members identified with the Psych et Po tendency.

In a similar way to the team of *Tb* 5, *la parole* ('the spoken word') was identified as a potential solution to this impasse (*Tb* 5, p. 15). Before proceeding to further public actions, the group had to resort to *la parole* to be able to overcome its definitional and organisational issues. Unsurprisingly, one of the most efficient activities of the group, at its beginnings, were discussions:

> Nous avions abandonné la préparation du marché suivant... *Nous avons toutes davantage parlé de nous*; ce n'étaient encore que la mise en commun d'expériences; mais nous expérimentions à nouveau *l'effet libérateur de cette mise en commun*. (*Tb* 3, p. 7, italics mine)

> We gave up preparing the next market... Instead, we all spoke more about ourselves; at that point, it was only the sharing of our experiences, but we were trying out once more the liberating effect of this sharing.

This *mise en commun* ('sharing') is a way of generating knowledge of the self and of the group. The *mise en commun* does not mean an attempt to find the common thread that links the experiences of all women while neglecting their differences and singularities. On the contrary, it means drawing strength from this very diversity, finding *l'effet libérateur* ('the liberating effect') through sharing with, supporting and valuing the other. Nonetheless, this experience of sharing occurs with fewer difficulties at the beginning of a group's existence, when getting to know the other fuels the development of the group. Reconnecting with the liberating effect of the spoken word is much more difficult after months of disagreements. Moreover, re-engaging with group discussions would entail an inward look rather than an outward one, further delaying other militant activities. However, delaying the discussions would significantly affect the group dynamic and the quality of the militant activities they might be able to organise. These activities would have to follow organically from the discussions (*Tb* 5, p. 15). It is also worth noting that the very publication of the article about the issues of the *groupe du 12e* is a way of engaging in these discussions. Rather than disbanding the group and joining others, the members were willing to attempt resolving their issues in a non-exclusionary manner. The article contributes to the group's re-engagement with *la parole*, while simultaneously acting as a cautionary tale for future groups. The article is both inward and outward looking; it becomes a militant act by promoting self-awareness and self-reflexivity within the MLF. The final part of this chapter was inspired by this group's article and their observation that before organising nurseries for others they had to be able to coordinate child-care at the level of the group (*Tb* 5, p. 15).

Crèches sauvages – The Rewards and Challenges of Autogestion ('Self-sufficiency')

The existence of *crèches sauvages* precedes the publication of any issue of *Tb*, dating back to the May 1968 protests that saw their emergence at the Sorbonne. By the time of the first independent issue of *Tb*, only two such *crèches* were still functioning in Paris – at Censier and the Beaux-Arts (*Tb* 1, p. 15). Two issues – *Tb* 1 and 3 – offer extensive space to articles dealing with the practicalities, as well as the ideological aims of these *crèches*. In *Tb* 1, there is first an appeal from 'a mother, a grandmother and a worker' to other 'women, sisters, mothers and grandmothers' (p. 14) to contribute to the functioning and creation of other *crèches sauvages*. This is followed on page 15 by an article written by 'a woman from the Beaux-Arts and Censier *crèches* after 2 years of meetings and of running such a *crèche*'. While the article gives practical details about these *crèches*, it is focused mostly on ideological issues, showing how the *crèches sauvages* go against bourgeois pedagogy and create revolutionary relationships with children (*Tb* 1, p. 15).[27] In *Tb* 3, one article outlines in much more detail the day-to-day running of the Censier *crèche*. This article was meant to be the first in a series on this topic (*Tb* 3, p. 19),[28] but unfortunately no further *Tb* issues return to this subject in as much detail.

The main characteristic of a *crèche sauvage* is the fact that parents (or someone on their behalf) must be on nursery duty for half a day per week (*Tb* 3, p. 19). The only way that the *crèches* can be self-sufficient is through the parents' active participation and through the daily fee of three francs that was used for food, toiletries and other necessities.[29] There was an acknowledgement that the need for the parents' involvement would exclude parents who worked full time on regular and strict schedules (*Tb* 3, p. 19). The *crèches* provided a solution that was functional only if everyone brought a minimum contribution, both financial and personal (as time given to the *crèches*). In as much as their work was unpaid, the parents could be considered *bénévoles*; moreover, there is also an element of *militantisme*, since the ideological and political underpinnings of the *crèches* aimed to demonstrate that structural and systemic changes are possible. However, there was also a direct gain for the families, in the form of childcare (especially when places in other *crèches* were scarce and waiting lists lengthy). This direct gain might not be as immediately visible in the case of the other two examples of *bénévolat militant* described in this chapter. We can also argue that this direct gain contributed to the longevity of the *crèches* (which had already been running for at least two years when *Tb* 1 was published). Nonetheless, we should not ignore that the set-up of the *crèches* is exclusionary, as many parents (especially working-class parents) would be unable to take half a day off every week. There is some acknowledgement of this in the article, but it is quickly dispensed with, following an enumeration of the categories of who can afford such flexibility: temporary workers, teachers, the unemployed, students or stay-at-home women (*Tb* 3, p. 19). One of the political demands of the *crèches sauvages* was the emergence of a system where employees would have sufficient free time to look after their children, even during the day (*Tb* 3, p. 19). However, it is naive to assume that the mere existence of the *crèches* would provoke such huge systemic changes. Most of the parents involved in the *crèches* would still have to remain part of the capitalist system, through their paid employment. Furthermore, the indication that the aim of the *crèches* was 'd'amener les gens à l'autogestion et non pas de "soulager la misère des prolétaires" et de résoudre les problèmes à leur place' (*Tb* 3, p. 19) ('to get people to be self-sufficient and not to relieve "the misery of the working classes" nor to solve their problems in their place') can be read as condescending. And it fails to recognise that they are in fact quickly excluding the families who might benefit most from the existence of these *crèches*. While the system promotes self-sufficiency through active parental involvement, it excludes those for whom the latter is not a viable option.

Nonetheless, parents were not the only ones who could get involved, as the *crèches* welcomed anyone who wanted to volunteer (*Tb* 1, p. 15). Therefore, the groups of *bénévoles* were mixed (which was not the case for the other two examples discussed in this chapter) and often intergenerational. While this composition had its advantages, ensuring that the children had heightened social abilities by interacting with a multitude of people, it also came with its challenges. First, due to the diversity of volunteers, sustaining a continuous programme of learning proved difficult: 'Chez nous on n'apprend rien aux gosses, c'est vrai aussi; mais nous faisons pleinement aussi s'exercer la meilleure fonction d'apprentissage qui est le jeu' (*Tb* 1, p. 15) ('It's true that we don't teach the kids anything here; but we get them to make full use of the best learning tool there is – playing'). This was due to the limited number of volunteers and to their daily rotation, which precluded a sense of continuity. However, the article in *Tb* 3 highlights another issue as well, relating to the volunteers' experience (or rather lack thereof) of looking after children. The simple desire of volunteering or of being a militant was not always enough to ensure the smooth running of the *crèches*. People found themselves thrown in at the deep end,[30] responsible for the children's wellbeing, regardless of any prior experience of care giving. The training available to the volunteers was very much on the job, rather than before starting it. Due to the limited number of volunteers and to their numerous tasks (which included shopping, cooking and looking after the children), certain practical concerns could not be prioritised: 'Chez nous c'est sale ... Chez nous c'est dangereux' (*Tb* 1, p. 15) ('Our place is dirty ... our place is dangerous'). While both dirt and danger can have educational value (as highlighted by the same article), there is a clear sense (albeit expressed with a touch of sarcasm) that more volunteers would help improve the situation: 'nous ne sommes pas assez nombreux alors les fanatiques de l'hygiène n'ont qu'à intervenir avec leurs petits balais et leur éponge' (*Tb* 1, p. 15) ('there aren't enough of us, so the cleanliness police can intervene if they really want to, with their little brooms and sponge'). More volunteers, with a clear interest in early-years development, would have brought a positive contribution to an already successful initiative[31] that was trying to provide a practical and ideological alternative to the state-run system.

Conclusion

Bénévolat militant was an integral part of the MLF, contributing to the success of the movement and to some of the major changes that we have come to associate with the feminism of the 1970s. It also created opportunities for discussions and sharing that were not available in other forums (i.e., labour unions or educational institutions). Nonetheless, as was shown by the three activities analysed in this chapter, *bénévolat militant* had its own challenges and difficulties that could lead to conflicts, burnout and even exclusions. One of the exclusions mentioned above was that of working-class parents, especially in the context of the *crèches sauvages*. We also need to consider that, within the working classes, there is a high concentration of families with an immigrant background, which leads us to another exclusion at work here: the exclusion of women of colour. The inclusion or exclusion of these groups is not explicitly mentioned in any of the texts studied in this chapter. However, other scholars have highlighted the fact that, despite the diversity of groups in the MLF, the movement was dominated by white feminist concerns,[32] ignoring racial and colonial questions and the intersection of these questions with sexism and heteronormativity. Thinking back to the desire expressed by the *groupe du 12e* to expand the group beyond 'intellectuals, students, *petites bourgeoises*', the exclusion of women of colour would have significantly affected the way women's liberation was understood and enacted. This exclusion had effects that resonate until today, if we look at the 'feminist camps' created around questions such as the wearing of the veil in the French public space.[33]

As mentioned in the first half of the chapter, the availability of time often affected who could get involved with *bénévolat militant* and for how long. The more time women dedicated to *militantisme*, the higher the chance that they would be juggling lengthier periods of study, part-time jobs and even unemployment, the latter two not being conducive to establishing a career path that would lead to a reasonable pension. Pensions depend on the amount of contributions made to a retirement fund during one's working life. However, starting one's working life later to accommodate activism or starting it with a series of part-time jobs will negatively affect the amount available in the retirement fund. Many former MLF activists are currently retired, and some of them have lower pensions due to combining *militantisme* with employment during the 1970s.[34] Acknowledging this effect, which was felt only decades after the heyday of the MLF, is part of the reason why this chapter has mentioned intergenerational dialogue more than once. The latter can help current feminist movements avoid past mistakes (linked, for example, to organisational and leadership issues as discussed in the first and second parts of this chapter), or find solutions to their setbacks (through effective discussion groups (as was the case with the *groupe du 12e* and the editorial team of *Tb* 5) or even volunteer training (which could have helped the functioning of the *crèches sauvages*). More importantly, this intergenerational dialogue will ensure that we do not forget the material and symbolic costs of women's *bénévolat militant* during the 1970s, especially when some of the advancements of the decade are brought into question by contemporary sociopolitical decisions and discourses. The recent return to second-wave feminism mentioned at the beginning of this chapter can be both grateful and critical, challenging the exclusions that were at play during the movement; gratefulness and criticism can help us create a truly intersectional movement, fighting to protect the accomplishments of the past and ceaselessly pushing forward for new ones.

Works Cited

Archambault, Édith, 'Le bénévolat en France et en Europe', *Pensée plurielle*, 9/1 (2005), 11–34.

Associathèque, 'Le bénévolat c'est quoi' (2020), *www.associatheque.fr/fr/association-et-benevoles/benevolat-cest-quoi.html* (accessed 12 December 2021).

Atack, Margaret, Alison S. Fell, Diana Holmes and Imogen Long (eds), *French Feminisms 1975 and After: New Readings, New Texts* (Bern: Peter Lang, 2018).

—— *Making Waves: French Feminisms and Their Legacies 1975–2015* (Liverpool: Liverpool University Press, 2019).

Bard, Christine, *Féminismes: 150 ans d'idées reçues* (Paris: Le Cavalier Bleu, 2020).

Benfarah, Khadija, 'Po(é)litiser la parole des femmes depuis les mouvements de libération. Rencontre avec Xavière Gauthier, le 19 octobre 2019', *https://lesparleuses.hypotheses.org/1363* (accessed 12 December 2021).

Bonnet, Marie-Jo, *Mon MLF* (Paris: Éditions Albin Michel, 2018).

Delphy, Christine, 'Antisexisme ou antiracisme? Un faux dilemme', *Nouvelles questions féministes*, 25/1 (2006), 59–83.

Kandel, Liliane, 'L'explosion de la presse féministe', *Le Débat*, 1/1 (1980), 105–28.

—— 'Journaux en mouvement: la presse féministe aujourd'hui', *Questions Féministes*, 7 (1980), 14–36.

Lasserre, Audrey, 'Quand la littérature se mit en mouvement: écriture et mouvement de libération des femmes en France (1970–1981)', *Les Temps modernes*, 3 (2016), 119–41.

Lowthorpe, Philippa (dir.), *Misbehaviour* (2019).

Mrs. America (FX, created by Dahvi Waller, 2020).

Prouteau, Lionel, François-Charles Wolff, 'Adhésions et dons aux associations: permanences et évolutions entre 2002 et 2010', *Economie et Statistique*, 459 (2013), 27–57.

Le Torchon brûle, issues 0–6, *https://archivesautonomies.org/spip.php?article589* (accessed 12 December 2021).

Taymor, Julie (dir.), *The Glorias* (2020).

Vergès, Françoise, 'Toutes les féministes ne sont pas blanches. Pour un féminisme décolonial et de marronnage', *Le Portique. Revue de philosophie et de sciences humaines*, 39/40 (2017), 1–18.

Notes

1 See, for example, the series *Mrs. America* (FX, created by Dahvi Waller, 2020), as well as the films *Misbehaviour* (dir. Philippa Lowthorpe, 2019) and *The Glorias* (dir. Julie Taymor, 2020).

2 See, for example, Margaret Atack, Alison S. Fell, Diana Holmes and Imogen Long (eds), *French Feminisms 1975 and After: New Readings, New Texts* (Bern: Peter Lang, 2018); Margaret Atack, Alison S. Fell, Diana Holmes and Imogen Long (eds), *Making Waves: French Feminisms and Their Legacies 1975–2015* (Liverpool: Liverpool University Press, 2019); Christine Bard, *Féminismes: 150 ans d'idées reçues* (Paris: Le Cavalier Bleu, 2020).

3 For links between second-wave and contemporary feminism, see the 'Introduction' to Margaret Atack et al., *Making Waves* (written by the editors), and the 2019 interview with Xavière Gauthier, by Khadija Benfarah, 'Po(é)litiser la parole des femmes depuis les mouvements de libération', *https://lesparleuses.hypotheses.org/1363* (accessed 12 December 2021).

4 A direct translation of this expression can be 'militant voluntary work'; due to the definitional challenges analysed in this introduction, the French version of *bénévolat militant* will be used throughout.

5 Hereafter, *Le Torchon brûle* will be referred to by the shortened version *Tb*, followed where necessary, by the relevant issue and page numbers.

6 Nonetheless, as highlighted by Bard in *Féminismes*, second-wave French feminism was much larger than the MLF (pp. 81–92).

7 Audrey Lasserre, 'Quand la littérature se mit en mouvement: écriture et mouvement de libération des femmes en France (1970–1981)', *Les Temps modernes*, 3 (2016), 127. See also Liliane Kandel, 'L'explosion de la presse féministe', *Le Débat*, 1/1 (1980), 105–28 (especially p. 105) and Liliane Kandel, 'Journaux en mouvement: la presse féministe aujourd'hui', *Questions Féministes*, 7 (1980), 14–36 (especially p. 25).

8 Marie-Jo Bonnet, *Mon MLF* (Paris: Éditions Albin Michel, 2018), pp. 11–13. Issue 0 of *Tb* was not a standalone issue, but rather stapled with smaller pages in the middle of *L'Idiot liberté*, 1, December 1970.

9 As a *menstruel* [word play on monthly/menstrual], attribute which appears on every cover.

10 The six issues do not include issue 0, published as part of *L'Idiot Liberté*. All issues are available at *https://archivesautonomies.org/spip.php?article589* (accessed 12 December 2021).

11 Kandel, 'L'explosion', p. 21.

12 I am extremely grateful to Dominique Samson, Suzette Robichon and Louise Turcotte for drawing my attention to these definitional issues.

13 Nonetheless, the later financial implications of the time spent contributing to the movement will be discussed in the conclusion of this chapter.

14 Associathèque, 'Le bénévolat c'est quoi' (2020), *www.associatheque.fr/fr/association-et-benevoles/benevolat-cest-quoi.html* (accessed 12 December 2021).

15 Lionel Prouteau, François-Charles Wolff, 'Adhésions et dons aux associations: permanences et évolutions entre 2002 et 2010', *Economie et
Statistique*, 459 (2013), p. 43 (italics mine).

16 Édith Archambault, 'Le bénévolat en France et en Europe', *Pensée plurielle*, 9/1 (2005), 14.

17 With the variation *bénévole(s) militant(e.s)* for the militant volunteers
themselves. The (s) marks the plural, while the (e) marks the feminine
in French.

18 Kandel, 'L'explosion', p. 7.

19 Collectively run alternative childcare.

20 Lasserre, 'Quand la littérature', pp. 130–1. See also Kandel,
'L'explosion', p. 7.

21 Kandel, 'L'explosion', p. 7 (italics mine).

22 Choice of punctuation and formatting in the original.

23 For more on the work on issue 5 of *Tb* see also Marie-Jo Bonnet, *Mon
MLF*, pp. 158–63.

24 There had been appeals in previous issues to include more contributions from outside Paris (including in the editorial note of issue 5), to
embrace a larger variety of issues and opinions.

25 Intergenerational dialogue is not often discussed in analyses of the
MLF. However, given that the heyday of the MLF was the 1970s, many of
its militants are still alive and willing to continue their involvement with
current feminist movements. Fruitful intergenerational dialogue could
become a feature of contemporary movements.

26 Françoise Vergès, 'Toutes les féministes ne sont pas blanches. Pour un
féminisme décolonial et de marronnage', *Le Portique. Revue de philosophie et de sciences humaines*, 39/40 (2017), 1–18; and Bard, *Féminismes*,
especially pp. 90–2.

27 Engaging with the ideological discussion presented in the quoted
article is beyond the scope of this chapter. Nonetheless, the article
presents opportunities for further research, by reading it in parallel
with Marxist ideas of pedagogy, but also with more recent developments surrounding alternative education.

28 On page 19 of the same issue, there is another article about the lack of
crèches in the tenth *arrondissement* of Paris and a note about the meaning
of *autogestion* in relation to the *crèches*.

29 There was no government funding for these *crèches*. The Censier one
benefitted from some initial help from the university, in terms of essen-
tials such as bathroom facilities, a stove and a fridge (*Tb* 3, p. 19).

30 Usually, a minimum of three people on duty for fifteen to twenty children (*Tb* 3, p. 19).

31 Evaluating the success of the initiative needs to bear in mind the exclusions mentioned above.

32 Vergès, 'Toutes les féministes', especially pp. 4–5, and Bard, *Féminismes*,
especially pp. 90–2.

33 For an in-depth discussion of the discourses and 'feminist camps'
created around the issue of the veil in public schools in France, see

Christine Delphy's seminal article, 'Antisexisme ou antiracisme? Un faux dilemme', *Nouvelles questions féministes*, 25/1 (2006), 59–83.
34 I am extremely grateful to Suzette Robichon for bringing this issue to my attention.

Chapter 14

Women Working: Women Rebelling – Female Community and Gender Relations in *Ah! Nana*

VALENTINA DENZEL

In October 1976, the French feminist comic magazine *Ah! Nana* published its first issue. The editorial column not only announced the magazine's intention to discuss uncommon topics, such as racism, sexual harassment, sado-masochism and incest, but also underscored the importance of giving voice to an international body of women artists, citing contributions from France, Italy and the United States in the inaugural issue.[1] This international collaboration of women artists tackling taboo topics highlights the innovative character of *Ah! Nana* in a male-dominated comic scene. In fact, the goal for the exclusively female editorial staff of this magazine was the professional enhancement of women in the comic scene and the critical deconstruction of and liberation from sexual objectification of women at the workplace and in the media. The editors of *Ah! Nana* were determined to contribute to the practice of women expressing themselves freely in an intellectual and artistic way.[2]

Unfortunately, this feminist project came to an end in September 1978 with volume 9. *Ah! Nana* journalist Carine Lenfant chose the prominent location of the inside of the cover page for her article announcing a ban on sales of the magazine to minors, representing a 30 per cent loss of profit. *Ah! Nana*, an already fragile venture kept afloat only through financial concessions by its female contributors, was thereby brought to an abrupt end. Lenfant's short article, depicting men opposing women in the exercise of their rights to self-expression and full participation in society, was accompanied by a drawing by Chantal Montellier, a former illustrator of left-wing publications. In the same issue, Montellier contributed her own six-page long *bande dessinée* or comic strip entitled *Game Over*, which represented a similar antagonism between men and women. In *Game Over*, Montellier depicts the invisibility and objectification of women at the workplace. Yet, it also features an inversion of societal perception of economic dependence by depicting men relying financially on women.

This chapter focuses on a comparison between Montellier's illustration for Lenfant's article and her comic strip *Game Over*. Both stress the importance of a feminist community and criticise the objectification of women and their marginalisation and invisibility in the workforce. They represent two of *Ah! Nana*'s main goals, described in its inaugural issue, namely the professional advancement of women and the right to criticise the misogynist society they live in. *Game Over* furthermore complicates power relations by stressing a vulnerable masculinity that can be read as a satirical comment on male hegemony. It also functions as an invitation to male readers to empathise with their female counterparts, thereby going beyond the polemic opposition of men and women in Lenfant's article. Instead, *Game Over* highlights the importance of a supportive community and egalitarian relationships between the sexes. These two illustrations, appearing in the final volume, represent a complementary statement against the demise of *Ah! Nana* and, when read together, emphasise the negative consequences of gender inequality and the importance of dismantling patriarchal myths.

In her article on *Ah! Nana*'s demise, Lenfant stated with regret: '*Ah! Nana* va mourir' ('*Ah! Nana* will die'). The 'murderers' of *Ah! Nana* were identified as unitarily male. According to Lenfant, contemporary society was not used to women working in a male-dominated field, and even less to women making it their professional goal to rebel against a misogynist society by tackling controversial topics in an iconoclastic manner. Therefore, the magazine was being 'punished' by the strict censorship laws of a misogynist juridical system. Little progress had been made since the social revolution in 1968 regarding women's acceptance and fulfilment in the workforce. Women, at least in the comic industry, still did not seem to have 'the same right to work or [to find] the same personal fulfil-ment in a career as men'.[3]

To remedy this *Ah! Nana* made it a point to promote women in the comic industry, even inexperienced and unpublished artists. This emphasis on gynocentrism aligned with the female centred philos-ophy of prominent French second-wave movements such as the *Mouvement de libération des femmes* (MLF) ('Movement for women's liberation') and the *Féminisme, Marxisme, Action* (FMA) ('Feminism, Marxism, Action') formerly known as *Féminin, Masculin, Avenir* ('Feminine, Masculine, Future'), both founded in 1970. As Françoise Picq pointed out, the MLF and the FMA decided soon after their foundation to work in a women-only environment to analyse their oppression and discuss strategies to overcome it without the pres-ence of the oppressor, that is, men.[4] Even though *Ah! Nana*, in the editorial column of volume 2, denounced the practice of 'hyper-feminism', which would exclude male collaborators, their magazine was directed mainly towards a female audience.[5] While the comic magazine did not claim any adherence to a particular feminist move-ment, second-wave feminism was one of the major factors contributing to the creation of *Ah! Nana*, together with the influ-ence of American feminist underground comics.[6] The American underground comic scene served as a model for the European contributors of *Ah! Nana* because the absence of commercial benefit allowed artists to explore taboo topics and express their political views in a censorship-free environment. Furthermore, it enabled female artists to create collectives and establish themselves in a male-orientated field.[7] These collectives were also international as shown by the collaboration of Trina Robbins and other American artists with their European counterparts of *Ah! Nana*. This collaboration enriched the content of *Ah! Nana* through various styles and tech-niques, and enhanced references to American cultural products.

Allusions to American counterculture and particularly to Trina Robbins's work are also present in Montellier's drawing for Lenfant's article that occupied two-thirds of the page. The left side of the page shows an isolated young woman, dressed in an unconventional style that refers to the American underground scene: she is wearing a short-sleeved T-shirt over a long-sleeved shirt, large trousers and sandals. Her T-shirt features an image of Rosie the Riveter, the iconic figure representing feminism, in general, and the prominence of women taking over male employment in factories during the Second

World War, more specifically. As Claire Duchen states, the last two years of the Second World War were filled with the hope that women 'would become equal citizens, equal partners at work and even (maybe) at home'.[8] As Duchen has shown, this hope was disappointed during the two decades after the Second World War. Despite their efforts, women's demands for better education, contraception, abortion and political representation were mainly ignored by the post-war government.

Given the context of *Ah! Nana*'s own demise to establish a lasting feminist comic magazine, Montellier's choice of including a reference to Rosie the Riveter in the article announcing *Ah! Nana*'s termination is telling. The image of Rosie the Riveter in Montellier's drawing stands for the attempt of women to assert themselves in the workforce, despite their disappointment of 'the tremendous hopes of 44–5'[9] that did not lead to gender equality. Furthermore, the reference to Rosie the Riveter also creates a connection to Trina Robbins's work whose image of Rosie Montellier had copied in her illustration. As Robbins recalls, 'the last issue featured a cartoon by Chantal Montellier: a woman dressed in one of my Rosie the Riveter T-shirts walks past five smirking men. She says, "**Ah! Nana** the only comic magazine made by women!" and they continue, "**Forbidden** by men !!!!"[10] This artistic cross-reference to Robbins's work shows the influence American feminist artists had on their French counterparts and proves that *Ah! Nana*, despite its short-lived existence, was able to create a professional network and a sense of collectivity among female comic artists.

In Montellier's illustration, the ambivalent and successive feelings of hope and disappointment of becoming equal partners in the workforce are expressed through the body language of the two female characters in Montellier's drawing. Rosie is standing in a defiant manner, holding a metal tool across her lower abdomen, ready to use it for work or to beat whoever gets in her way or harasses her. She is wearing a work suit and her figure dominates over an industrial landscape in the background. Her attitude is self-confident, showing that she owns the space she is inhabiting. By contrast, Montellier's second female character is not actually walking, as Robbins remembered, but standing with her feet close together, her hands in her pockets. Her expression is static, almost indifferent, or even disappointed. She pouts as she looks straight into the reader's eyes, her speech bubble stating that *Ah! Nana* is the only comic magazine for women: '*Ah! Nana* le seul journal de bandes dessinées fait par des femmes!'. Through her direct gaze, she seems to elicit empathy and support from the reader.

Five men, wearing casual to elegant outfits, confidently occupy the remaining two-thirds of the drawing. They are all turned towards the woman, cornering her as a closed group on one side of the page, a sneer on their faces. The man closest to the woman seems to step towards her and lift his sunglasses to take a better look at her. His gesture has a sexual undertone, and his speech bubble contains nothing more than four suspension points. Perhaps they indicate that he is hesitating as he judges her sexual attractiveness and function as a sarcastic comment on the fact that he is not using his intellectual capacities to evaluate the situation. Maybe the suspension points also represent a sort of censorship against sexist language. The other four men share a speech bubble that continues the sentence of the young woman by asserting that the magazine is forbidden by men: 'Interdit par des hommes.' The two words at the beginning of each speech bubble, '*Ah! Nana*' and 'Forbidden', are highlighted in bold characters, creating two different levels of text: a headline, *Ah! Nana Forbidden!!!*, and a sentence explaining the purpose of the magazine and who caused its demise. The fact that the woman's enunciation focuses on the magazine's feminist endeavour (*Ah! Nana* the only comic magazine made by women), however, seems to stress the achievements of *Ah! Nana*, namely its feminocentric universe. While the woman is outnumbered and her static posture expresses disappointment, she is not afraid of her male harassers and strikes a stoic pose.[11] The reason for her fearlessness might be the picture of the combative Rosie on her T-shirt as well as her dress-code referring to the American feminist underground scene: these references allude to female solidarity and community with the goal of advancing women professionals in male-dominated fields. Furthermore, they enhance the importance of metaphors and icons to foster feminist networks that continue to exist despite occasional failures such as *Ah! Nana*'s termination.

On the one hand, Montellier's drawing accentuates the opposition between men and women, accusing the former of preventing the latter from making any intellectual and artistic contribution to society, reducing women to mere sex objects. On the other hand, the reference to Rosie the Riveter and the American underground scene integrates her into a framework that does not rely solely on physical presence but also on an analytical and theoretical connect-edness between feminists. The repetition of signs and icons also helps create a sense of collectivity. As Sara Ahmed explains, 'the repetition of signs is what allows others to be attributed with emotional value'.[12] According to Ahmed, 'emotions *do* things and work to align individuals with collectives – or bodily space with social space – through the very intensity of their attachments'. More specif-ically it is 'how we feel about others' that 'aligns us with a collective'.[13] The men build a group **against** the woman, relying on histories of sexism 'in which the presence of others is already read as an invasion of bodily territory', whereas the woman connects **with** other femi-nists through the impression they literally have left upon her. In Ahmed's words, 'impression is a sign of the persistence of others even in the face of their absence'.[14]

The hateful connectivity between men is opposed to the supportive feminist bond on which the woman is relying. What is more, the fact that the woman takes up (work) space in the comic universe that according to the men she is not allowed to inhabit, may enable the arrival of 'new impressions, for new lines to emerge, new objects, or even new bodies'.[15] In fact, as Laurence Brogniez has shown, the female 'bande dessinée d'auteur' of the 1960s and 1970s paved the way in the 1990s for a resurgent feminist and female *bande dessinée* by independent publishers, including L'Association, Les Requins Marteaux and Frémok, with a specific focus on autobiog-raphy and diaries.[16] According to Brogniez, these genres allow for a greater freedom of expression due to the lack of codification and enhance the revendication of female authors to be taken seriously in a still male-dominated field.[17]

While the American underground scene was hailed in *Ah! Nana* for defying conventional representations of femininity, as we have seen in Montellier's illustration of Lenfant's article, allusions to American mainstream culture were generally used to criticise social injustice, consumerism and lack of community and solidarity.[18] For instance, in Montellier's series entitled *Andy Gang* and published in *Ah! Nana* Montellier lampoons the titular hero, constable Andy Gang for his ignorance, machismo and blatant racism. Her parody of an incompetent 'wanna-be-superhero', inspired by American mainstream culture, takes a clear stand against the glorification of a patriarchal system that promotes white supremacy and misogyny. While Catriona MacLeod describes Montellier's series as lacking any

'feminist' message,[19] it is important to understand Montellier's feminism as being part of a larger feminist critique that evolved during
the second wave and of which Danièle Kergoat is one of the major
exponents. Kergoat's notion of 'co-substantiality' was coined in 1978
and emphasises the importance of analysing the complexity of social
power relations and the ways in which they overlap to find an efficient strategy for emancipation.[20]

Montellier applies Kergoat's theory of 'co-substantiality' in her
analysis of power structures in *Andy Gang* and, as we will see, also in
Game Over. Montellier's feminism, therefore, needs to be understood in the complex entanglement of the various power struggles
during the 1960s and beyond, such as May 1968, the anti-colonial
movements and the workers' revolt in France (1972–5).
Furthermore, Montellier's work aligns itself with the second-wave
slogan of 'The Personal is Political'. This analysis of private and
public power structures was a successful strategy in second-wave
feminism to work towards more egalitarian relations between men
and women.[21]

In *Game Over*, the opposition between the two genders is more
subtle – it does not focus on the exclusion of women in the comic
industry but on working women in general and on women's invisibility in society. Montellier experiments with the form of the comic
by presenting two different types of reality: the upper strip represents the screen of a video game in which two opposed players whose
avatars are two little cowboy figures shoot at each other in a rural
landscape. The lower strip occupies four-fifths of the remaining
page and features the interior of a bar filled with a diverse group of
customers during a rainy night – the subtitle of *Game Over* is 'un
instant de pluie' ('a moment of rain'). The first two one-page panels
give an overview of the scene and the three dimensions of the space:
the foreground features a man and a woman sitting at a table; the
middle-ground, from left to right, shows two teenagers playing at a
pinball machine, a man sitting by himself on a bar stool and two
men and a woman standing at the counter of the bar; and the background is occupied by a barmaid who is working behind the bar,
wearing a hair band and a dotted dress with a low cleavage revealing
part of her breasts. Her outfit is reminiscent of the 1950s and seems
outdated compared to that of the other characters. The combative
environment of the video game featured in the upper strip foreshadows tensions between a man and a woman in the lower strip, as

well as internal tensions in individual characters that are also highlighted by references to American mainstream culture. The
diner-like ambience, the pinball machine, the video game and the
cowboy figures set the scene for a cold, consumeristic place in which
different individuals struggle in a capitalistic, heteronormative
society.

Besides the two teenagers, the barmaid is the only character
without a speech or thought bubble. She is therefore marginalised
through her sexual objectification and her silence. Throughout the
comic strip, her gaze is averted while she focuses on her tasks, which
diminishes her subjectivity as she seems to blend in with the background and with the objects that surround her. According to
Ahmed, 'bodies do not dwell in spaces that are exterior but rather
are shaped by their dwellings and take shape by dwelling'.[22] The
barmaid's existence is eerily joined to and inseparable from the
space of the bar. Most of her activities are hidden by the characters
occupying the middle ground. Her work is therefore made invisible
to the reader and loses its value of exchange. As Jeremy Lane and
Sarah Waters remind us, work is strongly linked to our sense of
subjectivity. 'Work can offer the potential for individual fulfilment
and emancipation, but conversely, it can also encroach on complex
and fragile processes of subjectivisation.'[23] The processes of subjectivisation might become even more fragile when work tasks are
judged under a gendered hierarchy. In this panel, Montellier creates
a parallel between the invisibility of the barmaid's work and 'the
unpaid labor of women for domestic services and child-rearing' that
'are excluded from the realm of exchange and consequently have
no *value*', yet serve as society's foundation, according to French
materialist feminist Christine Delphy.[24] Even though the barmaid's
work is paid, it is reminiscent of domestic work. The existence of the
barmaid remains unnoticed by the other characters, yet it is through
her services that they find shelter from the rain in the space of her
bar that functions as a micro-society.[25]

The invisibility of her work is linked to the invisibility of another
fictional female character who does not appear in the comic but
who is mentioned by the two men standing at the bar with another
woman. The barmaid is listening to their conversation, while the
man on the left tells his interlocutors about his recent visit to Jean-
Louis's atelier. He is shown in profile with his left foot posed on the
lower end of a bar stool, thereby demonstrating his dominance and

his ease in occupying the room physically. He describes Jean-Louis's atelier in detail, its convenient features, and defines it as 'un vrai paradis' ('a real paradise').[26] The other man, positioned on the far right of the comic page and whose face is shown in a three-quarters portrait, is the first to introduce the invisible and nameless female character 'la fille' ('the girl'), Jean-Louis's lover who died by suicide in that apartment. He asks the man to the left if her belongings have been moved out of the atelier, which the latter denies.

The insignificance of Jean-Louis's lover is highlighted by the fact that the man to the left describes her place of suffering and death as paradise and that he does not hesitate to move in. Yet, her letters to Jean-Louis that she never sent are still in the apartment, as well as her syringes that are piling up in the drawers, the wardrobe and behind the electric heater. He is therefore invading a room that is still inhabited by the traces of la fille. As Ahmed has pointed out, the work of inhabitance is 'a process of becoming intimate with where one is: an intimacy that feels like inhabiting a secret room that is concealed from the view of others'.[27] Ironically, la fille's 'secret room' has been penetrated. While her interior life remains tragically invisible to Jean-Louis because of her unsent letters, it is exposed by the new tenant, according to whom her abuse of drugs and Jean-Louis's departure are the causes of her suicide. It is unclear whether she was an artist herself, a profession that might explain the atelier as her residence. Yet, information about la fille is limited to the voyeuristic revelations of the new tenant and to her fatal relationship with Jean-Louis. In fact, the reference to this character as la fille instead of her name infantilises her and denies access to a professional identity.

The woman standing in between the two men is mainly listening to their conversations. Her back is to the reader, making her thoughts and expressions invisible, which links her to la fille. Her head moves from left to right while she is paying attention to the speech acts of the two men, revealing as a result only one-third of her face. Her only contribution to this conversation is her question whether the new tenant knew the girl well, which he denies. She refused to meet with him because she was crazy ('dingue'). La fille is therefore marginalised by her queerness and a life course that went against societal expectations, as described by the adjective 'dingue'. As Ahmed reminds us, 'for a life to count as a good life … it must return the debt of its life by taking on the direction promised as a social good, which means imagining one's futurity in terms of reaching certain points along a life course'.[28] Through her suicide, la fille refused to commit to certain points requested by heteronormativity, namely marriage and reproduction. Her tragic ending seems to indicate that la fille failed in creating an 'intimacy that feels like inhabiting a secret room', in 'feeling at home' not only in the confined space of the atelier but in the world, in general.[29] The title *Game Over* might even imply an eerie reference to la fille's suicide. La fille, as well as the speechless barmaid and the woman standing at the bar, in a paradoxical way all embody the invisibility of women, their work and their contributions to society.

Montellier emphasises the barmaid through the *mise en page* of the last page, focusing entirely on her as the only fictional character inhabiting the space after the rain stopped and the customers have left. Reminiscent of paintings including *Nighthawks* (1942) by the American artist Edward Hopper, known for his ability to represent deserted places, isolation and melancholy, Montellier underlines in this ambience the shortcomings of a consumerist and individualistic society as represented in American culture. The final panel of *Game Over* portrays the barmaid, leaning slightly forward, with her right arm lying on the counter while her chin rests on her left hand, a gesture that represents sorrow and frustration. Maybe it also conveys defeat, as indicated by the title *Game Over*. Just like la fille, she has failed in the struggle to create a place for herself in society. Her expression is sad, her gaze, avoiding the reader again, is directed towards the right of the drawing, into the void. On the table in the foreground are two empty coffee cups and empty bags of snacks, abandoned after being used, like the abandoned barmaid that is left behind after having served her customers. Her dissatisfaction is therefore linked to her work that requires repetitive and mechanic actions, likening her to a robot. As Ahmed states, 'our body takes the shape of this repetition; *we get stuck in certain alignments as an effect of this work*'.[30] Like the two avatar cowboys featured in the upper strip of the *bande dessinée*, the barmaid seems to act like an automaton, imprisoned in a timeless bubble where nothing changes or evolves. This impression is reinforced by her old-fashioned summer dress that distinguishes her even further from the other characters wearing winter clothes in the style of the 1970s. The circular movement between the first and the last panel representing the space of the bar on one page seem to confirm the recurring monotony of her trapped existence. She shares this lack of connectedness with

Jean-Louis's girlfriend who did not send her letters or engage with Jean-Louis's friends but chose instead to cut ties with the world by taking her own life. The tragic story of Jean-Louis's lover that she overheard might also have contributed to the barmaid's frustration. Indeed, in the panel where Jean-Louis's friend mentions the girl's unread letters and her syringes, the barmaid's eyes are directed towards the man telling the story.[31]

Contrary to Montellier's drawing that accompanied Lenfant's article, *Game Over* stresses the lack of a feminist community, highlighting instead the absence of Jean-Louis's lover, the isolation of the barmaid, as well as the invisibility of the woman standing between the two men, who is shown mostly with her back to the reader. Montellier's emphasis on women's invisibility in society aligns with the feminist recuperation of other (symbolic) invisible female characters, most notably the deposit of a wreath for the wife of the unknown soldier at the Arc de Triomphe by members of the MLF on 26 August 1970.[32] It is also linked to materialist feminist endeavours, including Christine Delphy's, to unmask 'the existence of a noncapitalist system of production'; namely, unpaid domestic work delivered by women, making outside work an additional burden.[33] The invisibility of the barmaid's work is a metaphor for the invisibility of domestic work, whose familiarity makes it go unnoticed.[34]

Invisibility, isolation and vulnerability, however, are not limited to female characters in Montellier's *Game Over*. An elderly man, with his back to the reader in the first two panels, is sitting by himself. His thought bubble expresses existential anxiety over his job as a taxi driver and the fact that he is not making enough money to survive ('tenir le coup'). The panel on page 31 shows his profile, covered mostly by his coat and hat, his invisibility creating a link to the woman at the bar, la fille and the barmaid. While he is walking away, he repeats the expression 'tenir le coup', this time highlighted in bold, capital letters and with an exclamation mark in his thought bubble. The barmaid is watching him, almost as if she could read his mind, while Jean-Louis's friend relates the suicide of la fille. In this one-page panel Montellier creates a triangle between the taxi driver in the foreground, Jean-Louis's lover mentioned in the speech bubble of his friend in the middle-ground and the barmaid in the background. These three characters are linked through their isolation, and the taxi driver and the suicide victim through the impossibility of living or making a living.

The foreground, as mentioned earlier, focuses on a couple, whose relationship seems to be tense. Their gaze never meets and they rarely exchange a word. The woman is wearing dark sunglasses, which is surprising for a rainy winter's night. Her right elbow rests on the table, her left on a book and a magazine, while the fingers of her two hands intercross into a fist, thereby creating a further barrier between her and the man, in addition to the sunglasses. The man has long hair, kept back by a ponytail. His thought bubble reveals that he is an artist in need of money who is secretly planning on leaving the woman and renting an atelier in an unnamed country for which he needs a visa. In his thoughts he complains about the woman not uttering a word and keeping her eyes on her watch instead. The woman also complains about the man being silent and she is aware of his money problems as well as of his desire to leave her. While he is wondering who could lend him money, she is telling herself that she should find the courage to fire him. She uses the word 'virer' that besides 'to fire' also means 'to get rid of somebody', 'to turn' and 'to swing'.[35] This suggests that the woman is his employer and that she is thinking of terminating her professional and romantic relationship with him. His economic dependence on her is emphasised by his secret wish that as a last favour the woman would accept to take care of his visa (p. 29). Furthermore, the definition of 'virer' as turn or swing could indicate that the woman is at a turning point in her life. According to Ahmed, 'the work of inhabiting space involves a dynamic negotiation between what is familiar and unfamiliar, such that it is still possible for the world to create new impressions, depending on which way we turn, which affects what is within reach'.[36] Her consideration of terminating something familiar to her and to expand what is within her reach likens her desire for freedom to her partner's wish to leave the country and stands for the possibility of agency to put an end to an unbearable situation.

The last panel featuring the couple shows a sticker on the man's coat saying 'Stinky Toys', a French punk-rock band formed in Paris in 1976. This sticker functions like the icon Rosie the Riveter in creating an attachment to a social group. In the case of the artist, it is the anti-establishment punk scene that highlights his marginalisation from mainstream society. Through his relation to the punk and art scene, the man is linked to the world of *Ah! Nana* and its abundant references to punk,[37] and to Montellier herself who had studied

Fine Arts for seven years before entering the comic industry. The emphasis on the printed press, the book and the magazine, could link the woman to the world of editing, maybe even to the editors of *Ah! Nana*. This suggests that Montellier is identifying with the male artist and his female partner alike, highlighting a universal fragility that denies the stereotypical representation of strong male figures, similarly to Montellier's critique of patriarchy in *Andy Gang*, and the need of solidarity between the sexes. In addition, *Game Over* complicates power relations as dynamic and interconnected with categories of class (the artist and the taxi driver both lack financial security and the artist adheres to the punk counterculture) and age (in the case of the taxi driver). As Kergoat has shown, it is important to analyse 'the interlocking of different systems of oppression from a dynamic understanding of power relations'.[38] In Michel Foucault's words, power does not follow a monolithic top-down structure, but consists of 'a subtle network of discourses, special knowledges, pleasures, and powers'.[39]

This is evident in the case of the woman in the foreground: she does not dare to separate professionally and romantically from the man who financially depends on her. While economically in a superior position to her male counterpart, her relationship demonstrates an investment and the consequences of failure if she gives up on it.[40] Her anxiety of separation might not be limited to a personal feeling, but also 'rehearse associations that are already in place';[41] namely, that a woman alone is not viable in a male-centred society. She could be cornered just like the woman in Montellier's previous drawing. At the same time, Montellier's portrayal of male vulnerability might incite male readers to empathise with the exploitation of women and to identify with a comparable status of fragility. Furthermore, her emphasis on co-substantiality of social relations could be an invitation to male and female readers to collaborate instead of opposing each other and hampering each other's possibilities and potentials, as was shown in her drawing accompanying Lenfant's article. In *Game Over*, Montellier strives to make visible what a capitalistic, heteronormative society is eager to hide: unconventional lifestyles and struggles, as exemplified by the artist, the taxi driver, la fille and the barmaid who are all marginalised from a consumeristic society. A comparative reading of *Game Over* with Montellier's illustration of Lenfant's article highlights the shortcoming and sometimes fatal exclusions caused by a capitalistic society and the importance of equal rights, for men and women. Furthermore, Montellier's illustration and comic strip in the last issue of *Ah! Nana* could encourage the readers to refuse 'the very requirement that we follow what is already given to us'[42] and choose instead a path less well trodden leading to gender equality and social justice.

Works Cited

Ahmed, Sara, 'Collective Feelings, or the Impressions left by Others', *Theory, Culture & Society*, 21/2 (2004), 25–42.

—— *Queer Phenomenology: Orientations, Objects, Others* (London and Durham NC: Duke University Press, 2006).

Alessandrini, Marjorie 'Images de Patti', *Ah! Nana*, 1, (1976), 22–3.

Brogniez, Laurence, 'Féminin singulier: les desseins du moi. Julie Doucet, Dominique Goblet', *Textyles*, 36/37 (2010), 117–38.

Collectif des créatrices de BD contre le sexism, *http://bdegalite.org/* (accessed 31 December 2021).

Chute, Hillary L., 'Introduction', in *Graphic Women: Life Narrative and Contemporary Comics* (New York: Columbia University Press, 2010), pp. 1–28.

Delphy, Christine, 'The main enemy', *Feminist Issues*, 1 (1980), 23–40.

Duchen, Claire, *Women's Rights and Women's Lives in France 1944–1968* (London and New York: Routledge, 2003).

Foucault, Michel, *The History of Sexuality, Volume 1: An Introduction*, Trans. Robert Hurley, (New York: Pantheon Books, 1978).

Galer, Elsa, and Danièle Kergoat, 'Consubstantialité vs intersectionnalité? À propos de l'imbrication des rapports sociaux', *Nouvelles pratiques sociales*, 26/2 (2014), 44–61.

Husson, Anne-Charlotte and Thomas Mathieu, *Le féminisme: en sept slogans et citations*, (Bruxelles: Le Lombard, 2016).

Kukkonen, Karin, *Studying Comics and Graphic Novels* (Oxford: Whiley-Blackwell, 2013).

Lane, Jeremy, and Sarah Waters (eds), 'Work in crisis: film, fiction and theory', *Modern and Contemporary France*, 3/26 (2018), 225–32.

MacLeod, Catriona '*Ah! Nana*: The Forgotten French Feminist Comic Magazine', *Comics Forum*, 16 September 2011, *https://comicsforum.org/2011/09/16/ah-nana-the-forgotten-french-feminist-comics-magazine-by-catriona-macleod* (accessed 31 December 2021).

Marjorie Alessandrini, 'Images de Patti', *Ah! Nana*, 1 (1976), 22–3.

Montellier, Chantal, 'Game Over (Un instant de pluie)', *Ah! Nana*, 9 (1978), 28–34.

Montellier, Chantal 'Andy Gang', *Ah! Nana*, 1 (1976), 17–22.

Picq, Françoise, *Libération des femmes: les Années-mouvement* (Paris: Seuil, 1993).

Robbins, Trina, 'The Two Glorious Years of *Ah! Nana*', 26 September 2011, *https://comicsforum.org/2011/09/26/the-two-glorious-years-of-ah-nana-by-trina-robbins* (accessed 31 December 2021).

Notes

1 The magazine was distributed in France, Belgium and the United States.
2 Edith Orial, 'Editorial', *Ah! Nana*, 1 (1976), 3.
3 Claire Duchen, *Women's Rights and Women's Lives in France 1944–1968* (London and New York: Routledge, 2003), p. 163.
4 Françoise Picq, *Libération des femmes: les Années-mouvement* (Paris: Seuil, 1993), pp. 14–15.
5 Edith Orial, 'Editorial', *Ah! Nana*, 2 (1977), 3.
6 Virginie Talet, 'Le magazine "*Ah! Nana*": une épopée féministe dans un monde d'hommes?', *Clio: Femmes, Genre, Histoire*, 24 (2006), 252–5.
7 For a more detailed account on the American feminist underground comics scene, see Hillary L. Chute, 'Introduction', in *Graphic Women. Life Narrative and Contemporary Comics* (New York: Columbia University Press, 2010), pp. 1–28.
8 Duchen, *Women's Rights*, p. 2.
9 Duchen, *Women's Rights*, p. 2.
10 Robbins, 'The Two Glorious Years of *Ah! Nana*', 26 September 2011, *https://comicsforum.org/2011/09/26/the-two-glorious-years-of-ah-nana-by-trina-robbins* (accessed 31 December 2021).
11 According to Karin Kukkonen, the pose of having one's hands in one's pockets 'signals being relaxed', Karin Kukkonen, *Studying Comics and Graphic Novels* (Oxford: Whiley-Blackwell, 2013), p. 8.
12 Sara Ahmed, 'Collective Feelings, or the Impressions left by Others', *Theory, Culture & Society*, 21/2 (2004), 32.
13 Ahmed, 'Collective Feelings', 26–7.
14 Ahmed, 'Collective Feelings', 30.
15 Sara Ahmed, *Queer Phenomenology: Orientations, Objects, Others* (London and Durham NC: Duke University Press, 2006), p. 62.
16 Laurence Brogniez, 'Féminin singulier: les desseins du moi. Julie Doucet, Dominique Goblet', *Textyles*, 36/37 (2010), 118.
17 Brogniez, 'Féminin singulier', 122 and 138. Despite this positive development, Brogniez emphasises the danger of creative limitations of female artists through diaries and autobiographies. More recently in 2015, 250 international female artists created the website *Collectif des créatrices de BD contre le sexisme* against sexual harassment, work inequality and creative confinement of female artists to so-called 'female genres', *http://bdegalite.org/* (accessed 31 December 2021).
18 In his films, including *Mon Oncle* (1958) and *Play Time* (1967), Jacques Tati criticises in a similar vein Americanisation and modernisation. See, for instance, Malcolm Turvey, *Play Time: Jacques Tati and Comedic Modernism* (New York: Columbia University Press, 2020).
19 Catriona MacLeod, '*Ah! Nana*: The Forgotten French Feminist Comic Magazine', *Comics Forum*, 16 September 2011, *https://comicsforum.org/2011/09/16/ah-nana-the-forgotten-french-feminist-comics-magazine-by-catriona-macleod* (accessed 31 December 2021).

20 Elsa Galer and Danièle Kergoat, 'Consubstantialité vs intersection-nalité? À propos de l'imbrication des rapports sociaux', *Nouvelles pratiques sociales*, 26/2, (2014), 47.

21 For instance, this strategy finally led in 1975 to the depenalisation of abortion in France through the publicisation of a rape case. In 1972, the sixteen-year-old Marie-Claire C. was raped and had to resort to a life-risking illegal abortion to terminate the ensuing pregnancy. In the famous juridical process of Bobigny, the feminist lawyer Gisèle Halimi successfully defended her and several other women who were put on trial for illegal abortion. Anne-Charlotte Husson and Thomas Mathieu, *Le féminisme: en sept slogans et citations* (Bruxelles: Le Lombard, 2016), pp. 32–7.

22 Ahmed, *Queer Phenomenology*, p. 9.

23 Jeremy Lane and Sarah Waters (eds), 'Work in crisis: film, fiction and theory', *Modern and Contemporary France*, 3/26 (2018), 229.

24 Christine Delphy, 'The main enemy', *Feminist Issues*, 1 (1980), 25. Originally published in a special double issue of the journal *Partisans*, entitled *Libération des femmes: année zéro*, 1970.

25 According to Delphy, 'the transformation of raw materials into consum-able products have been industrialized', such as dressmaking and the preparation of preserved food. Yet, there is no difference between these services and domestic services, with the exception that the former possesses an exchange value whereas the latter does not. Delphy, 'The main enemy', 30.

26 Chantal Montellier, 'Game Over (Un instant de pluie)', *Ah! Nana*, 9 (1978), 29.

27 Ahmed, *Queer Phenomenology*, p. 11.

28 Ahmed, *Queer Phenomenology*, p. 21.

29 Ahmed, *Queer Phenomenology*, p. 20.

30 Ahmed, *Queer Phenomenology*, p. 57.

31 Montellier, 'Game Over (Un instant de pluie)', 32.

32 Picq, *Libération des femmes*, p. 11.

33 Delphy, 'The main enemy', 36, 38.

34 Ahmed, *Queer Phenomenology*, p. 37.

35 Montellier, 'Game Over (Un instant de pluie)', 31.

36 Ahmed, *Queer Phenomenology*, pp. 7–8.

37 For instance, in volume 1 *Ah! Nana* journalist Marjorie Allesandrini hailed punk icon Patti Smith for defying conventional representations of femininity. Marjorie Alessandrini, 'Images de Patti', *Ah! Nana*, 1 (1976), 22–3.

38 Kergoat, 'Consubstantialité vs intersectionnalité?', 45.

39 Michel Foucault, *The History of Sexuality, Volume 1: An Introduction*, Trans. Robert Hurley, (New York: Pantheon Books, 1978), p. 72.

40 Ahmed, *Queer Phenomenology*, p. 18.

41 Ahmed, 'Collective Feelings', 39.

42 Ahmed, *Queer Phenomenology*, p. 21.

Chapter 15
'Putting Us Back in Our Place': #MeToo, Women and the Literary/Cultural Establishment

MERCÉDÈS BAILLARGEON

With the publication of *Le Consentement* ('*Consent*') in January 2020, Vanessa Springora blew the lid off of the literary world's culture of silence around sexual abuse and assault. In her explosive memoir, Springora recounts the now infamous tale of her relationship with the French writer Gabriel Matzneff, fifty at the time, when she was just fourteen. According to Homayra Sellier, an advocate for child victims of sexual violence, '[t]his is a very important book. It's France's #MeToo moment'.[1] Unlike Harvey Weinstein or Jeffrey Epstein, Matzneff's actions were not just quietly tolerated; they were at the heart of his writing. For decades, he received literary accolades and, in November 2019, Gallimard, one of France's most esteemed publishers, published his new book. Prominent essayists, critics and politicians likened his explicit paedophilia to 'unrepentant seduction' and 'libertinism' – a culture of indulgent pleasures considered central to French identity and sexual freedom.[2] In 1977, some of France's most prominent cultural figures, including Jean-Paul Sartre and Simone de Beauvoir, future Foreign Minister Bernard Kouchner and dozens of others, joined Matzneff in signing a petition, published in *Le Monde*, that defended three men who were detained ahead of their trial for sexual activity with minors.[3] In 1990, Matzneff was confronted by Québec writer Denise Bombardier on the French literary show *Apostrophes*, who said that, if Matzneff were an anonymous employee at a regular workplace, he would be held accountable for the actions that he describes in his books.[4] At the time, people defended Matzneff and Bombardier was ridiculed. As recently as 2013, Matzneff was still taken care of by his connections within the literary elite and, after two previous failed attempts, he was finally awarded the Prix Renaudot essai. Now, the elites who long welcomed him into their exclusive circles are distancing themselves as the eighty-four-year-old author is now being charged with promoting the sexual abuse of children.[5]

Beyond the notion of consent, Springora's book uncovers a culture of promiscuity and grooming, made partly possible by an anti-conformist and hedonistic background that defines the way (some, mostly male) authors and cultural figures define themselves against society's norms and code of conduct, and more specifically on the sexual level. Taking the controversy of the #MeToo movement in France as its backdrop, and the publication of *Consent* as its starting point, this chapter will identify and examine the kind of sexual culture that exists in the literary, cultural and publishing worlds. It appears as though the time was ripe for Vanessa Springora's testimony, which touched on many questions including the separation of the work and the artist while responding to a writer on the same ground as him, with his own weapon. Although this chapter discusses sexual abuse and paedophilia within literary and cultural establishment, the rise of the #MeToo movement in France, as well as the effects of the publication of a book such as *Consent* in the French cultural landscape, it is necessary not to forget that art itself (writing, acting, painting, etc.) is, in fact, labour (i.e., work for compensation) and should be approached as such; it is important not to fall into the belief of the 'inspired artist' or the 'pseudo-genius'. This chapter, among the many questions it will try to answer, will be interested in how this false belief, or 'aura' of the artist, impacts women and how it leads to a toxic sexual culture. More specifically, I will first situate the Matzneff scandal and the publication of *Consent* in the context of the #MeToo movement and of feminism's fourth wave in order to better understand its reception; second, I will look at Delvaux's concept of the 'boys' club' as a way to better understand the way that the French cultural elite works as a network and how this can create a breeding ground for toxic masculinity to develop; and finally, through Geneviève Fraisse's examination of consent, I will look at the literary itself, as a site of disempowerment for Matzneff's victims, but also a way for Springora to reclaim her own narrative. The question of power will also traverse this analysis.

Situating the Matzneff Scandal in the Context of Fourth-Wave Feminism and #MeToo

Marked by a renewed interest in 'everyday sexism', to borrow Laura Bates' expression,[6] feminism's 'fourth wave' emerged in the early 2010s and represents:

> an era of feminist thinkers, writers, artists, and activists who have embraced inclusionary and pragmatic approaches to theory – including social media activism – and whose works especially signal a necessary vigilance that must be maintained in the wake of ongoing misogyny, ageism, racism, sexism, ableism, and other forms of exclusion.[7]

Questions at the heart of fourth-wave feminism include, but are not limited to, street and workplace harassment, sexual assault on college campuses, and rape culture more generally. This also led to the emergence of the #MeToo movement, which encourages people to share their experiences of sexual harassment and assault. The explosion of the hashtag #MeToo in the English-speaking world, and its variations elsewhere (#BalanceTonPorc in France), point to a desire to break the silence and speak up about past abuse, and to reclaim one's own narrative. As Tarana Burke, who first used the hashtag in 2006, explained, her objective was to empower women, especially young and vulnerable women, through strength in numbers, by visibly demonstrating how many women have survived sexual assault and harassment.[8] #MeToo, moreover, puts the spotlight on a toxic culture in which some powerful men use their power and influence to either force themselves onto, coerce or otherwise sexually intimidate or harass women into sexual relations or assault.

The effects and effectiveness of the #MeToo movement are still up for debate: some call it a 'witch hunt', others refer to it as part of a larger, problematic 'cancel culture', while others again consider it to be an unfair 'trial of public opinion' with its main goal to slander, in the public eye, some powerful men without having to meet the burden of proof that filing a police report and going to court would require. In France, #MeToo and #BalanceTonPorc have been welcomed with mixed feelings and have generated considerable commentary in the media and online. In 2019, the journalist Sandra Muller – who instigated the hashtag #BalanceTonPorc, which, much like #TimesUp in the English-speaking world, incited women to divulge details of sexual harassment in the workplace as well as the identity of the alleged perpetrator – was found guilty of defamation and sentenced to pay €15,000 to her ex-boss Eric Brion.[9] In January 2018, a group of French women, including Catherine Deneuve, Catherine Millet and Catherine Robbe-Grillet, signed an open-letter in *Le Monde*, decrying a new puritanical sexual climate, imported from the United States, which – according to them – threatens the French art of seduction. They claim, 'Nous défendons une liberté d'importuner, indispensable à la liberté sexuelle', meaning that they consider men pestering women, and women feeling annoyed by it, as a justifiable part of sexual freedom and decry that the movement has led to the public indictments in the press and on social networks of individuals without them going on trial.[10] The reception of #MeToo in France has been far different from that in any other country. As the feminist blogger Marion Seclin noticed, many of these cultural beliefs seem intractable, deeply embedded within the French collective psyche.[11] For Karina Piser, '[t]he country claims to champion gender equality and sexual freedom – as long as men control the narrative'.[12] Moreover, France's reaction to #MeToo has also produced much commentary coming from abroad where many English-speaking newspapers and web publications have seemingly been puzzled by the difficulty of the movement to take root in France.

The Matzneff scandal erupted in France concurrently with a change in the tide of public opinion regarding sexual harassment and, more specifically, regarding powerful men taking advantage of their position to abuse underage girls. November 2019 marked a major turning point in the #MeToo movement in France when Mediapart published an investigation into actress Adèle Haenel's complaint against director Christophe Ruggia, whom she accuses of sexually harassing and assaulting her when she was between twelve and fifteen years old.[13] Furthermore, Haenel, alongside director Céline Sciamma and actress Aïssa Maïga, created an uproar when they left the forty-fifth César ceremony, in February 2020, following the award of the César for best director to Roman Polanski, who is the subject of an open court case for drugging and raping a thirteen-year-old girl in the United States in the late 1970s.[14] This galvanised the division within French cinema about the status granted to Polanski, and more generally about the fight against sexual violence, bringing to the forefront the complicated question of separation between artist and work – a troubling question often evoked in discussions regarding *Consent* and the Matzneff scandal, as well as the literary establishment itself.

France's Literary Elites, Toxic Masculinity and the 'Boys' Club'

As many readers and critics have pointed out, it is close to impossible not to wonder how Matzneff was able to get away with his paedophilic behaviour for so long?[15] When received at *Apostrophes*, in 1990, Pivot introduced Matzneff as a true sex-education teacher who loved giving private lessons to his students.[16] Guests laughed as if nothing was wrong, well-aware of both Matzneff's works and of his reputation. What seems to provoke outrage though, in Vanessa Springora's account in *Consent*, is not so much the divulgation of Matzneff's behaviour since it was already known, but the indifference, both within her family and in the literary world, with their affair. How was he not considered a pariah in the literary world, but instead was protected, defended and even celebrated for his 'art of seduction'?

As Norimitsu Onishi's and Constant Méheut's article, published in *The New York Times*, highlights, for 'a nation that places literature at the heart of its sense of grandeur and global standing', France's literary institutions, including the close ties between publishers, critics and jurors for prestigious literary prizes, largely lack diversity of representation and consist mostly of a 'clubby' Parisian elite that tends to celebrate and protect the members of its own inner circle.[17] Not unlike other cultural institutions (e.g., the film industry), the literary world appears to be a 'boys' club', to borrow Martine Delvaux's expression. According to her, the boys' club works as a network of exchange, as an apparatus in a Foucauldian perspective, seen as a network or an organisation typically controlled by a group of older and wealthy men who use their political power for their own benefit, most often indirectly, as a way to preserve the elites and look after 'their own'.[18] It is thus unsurprising that literary prizes are set up in a way in which favours seem to be exchanged; publishers 'congratulate' their own writers, writers favour books from their own publishers, and so on.[19] These are all ways of upholding the status quo, and for men in power to defend things as 'normal' while maintaining their power. Moreover, they largely have control of the narrative of what's going on inside their walls as another way of holding on to control and power. In this context, it is thus unsurprising to hear author Frédéric Beigbeder, who has served as a Renaudot juror since 2011, explain that the 2013 prize was awarded to Matzneff as a way of 'cheering up' an 'old friend,' who was 'sick and broke' at the time. Beigbeder also derides suggestions that the Renaudot, and French literary prizes in general, need to be overhauled 'as representing an American-influenced desire for "purity" and "perfection"'.[20] Moreover, influential men are able to keep their behaviour outside the realm of prosecution by having their victims and entourage keep quiet and, in some cases, even defend them. They also largely have control of the narrative of what's going on inside their walls, which is yet another way of holding on to control and power.

As an op-ed (opinion piece) recently published in the Montréal-based newspaper *Le Devoir* pointed out, we must recognise that sexual violence is widespread, protean, trivialised and tacitly accepted in the literary world. Signed by more than 150 women related to the literary world, the open letter, entitled 'La culture du silence au sein du milieu littéraire doit cesser' ('The culture of silence within the literary world must end)', points the finger at patriarchal oppression and its many myths, which serve to banalise different forms of sexual violence. Much like in Hollywood, the literary world is precarious and people in power (cultural attachés, editors, other writers, etc.) often have the prestige and the means to exert considerable influence on one's literary career. This kind of environment fosters a toxic and unhealthy climate in which women are made to be fearful and toxic masculinity can flourish.[21] It also appears to be intrinsically tied to the boys' club, which strives to keep power between men while excluding women from places of power. Breaking the code of silence that reigns within the literary world to speak up against one of its perpetrators can be tantamount to putting an end to one's literary career since so much depends on relationships and who you know.

The co-signers of the op-ed published in *Le Devoir* denounce the supposed mystique of the 'poète maudit' ('damned poet'), to whom everything is forgiven in advance because of his pseudo-genius or his notoriety, and identify it as one of the main reasons behind the culture of silence and of the banalisation that prevails around sexual violence in the literary world. Similarly, the film critic Iris Brey argues that the separation of the artist and his work, which presents itself in a very specific way in the French context, is often used to gloss over allegations of sexual assault against artists such as Polanski, but also Matzneff.[22] Indeed, in France, it is common to hear that one cannot judge an artist's work based on the actions of the artist itself. As Jess McHugh writes in *The Guardian*, 'there is a tradition in the French public and press alike to ignore – or briefly mock and then ignore – the checkered personal lives of powerful men'.[23] Though initially understood as a way to protect the artist's freedom, primarily from legal consequences, it appears that 'la théorie de l'art pour l'art' ('art for art's sake') can also be used as a way to protect powerful men from the consequences of their actions. Moreover, it appears as though some of these powerful men not only use their aura, influence or notoriety as leverage to impose themselves, intimidate their victims or, in cases like Vanessa Springora's, to seduce them, they also use their position as a shield, their art seemingly being more valuable and impactful than the abuse they could have imposed to their victim:

> Il faut croire que l'artiste appartient à une caste à part, qu'il est un être aux vertus supérieures auquel nous offrons un mandat de toute-puissance, sans autre contrepartie que la production d'une œuvre originale et subversive ... Tout autre individu, qui publierait par exemple sur les réseaux sociaux la description de ses ébats avec un adolescent philippin ou se vanterait de sa collection de maîtresses de quatorze ans, aurait affaire à la justice et serait immédiatement considéré comme un criminel. En dehors des artistes, il n'y a guère que chez les prêtres qu'on ait assisté à une telle impunité. La littérature excuse-t-elle tout?[24]

> It seems that an artist is of a separate caste, a being with superior virtues granted the ultimate authorisation, in return for which he is required only to create an original and subversive piece of work ... Were any other person to publish on social media a description of having sex with a child in the Philippines or brag about his collection of fourteen-year-old mistresses, he would find himself dealing with the police and be instantly considered a criminal. Apart from artists, we have witnessed only Catholic priests being bestowed with such a level of impunity. Does literature really excuse everything?[25]

As Springora herself points out in *Consent*, despite the scandalousness of Matzneff's behaviour, their relationship was accepted and
even admired in the community of artists and intellectuals that her
and her mother inhabited and, to them, artists existed outside the
social norms that governed other people's – 'regular people's' – lives
(pp. 66; 53). From that perspective, as the op-ed in *Le Devoir* pointed
out, it appears as though the literary world will often use values such
as freedom, transgression, open-mindedness and anti-conformism –
all considered forms of liberation – to gloss over, legitimise and
facilitate abusive behaviour. [26]According to the sociologist Pierre
Verdrager, the culture of transgression that reigns within the French
intelligentsia is an artefact of 1968, a time during which transgression was seen as the equivalent to liberation;[27] and, if this false
equivalency has gone as widely accepted up until now, the reckoning
brought upon by the #MeToo movement in France is definitely
questioning this belief. Verdrager explains how, in the context of the
sexual liberation of the 1960s and 1970s, paedophilia became the
ultimate taboo to transgress.[28] This, to him, explains the silence, and
even widespread acceptance of Matzneff's relationships with
underage girls. Thus, what the publication of *Consent* uncovers is
also a misogynistic sexual culture that is justified as being supposedly
countercultural;[29] the rules of the game are written by men for their
own pleasure; and to be part of the 'club' women are taunted and
gaslighted, pushed to prove how 'truly free' and how 'truly liberated'
they really are, often by agreeing to sexual encounters that they
would have otherwise refused. Thus, it appears that the global movement caused by #MeToo could mark the end to the sacro-sanctity of
the artist, who can do no wrong, and help reconsider writing and art
as another form of labour, subject to the same kinds of law as any
other workplace.

Consent: the Power of the Object Itself

This brings us to the book *Consent* itself, as an object that exists
within the current cultural and political zeitgeist brought about by
the #MeToo movement. An object that also has power, in and of
itself. With her book, Springora uncovers a culture of promiscuity
and grooming, made partly possible by an anti-conformist and
hedonistic perspective, a countercultural posture that often defines
the way artists, writers and cultural figures see themselves, and adds

to the myth of the 'enlightened' artist. As Luc Le Vaillant describes it in *Libération*, the title of the book is a red herring to say the opposite;[30] this is also addressed by Springora: 'Comment admettre qu'on a été abusée quand on ne peut nier avoir été consentante? Quand, en l'occurrence, on a ressenti du désir pour cet adulte qui s'est empressé d'en profiter?' (p. 163) ('How is it possible to acknowledge having been abused when it's impossible to deny having consented, having felt desire, for the very adult who was so eager to take advantage of you?' (p. 145)). Springora depicts a process of relentless psychic manipulation and the frightening ambiguity in which the consenting victim, feeling in love, is placed. On the set of *La Grande Librairie*, Springora discusses the notion of consent, underscoring how you must be free in your choices, but you also have to be equal in order to be able to give valid consent.[31] As French philosopher Geneviève Fraisse points out in her book *Du Consentement*, the question of consent is far more complicated than meets the eye. If the notion seemingly appears with Pascal in the seventeenth century, alongside the idea of the Cartesian subject ('C'est le consentement de vous à vous-même et la voix constante de votre raison, et non des autres qui vous doit faire croire', ('It is consent with yourself, and with your own voice of reason, and not that of others, which you must believe')), it also exists alongside logics of revolt, of liberation and of transgression at the heart of the sexual liberation of the 1960s and 1970s. Fraisse raises the question that, in order to be granted, consent must be given freely, without constraint; and given in light of all information available.[32] Yet, she also mentions the age-old proverb, 'qui ne dit mot consent' ('silence is consent'), as well as the feminist slogan, 'quand une femme dit non, c'est non' (p. 27) ('when a woman says no, it means no'). Moreover, consent necessarily implies a relationship between at least two individuals and this relationship is not always equal; as Fraisse points out, referencing French feminist Nicole-Claude Mathieu, to give in is not necessarily the same as to consent.[33] Thus, consent can only be given in an egalitarian context, which was clearly not the case for Springora with Matzneff given their age and power difference. Consent thus being a fraught concept to some degree, it is unsurprising then that victims resist coming forward:

> Ce silence semble corroborer les dires de G., prouver qu'aucune adolescente n'a jamais eu à se plaindre de l'avoir rencontré ... Toute l'ambiguïté de se sentir complice de cet amour qu'on a

forcément ressenti, de cette attirance qu'on a soi-même suscitée, nous lie les mains plus encore que les quelques adeptes qui restent à G. dans le milieu littéraire. En jetant son dévolu sur des jeunes filles solitaires, vulnérables, aux parents dépassés ou démissionnaires, G. savait pertinemment qu'elles ne menaceraient jamais sa réputation. Et qui ne dit mot *consent*. (p. 203)

The silence apparently corroborates what G. has always claimed, offering proof that no teenage girl has ever had reason to complain of having been in a relationship with him ... It is hard to shake the feeling of self-doubt, the sense of being complicit in a love that one felt oneself, in the attraction that we once aroused in him; this is what held us back, even more than the few fans that G. still has in the Parisian literary world. By setting his sights on young, lonely, vulnerable girls, whose parents either couldn't cope or were actively negligent, G. knew that they would never threaten his reputation. And silence means consent. (pp. 183–4)

With this passage almost at the end of the book, Springora finishes depicting Matzneff as a predator who, as he described in *Les moins de seize ans*, which appears almost as a kind of 'how to' manual for paedophiles, preys on the most vulnerable girls, the ones that it would be easiest to take advantage of, and who would almost unequivocally remain silent, blaming themselves for their complicity.

Much like #MeToo's objective to give women the power to reclaim their own narrative by denouncing their assailant, the book also exists as a way for Springora to take back her own narrative after having been dispossessed of it so many times by Matzneff, as he did for the many other boys and girls he seduced, every time she saw herself reappear in a new book that he had just published. Indeed, Matzneff's predatory behaviour is double: not only is he a sexual predator, but he is also a literary predator, as Chantal Guy puts it.[34] Not only did he dispossess his victims of their sexuality from a very young age – something he misrepresented as a gift or initiation – but he continued to dispossess them by incorporating his sexual 'exploits' in his books. Matzneff would even go as far as including in their entirety the letters that he and his victims had exchanged, thus exploiting these young victims' words and, in a twisted way, turning their own words against them for his own literary gain. Springora herself is constantly reinvented; Vanessa S. or 'little V.': 'Cette initiale résume désormais mon identité. J'aurai quatorze ans pour la vie. C'est écrit' (p. 123) ('my initial, V., which encapsulated my identity from then on' (p. 167)). Moreover, when she starts questioning him, Matzneff turns her into a horrible character:

> Par la force de l'écrit, il fait de la 'petite V.' une fille instable rongée par la jalousie, raconte ce qui lui chante. Je ne suis maintenant plus qu'un personnage en sursis, comme les filles précédentes, qu'il ne tardera pas à gommer des pages de son maudit journal. Pour ses lecteurs, ce ne sont que des mots, de la littérature. Pour moi, c'est le début d'un effondrement. (pp. 134–5)

> With the power of the written word, he turned his 'little V.' into an unstable teenage girl eaten up with jealousy. He said whatever he wanted; I was just a character now, living on borrowed time, like every other girl who'd come before me. It wouldn't be long before he erased me completely from the pages of his wretched diary. For his readers, it was merely a story, words. For me, it was the beginning of a breakdown. (p. 117)

In *Consent*, he is G.M., 'à son tour l'écrivain est réduit à une projection littéraire, enfermée par deux petites lettres' ('reduced to a literary projection, the prisoner of two little letters'),[35] turned into the object of Springora's investigation into the causes that brought her to living out this traumatising experience; but also an object in relation to Springora herself who, as a writer, asserts a strong 'je' ('I') within her text, taking the pen to tell her own story. This is precisely the goal that Springora sets out in her prologue to *Consent*: 'Depuis tant d'années, je tourne en rond dans ma cage, mes rêves sont peuplés de meurtre et de vengeance. Jusqu'au jour où la solution se présente enfin, là, sous mes yeux, comme une évidence: prendre le chasseur à son propre piège, l'enfermer dans un livre' (p. 10) ('For many years I paced around my cage, my dreams filled with murder and revenge. Until the day when the solution finally presented itself to me, like something that was completely obvious: Why not ensnare the hunter in his own trap, ambush him within the pages of a book?' (p. viii)). As she reflects, nearing the end of her book, on her literary project, she writes:

> Pour me donner du courage, j'ai fini par m'accrocher à ces arguments: si je voulais étancher une bonne fois pour toutes ma colère et me réapproprier ce chapitre de mon existence, écrire était sans doute le meilleur remède … C'est l'homme que j'aime qui m'en a finalement convaincue. Parce qu'écrire, c'était redevenir le sujet de ma propre histoire. Une histoire qui m'avait été confisquée depuis trop longtemps. (p. 202)

> To give myself courage, I clung to this argument: if I wanted to
> assuage my fury once and for all, and reclaim this chapter of my
> life, writing was without a doubt the best way to do it ... [W]riting
> meant becoming once more the subject of my own story. A story
> that had been denied me for too long. (p. 183)

These words seem to echo the specific place that not only women
have occupied, but all dominated people, have occupied in history.
Through repeated humiliation and dispossession of her narrative,
Matzneff was trying to remind Springora of 'who's boss' – he was the
writer, the person of standing and influence, not her. As Sandra
Muller says, the #MeToo movement tries to remind us that men in
power have long used that position to abuse women who were subor-
dinated to them. Moreover, in their capacity to control the narrative,
many powerful men (and women, serving as accomplices) portray
#MeToo as a witch hunt; doing so, they essentially present aggressors
as victims.

As the writer Virginie Despentes puts it in an op-ed reacting to
Polanski's win at the Césars, it seems as though the powerful demand
both constant and unequivocal respect as well as the silence of their
victims to uphold the old sexual order: 'quand Adèle Haenel s'est
levée, c'était le sacrilège en marche. Une employée récidiviste, qui
ne se force pas à sourire quand on l'éclabousse en public, qui ne se
force pas à applaudir au spectacle de sa propre humiliation' ('what a
sacrilege it was when Adèle Haenel stood up. A disgruntled
employee, repeat offender, who does not force herself to smile when
taunted in public, who does not force herself to applaud at the spectacle of her own humiliation').[36] Writing about Polanski's win at the
Césars, queer philosopher Paul B. Preciado reflects on the ceremony as a political ritual, a 'social paralanguage', to borrow
Lévi-Strauss' expression, that serves to reassert the power of the
heteropatriarchy, defined by 'le déni de la souveraineté sexuelle et
politique des femmes hors de la relation hétérosexuelle et du plaisir
masculin' ('the denial of the sexual and political sovereignty of
women outside heterosexual relationships and of male pleasure').[37]
Heteropatriarchy being put into question by different social movements, including #MeToo, Haenel's testimony, as well as the
publication of *Consent*, it needs to constantly reaffirm itself in order
to maintain its power. Thus, if the boys' club is defined by a hatred of
women, as Delvaux writes, why would men in power oppose the
abuse of women and children then? This reversal of victimisation

appears as another form of gaslighting, a kind of manipulation that forces someone to question their thoughts, memories and the events occurring around them, hence leaving a person or group pathologically dependent on the gasligther for their thoughts and feelings.[38] All these things serve them, directly and indirectly, by keeping women 'in their place'.

Finally, I would like to reflect on the name that we have been giving this affair, 'the Matzneff scandal' or 'l'affaire Matzneff' in French. Certainly, Matzneff's notoriety as a well-known literary figure into 1970s and 1980s has something to do with the 'scandalousness' of this affair, but it is interesting to note that he had been largely forgotten since and that, only now, in the wake of this scandal, are we taking back out terms like 'un grand écrivain' ('a great writer') to speak of him; propping up, once again, the myth of the artist and thus reasserting his (now disgraced) belonging to the dominating class of the literary French elite. According to the Merriam-Webster dictionary, the simple definition of 'scandal' is: 'a circumstance or action that offends propriety or established moral conceptions or disgraces those associated with it ... loss of or damage to reputation caused by actual or apparent violation of morality or propriety ... indignation, chagrin, or bewilderment brought about by a flagrant violation of morality, propriety, or religious opinion.'[39] That a great writer can do harm, as Springora herself points out in her book, certainly does that. But, looking at the definition of François Laplantine, in *De tout petits liens*, it seems that scandal goes one step further; according to Laplantine, true scandal appears when one brings to light how the ruling class is breaking its own rules and denounces the hypocrisy of this class, which, to keep its power and maintain its domination, hides its own crimes, since they precisely hold the power to punish or not to punish an individual.[40] As such, if Springora's book has caused such a controversy, it appears as though it is not so much because it exposes Matzneff's paedophilia, but because she dares to break the silence, the omertà that prevails within the literary world, certainly, but more so within spheres of power, where men maintain their 'boys' club'. Feminism's fourth wave, with the global #MeToo movement that followed, set the stage for the publication, but even more so, for the reception of Vanessa Springora's *Consent.*

Up until now, power, sex and gender had been intertwined in the literary world, where men held the balance of power. Against the 'boys' club', women are now able to organise in a transnational network of feminist solidarities capable of speaking up against their aggressors and of saying 'me too', thanks to the possibilities offered by social media and the internet. 'Ce qui a changé aujourd'hui, et dont se plaignent, en fustigeant le puritanisme ambiant, des types comme lui et ses défenseurs, c'est qu'après la libération des mœurs, la parole des victimes, elle aussi, soit en train de se libérer' (pp. 203–4) ('What has changed today – something that men like he and his defenders complain about constantly, excoriating the general atmosphere of puritanism – is that following the sexual revolution, it is now, at last, the turn of the victims to speak out' (p. 184)), writes Springora in *Consent*. But we must also be careful. From the neoliberal logic of hashtags, performative activism and retweeting, there is a key element to keep in mind if we want to continue the struggle: the mixed reception of #MeToo and #BalanceTonPorc reveals much about France's contradictions as well as its conservatism when it comes to women's emancipation. As Sandra Muller explains, #MeToo has largely been criticised as a man-hating crusade led by 'radical feminists' importing American puritanism into 'le pays de la galanterie' ('the country of seduction').[41] Holding up the old scarecrow of American puritanism against the #MeToo movement and accusing it of being a form of cultural imperialism against French exceptionalism only allows for France's 'old order' to be defended. As Despentes explains in her op-ed, this is not a war between men and women, it is a war between those who dominate and those who are dominated, those who benefit from a particular social and sexual order and who intend to silence those who threaten this said order.[42] Whether it is the promotion of sexual transgression and anti-conformism, the defence of 'la liberté d'importuner' ('the freedom to pester'), to use Deneuve's op-ed's expression, or the aura that French culture cultivates around its artist's as 'inspired' or pseudo-geniuses; all these elements have the effect of maintaining, justifying and legitimising unequal relationships between the sexes. Moreover, the invisibility of Black and brown women in the #BalanceTonPorc movement in France adds yet another layer of silencing. In doing so, the ruling class retains its power by abusing others. So, it seems that, despite its best intentions, the ideology of 1968 and its figures have themselves become the guardians of elitist and bourgeois values.

Works Cited

'1990: Gabriel Matzneff face à Denise Bombardier dans "Apostrophes"', *Archives INA*, 26 December 2019, *www.youtube.com/watch?v=H0LQiv7x4xs* (accessed 9 December 2021).

Breeden, Aurélien, 'French #MeToo Movement's Founder Loses Defamation Case', *New York Times*, 25 September 2019, *www.nytimes.com/2019/09/25/world/europe/france-sandra-muller-verdict.html* (accessed 9 December 2021).

Brey, Iris, 'Polanski: l'impossible séparation entre l'homme et l'artiste', *Mediapart*, 13 November 2019, *www.mediapart.fr/journal/france/131119/polanski-l-impossible-separation-entre-l-homme-et-l-artiste?onglet=full* (accessed 9 December 2021).

Busnel, François, 'Autour de Vanessa Springora', *La Grande Librairie*, France TV, 15 January 2020, *www.france.tv/france-5/la-grande-librairie/la-grande-librairie-saison-12/1143743-la-grande-librairie.html* (accessed 9 December 2021).

Chiche, Sarah, *et al.*, 'Nous défendons une liberté d'importuner, indispensable à la liberté sexuelle', *Le Monde*, 9 January 2018, *www.lemonde.fr/idees/article/2018/01/09/nous-defendons-une-liberte-d-importuner-indispensable-a-la-liberte-sexuelle_5239134_3232.html?_ga=2.222423256.298773082.1608237014-139048590.1608237013* (accessed 9 December 2021).

Delvaux, Martine, *Le Boys Club* (Montreal QC: Remue-ménage, 2019).

Despentes, Virginie, 'Césars: "Désormais on se lève et on se barre"', *Libération*, 1 March 2020, *www.liberation.fr/debats/2020/03/01/cesars-desormais-on-se-leve-et-on-se-barre_1780212* (accessed 9 December 2021).

Desta, Yohana, 'Can the César Awards Ever Recover from Roman Polanski Catastrophe?', *Vanity Fair*, 2 March 2020, *www.vanityfair.com/hollywood/2020/03/cesar-awards-adele-haenel-roman-polanski* (accessed 9 December 2021).

Douaphars, Hélène, '#MeToo? The French Resistance', *BBC World News*, 5 April 2019, *www.youtube.com/watch?v=JHRPCBXJSng* (accessed 9 December 2021).

Erner, Guillaume, 'Vanessa Springora: Matzneff "était bien ce qu'on apprend à redouter dès l'enfance: un ogre"', *L'Invité des matins*, France Culture, 3 January 2020, *www.youtube.com/watch?v=M5vh4aTl8XE* (accessed 9 December 2021).

Fraisse, Geneviève, *Du Consentement* (Paris: Seuil, 2007).

'Gaslighting', *Healthline*, *www.healthline.com/health/gaslighting#:~:text=Gaslighting%20is%20a%20form%20of,they%20question%20their%20own%20sanity* (accessed 9 December 2021).

Gill, Gurvinder, and Imran Rahman-Jones, 'Me Too founder Tarana Burke: Movement is not over', 9 July 2020, *www.bbc.com/news/newsbeat-53269751* (accessed 9 December 2021).

Guy, Chantal, 'Vanessa Springora, Le Consentement et l'influence d'un livre', *La Presse*, 5 February 2020, *www.lapresse.ca/arts/litterature/2020-02-05/vanessa-springora-le-consentement-et-l-influence-d-un-livre* (accessed 9 December 2021).

'La culture du silence au sein du milieu littéraire doit cesser', *Le Devoir*, 16 July 2020, *www.ledevoir.com/opinion/libre-opinion/582503/la-culture-du-silence-au-sein-du-milieu-litteraire-doit-cesser* (accessed 9 December 2021).

Laplantine, François, *De tout petits liens* (Paris: Mille et une nuits, 2003).

Leicester, John, 'France's #MeToo: Book on child-sex writer prompts outcry', *AP News*, 12 January 2020, *https://apnews.com/article/aeea1b-d377966a3eae3ed1f887a8a08f* (accessed 9 December 2021).

Le Vaillant, Luc, '"Le consentement" sans concession de Vanessa Springora', *Libération*, 29 December 2019, *https://next.liberation.fr/livres/2019/12/29/le-consentement-sans-concession-de-vanessa-springora_1771343* (accessed 9 December 2021).

Marcotte, Amanda, 'Overcompensation Nation: It's time to admit that toxic masculinity drives gun violence', *Salon*, 13 June 2016, *www.salon.com/2016/06/13/overcompensation_nation_its_time_to_admit_that_toxic_masculinity_drives_gun_violence/* (accessed 9 December 2021).

Marcovich, Malka, *L'Autre héritage de 68: La face cachée de la révolution sexuelle* (Paris: Albin Michel, 2018).

Mathieu, Nicole-Claude, *L'anatomie politique: Catégorisations et idéologies du sexe* (Paris: Côté-femmes, 1991).

McHugh, Jess, 'The Polanski protests have brought France's #MeToo reckoning a step closer', *Guardian*, 8 March 2020, *www.theguardian.com/commentisfree/2020/mar/08/roman-polanski-metoo-france* (accessed 9 December 2021).

Piser, Karina, 'France could finally be on the brink of a #MeToo reckoning', *Washington Post*, 13 February 2020, *www.washingtonpost.com/opinions/2020/02/13/france-could-finally-be-brink-metoo-reckoning/* (accessed 9 December 2021).

Preciado, Paul B., 'L'ancienne académie en feu', *Libération*, 1 March 2020, *www.liberation.fr/debats/2020/03/01/l-ancienne-academie-en-feu_1780215* (accessed 9 December 2021).

Onishi, Norimitsu, 'A Pedophile Writer is on Trial. So Are the French Elites', *New York Times*, 11 February 2020, *www.nytimes.com/2020/02/11/world/europe/gabriel-matzneff-pedophilia-france.html* (accessed 9 December 2021).

Onishi, Norimitsu, and Constant Méheut, 'Pedophile Scandal Can't Crack the Closed Circles of Literary France', *New York Times*, 28 November 2020, *www.nytimes.com/2020/11/28/world/europe/france-literary-prizes-matzneff.html* (accessed 9 December 2021).

'Scandal', *Merriam-Webster.com Dictionary*, Merriam-Webster, *www.merriam-webster.com/dictionary/scandal* (accessed 9 December 2021).

Schaal, Michèle and Adrienne Angelo, 'Editors' introduction: Alive and Kicking: French and Francophone Feminisms Now', *French Cultural Studies*, 31/4 (2020), 259–74.

Springora, Vanessa, *Le Consentement* (Paris: Grasset, 2020).

—— *Consent*, trans. Natasha Lehrer (New York: HarperCollins, 2021).

Talabot, Jean, and Alice Develey, 'Affaire Matzneff: que découvre-t-on dans *Le Consentement* de Vanessa Springora?', *Le Figaro*, 31 December 2019, *www.lefigaro.fr/livres/affaire-matzneff-que-decouvre-t-on-dans-le-consentement-de-vanessa-springora-20191231* (accessed 9 December 2021).

The Everyday Sexism Project, www.everydaysexism.com (accessed 9 December 2021).

Turchi, Marine, 'Une enquête singulière', *Mediapart*, 3 November 2019, *https://blogs.mediapart.fr/marine-turchi/blog/031119/une-enquete-singuliere* (accessed 9 December 2021).

Vaton, Marie, 'Sandra Muller: "La France n'a rien compris à #MeToo"', *Nouvel Observateur*, 8 October 2018, *www.nouvelobs.com/rue89/notre-epoque/20181008.OBS3590/sandra-muller-la-france-n-a-rien-compris-a-metoo.html* (accessed 9 December 2021).

Verdrager, Pierre, *L'Enfant interdit: comment la pédophilie est devenue scandaleuse* (Paris: Armand Colin, 2013).

Notes

1   John Leicester, 'France's #MeToo: Book on child-sex writer prompts outcry', *AP News*, 12 January 2020, *https://apnews.com/article/aeea1b-d377966a3eae3ed1f887a8a08f* (accessed 9 December 2021).
2   Karina Piser, 'France could finally be on the brink of a #MeToo reckoning', *Washington Post*, 13 February 2020, *www.washingtonpost.com/opinions/2020/02/13/france-could-finally-be-brink-metoo-reckoning/* (accessed 9 December 2021).
3   Leicester, 'Book on child-sex writer prompts outcry'.
4   '1990: Gabriel Matzneff face à Denise Bombardier dans "Apostrophes:"', *Archives INA*, 26 December 2019, *www.youtube.com/watch?v=H0LQiv7x4xs* (accessed 9 December 2021).
5   Piser, '#MeToo reckoning'.
6   *The Everyday Sexism Project, www.everydaysexism.com* (accessed 9 December 2021).
7   Michèle Schaal and Adrienne Angelo, 'Editors' introduction: Alive and Kicking: French and Francophone Feminisms Now', *French Cultural Studies*, 31/4 (2020), 264.
8   Gurvinder Gill and Imran Rahman-Jones, 'Me Too founder Tarana Burke: Movement is not over', 9 July 2020, *www.bbc.com/news/newsbeat-53269751* (accessed 9 December 2021).
9   Aurélien Breeden, 'French #MeToo Movement's Founder Loses Defamation Case', *New York Times*, 25 September 2019, *www.nytimes.com/2019/09/25/world/europe/france-sandra-muller-verdict.html* (accessed 9 December 2021).
10 Sarah Chiche *et al.*, 'Nous défendons', *Le Monde*, 9 January 2018, *www.lemonde.fr/idees/article/2018/01/09/nous-defendons-une-liberte-d-importuner-indispensable-a-la-liberte-sexuelle_5239134_3232.html?_ga=2.22242 3256.298773082.1608237014–139048590.1608237013* (accessed 9 December 2021).
11 Hélène Douaphars, '#MeToo? The French Resistance', *BBC World News*, 5 April 2019, *www.youtube.com/watch?v=JHRPCBXJSng* (accessed 9 December 2021).
12 Piser, '#MeToo reckoning'.

13 Marine Turchi, 'Une enquête singulière', *Mediapart*, 3 November 2019, *https://blogs.mediapart.fr/marine-turchi/blog/031119/une-enquete-singuliere* (accessed 9 December 2021).

14 Yohana Desta, 'Can the César Awards Ever Recover from Roman Polanski Catastrophe?', *Vanity Fair*, 2 March 2020, *www.vanityfair.com/hollywood/2020/03/cesar-awards-adele-haenel-roman-polanski* (accessed 9 December 2021).

15 Norimitsu Onishi, 'A Pedophile Writer is on Trial. So Are the French Elites', *New York Times*, 11 February 2020, *www.nytimes.com/2020/02/11/world/europe/gabriel-matzneff-pedophilia-france.html* (accessed 9 December 2021).

16 '1990: Gabriel Matzneff face à Denise Bombardier dans 'Apostrophes'', *Archives INA*, 26 Decemder 2019, *https://www.youtube.com/watch?v=H0LQiv7x4xs* (accessed 9 December 2021).

17 Norimitsu Onishi and Constant Méheut, 'Pedophile Scandal Can't Crack the Closed Circles of Literary France', *New York Times*, 28 November 2020, *www.nytimes.com/2020/11/28/world/europe/france-literary-prizes-matzneff.html* (accessed 9 December 2021).

18 Martine Delvaux, *Le Boys Club* (Montreal QC: Remue-ménage, 2019), pp. 16–25.

19 Onishi and Méheut, 'Pedophile Scandal'.

20 Onishi and Méheut, 'Pedophile Scandal'.

21 Amanda Marcotte, 'Overcompensation Nation: It's time to admit that toxic masculinity drives gun violence', *Salon*, 13 June 2016, *www.salon.com/2016/06/13/overcompensation_nation_its_time_to_admit_that_toxic_masmasculin_drives_gun_violence/* (accessed 9 December 2021).

22 Iris Brey, 'Polanski: l'impossible séparation entre l'homme et l'artiste', *Mediapart*, 13 November 2019, *www.mediapart.fr/journal/france/131119/polanski-l-impossible-separation-entre-l-homme-et-l-artiste?onglet=full* (accessed 9 December 2021).

23 Jess McHugh, 'The Polanski protests have brought France's #MeToo reckoning a step closer', *Guardian*, 8 March 2020, *www.theguardian.com/commentisfree/2020/mar/08/roman-polanski-metoo-france* (accessed 9 December 2021).

24 Vanessa Springora, *Le Consentement* (Paris: Grasset, 2020), pp. 193–4.

25 Vanessa Springora, *Consent*, trans. Natasha Lehrer (New York: HarperCollins, 2021), p. 175.

26 'La culture du silence au sein du milieu littéraire doit cesser', *Le Devoir*, 16 July 2020, *www.ledevoir.com/opinion/libre-opinion/582503/la-culture-du-silence-au-sein-du-milieu-litteraire-doit-cesser* (accessed 9 December 2021).

27 Guillaume Erner, 'Vanessa Springora: Matzneff "était bien ce qu'on apprend à redouter dès l'enfance: un ogre"', *L'Invité des matins*, France Culture, 3 January 2020, *www.youtube.com/watch?v=M5vh4aTl8XE* (accessed 9 December 2021).

28 Pierre Verdrager, *L'Enfant interdit: comment la pédophilie est devenue scandaleuse* (Paris: Armand Collin, 2013), p. 21.

29 Malka Marcovich, *L'Autre héritage de 68: La face cachée de la révolution sexuelle* (Paris: Albin Michel, 2018).

30 Luc Le Vaillant, '"Le consentement" sans concession de Vanessa Springora', *Libération*, 29 December 2019, *https://next.libération.fr/livres/2019/12/29/le-consentement-sans-concession-de-vanessa-springora_1771343* (accessed 9 December 2021).

31 François Busnel, 'Autour de Vanessa Springora', *La Grande Librairie*, France TV, 15 January 2020, *www.france.tv/france-5/la-grande-librairie/la-grande-librairie-saison-12/1143743-la-grande-librairie.html* (accessed 9 December 2021).

32 Geneviève Fraisse, *Du Consentement* (Paris: Seuil, 2007), p. 26.

33 Nicole-Claude Mathieu, *L'anatomie politique: Catégorisations et idéologies du sexe* (Paris: Côté-femmes, 1991), p. 207; cité par Fraisse, *Du Consentement*, p. 75–6.

34 Chantal Guy, 'Vanessa Springora, *Le Consentement* et l'influence d'un livre', *La Presse*, 5 February 2020, *www.lapresse.ca/arts/litterature/2020–02–05/vanessa-springora-le-consentement-et-l-influence-d-un-livre* (accessed 9 December 2021).

35 Jean Talabot and Alice Develey, 'Affaire Matzneff: que découvre-t-on dans *Le Consentement* de Vanessa Springora?', *Le Figaro*, 31 December 2019, *www.lefigaro.fr/livres/affaire-matzneff-que-decouvre-t-on-dans-le-consentement-de-vanessa-springora-20191231* (accessed 9 December 2021).

36 Virginie Despentes, 'Césars: "Désormais on se lève et on se barre"', *Libération*, 1 March 2020, *www.liberation.fr/debats/2020/03/01/cesars-desormais-on-se-leve-et-on-se-barre_1780212* (accessed 9 December 2021).

37 Paul B. Preciado, 'L'ancienne académie en feu', *Libération*, 1 March 2020, *www.liberation.fr/debats/2020/03/01/l-ancienne-academie-en-feu_1780215* (accessed 9 December 2021).

38 'Gaslighting', *Healthline*, *www.healthline.com/health/gaslighting#:~:text=Gaslighting%20is%20a%20form%20of,tthe%20question%20their%20own%20sanity* (accessed 9 December 2021).

39 'Scandal', *Merriam-Webster.com Dictionary*, Merriam-Webster, *www.merriam-webster.com/dictionary/scandal* (accessed 9 December 2021).

40 François Laplantine, *De tout petits liens* (Paris: Mille et une nuits, 2003), p. 366.

41 Marie Vaton, 'Sandra Muller: "La France n'a rien compris à #MeToo"', *Nouvel Observateur*, 8 October 2018, *www.nouvelobs.com/rue89/notre-epoque/20181008.OBS3590/sandra-muller-la-france-n-a-rien-compris-a-metoo.html* (accessed 9 December 2021).

42 Virginie Despentes, 'Césars: "Désormais on se lève et on se barre"', *Libération*, 1 March 2020, *www.liberation.fr/debats/2020/03/01/cesars-desormais-on-se-leve-et-on-se-barre_1780212* (accessed 9 December 2021).

Chapter 16

Breaking Down Barriers and Advocating for Change in the French Film Industry: the Career and Activism of Actress Aïssa Maïga

LESLIE KEALHOFER-KEMP

As France's first successful Black actress (and still one of very few Black actresses) with a career spanning nearly twenty-five years, Aïssa Maïga has faced many challenges and broken barriers in the French film industry. During the 2020 French César Awards Ceremony, where she had been invited to present an award, Maïga took advantage of her presence on stage to give an impassioned speech about the lack of diversity in the French film industry. Her remarks were met with a very cold reception at the ceremony and went viral on social media, generating strong criticism, notably from people who did not agree with how Maïga addressed race and privilege – taboo subjects in a country that allows very limited collection of ethnic statistics and prides itself on universal ideals and a colour-blind ideology. The most commented upon part of her remarks came at the beginning of her nearly five-minute speech, when she said hello to the very few Black people present and then shared that for more than twenty years, she had been unable to stop herself from counting the number of Black people in a room whenever she was at an important event in the industry.[1]

The controversy that Maïga's speech generated – as well as the actress's near invisibility in the French media for several weeks following the ceremony – stood in stark contrast to the reception that she received in the media in 2018 around the publication of the collection of essays that she initiated, *Noire n'est pas mon métier* (*'Black is Not My Job'*).[2] This collective endeavour includes chapters by sixteen Black actresses who recount their experiences with discrimination in the French film industry. It begins with a prologue by Maïga, who also contributed a chapter. The book was published by the prestigious Parisian publishing house Les Éditions du Seuil, was commercially successful and generated a significant amount of positive attention in the media in France. An important contributing factor to the visibility of the project was the women's participation in a symbolic moment and collective gesture at the 2018 Cannes Film Festival shortly after the book's release. Dressed in designer garments and dancing to 'Diamonds' by Rihanna, they ascended the steps of the red carpet together and posed for photos in front of the international media. In the weeks leading up to and following the festival, Maïga was invited to speak about the project to diverse media outlets.

This chapter will revisit these very visible moments of engagement and their reception by considering them within the broader arc of the actress's career. I will suggest that the language that Maïga employed in her Césars speech – notably referring to the French film industry as a closed space to which not everyone has the key – is part of a much more sustained commentary and engagement about discrimination and exclusion in the industry. An important aspect of Maïga's activism has been to name and shed light on barriers to inclusion through her interviews and media engagements, and a recurring theme is the metaphor of the French cinema industry as a space with doors, barriers, walls or (glass) ceilings that exclude certain people or inhibit their full participation. Although Maïga eventually gained access to this coveted space, this did not open the floodgates for Black actresses who came after her. In what follows, I will examine Aïssa Maïga's discourse about the contours and barriers to access the French film industry, as expressed primarily through interviews, as well as potential drawbacks of the interview platform itself as an activist space. I will then consider how in her activism since 2018, Maïga has leveraged alternative spaces outside of the interview platform to advocate for change.

Breaking Down Barriers and Opening Doors

Aïssa Maïga was cast in her first téléfilm in 1993, and part of the preparation for this project involved travelling to Zimbabwe and meeting with socially engaged theatre performers.[3] In 2018, Maïga underscored that this was a decisive experience for her for two reasons: first, she decided that she wanted to pursue acting as a career, and second, from the very start of her career path, acting was intertwined with the idea of engagement and the possibility of bringing about change (*'La Poudre'*). However, this was not yet specifically rooted in questions of inclusion, diversity or being a Black actress in the French film industry, as Maïga said in a 2020 interview:

> [J]'étais loin de m'imaginer au départ que l'acte militant, il allait non pas s'exprimer forcément dans les films en eux-mêmes, mais à la porte, aux portes du milieu, dans le fait d'avoir à revendiquer une place, revendiquer un droit à l'égalité finalement.[4]

> In the beginning, I never imagined that the militant action would be expressed not necessarily through the films themselves, but at the door, at the doors of the industry, in having to fight for a place and fight for the right to equality.

This reality came as a shock to her, as she explained in a 2017 interview:

> When I was a kid ... I didn't realise there was a problem, I just watched movies like any other kid and could identify ... with French white actresses ... I started realizing that there was a problem when I became an actress myself.[5]

Maïga has said that her co-authors of *Noire n'est pas mon métier* had not anticipated facing discrimination in the French film and theatre industries either.[6] She attributed this to the fact that they had been raised and educated to believe in the egalitarian ideals of the French Republic.[7] In 2019, Maïga explained that actresses in France all go through the same schooling and formation, during which time they study 'classic' texts of French literature, but when Black actresses enter the professional realm, they find that the same roles are off limits to them because people 'sont conditionnés, ils sont dans l'idée reçue que Molière ne peut être joué que par des blancs' ('are conditioned to the preconception that Molière can only be played by white people').[8] A useful way of conceptualising the divide that Maïga describes is through the lens of Sara Ahmed's discussion of the idea of 'inhabit[ing] a category of privilege'.[9] She argues:

> When we fail to inhabit a category ... then the category becomes more apparent, rather like the institutional wall: a sign of immobility or what does not move ... When a category allows us to pass into the world, we might not notice that we inhabit that category. When we are stopped or held up by how we inhabit what we inhabit, then the terms of habitation are revealed to us. (p. 176)

Film roles represent a major access point to the industry and are a gateway to opportunities, visibility and professional success. Although gaining entry into the privileged space of the French film industry is no easy feat for any actor, Aïssa Maïga's discourse on the subject points to specific, and sometimes multiple, hindrances in various forms that actors and actresses of colour can face and that prevent them from 'passing into' this world. Throughout her career, she has emphasised two things in particular that in her view hinder the careers of Black actresses: on the one hand, a lack of roles, and on the other, roles that are stereotyped, clichéd or lacking in depth or complexity.[10] With regard to recurrent stereotypes, Maïga has cited, among others, the prevalence of ultra-sexualised roles as well as those in which Black women are victims of their 'communauté d'origine' ('community of origin').[11]

In a 2000 televised interview following the release of *Jonas et Lila, à demain* ('*Jonas and Lila, Til Tomorrow*') (Alain Tanner), in which she had a lead role, Maïga was asked about being one of the only Black actresses in France. She responded:

> c'est parce que déjà, il y a très peu de rôles ... et il y a très peu de rôles qui sont écrits pour nous, et les rôles qui sont écrits la plupart du temps sont très réduits ou réducteurs. Finalement on n'a pas une réelle place ici.[12]

> for a start, it's because there are very few roles ... and there are very few roles that are written for us, and most of the time, the roles that are written are limited or over-simplistic. In the end, we do not have a real place here.

The way that she is introduced at the beginning of the segment, as 'l'actrice africaine la plus en demande en Europe et en France en particulier' ('the most in-demand African actress in Europe, and especially in France'), hints at the challenge she faced with regard to being considered to play roles of French women.[13] Introducing her as an African actress (as opposed to a Black actress) in Europe or France situates her as an outsider and as not French.

The subject of the lack of diversity and representation in cinema and the media in France would be raised in a more public way a few weeks after this interview. Writer Calixthe Beyala and actor/director Luc Saint-Éloy made an uninvited speech during the 2000 César Awards as representatives of the group Collectif Égalité.[14] Saint-Éloy explained that Collectif Égalité was fighting 'pour une véritable représentation de la réalité multiraciale de la France dans tous les médias, dans tous les lieux de culture' ('for a true representation of the multiracial reality of France in all media forms and cultural spaces').[15] An important commonality between this speech and Maïga's aforementioned interview is the act of naming the paucity of roles available to actors of colour and pointing out their overall invisibility at a time when this was largely absent from public discourse. Sara Ahmed's writings concerning barriers to inclusion and doing 'diversity work' in academic institutions provide a useful way to think about the kind of work that Collectif Égalité and Maïga, respectively, engaged in in this particular context, as well as the specific challenges involved. In the words of Ahmed, 'You come up against what others do not see; and (this is even harder) you come up against what others are often invested in not seeing ... Diversity work is hard because what you come up against is not revealed to others'.[16] With regard to the French film industry, there is thus a twofold challenge: the first involves shedding light on barriers that themselves are not visible to most people; the second entails addressing the consequences of these unseen barriers, and namely, the invisibility or absence of people of colour on the big and small screens. The idea of trying to make visible 'what others do not see' has additional implications when considered within the French context, since for many, simply talking about ethnic or racial differences flies in the face of France's tradition of a universalist and colour-blind ideology (even if the end goal of those doing the work is to actually make these ideals a reality).

In an interview published shortly after Beyala and Saint-Éloy's intervention, Maïga stated: 'Je suis contente que le Collectif Égalité ... ait pris la parole pour ouvrir le débat' ('I am happy that Collectif Égalité ... spoke out to initiate the discussion').[17] She also made reference to invisible barriers that she felt had an impact on her career. For example, she noted that while she could not complain about her own career because she had worked on a regular basis for the previous four years, there was significant disparity between the number of auditions she had had as compared to a white counterpart. A major contributing factor, she argued in the same interview, was how the roles were written in the first place. When directors 'écrivent un rôle de fille de vingt ans, c'est forcément une Blanche' ('write a role of a twenty-year-old girl, it's inevitably a white girl'), and as a result, Black actresses were not considered for roles unless the script specified that the character was Black. As recently as 2018, Maïga reiterated that when it comes to casting choices and how roles are written, 'l'universel est blanc' ('the universal is white').[18]

The years 2005 and 2006 represented an important period in Maïga's career and activist path. She gained entry to important access points in the industry, with roles in films by well-known directors such as Michael Haneke, Cédric Klapisch, Claude Berri, Philippe Lioret and Abderrahmane Sissako. She earned a Most Promising Actress César nomination for her role in Sissako's *Bamako* and represented this film and the international collection of short films *Paris je t'aime* ('*Paris, I Love You*') at the 2006 Cannes Film Festival. Her media engagements from 2006 and 2007 highlight this forward momentum and reflect that she felt that things were finally opening up for her, notably with regard to casting opportunities. This included being asked to audition for roles that were not specified as being Black women in the script. Then came another key moment: she was cast in a lead role in a romantic comedy alongside bankable actor Romain Duris and would play a trendy photographer, and not, Maïga emphasised, 'une fille mariée de force et excisée! Il était temps, car dans les rôles écrits pour les Noirs, on est souvent traité comme l'étrange étranger' ('a girl forced into marriage and excised! It's about time, because in roles written for Black people, we are often treated as the strange foreigner').[19] Yet this period was not without its setbacks. When it came time to promote the film, Maïga discovered that her image had been excluded from the poster, with the supposed reason being that the public was not ready (and thus would not have gone to see the film had they seen her on the poster).[20] Maïga has discussed this barrier to inclusion (i.e., the perception that having Black actors in prominent roles represents a financial risk) at different points throughout her career and has highlighted the inherent paradox of this argument; namely, that American television programmes and films starring Black actors have a history of success in France.[21]

It was also during this first sustained period of success in Maïga's career that there was an increased awareness of and discussions about equal opportunity, discrimination and the representations of minoritised populations in the media and on television in France. This occurred in the wake of three weeks of civil unrest in 2005 in disadvantaged suburbs commonly referred to as *les banlieues*, which were sparked after two young French men of Mauritanian and Tunisian descent were electrocuted while being pursued by the police.[22] The heavily mediatised events led to a plethora of debates and discussions about the root causes and what to do about it. A recurrent subject of discussion was representation in the media and on television. The French government sought to take concrete steps to address inequalities, some of which touched the media industry directly.[23] For example, decreed in the 31 March 2006 'loi pour l'égalité des chances' ('equal opportunities law') was the mission of publicly owned television networks to promote social cohesion, fight discrimination and reflect the diversity of French society through their programming.[24] Other measures had a more direct impact on the cinema industry, such as funding opportunities designed to promote diversity.[25]

These events and their aftermath would also have an impact on Maïga's activism and career more broadly. First, they raised awareness about issues that she had been talking about since the beginning of her career. Second, Maïga felt that they led to more interest in her as an individual. She even surmised that her César nomination for her role in *Bamako* – the first for a Black actress – was in part due to the increased awareness of and attention to the question of visible minority representation.[26] Third, Maïga was regularly invited to comment upon these questions in the media (and to serve as a kind of *de facto* spokesperson about diversity), sometimes at the expense of being asked about her work as an actress. Her participation in an April 2006 televised roundtable discussion entitled 'Le cinéma français est-il vraiment en couleur?' ('Is French Cinema Really in Colour?') highlights this dynamic with particular clarity. There were two other participants in addition to Maïga: director Yamina Benguigui, whose 2006 documentary *Le Plafond de verre/Les Défricheurs* ('*The Glass Ceiling*') addressed the impact of employment discrimination on minority ethnic youth in France, and actor Saïd

Taghmaoui, best known for his role as one of three *banlieue*youth in the 1995 film *La Haine* ('*Hate*') (Mathieu Kassovitz). Despite being nominated for a Most Promising Actor César for the role, Taghmaoui's career did not take off, and he moved to the United States in search of acting opportunities. During the roundtable, he described how he had been offered – and rejected – clichéd and stereotyped roles when he was in France.[27]

During the discussion, Maïga spoke about her audition experiences as a young actress, describing the 'vent glacial' ('glacial wind') that she had faced when she auditioned for roles that were not specified as being Black characters. She also alluded to the interview platform as a space of potential inclusion or exclusion for actors and actresses of colour and made a pointed critique directed at journalists: instead of inviting Maïga, Taghmaoui and Benguigui on television to talk about the presence and representations of minorities in French cinema, she argued, that they should invite them to talk about and promote their films.[28] Six months later, Maïga touched on this question again when she underscored the risks of being 'engaged' with regard to these issues, stating:

> [J]e ne voudrais pas que mes engagements me vampirisent … Souvent, on m'invite sur les plateaux télé pour parler non de mon cinéma, mais de la condition des Noirs en France, comme si j'étais sociologue! Ne parler que de ça serait une nouvelle prison. Je suis comédienne, j'ai avant tout une démarche artistique.[29]

> I do not want my engagements to consume me … I am often invited on television to speak not about my films, but about the condition of Black people in France, as if I were a sociologist! Speaking only about that would be a new prison. I'm an actor, and I have first and foremost an artistic approach.

Paradoxically, then, something that might at first seem to be a gesture of inclusion (inviting Maïga to participate in a television programme) can actually result in exclusion and marginalisation if the topic of the interview relates not to the work that she does as an actress, but rather is rooted in the fact that she is Black. Maïga would voice a similar concern about interviews more than thirteen years later, following the success of *Noire n'est pas mon métier*. She wondered if she had not recreated the very situation that she had been trying to avoid, wherein she would no longer be asked about her work as an actress during interviews. The space of the interview platform has thus represented a double-edged sword for Maïga and has not always been compatible with simultaneously promoting her career as an actress and her position as an activist. In fact, at one point during her career, before the publication of *Noire n'est pas mon métier*, Maïga had actually made a conscious decision to step back from talking about questions relating to diversity in the film industry, as she wanted the journalists to listen to the actress, as opposed to the activist. She also felt that her speaking out had not brought about change, and this led her to turn to a collective approach to activism and the book project.[30]

Forging a Collective Activist Path and Leveraging Alternate Spaces

The publication of *Noire n'est pas mon métier* in 2018 represented a shift to collective action, with Maïga taking a lead role, as well as a higher profile approach to advocating for change that expanded to include spaces beyond interview platforms. Although Maïga had previously contemplated doing something collective with other actresses, what sparked this concrete action was seeing a teaser for the documentary film *Ouvrir la voix* ('*Speak Up*') (Amandine Gay, 2017) entitled 'Aïssa Maïga'. In it, young Black women in France are asked to name five Black French actresses, and none is able to do it. Yet Maïga's name comes up several times. Speaking about the book project, Maïga said: '[J]'ai eu envie de faire quelque chose de marquant et quelque chose de durable' ('I wanted to do something memorable and something lasting').[31] She also felt that the timing was right for collective action by women in cinema, in the wake of the #MeToo movement.[32] Nevertheless, the women who contributed to the book knew that their participation did not come without risks for their careers and that their desire to open doors could very well have the opposite outcome.[33] The book met with commercial success and was treated very favourably in the media, and this success – from *outside* of the walls of the cinema industry – made their symbolic moment at the 2018 Cannes Film Festival possible.

Maïga and her co-authors used the international platform of Cannes to address inequality and promote change specifically within the French (national) film industry.[34] At the same time, Maïga's discourse about this moment at Cannes reflects a widening of the aims and scope of her activist approach, as well as the goal of connecting their endeavour to people outside of the film industry. For example, in one interview, she framed the event at Cannes through the lens of workplace discrimination, referring to the space of the red carpet itself as symbolising the women's workplace.[35] She went on to say that the experiences the women faced were shared by people outside of cinema and television, including those who faced discrimination due to gender, sexual orientation or the colour of their skin. Elsewhere, Maïga pointed to the larger questions that the project raised that went beyond the experiences of Black actresses, asking: 'Quelles sont les valeurs qu'on défend?' ('What are the values we are defending?'). In the months after Cannes, Maïga again underscored the importance of collective action and said that within the context of the film industry, solutions could only be put in place collectively and with the help of allies.[36]

A year and a half after Cannes, Maïga decided to capitalise on her presence in another symbolic and visible space of French cinema – the stage of the 2020 César Awards, as mentioned earlier – to give a speech about diversity, representation and inclusion. The content and message of Maïga's speech did not in and of itself diverge from the path she had been tracing throughout her career. She criticised the lack of diversity in French cinema, as well as the history of stereo-typed roles, and called for inclusion, stating: 'faisons une maison plutôt qu'une vitrine, une maison qui soit fière d'inclure toutes les différences' ('Let's make a house, rather than a window, a house that is proud to include all differences').[37] What distinguished this moment of activism from previous ones in Maïga's career, however, was the cold reception of the speech during the ceremony, and the treatment of her words (and her personally) in the media, and espe-cially social media afterwards. Her comments went viral and were much commented upon in the written press and debated on tele-vised platforms. This was no doubt fuelled by the large television audience that the 2020 Césars garnered, due in large part to medi-atised events prior to the ceremony. These related to the lack of transparency of the Césars voting body, gender discrimination in the industry, and the nomination of Roman Polanski and his film *J'Accuse* ('*An Officer and a Spy*') for twelve César Awards two months after the director was accused (again) of sexual assault. The cere-mony was very much in the headlines leading up to the event, and a record television audience – more than 2 million spectators – tuned in to watch it.[38]

Maïga thus stepped into what was already a very mediatised context and spoke on live television. She also did so alone. Although in interviews about *Noire n'est pas mon métier* she had underscored the necessity of using collective action involving allies to bring about change in the industry, her approach at the ceremony diverged from this. Two days earlier, Maïga had been involved in a collective gesture as one of thirty signatories of a tribune published in *Le Parisien*, which presented the hashtag #BlackCesars and called for the adoption of 'mesures d'inclusion' ('inclusionary measures') in French cinema that would include but go beyond gender parity (a main focus of the debates leading up to the ceremony).[39] Maïga did not appear to collaborate with any of the other signatories on her speech, however, and no one accompanied her on stage or manifested their support in any recognisable way during the ceremony itself.[40] Maïga has said that even if she knew that her words would strike a nerve with some members of the academy, she did not anticipate the very cold and uncomfortable reception that she encountered.[41]

This lack of solidarity was nothing compared to the reactions that her words provoked on social media, as well as through some traditional media outlets. Her speech took on huge proportions, and this made her a target for criticism on social media (notably on the part of the 'fachosphère', according to Maïga[42]). Although there were some people who supported her efforts and message, right wing politicians and public figures (Nadine Moreno, Alain Finkielkraut and Eric Zemmour, among others), vehemently criticised her for promoting a 'racialising' discourse (and being racist), playing into identity politics, and creating divisions in society (thus breaking from France's universalist tradition).[43] It was thus Maïga herself who became the object of criticism for many because, to borrow Ahmed's theorisation of the act of speaking out about racism and sexism, she 'bec[a]me a problem' by 'giv[ing] problems their names'.[44]

With regard to the reactions to Maïga's speech, on the other side of the coin was silence. Notably absent in the aftermath were public shows of support for Maïga from people within the French cinema industry (an exception was Sonia Rolland).[45] Maïga virtually disappeared from her social media accounts and had no official media appearances until nearly three months later, when she gave an interview in English to the American publication *Essence*.[46] She later said that the fallout was so extreme that at one point she feared for her safety.[47] She would be visible in the French media again on 2 June, however, when she gave a short but powerful speech at a rally for justice and against racism and police violence in Paris in the wake of the death of George Floyd. It brought together more than 20,000 people and was organised by the Comité vérité et justice pour Adama ('Justice and Truth for Adama Committee'), a group created to seek justice for Adama Traoré, who died in police custody in 2016. In her short remarks delivered to the crowd, Maïga wove in ideas from her Césars speech – about the fight for representation in the arts – to a larger fight for justice, echoing a line that she had said at the Césars (indicated in italics): '*Nous ne laisserons pas le cinéma français tranquille.* Nous ne laisserons pas la justice française tranquille, nous ne laisserons pas la France tranquille tant qu'il y aura des injustices' ('*We will not leave French cinema alone.* We will not leave the French justice system alone. We will not leave France alone as long as there is injustice').[48]

In contrast to the Césars, here Maïga delivered her speech surrounded by a mass of people who stood together in solidarity around these issues, and what was particularly striking about this activist moment was that several recognisable figures from the French film industry were also present. This included Leïla Bekhti, Camélia Jordana, Géraldine Nakache, JoeyStarr, Céline Sciamma, Ladj Ly and Adèle Haenel. This gathering was widely covered in the media, and Maïga's speech was cast in a favourable light.[49] Maïga's activist agenda in 2020 also included wrapping up her first documentary film project, which stemmed from her work on *Noire n'est pas mon métier*. Entitled *Regard Noir* ('*Black Gaze*'), the film includes international perspectives on the representations of Black women in cinema with interviews by American directors Ava DuVernay and Ryan Coogler, Brazilian star Taís Araújo, and French actresses Firmine Richard, Sonia Rolland and Adèle Haenel, among others. It was broadcast in France on 16 March 2021 on Canal+, the same network that had televised Maïga's speech at the Césars just over one year earlier. The film project marked a return to a collective activist approach for Maïga and leveraged another kind of medium through which to express her activist perspective. It involved allies from the French film industry, including her co-director, Isabelle Simeoni.

Although in the months following the César Awards it seemed that Maïga's career could very well be negatively impacted due to her speech and the subsequent backlash, ultimately this has not been the case. Indeed, the marches for justice in summer 2020 (in France and abroad) and their treatment in the media lent weight to Maïga's activist message as expressed during the César awards. In addition, Maïga's activism subsequently expanded in a new direction and took shape in a second documentary (her first as solo director), called *Marcher sur l'eau* ('*Above Water*'). Filmed in the village of Tatiste in Niger, West Africa, it focuses on the effects of climate change, and drought in particular, on the lives of the families in the village. The film was an official selection of the 2021 Cannes Film Festival, as well as several other festivals in France and abroad, received significant media attention, and was released in French cinemas in November 2021. Aïssa Maïga has found a way to productively weave together her work as an actress and director with her position as an activist, and this work is increasingly global in scope.

Works Cited

'Adama Traoré. Le discours percutant d'Aïssa Maïga lors du rassemblement contre les violences policières', *Ouest France*, 3 June 2020.

Ahmed, Sara, *Living a Feminist Life* (Durham NC and London: Duke University Press, 2017).

—— *On Being Included: Racism and Diversity in Institutional Life* (Durham NC and London: Duke University Press, 2012).

'Aïssa Maïga', *La Poudre*, episode 30, podcast, 17 May 2018.

'Aïssa Maïga', *Women in Motion Podcast*, S1E4, Kering Group, released 13 May 2019.

'Aïssa Maïga: après son discours aux Césars', *Club 21e siècle*, Webinar, 18 September 2020, *www.youtube.com/watch?v=kvs6F2I07EI* (accessed 30 November 2021).

'Aïssa Maïga: "Citez moi le nom de 5 actrices noires françaises!"', *She Cannes*, podcast, 7 June 2019, *https://podtail.com/fr/podcast/she-cannes/aissa-maiga-citez-moi-le-nom-de-5-actrices-noires-/* (accessed 30 November 2021).

'Aïssa Maïga: noire n'est pas son métier', *France Culture*, 19 June 2018, *www.youtube.com/watch?v=wNjoziYh5x4* (accessed 30 November 2021).

'Aïssa Maïga: On l'aime déjà …', *L'Express*, 19 October 2006, p. 26.

'Aissa Maïga se bat pour la diversité dans le cinéma', Simone Media, 22 January 2020, *www.youtube.com/watch?v=DzFG6i2NE5A* (accessed 30 November 2021).

'Aïssa Maïga: "Un réalisateur qui veut faire un film avec une comédienne noire aura un mal fou à avoir de l'argent"', *France Culture*, 'Par les temps qui courent par Marie Richeux', 6 November 2018, *www.franceculture.fr/emissions/par-les-temps-qui-courent/aissa-maiga* (accessed 30 November 2021).

Balle, C., '#BlackCesars: une tribune dénonce le manque de diversité dans le cinéma français', *Le Parisien*, 26 February 2020, *www.leparisien.fr/culture-loisirs/cinema/blackcesars-une-tribune-denonce-le-manque-de-diversite-dans-le-cinema-francais-26–02–2020–8267550.php* (accessed 30 November 2021).

'César 2020 – Le discours engagé d'Aïssa Maïga', Canal+, 28 February 2020, *https://fr-fr.facebook.com/canalplus/videos/c%C3%A9sar-2020-le-discours-engag%C3%A9-da%C3%AFssa-ma%C3%AFga/1108613199477617/* (accessed 30 November 2021).

Davis, R. A., 'We Remember Aïssa Maïga's Black Girl Magic Moment at Cannes', *Essence*, 22 May 2020, *www.essence.com/feature/watch-actress-aissa-maiga-on-being-an-activist-for-diversity-in-french-cinema/* (accessed 30 November 2021).

'Débat du mois: Le cinéma français est-il vraiment en couleur? Avec la réalisatrice Yamina Benguigui et les acteurs Saïd Taghmaoui et Aïssa Maïga', France 2, 'Jour de fête', 11 April 2006, Institut National de l'Audiovisuel.

Daumas, C. *et al.*, '"Pourquoi ne se pense-t-on pas comme des alliés spontanés et nécessaires?"', *Libération*, 13–14 June 2020.

Dubois, Régis, *Les noirs dans le cinéma français: de Joséphine Baker à Omar Sy* (La Madeleine, France: Éditions LettMotif, 2017).

'En février 2000, Luc St. Eloy bousculait "la grande famille du cinéma". Depuis, rien n'a change …' 97LAND, 9 March 2020, *https://97land.com/il-y-a-20-ans-luc-st-eloy-chers-amis-de-la-grande-famille-du-cinema/* (accessed 30 November 2021).

Finkielkraut, A., 'L'effroyable soirée des César', *Le Figaro*, 2 March 2020.

Frachon, Claire, and Virginie Sassoon (eds), *Médias et diversité: de la visibilité aux continus. Etat des lieux en France, au Royaume-Uni, en Allemagne et aux États-Unis* (Paris: Institut Panos and Karthala, 2008).

'France: Culture: Aïssa Maïga vedette du film d'Alain Tanner', France Ô, RFO, 22 January 2000, Institut National de l'Audiovisuel.

Hargreaves, Alec G., *Multi-Ethnic France: Immigration, Politics, Culture and Society*, 2nd edition (New York and London: Routledge, 2007).

'In Conversation: Aïssa Maïga', Focus on French Cinema, Interview, 6 April 2017, *https://m.facebook.com/FocusOnFrenchCinema/posts/10155321836074 203* (accessed 30 November 2021).

'L'intervention magistrale d'Aïssa Maïga durant la manifestation pour Adama Traoré', *Vanityfair.fr*, 3 June 2020.

Maïga, A., 'Expulsée', in A. Maïga (ed.), *Noire n'est pas mon métier* (Paris: Éditions du Seuil, 2018), pp. 57–63.

Maïga, Aïssa (ed.), *Noire n'est pas mon métier* (Paris: Éditions du Seuil, 2018).

Marlier, F., '[Vidéo] Le discours poignant d'Aïssa Maïga lors de la manif contre les violences policières', *Les Inrockuptibles*, 3 June 2020.

McGonagle, Joseph, *Representing Ethnicity in Contemporary French Visual Culture* (Manchester: Manchester University Press, 2017).

Niang, Mame-Fatou, *Identités françaises: Banlieues, féminités et universalisme* (Leiden: Brill-Rodopi, 2019).

'Noire n'est pas mon métier!', 'C'est à vous', France 5, 4 May 2018, *www.youtube.com/watch?v=bqNvW1cMGAQ* (accessed 30 November 2021).

Potdevin, P., 'Aïssa Maïga, Camélia Jordana, Olivier Rousteing: la culture et la mode marchent contre le racisme', *Madame Le Figaro*, 3 June 2020.

'"Qu'on nous donne des rôles!": Entretien de Frédéric Darot avec Aïssa Maïga', Africultures.com, Article 1324, 31 March 2000, *http://africultures.com/quon-nous-donne-des-roles-1324/* (accessed 30 November 2021).

Suaudeau, Julien, 'Aïssa Maïga a raison', *Slate.fr*, 2 March 2020, *www.slate.fr/story/188070/cinema-francais-ceremonie-cesar-discours-aissa-maiga-racisme-representations* (accessed 30 November 2021).

Ubertalli, O., 'Toledano-Saada: 'Les César ne sont plus un club de bridge fermé', *Le Point*, 1 March 2021, *www.lepoint.fr/culture/toledano-saada-les-cesar-ne-sont-plus-un-club-de-bridge-ferme-01-03-2021-2415832_3.php* (accessed 1 March 2021).

'Vidéo: on a posé six questions reloues à Aïssa Maïga', *Konbini*, 28 January 2020, *www.konbini.com/fr/cinema/video-on-a-pose-six-questions-reloues-a-aissa-maiga/* (accessed 30 November 2021).

Wessbecher, L., 'Adama Traoré: Le discours fort d'Aïssa Maïga contre les injustices', *Huffingtonpost.fr*, 3 June 2020, *www.huffingtonpost.fr/entry/adama-traore-le-discours-fort-daissa-maiga-contre-les-injustices_fr_5ed7571fc5b600fead0e5f82* (accessed 30 November 2021).

Notes

1   'César 2020 – Le discours engagé d'Aïssa Maïga', Canal+, 28 February 2020, *https://fr-fr.facebook.com/canalplus/videos/c%C3%A9sar-2020-le-discours-engag%C3%A9-da%C3%AFssa-ma%C3%AFga/1108613199477617/* (accessed 30 November 2021).

2   Aïssa Maïga (ed.), *Noire n'est pas mon métier* (Paris: Éditions du Seuil, 2018).

3   'Aïssa Maïga', *La Poudre*, episode 30, podcast, 17 May 2018.

4   'Aïssa Maïga se bat pour la diversité dans le cinéma', Simone Media, 22 January 2020, *www.youtube.com/watch?v=DzFG6i2NE5A* (accessed 30 November 2021).

5   'In Conversation: Aïssa Maïga', Focus on French Cinema, Interview, 6 April 2017, *https://m.facebook.com/FocusOnFrenchCinema/posts/10155321836074203* (accessed 30 November 2021).

6   'Aïssa Maïga: "Un réalisateur qui veut faire un film avec une comédienne noire aura un mal fou à avoir de l'argent"', *France Culture*, 'Par les temps qui courent par Marie Richeux', 6 November 2018, *www.france-culture.fr/emissions/par-les-temps-qui-courent/aissa-maiga* (accessed 30 November 2021).

7   'Aïssa Maïga: "Un réalisateur"', *France Culture*.

8   'Aïssa Maïga', *Women in Motion Podcast*, S1E4, Kering Group, released 13 May 2019.

9   Sara Ahmed, *On Being Included: Racism and Diversity in Institutional Life* (Durham NC and London: Duke University Press, 2012), p. 176.

10   See Régis Dubois, *Les noirs dans le cinéma français: de Joséphine Baker à Omar Sy* (La Madeleine, France: Éditions LettMotif, 2017), for further

contextualisation of this trend in French cinema. See also chapter 5 of Mame-Fatou Niang's *Identités françaises: Banlieues, féminités et universalisme* (Leiden: Brill-Rodopi, 2019) for a discussion of casting and roles attributed to Black actresses in France within the context of an analysis and critique of Céline Sciamma's 2014 film *Bande de filles* (*'Girlhood'*).

11 'Aïssa Maïga: noire n'est pas son métier', *France Culture*, 19 June 2018, *www.youtube.com/watch?v=wNjoziYh5x4* (accessed 30 November 2021).

12 'France: Culture: Aïssa Maïga vedette du film d'Alain Tanner', France Ô, RFO, 22 January 2000, Institut National de l'Audiovisuel.

13 'France: Culture: Aïssa Maïga vedette', France Ô.

14 For further information about Collectif Égalité and their activism, see Claire Frachon and Virginie Sassoon (ed.), *Médias et diversité: de la visibilité aux continus. État des lieux en France, au Royaume-Uni, en Allemagne et aux États-Unis* (Paris: Institut Panos and Karthala, 2008), pp. 38–40.

15 'En février 2000, Luc St. Eloy bousculait "la grande famille du cinéma". Depuis, rien n'a change …' 97LAND, 9 March 2020, *https://97land.com/il-y-a-20-ans-luc-st-eloy-chers-amis-de-la-grande-famille-du-cinema/* (accessed 30 November 2021).

16 Sara Ahmed, *Living a Feminist Life* (Durham NC and London: Duke University Press, 2017), p. 138.

17 '"Qu'on nous donne des rôles!": Entretien de Frédéric Darot avec Aïssa Maïga', Africultures.com, Article 1324, 31 March 2000, *http://africultures.com/quon-nous-donne-des-roles-1324/* (accessed 30 November 2021).

18 'Noire n'est pas mon métier!', 'C'est à vous', France 5, 4 May 2018, *www.youtube.com/watch?v=bqNvW1cMGAQ* (accessed 30 November 2021).

19 'Aïssa Maïga: On l'aime déjà …', *L'Express*.

20 A. Maïga, 'Expulsée', in A. Maïga (ed.), *Noire n'est pas mon métier* (Paris: Éditions du Seuil, 2018), pp. 60–2.

21 For example, she has cited the success of *The French Prince of Bel-Air* and *The Cosby Show* ('In Conversation: Aïssa Maïga', *Focus on French Cinema*), as well as the success of films starring African-American actors such as Will Smith and Denzel Washington in France ('Expulsée', p. 62).

22 For further contextualisation, see Alec G. Hargreaves, *Multi-Ethnic France: Immigration, Politics, Culture and Society*, 2nd edition (New York and London: Routledge, 2007), pp. 1, 135–7.

23 For further discussion, see Joseph McGonagle, *Representing Ethnicity in Contemporary French Visual Culture* (Manchester: Manchester University Press, 2017), pp. 62–4.

24 Frachon and Sassoon, *Médias et diversité*, pp. 51–2.

25 Dubois, *Les noirs dans le cinéma français*, p. 68n.

26 'Aïssa Maïga: "Un réalisateur"', *France Culture*.

27 'Débat du mois: Le cinéma français est-il vraiment en couleur? Avec la réalisatrice Yamina Benguigui et les acteurs Saïd Taghmaoui et Aïssa Maïga', France 2, 'Jour de fête', 11 April 2006, Institut National de l'Audiovisuel.

28 She was invited back to the programme the following year (6 March 2007) to talk about the first film that she planned to direct. This was shortly after the César Awards for which she had been nominated for her role in *Bamako*.

29 'Aïssa Maïga: On l'aime déjà …', *L'Express*, 19 October 2006, p. 26.

30 'Vidéo: on a posé six questions reloues à Aïssa Maïga', Konbini, 28 January 2020, *www.konbini.com/fr/cinema/video-on-a-pose-six-questions-reloues-a-aissa-maiga/* (accessed 30 November 2021).

31 'Aïssa Maïga: "Citez moi le nom de 5 actrices noires françaises!"', *She Cannes*, podcast, 7 June 2019, *https://podtail.com/fr/podcast/she-cannes/aissa-maiga-citez-moi-le-nom-de-5-actrices-noires-/* (accessed 30 November 2021).

32 'Aïssa Maïga: "Un réalisateur"', *France Culture*.

33 'Aïssa Maïga', *La Poudre*.

34 There was another women's march up the steps of the red carpet that took place at the festival just a few days before and was international in scope. It was led by Cate Blanchett and Agnès Varda and focused on gender inequality in the industry.

35 'Aïssa Maïga: "Citez moi le nom"', *She Cannes*.

36 'Aïssa Maïga: "Un réalisateur"', *France Culture*.

37 'César 2020 – Le discours engagé d'Aïssa Maïga', Canal+.

38 O. Ubertalli, 'Toledano-Saada: 'Les César ne sont plus un club de bridge fermé', *Le Point*, 1 March 2021, *www.lepoint.fr/culture/toledano-saada-les-cesar-ne-sont-plus-un-club-de-bridge-ferme-01–03–2021–2415832_3.php* (accessed 1 March 2021).

39 C. Balle, '#BlackCesars: une tribune dénonce le manque de diversité dans le cinéma français', *Le Parisien*, 26 February 2020, *www.leparisien.fr/culture-loisirs/cinema/blackcesars-une-tribune-denonce-le-manque-de-diver-site-dans-le-cinema-francais-26–02–2020–8267550.php* (accessed 30 November 2021).

40 This stands in contrast to the experience of Saint-Éloy and Beyala of Collectif Égalité on stage during the César Awards in 2000. They gave their speech in the presence of the Masters of Ceremonies, Alain Chabat and Édouard Baer, who did not attempt to stop them or rush them off the stage (see Suaudeau). Their speech was followed by enthusiastic applause from the audience and a handshake between Saint-Éloy and Baer.

41 'Aïssa Maïga: après son discours aux Césars', Club 21e siècle, Webinar, 18 September 2020, *www.youtube.com/watch?v=kvs6F2I07EI* (accessed 30 November 2021).

42 'Aïssa Maïga: après son discours aux Césars', Club 21e siècle.

43 See for example, A. Finkielkraut, 'L'effroyable soirée des César', *Le Figaro*, 2 March 2020.

44 Ahmed, *Living a Feminist Life*, p. 34.

45 Maïga found an important ally in the aftermath of the César Awards in the form of Adèle Haenel, who reached out to Maïga privately after the ceremony to express her solidarity. Haenel is one of France's best-known actresses, and in November 2019, she had made public that she

was sexually abused by a film director as an adolescent. She walked out of the ceremony when Polanksi's Best Director award was announced, and this reaction was widely mediatised. Maïga and Haenel were subsequently featured on the cover of *Libération* and gave an in-depth joint interview. Cécile Daumas *et al.*, '"Pourquoi ne se pense-t-on pas comme des alliés spontanés et nécessaires?"', *Libération*, 13–14 June 2020, p. 2.

46   R. A. Davis, 'We remember Aïssa Maïga's Black Girl Magic Moment at Cannes', *Essence*, 22 May 2020, *www.essence.com/feature/watch-actress-aissa-maiga-on-being-an-activist-for-diversity-in-french-cinema/* (accessed 30 November 2021). Maïga participated in the 8 March 2020 women's march in Paris in the company of Céline Sciamma, Adèle Haenel and Nadège Beausson-Diagne.

47   'Aïssa Maïga: après son discours aux Césars', Club 21e siècle.

48   L. Wessbecher, 'Adama Traoré: Le discours fort d'Aïssa Maïga contre les injustices', *Huffingtonpost.fr*, 3 June 2020, *www.huffingtonpost.fr/entry/ adama-traore-le-discours-fort-daissa-maiga-contre-les-injustices_ fr_5ed7571fc5b600fead0e5f82* (accessed 30 November 2021).

49   For example, see F. Marlier, '[Vidéo] Le discours poignant d'Aïssa Maïga lors de la manif contre les violences policières', *Les Inrockuptibles*, 3 June 2020; 'Adama Traoré. Le discours percutant d'Aïssa Maïga lors du rassemblement contre les violences policières', *Ouest France*, 3 June 2020; L. Wessbecher, 'Adama Traoré'; 'L'intervention magistrale d'Aïssa Maïga durant la manifestation pour Adama Traoré', *Vanityfair. fr*, 3 June 2020; P. Potdevin, 'Aïssa Maïga, Camélia Jordana, Olivier Rousteing: la culture et la mode marchent contre le racisme', *Madame Le Figaro*, 3 June 2020.

Chapter 17
Unapologetically Visible? Representing and Reassessing Contemporary French Womanhood in *Dix Pour Cent*

LOÏC BOURDEAU

A government-certified survey spanning nine years (2010–19) found that the median percentage of women speaking on French television lies at 32.9 per cent.[1] A study led by the Conseil Supérieur de l'Audiovisuel (CSA), from 2014 to 2018, confirmed similar results and noted that only 29 per cent of women were represented in prime time slots.[2] For Géraldine Poels, television has played a significant, pedagogical role since the 1970s, yet it 'a contribué, dans le même temps, à naturaliser un certain nombre de rôles sociaux, de modes de relations entre les sexes ou d'institutions (comme la famille patriarcale) ('has contributed, at the same time, to naturalise a certain number of social roles, gender relations and institutions (such as the patriarchal family)').[3] Created by Fanny Herrero and based on an original idea by Dominique Besnehard, Michel Vereecken and Julien Messemackers, the television series *Dix Pour Cent* (henceforth, '*DPC*') offers an alternative discourse that, in effect, embraces women's empowerment and seeks to deconstruct gendered expectations. Comprising four seasons[4] of six episodes each, *DPC* received public and critical acclaim.[5]

Known internationally as *Call My Agent!* (Netflix), the show follows four main talent agents from ASK (Samuel Kerr Agency, named after its founder) – Andréa Martel (Camille Cottin), Mathias de Barneville (Thibault de Montalembert), Gabriel Sarda (Grégory

Montel) and Arlette Azémar (Liliane Rovère) – as they work with major French actors (e.g., Isabelle Hubert, Jean Dujardin, Juliette Binoche) playing exaggerated or fictional versions of themselves.[6] *DPC* offers an almost equal number of actors and actresses each season, with a slight majority in favour of women. Herrero adds in that regard: 'j'avais envie de personnages féminins forts, libres, indépendants: une femme scénariste est plus sensible à ça' ('I wanted strong, free and independent female characters: a woman show writer is more sensitive to this issue').[7] Despite a clear commitment to producing a diverse show, Herrero maintains that '*Dix Pour Cent* n'est pas une série militante' ('*Dix Pour Cent* is not a militant show').[8] This chapter argues, on the contrary, that to make room for and to give more visibility to women, to their desires, sexuality and subjectivities, is militant in itself. And such an endeavour is not without its share of attendant, ethical concerns. To refuse to inscribe these women into an essentialised narrative of care and to allow them to be selfish and fail at patriarchal womanhood expands the existing, limited spectrum of representation. As such, the show allows for a reassessment of women's status both in the workplace (i.e., the office of the agency) and in French society today. It gives necessary time and attention to 'imperfect' models, which, in turn, speaks about and to French society at large.

Considering the violent pushback against gay marriage (passed in 2013), the ongoing opposition to medically assisted procreation for all women (adopted in 2021) or more broadly, the powerful masculinist rhetoric – heralded by such public figures as Eric Zemmour who bemoan the alleged feminisation of society and lament women's taking too much space – *DPC* plays an important role in giving a voice to underrepresented issues, such as salary inequalities, racial discrimination in the industry, homosexuality, single-parent families and non-normative sexuality. As such, although the show affords needed visibility to powerful, strong, lesbian or old women, it bears keeping in mind that they benefit from class and race privilege and have access to dominant cultural capital. In what follows, I focus on two main characters, who, at different points of the age spectrum, share many similarities, including an unapologetic desire to live fully and freely: they satisfy their sexual desires, refuse to submit to patriarchal order and exhibit professional ambition. They come to represent what Lisa Downing calls 'female selfishness', that is, 'a radical and deviant departure from the expected qualities of "woman," [which] may indeed be properly considered to be a strategic, political, and personal *achievement*.[9] As Sofia Leprince (Stéfi Celma), the receptionist and aspiring actress explains, one is 'trop dure' ('too tough') and the other 'trop vieille' ('too old'): Andréa Martel, a successful, driven, at-times abrasive lesbian and Arlette Azémar, an established, nonchalant and independent, straight, older woman. Both agents demonstrate a true passion for cinema and prioritise their professional goals. In the end, these representations both reflect and test contemporary conceptions of French womanhood.

'LES-BI-ENNE':[10] Andréa Martel and Lesbian Visibility

In her hotly debated book, *Le Génie lesbien*, lesbian and LGBTQI-rights activist, feminist and journalist Alice Coffin exposes men's domination in the media and in power structures overall, which French society is refuses to see. She further remarks on the invisibilisation of lesbians in politics, journalism and even in cinema.[11] Clara-Bradbury Rance confirms that 'the figure of the lesbian in contemporary cinema is marked by a paradoxical burden of visibility and invisibility produced at the convergence of queer and feminist discourses'.[12]

Thirty-four-year-old Andréa Martel is not one to prevaricate when it comes to her sexual orientation or experiences. Within the first five minutes of season one, episode one, a tracking shot follows the main characters in the agency, including Andréa who is moving quickly from one office to the next, drinking coffee and assigning tasks to her assistant, such as cancelling a date with a woman. Unable to find an excuse, the assistant is chastised by the strong-headed, busy and assertive lesbian character who engages in one-night stands. The tracking-shot, in its linearity, first blurs the lines between professional and personal life effectively and posits her sexual identity as a non-issue. It stands out to viewers, however, who seldomly encounter lesbian characters on French television, and even less so in a professional context derived of any eroticised undertones. Even American models only account for a minute percentage.[13] Andréa's on-screen and unquestioned presence gathered positive responses because for once a show has 'réussi à introduire un personnage clairement lesbien ... avec ses joies et ses peines, de cœur ou de boulot' ('successfully managed to introduce an openly lesbian character ... with its emotional and professional highs and lows').[14] Later, she appears in a bar with her colleague Gabriel on the lookout for a night-time encounter and starts exchanging seductive gazes with a woman. While the scene cuts to another sequence, relying on the viewer's imagination to fill in the gaps, *DPC* affords its character real moments of intimacy. In season two, episode two, after meeting and kissing an old lover at a club, the show cuts to a sensual, yet somewhat comical, bedroom scene. Andréa appears from under the covers with a vibrator that stopped working. Noting that she 'aurai[t] dû acheté des piles rechargeables' ('should have bought rechargeable batteries'), she nevertheless proceeds with 'la méthode traditionnelle' ('the traditional method') (00:28:00–00:29:10).

For a prime-time show on public television to showcase such a sexually free character and to also include intimate scenes in the bedroom proves a powerful stance. As this volume looks at notions of 'place' and 'space', to bring the camera inside the space of same-sex sexual acts is somewhat radical. More generally, it also bears noting Andréa's easiness to move from one place to the next. Whether in her office, at the agency, on film sets, in bars, or in the albeit progressive and diverse city of Paris, her belonging remains uncontested. Within the professional space of the agency, she also makes it clear that she wishes to take over CEO Samuel Kerr's office, upon his death. The office walls may be made of glass, but there is no glass ceiling for Andréa.

In light of a controversy following the end of season two, to which we will return shortly, Cottin explained her enthusiasm to be playing such an independent character on television, regardless of her sexual orientation, and remarked that: 'On s'en fout qu'elle aime les femmes, ce n'est pas un sujet et ça fait du bien! Je pense que c'est un rôle éminemment politique' ('No one cares that she likes women, it's not a topic and that feels good! I think it's an eminently political role').[15] For Cottin, the political dimension of the role lies, among other things, in its normality, in its unchallenged nature. This claim is slightly inaccurate from a mere plot perspective insofar as her sexual orientation does inform narrative development. More importantly, while her position is laudable and valid, it reflects a French Republican take on the matter, one that is grounded in universalism, blind to communitarian specificities and reluctant to engage in identity politics or identitary discourse. It is not surprising then that the word 'lesbian' is never uttered in three seasons, or in fact, by the actress herself. During one encounter with actor Fabrice Luchini, a talent from another agency, who called on her in the middle of the night, interrupting the aforementioned sex scene, he asks, surprised: 'Vous êtes gouine' ('You're a dyke?') to which she responds: 'Je ne sais pas si le mot existe encore, mais...' ('I don't know if the word still exists, but...') (00:33:30). Not once does she use the word that actually exists.

On the 2019 *Journée de la visibilité lesbienne* ('International Lesbian Day'), Coffin called on French media and public figures to encourage everyone to use the word 'lesbian', rather than avoiding it or not using it altogether. Not only are they invisibilised and absent from television and from political debates that concern them directly, but also from language itself. The absence or recourse to euphemisms proves damaging if only for the mere fact that it effaces or unsettles part of one's identity. To that extent, *DPC*, too, operates a form of discursive marginalisation; to not-name or to misname creates a hierarchy and posits otherness at its bottom.

I return to Luchini's character who goes on to provide a history of other terms used in the past such as 'brioche maudite' ('accursed brioche') or 'les femmes damnées de Baudelaire' ('Baudelaire's doomed women') (00:34:00), enquires about Andréa's discovery of her sexual orientation and explains that 'la libido masculine n'a rien à voir avec la libido féminine' ('male libido is nothing like female libido') (00:34:00–00:35:00). Andréa listens, quietly. Considering that she is at the time trying to sign Luchini with her agency, her attentive demeanour can be read as a recruitment strategy. Putting her usual assertiveness aside – because of the professional stakes and hierarchy at play – she certainly manages to create a bond with him and to eventually win him over. It is nevertheless a missed opportunity for the character to own her narrative. This scene, with its references to derogatory euphemisms (coined by men) along with a *mansplanation* of the alleged differences between women's and men's sexual urges, fails its lesbian character insofar as she does not respond or address these comments. Her way of life may be unproblematic and on par with her heteronormative colleagues, but a degree of secrecy or restraint is required for her to succeed with her clients. For viewers, Andréa also acts as a representative for a community, whether the show creators, writers and actors want it or not. Alison Darren reminds us that for too long 'lesbians have been *inadequately* served by the cinema ... [they] might be sadistic, ruthless, antisocial, perverse, lacking in maternal instinct, predatory, anti-male, lecherous and sick'.[16] It is not to say that, on the one hand, *DPC* is not serving its lesbian character well, because it clearly is having a positive impact, or on the other hand, that negative portrayals should not exist; rather, it is about allowing these figures to speak (up), to own their stories and to be more than stereotypical projections. Andréa is ruthless, antisocial and lacks maternal instincts, but she is a, if not *the*, main character who lives as she pleases. For many (underrepresented) viewers, Andréa, as a lesbian and a feminist, embodies the promise of visibility and social acceptance. In the professional context, however, she does not quite deliver because being a feminist can hinder one's accomplishments. For Sara Ahmed, 'the one who speaks as a feminist is usually heard as the cause of the argument … She makes things tense'.[17] Andréa, and the show, cannot afford to draw too much attention to her sexual orientation, to 'make things tense', because '[w]hen you speak as a feminist, you have to deal with strong reactions'.[18]

With regard to missed opportunities, Mégane Choquet deplores the fact that *DPC* 'jumped head first into the trope of the "lesbian woman who ends up sleeping with a man"'.[19] Indeed, season two of *DPC* introduces Hicham Janowski (Assaâd Bouab) as ASK's new majority shareholder, a former schoolmate of Andréa's, and now, her new boss. Unfamiliar with the industry and concerned with profits, Hicham ruffles feathers with the disgruntled agents, in particular with Andréa whom he constantly belittles, mocks or harasses. In the third episode, forced to attend Hicham's son's birthday party, Andréa stumbles upon him as he is about to go to the bedroom with a model. She says, in her competitive tone: 'Tu pensais l'avoir pour toi tout seul?' ('Thought you'd have her all to yourself?') (00:38:50). Soon after they initiate the threesome, the model is left unattended. She leaves as the camera pans to Hicham and Andréa having sex. This trope is not novel. Darren explains about cinema that the lesbian's 'fate has included humiliation, rape, miraculous conversion to heterosexuality or, if not, death'.[20] Many viewers were disappointed with this scene: 'Il est dommage que des personnages présentés comme explicitement gays ou lesbiens doivent à chaque fois faire face à un moment de doute et qu'ils ne puissent pas vivre pleinement leur homosexualité' ('It is a pity that an explicitly gay or lesbian character should always face a moment of doubt and that they should not be able to fully live their homosexuality').[21] As much as the competition underlines Andréa's rejection of authority – especially that of a businessman who is not a true cinephile – and even if she reasserts her homosexuality in later episodes, claiming to have not enjoyed the moment, this scene initially feels incongruous, unnecessary and problematic given the strong hatred she expresses towards Hicham.

In response to the backlash, Herrero listened to the complaints, expressed sympathy and noted, however, that:

> chaque fois qu'on a des personnages qui sont issus d'une minorité, il y a toujours une frange très militante et extrêmement sensible qui s'exprime. Je le comprends, mais on ne maîtrise pas tout. On essaye d'avoir un discours politique tout en étant divertissant, ce qui peut conduire à une certaine maladresse.[22]

> every time there is a minoritised character, there's always a very militant and extremely sensitive group of activists that expresses itself. I understand them, but we do not master everything. We try to have a political discourse while entertaining, which can be clumsy.

This apology is also clumsy. Using words such as 'militant' and 'extremely sensitive' somewhat delegitimises the complaints and fails to acknowledge that the lives of minorities are not simply here to entertain the majority. Furthermore, it fails to acknowledge that viewers invest, emotionally and personally, in the characters, especially LGBTQI viewers who finally see themselves on screen. Mélanie Bourdaa, in her analysis of fan reactions to the breakup of the only lesbian couple (at the time) on *Grey's Anatomy* – a US television series and international phenomenon that offered lesbian visibility on French screens – provides a telling example of how fans, and lesbian viewers in particular, were scared 'de perdre un couple fictif représentant un orientation sexuelle' ('of losing a fictional couple representative of a sexual orientation').[23] After the breakup, many lesbian viewers noted that it was easy for these heterosexual, women showrunners to put an end to the lesbian couple narrative, but it was not easy for them to witness it when television, including *Grey's Anatomy*, offers so few examples of non-straight relationships.[24] The French context is no exception and emotional investment occurs in similar ways. Nevertheless, in this instance, *DPC*'s narrative investment in Andréa and Colette's relationship does offer a continued and positive presence for non-straight viewers (though somewhat less so in season four).

Notwithstanding the aforementioned plot (and even ethical) slip
up, *DPC* does use it to bring forth a discussion of non-heteronorma-
tive families as Andréa falls pregnant and rekindles her love with
fiscal inspector Colette Brancillon (Ophélia Kolb). Featured in the
first season, the two enter a monogamous relationship. Eventually,
Andréa loses her by prioritising her work. In season three, Colette
has returned to take care of pregnant Andréa. As Hicham finds out
that he is the genitor, he initiates a battle to recognise the child as his
own, thus bringing forth the thorny question of parental rights for
lesbian parents. After the delivery in episode four, the two women
are informed that Hicham is allowed to recognise the child as his
own whenever he wishes to. Colette, triggered, complains about the
many obstacles she is facing to be recognised as a legal guardian and
the fact that a judge (a man) has her fate in his hands (00:48:32–
00:50:40) The scene effectively appeals to the viewer's sympathy in
the face of injustice. A kind and invested character, Colette comes to
represent distraught lesbian co-parents whose legal status is in limbo:
her fate lies in the hands of the genitor and in the hands of a judge.
While the remainder of the season relies on the tension of not
knowing what Hicham will do, in the penultimate episode, he writes
a letter '[pour] renonc[er] à reconnaître Flora pour que Colette
puisse le faire à l'avenir en toute légitimité et être officiellement le
deuxième parent de Flora' ('[to] renounce [his] rights to Flora, so
that Colette can make a legitimate claim and officially become
Flora's second parent)'(00:46:10). Combining shots of Andréa and
Colette reading the letter with shots of Hicham facing the camera
and delivering his message directly to the viewer, *DPC* takes a stand
in favour of equal parental rights, thus reflecting a similar position
in French society.[25]

Overall, Andréa's character marks an important turn for television and for women. Despite some narrative flaws, she comes to
represent womanhood detached from essentialised preconceptions
such as femininity, ambition or care. She makes up a novel trope,
that of the selfish woman who prioritises her ambition and personal
needs over the collective good. Lisa Downing writes: 'For women,
who are supposed … to be life-giving, to be nurturing, to be *for the
other*, and therefore literally *self-less*, it is a far more serious transgression to be selfish while a woman – indeed it is a category violation of
identity'.[26] Downing considers extreme models such as Ayn Rand or
Margaret Thatcher who 'attained a position of power for herself but

left intact the systems that prevent other women from progressing'.[27] Andréa certainly fits into her analysis insofar as she puts herself and her success first, yet she also acts as an ally to her female counterparts. She proves to be a fierce agent and competitor, ready to do whatever it takes to acquire what she wants. In season three, for instance, she works hard to sign more clients before the end of the year report, even though she is about to deliver her daughter. She is also shown drinking alcohol either because it helps her sign more talents or because she simply wants to. The delivery scene, taking place in the office lobby, not only further blurs the boundaries between personal and professional, but also attest to Andréa's transgressing workspaces. Once a mother, she refuses to put her career on hold, and, in episode five, brings her child along on a movie set. Overall, she might seem antisocial, ruthless or predatory – which Darren, cited above, deplores as recurring and limiting tropes – but she also lives for cinema (e.g., she reads every script) and she is at all times supportive of her actors. As a woman, a mother, a lover or an employee, she is a constant case of 'category violation'. Paris and the office as her playground, she defies social and spatial expectations.

To call her a feminist can at first seem invalid or counterintuitive if feminism is considered an endeavour that benefits not one but all women. Such a conception, Downing argues, shows 'the assumption of feminism as inevitably collectivist' and, instead, proposes that '[r]ecognizing and celebrating the singular female genius as offering a blueprint for reimagining *the potentiality of women as a group* is ... a properly feminist project'.[28] I would add, in this particular instance, that Andréa also transgresses or complicates Downing's model, insofar as she is in fact a strong supporter of women's empowerment. Not only does she train a new assistant, she is also a constant ally to French actresses, such as Béatrice Dalle who refuses to be naked in a film or Isabelle Huppert who wants to be in too many projects and faces a legal battle. Season two, episode six, featuring Juliette Binoche, offers one of the most important moments in television. Having been chosen as Master of Ceremony for the Cannes Festival, Binoche struggles with fashion diktats and tries to avoid a preying, rich donor. All the while, Andréa is a supportive ally trying to balance personal preferences and the consequences on Binoche's career (and by default, her own). Eventually Binoche delivers a powerful speech, shortly after having torn up her gown, in which she lauds the fact that '[la moitié des] films en compétition officielle sont réalisés par des femmes' ('[half of] the films in competition were directed by women'), because 'on a besoin de leur regard, de leurs histoires, de leur vérité' ('we need their perspective, their stories, their truth') (00:40:40–00:41:50).[29] Binoche's declaration could be viewed as a reflection of *DPC*'s own groundbreaking representation of women on screen. The show, too, is making history by featuring new stories, new perspectives and new truths. It showcases a chorus of strong women who disobey all the rules of patriarchy and who are not social failures for it.

Impresario, Not Agent: Arlette Azémar

If one character embraces the potential of disobedience it is the doyenne of ASK, Arlette Azémar, who acts as the memory of French cinema since the *Nouvelle Vague*. Shot for the most part at the agency, she is something of a haunting presence, a reminder of the history of cinema and a pillar for her fellow agents. And, while she might prefer the outdated term *impresario* to describe her role, this is not to say that she is old-fashioned and behind the times; she is a dynamic, determined and knowledgeable woman. Indeed, oftentimes she shares important information about older actors and past feuds, which, in turn, helps the younger agents solve problems. Overall, her character makes a significant contribution to widening the spectrum of womanhood at work. In 1999, Kathleen Woodward remarked that race, gender and sexuality have been at the heart of scholarship and university courses, yet age has often been left out.[30] The past decade has seen a growing interest in the subject, especially as care studies, feminist studies and the medical humanities have paid more attention to its cultural representations. Natalie Edwards confirms this recent turn to shed light on ageing characters and notes: 'When older characters appear [in literature], they rarely represent ageing as a positive experience and are instead associated with loss of beauty, charm, wit, independence or faculties'.[31] Ariane Beauvillard, in *Les Croulants se portent bien?*, offers an in-depth (and rare) study of the matter in TV programming from 1949 to 2002 and underlines how 'il est rare qu'un film ou un téléfilm abandonne le point de vue général pour s'intéresser particulièrement à la vieillesse' ('it is rare for a [prime time] film or series to abandon the global point of view to focus specifically on old age').[32] As such, *DPC* is inscribed in a longer history of television and representation, whereby 'chaque époque crée sa figure [de la vieillesse], reprenant toujours les codes de l'époque précédente' ('each era creates its image [of old age], always borrowing the codes from the preceding era').[33] Considering that seeing and being seen are inherent to the media, representing old age is urgently needed at a time when women continue to bear the stigma of ageing.

In the case of *DPC*, not only does the show explore this common and known discrimination in the film industry, it also tries to fix the problem by including older women. In the first episode forty-year-old actress Cécile de France almost loses a role because of her age and refusal to resort to cosmetic surgery. She only keeps it because Mathias blackmailed the producers. Throughout the show, ageing actresses are featured in significant numbers from Line Renaud and Françoise Fabian to Monica Bellucci and Isabelle Huppert. Season four follows the trend and includes Sandrine Kiberlain and Sigourney Weaver. One could argue that French viewers have grown so accustomed to their faces, over generations, that they do not really see them age; or, in the case of Bellucci and Huppert, they are such icons that they seem ageless and do not reflect the majority of women. Arlette's character, however, provides viewers with a relatable older woman who works and can also become a model. It is also quite noteworthy that Arlette owes much of her storyline to eighty-six-year-old Liliane Rovère, who plays the role, thus adding to the character's credibility. For instance, Rovère has spoken of her relationship with Chet Baker, which is used in season two. At all times Rovère/Arlette is fiercely committed to her own freedom and remains unchanged: 'je n'ai pas bougé d'un cheveu ... Je fais tout ce que je peux pour faire tout ce que je veux' ('I haven't budged an inch ... I do everything I can to do everything I want').[34]

An equal member of the agency, Arlette is indeed a supportive, strong-headed and independent woman who, by transgressing social expectations, serves as a reminder that '[o]ur culture has assigned different norms of behaviour to different ages'.[35] Arlette's first real intervention in the first episode sets the tone. During a meeting with her colleagues and ASK founder and director, Samuel Kerr, who is about to leave for a (soon-to-be-fatal) vacation in Brazil, she tells him to make the most of it, to forget about the agency, and instead to 'boi[re] des caïpi, des mojitos ... regarde[r] le cul des filles et passe[r] le bonjour à Pelé' ('[d]rink caipirinhas and mojitos ... look at girls' asses and say hello to Pelé') (00:11:00). Her suggestion may seem unexpected for a woman her age in a rather bourgeois milieu, especially to her boss. Yet, it becomes clear that she is close to him but also pays no heed to hierarchical conventions.

Shortly after, Gabriel shares the news about Cécile de France, to which she replies: 'Trop âgée pour un rôle? Et c'est quoi le rôle, un enfant?' ('Too old? What's the part, a kid?') (00:12:20). To a significant extent, she shares many character traits with Andréa; she is very direct and is not afraid to speak her mind or to talk about (self) pleasures and desires. Like Andréa, she is also a true cinephile, sticks to her opinions and never fears Mathias' threats even if she owns fewer shares in the agency: 'Je me fiche de tes menaces. Je ne parle pas d'argent, je parle de dignité et de loyauté' ('Your threats don't bother me. I'm not talking about money, I'm talking about dignity and loyalty') (00:14:00). Critics have pointed out the lack of character development for Arlette (and Gabriel) in favour of the duelling duo Andréa and Mathias. A valid criticism, it is still the case that her on-screen interventions prove impactful because powerful, ageing women are still a rare sight, but also because she has no filters and, oftentimes, no patience for whining.

Later in the first episode, she listens to Gabriel's complaints (having lost Cécile de France to his colleague Mathias) but soon leaves him alone and refuses to entertain his wallow: 'Ouais, t'as raison. Reste allongé ici et fais rien' ('Yeah, you're right, just lie there and do nothing!') (00:48:20). Throughout the three seasons, Arlette often fulfils a supporting role, in particular to Gabriel or Andréa. She cares for them. She often shares moments of joy, cannabis joints and professional and personal advice. However, the strength of *DPC*, as far as she is concerned, lies in its ability to not equate care with womanhood or motherhood. She is no mother substitute and refuses the idea that care is an innately feminine quality. The tight-knit community of ASK certainly 'lends [*DPC*] a family vibe',[36] yet Arlette never assumes a matriarchal position in this somewhat dysfunctional family, in part because she is so transgressive that she does not even come close to the perfect model of motherhood under patriarchal ideology (caring and selfless). As a matter of fact, if Downing urges women 'to stop doing the extra emotional labour of being for the other and to occupy themselves with the interests of the self',[37] Arlette (as does Andréa) embodies such a call. Her support is never limitless and her (self) interests matter. She only really cares for her dog named after the famous French actor Jean

Gabin. This nod to classic French cinema further reinforces her position of power. She is the one with the voice, giving orders and making decisions. In episode two, as the agents are looking for money to buy Kerr's shares, she tells Andréa that she will invest her savings in the agency and explains: 'Je n'ai pas d'enfants, à part Jean Gabin ... Ma famille, c'est vous. Vous et mes acteurs' ('I have no kids, apart from Jean Gabin ... You're all my family. All of you and my actors') (00:27:10). As such, like Andréa, the boundaries of Arlette's personal and professional life are quite non-existent. For instance, she has no issues making sexual comments in the workplace where they should not belong. In episode three, she comically tells off Mathias and Gabriel – who often wage ego wars against one another – stating: 'Les concours de zizi, si c'est pas dans mon lit, ça m'intéresse pas' ('Dick-size contests don't interest me outside [my] bedroom') (00:42:01).

Season two, episode five marks a turn in Arlette's storyline. Guest-starring Guy Marchand, the episode incorporates her past that she eventually reveals to Gabriel. On the rooftop of the office with a view of the Eiffel Tower, a medium close-up shows Arlette's made-up face, her coiffed hair in the wind and her refined jewellery. Holding a cigarette, she resembles a stereotypical Parisian beauty. She finally shares about her relationship with Guy and explains that she dumped him for Chet Baker: 'J'aimais la vie et les artistes, lui [Guy] il voulait se marier. Il m'a jamais pardonnée. C'est con la jalousie quand même' ([of old age], 'I loved life and artists, he [Guy] wanted to get married. He never forgave me. Jealousy is stupid') (00:14:15– 00:15:54). Thinking back to Edward's aforementioned comment about the negative representation of older characters (i.e., loss of beauty, charm, independence, etc.), this instance provides a welcome counter-narrative. Both the scene and the story showcase Arlette as a beautiful (then and now), charming, witty and independent woman, who prioritises her desires and happiness over stability and the social privilege (and expectation) of marriage. Likewise, motherhood is non-existent as a topic, it is a non-problem. To ignore it is noteworthy insofar as it prevents the show from falling into a problematic rhetoric of regret or incompleteness.[38] At no point does Arlette bring up or justify her status as childfree – except for a passing joke about having to deal with actors who are child-like – which, in itself, helps deconstruct the oppressive myths of maternal instincts or love. Downing reminds us that 'to refuse this [maternal] role places the individual woman in a position of being aberrant with regard to social expectations, and, in some discourses, viewed as a failed woman'.[39] On the contrary, Arlette is a fulfilled and successful woman, whose desires have yet to wane, as the show attests by resuming her relationship with Guy Marchand. By the end of the episode, Guy invites her for a drink after filming. He asks whether 10 p.m. is too late, to which she replies, with a smile, 'Non, c'est pas trop tard' ('No, it's not too late') (00:46:10). Here, Arlette's response speaks more broadly of the possibility of (loving and/or sexual) relationships in old age. Professionally, too, while her clientele is dwindling, she still has some successes. Hicham, in his end-of-year report, compares her to Jean Gabin, her dog: 'Elle vous attaque au mollet et elle vous emmène toujours où elle veut ... elle augmente son chiffre de 20% en plus d'être dans le *Gala* avec Guy Marchand' ('She lunges for your calf and she always takes you where she wants ... she increased her numbers by 20 per cent, in addition to featuring in *Gala* with Guy Marchand') (00:50:41). Overall, she is a positive influence and a mentor to her younger peers, including to Hicham who listens to her industry stories and expands his knowledge.

In the larger scheme of French television, Arlette's character also reveals a general lack of investment in stories focused solely on the aged. That being said, while the figure of the ageing woman surrounded by younger characters is very much at play in *DPC*, Arlette still effectively creates a sense of disruption as an unapologetically free and fearless woman – in a manner reminiscent of Netflix's successful *Grace and Frankie* or the newer French show *Family Business* in which Rovère herself plays a pot-growing Jewish grandmother – far from the classic tropes of the celibate, the widow or the virgin; she instead embodies a strong professional woman.[40] In the end, be it Arlette or Andréa, both resist and distort gender norms, offering viewers exceptional models, in all that 'exceptional' entails.

Conclusion

What *DPC* manages to do, beyond some of the issues that this analysis has underlined, is to de-essentialise genders and gender relations, while offering new models of womanhood. Indeed, Andréa and Arlette offer two powerful and necessary portrayals that reflect current social evolutions and tensions and remind us, as Juliette Binoche does in the show, that 'le corps des femmes est un enjeu de pouvoir, de conflits. Et le cinéma, les images, sont une façon pour elles de résister' ('women's bodies are at stake in power games and conflicts. And cinema, the movies, give us the means to resist') (00:41:50). Television offers the same promise of liberation and emancipation. In four seasons, the show has successfully engaged with important debates such as gender inequality and reproductive rights. It struggled, however, to really test France's universalist ideal. The lack of visible diversity among the cast remains a major issue. According to the 2018 CSA report on 'La représentation de la diversité de la société française à la télévision et à la radio: bilan 2013–2018' ('The Representation of Diversity in French Society on Television and the Radio' (2013–2018)), non-white individuals only make up 17 per cent of people on television.[41] In July 2020, Rokhaya Diallo released a documentary investigating the place of French actors of colour. Her hashtag #OùSontLesNoirs (#WhereAreOurBlackActors) raised the question on social media and deplored their absence as well as the limits and stereotypical nature of the fictional characters available to them.[42] *DPC* did not help make a difference. Indeed, while Sofia, who becomes a central character over time, never seems defined by the colour of her skin, her limited development reduces her to her Blackness.[43] As Aïssa Maïga would put it, 'noire n'est pas [s]on métier' ('Black is not [her] job').[44] In the end, future shows can certainly learn from *DPC*'s success, its advocating for progress and diversity, but they will also need to actually name things as they are – lesbian, old, Black, etc. – so that these lived experiences might manifest with their full transformative potential.

Works Cited

Ahmed, Sara, *Living a Feminist Life* (Durham NC: Duke University Press, 2017).

Beauvillard, Ariane, *Les Croulants se portent bien?* (Lormont: Le bord de l'eau, 2012).

Bourdaa, M., '"*The end of Calzona as we know it*': analyse de réception des fans du couple Callie-Arizona dans la série *Grey's Anatomy*', in M. Bourdaa and A. Alessandrin (eds), *Fan Studies/Gender Studies: La Rencontre* (Paris: Téraèdre, 2017), pp. 139–53.

Bradbury-Rance, Clara, *Lesbian Cinema After Queer Theory* (Edinburgh: Edinburgh University Press, 2019).

Cappelle, L., 'Call My Agent! Is a rare thing', 6 August 2020, *www.ft.com/content/9b03a8f7-eab1–4d9f-98fb-c4abfbfeddf2* (accessed 23 November 2021).

Carlesimo, C., 'Dix pour cent: "Andréa est et restera lesbienne"', 22 November 2018, *www.telestar.fr/serie-tv/dix-pour-cent/dix-pour-cent-andrea-est-et-restera-lesbienne-391836* (accessed 23 November 2021).

Choquet, M., 'Comment Dix pour cent est tombée dans la représentation stéréotypée du personage lesbien', 15 May 2017, *https://büinge.konbini.com/series/dix-pour-cent-stereotype-lesbien/* (accessed 23 November 2021).

Coffin, Alice, *Le Génie lesbien* (Paris: Grasset, 2020).

Darren, Alison, *Lesbian Film Guide* (London and New York: Cassell, 2000).

Dassonville, A., 'Pourquoi les lesbiennes sont-elles privées de paroles à la télé?', 26 April 2019, *www.telerama.fr/medias/pourquoi-les-lesbiennes-sont-elles-privees-de-parole-a-la-tele,n6227908.php* (accessed 23 November 2021).

Downing, Lisa, *Selfish Women* (London and New York: Routledge, 2019).

Edwards, Natalie, *Voicing Voluntary Childlessness: Narratives of Non-Mothering in French* (Bern: Peter Lang, 2016).

Langlais, P., '"Dix pour cent" domine les prix des critiques français de séries', 8 August 2016, *www.telerama.fr/series-tv/dix-pour-cent-domine-les-prix-de-l-association-francaise-des-critiques-de-series,143682.php* (accessed 23 November 2021).

'La représentation de la diversité de la société française à la télévision et à la radio. Bilan 2013–2018', 29 January 2019, *www.csa.fr/Informer/Collections-du-CSA/Travaux-Autres-publications/L-observatoire-de-la-diversite/La-representation-de-la-diversite-de-la-societe-francaise-a-la-television-et-a-la-radio-bilan-2013–2018* (accessed 23 November 2021).

'La représentation des femmes à la télévision et à la radio. Rapport sur l'exercice de 2018', *www.csa.fr/Informer/Collections-du-CSA/Travaux-Autres-publications/Rapports-au-gouvernement.-parlement.-etc/La-representation-des-femmes-a-la-television-et-a-la-radio-Exercice-2018* (accessed 23 November 2021).

Maïga, Aïssa, *Noire n'est pas mon métier* (Paris: Seuil, 2018).

Merle, S., 'Liliane Rovère, actrice dans "Dix Pour Cent"', 11 April 2019, *www.leparisien.fr/culture-loisirs/livres/liliane-rovere-actrice-dans-dix-pour-cent-je-suis-une-rescapee-11-04-2019-8050899.php* (accessed 23 November 2021).

Poels, G., 'La télévision, "alliée de la femme"?', 7 March 2019, *https://larevuedesmedias.ina.fr/la-television-alliee-de-la-femme* (accessed 23 November 2021).

Poitte, I., 'Fanny Herrero, scénariste: "Les rôles féminins sont souvents moins intéressants"', 24 February 2016, *www.telerama.fr/series-tv/fanny-herrero-scenariste-les-roles-feminins-sont-souvent-moins-interessants,138683.php* (accessed 23 November 2021).

Renault, J.-M., 'Dix Pour Cent "n'est pas une série militante" selon sa créatrice', 21 November 2018, *www.allocine.fr/article/fichearticle_gen_carticle=18677096.html* (accessed 23 November 2021).

'Sondage IFOP/ADFH Les français, les LGBT face à l'homoparentalité', *https://adfh.net/portfolio-items/sondage-ifop-adfh-les-francais-les-lgbt-face-a-lhomoparentalite/* (accessed 23 November 2021).

'Taux d'expression des femmes annuel à la télévision: 2010–2019', *www.data.gouv.fr/fr/datasets/r/5f4a8e22–7599–4789-bf60–7cf7df9a8e70* (accessed 23 November 2021).

'Where We Are on TV. 2018–2019', *www.glaad.org/whereweareontv18* (accessed 23 November 2021).

Wilkinson, A., '82 women protested gender inequity', 13 May 2018, *www. vox.com/culture/2018/5/13/17347738/cannes-womens-protest-march-film-festival-cate-blanchett-agnes-varda-timesup-red-carpet* (accessed 23 November 2021).

Woodward, Kathleen (ed.), 'Introduction', in *Figuring Age: Women, Bodies, Generations* (Bloomington IN and Indianapolis IN: Indiana University Press, 1999), pp. ix–xxviii.

Notes

1   'Taux d'expression des femmes annuel à la télévision: 2010–2019', *www.data.gouv.fr/fr/datasets/r/5f4a8e22-7599-4789-bf60-7cf7df9a8e70* (accessed 23 November 2021).

2   'La représentation des femmes à la télévision et à la radio. Rapport sur l'exercice de 2018', *www.csa.fr/Informer/Collections-du-CSA/Travaux-Autres-publications/Rapports-au-gouvernement.-parlement.-etc/La-representation-des-femmes-a-la-television-et-a-la-radio-Exercice-2018* (accessed 23 November 2021).

3   G. Poels, 'La télévision, "alliée de la femme"?', 7 March 2019, *https:// larevuedesmedias.ina.fr/la-television-alliee-de-la-femme* (accessed 23 November 2021).

4   Although this analysis does not include season four, which came out in the United States after the completion of this chapter, it appears that the arguments herewith remain pertinent. Andrea, in particular, has to take care of her daughter alone, yet she does not let it take precedence over her career (until the very last episode). As for the word 'lesbian', it has yet to be uttered.

5   P. Langlais, '"Dix pour cent" domine les prix des critiques français de séries', 8 August 2016, *www.telerama.fr/series-tv/dix-pour-cent-domine-les-prix-de-l-association-francaise-des-critiques-de-series,143682.php* (accessed 23 November 2021).

6   English translations of *DPC* quotes come from the subtitle function on Netflix. All other translations are my own.

7   I. Poitte, 'Fanny Herrero, scénariste: "Les rôles féminins sont souvent moins intéressants"', 24 February 2016, *www.telerama.fr/series-tv/fanny-herrero-scenariste-les-roles-feminins-sont-souvent-moins-interessants,138683. php* (accessed 23 November 2021).

8   J.-M. Renault, 'Dix Pour Cent "n'est pas une série militante" selon sa créatrice', 21 November 2018, *www.allocine.fr/article/fichearticle_gen_carticle=18677096.html* (accessed 23 November 2021).

9   Lisa Downing, *Selfish Women* (London and New York: Routledge, 2019), p. 2.

10   A. Dassonville, 'Pourquoi les lesbiennes sont-elles privées de paroles à la télé?', 26 April 2019, *www.telerama.fr/medias/pourquoi-les-lesbiennes-sont-elles-privees-de-parole-a-la-tele,n6227908.php* (accessed 23 November 2021).

11   Alice Coffin, *Le Génie lesbien* (Paris: Grasset, 2020), p. 141.

12   Clara Bradbury-Rance, *Lesbian Cinema After Queer Theory* (Edinburgh: Edinburgh University Press, 2019), p. 2.

13   Less than 10 per cent of characters identify as LGBTQ, and 25 per cent of these identify as lesbian. See, GLAAD, 'Where We Are on TV. 2018–2019', *www.glaad.org/whereweareontv18* (accessed 23 November 2021).

14   M. Choquet, 'Comment Dix pour cent est tombée dans la représenta-tion stéréotypée du personnage lesbien', 15 May 2017, *https://biiinge. konbini.com/series/dix-pour-cent-stereotype-lesbien* (accessed 23 November 2021).

15   C. Carlesimo, 'Dix pour cent: "Andréa est et restera lesbienne"', 22 November 2018, *www.telestar.fr/serie-tv/dix-pour-cent/dix-pour-cent-andrea-est-et-restera-lesbienne-391836* (accessed 23 November 2021).

16   Alison Darren, *Lesbian Film Guide* (London and New York: Cassell, 2000), p. 3.

17   Sara Ahmed, *Living a Feminist Life* (Durham NC: Duke University Press, 2017), p. 37.

18   Ahmed, *Living a Feminist Life*, p. 21.

19   Choquet, *https://biiinge.konbini.com/series/dix-pour-cent-stereotype-lesbien/* (accessed 23 November 2021).

20   Darren, *Lesbian Film Guide*, p. 3.

21   Choquet, *https://biiinge.konbini.com/series/dix-pour-cent-stereotype-lesbien/* (accessed 23 November 2021).

22   Renault, *www.allocine.fr/article/fichearticle_gen_carticle=18677096.html* (accessed 23 November 2021).

23   M. Bourdaa, '"*The end of Calzona as we know it*": analyse de reception des fans du couple Callie-Arizona dans la série *Grey's Anatomy*', in M. Bourdaa and A. Alessandrin (eds), *Fan Studies/Gender Studies: La Rencontre* (Paris: Téraèdre, 2017), p. 145.

24   Bourdaa, '*The end of Calzona as we know it*', p. 149.

25   For a breakdown of official polls, see *https://adfh.net/portfolio-items/ sondage-ifop-adfh-les-francais-les-lgbt-face-a-lhomoparentalitese* (accessed 23 November 2021).

26   Downing, *Selfish Women*, p. 1.

27   Downing, *Selfish Women*, p. 3.

28   Downing, *Selfish Women*, p. 121.

29   See, A. Wilkinson, '82 women protested gender inequity', 13 May 2018, *www.vox.com/culture/2018/5/13/17347738/cannes-womens-protest-march-film-festival-cate-blanchett-agnes-varda-timesup-red-carpet* (accessed 23 November 2021).

30   Kathleen Woodward (ed.), *Figuring Age: Women, Bodies, Generations* (Bloomington IN and Indianapolis IN: Indiana University Press, 1999), p. x.

31   Natalie Edwards, *Voicing Voluntary Childlessness: Narratives of Non-Mothering in French* (Bern: Peter Lang, 2016), p. 157.

32   Ariane Beauvillard, *Les Croulants se portent bien?* (Lormont: Le bord de l'eau, 2012), p. 127.

33   Beauvillard, *Les Croulants se portent bien?*, p. 85.

34 S. Merle, 'Liliane Rovère, actrice dans "Dix Pour Cent"', 11 April 2019, *www.leparisien.fr/culture-loisirs/livres/liliane-rovere-actrice-dans-dix-pour-cent-je-suis-une-rescapee-11–04–2019–8050899.php* (accessed 23 November 2021).

35 Woodward, *Figuring Age*, p. x.

36 Cappelle, 'Call My Agent! Is a rare thing', 6 August 2020, *www.ft.com/content/9b03a8f7-eab1–4d9f-98fb-c4abfbfeddf2* (accessed 23 November 2021).

37 Downing, *Selfish Women*, p. 123.

38 Edwards, *Voicing Voluntary Childlessness*, p. 160.

39 Downing, *Selfish Women*, p. 105.

40 Beauvillard, *Les Croulants se portent bien?*, p. 23.

41 'La représentation de la diversité de la société française à la télévision et à la radio. Bilan 2013–2018', 29 January 2019, *www.csa.fr/Informer/Collections-du-CSA/Travaux-Autres-publications/L-observatoire-de-la-diversite/La-representation-de-la-diversite-de-la-societe-francaise-a-la-television-et-a-la-radio-bilan-2013–2018* (accessed 23 November 2021).

42 One might not be surprised that concrete actions to make room for minorities are lagging if the government is effectively unable to identify or name what constitutes a minority.

43 Sofia sheds light on social prejudice, implicit bias and outright discrimination against historically underrepresented French citizens. Yet, whether she plays a slave in a period film or secures an audition because her agent assumed that she could hip hop dance, Sofia's character remains defined by her colour, even though *DPC* never addresses it overtly.

44 Aïssa Maïga (ed.), *Noire n'est pas mon métier* (Paris: Seuil, 2018).

Chapter 18
Tracées to Black Excellence? Black Women at Work in *Mariannes Noires* by Mame-Fatou Niang and Kaytie Nielsen

JOHANNA MONTLOUIS-GABRIEL

When people think about the highest spheres of French society, highly creative or intellectual professions often come to mind. In academia, France is well known for its *Académie française* and its many thinkers and philosophers; it is known for its culinary prowess and innovation; it is known for its contributions to the beauty and cosmetic industries; and perhaps most importantly, France is known for its artists and filmmakers. When thinking of France's achievements in these areas, which images are conjured up? Do we not think of white scholars and thinkers, white male chefs and white painters? Indeed, the most lauded professions in France are often imagined as the domains of white men. This view, however, is artfully and skilfully challenged by a documentary titled *Mariannes Noires* ('*Black Mariannes*'), directed by Mame-Fatou Niang and Kaytie Nielsen, and shot in 2015.[1] The documentary features a number of Black French women working in professions socially considered as prestigious and sheds light on their contributions to their fields. In this documentary, Niang and Nielsen give insights to Black womanhood(s) in contemporary France as they constantly navigate their race and gender in these spheres.

Mariannes Noires makes three important moves. First, by filming and documenting Black women working in Parisian professional spheres, it shows that their existence constitutes a form of resistance to the undervaluation of their labour. Second, it shows that Black women experience overt racism and microaggressions, even when they reach the higher tiers of society, and that their work – which I conceptualise as *tracées* – allows them to claim space in these spheres. Third, the documentary shows how entrepreneurship allows for different kinds of path, some that create space in professional domains. The power conferred by entrepreneurship, which grants control over one's creativity and talent, has allowed many of the Black women in the film to become successful and give back to their communities.

First, I will define what I mean by '*tracée*'. *Tracée* is a Creole term for a road or pathway that is not clearly marked. *Tracées* are theorised by Patrick Chamoiseau and Raphaël Confiant in *Lettres créoles* ('*Creole Letters*'), where the authors contend that *tracées* in the colonial era were next to colonial roads elaborated by maroons. According to them, these *tracées* 'témoignent d'une spirale collective que le plan colonial n'avait pas prévue' ('testify of a collective spiral that the colonial plan had not expected').[2] When using *tracées* in this chapter, I mean to define it as a synonym of an unexpected professional pathway that Black women take to achieve their professional goals, and which remedies Black women's invisibility and erasure in professional spheres. If I wish to draw a parallel between the Caribbean *tracées* and the professional pathways available to Black women in France, it is because many of these mainstream pathways have been conceptualised for white bourgeois men.

I therefore conceptualise *tracées* as one of the threads running through many of the Black women's trajectories in the documentary when they explain how they have achieved professional success: by forging a pathway forward – whether it is via self-publishing, self-producing or any other activity that includes self-advocacy or entrepreneurship – in a racist and sexist society that may not have envisioned Black women in these positions. While *tracées* are an aspect of the practice of *maronnage*,[3] this essay focuses on *tracées* as a way to valorise Black women's epistemologies and examine the various ways that Black women find professional success. There are many pathways to success: in fact, none of the Black women in *Mariannes Noires* use the same strategies or face the same challenges when it comes to establishing their professional voice and presence. The diversity of perspectives in the documentary therefore suggests that multiple systems of *tracées* have allowed these Black women to reach a certain professional freedom.

Black Women in the French Landscape

The making of *Mariannes Noires* was a form of rebellion because registering Black women's existence on screen is in itself an act of resistance against the status quo. Mame-Fatou Niang joined a film-making repertoire that Isabelle Boni-Claverie established with her first movie *Trop noire pour être française?* (*'Too Black to be French?'*) (2015),[4] with *Mariannes Noires* continuing the legacy of shedding light on Black women's experiences. While Niang's film can be viewed as a continuation of the work of Boni-Claverie, who is one of the 'Mariannes' in the documentary, Niang's work also highlights the specificity of Black women's experience in a variety of working and professional ventures and arenas. What distinguishes *Mariannes Noires* from its predecessor *Trop Noire pour être française?* is that in the latter, the question of national identity was one of the key components of the documentary, addressing questions of Blackness and French citizenship. *Mariannes Noires*, in fact, is less concerned with questions of national identity. The choice to call the documentary *Mariannes Noires* already implies that these Black women are French and therefore contests from the outset the assumption that the citizenship and belonging of these women can be doubted. The title and the narrative arc of the documentary focus not on whether these Mariannes are French, but rather on the ways that they experience Frenchness in their daily and professional lives.

The second reason why *Mariannes Noires* constitutes a form of resistance is because filmmakers in France who want to create documentaries about Black women face many obstacles. One of the biggest issues is often a lack of funds and other resources necessary to produce a film, especially when the film in question is not centred on stereotypes of Blackness in the particular locale of the Parisian *banlieue*. Directors of films that are produced in the periphery of Paris, for example, do not seem to have trouble finding funding. On the contrary, they tend to be financially successful because they perpetuate stereotypes about Black women from the *banlieues*.[5] Thanks to funding from her American institution and stepping away from French structures, which seldom provide access to funding – and thus forging her own *tracée* –Niang did not have to meet the public's appetite for stereotypes. The choice to film the seven Black women in their work environments in Paris proper is a clear departure from previously and contemporary filmic stereotypical images of the 'mama africaine' ('the African mama') or rebellious youth in the Parisian *banlieue*. In creating her documentary, she shows an unexplored and overlooked aspect of Black womanhoods on screen and disrupts the record of their representation in France. Niang's filmic debut allows the undervalued richness of Black experience to come to light. In filming the *tracées* of seven Black French women in contemporary France, Niang breaks with stereotypical images of Black women in France and shows pieces of Black womanhoods that many Afro-descendant producers and filmmakers would undoubtedly like to portray if it were not for the lack of financial support and backing from French institutions. In other words, dedicating a film to the existence of these Black women is, in itself, an act of resistance against narratives nurturing well-worn stereotypes.[6]

In opposition to these pernicious stereotypical images, Niang's film exemplifies the director's commitment to establishing a record of serious aesthetic treatment in the realm of visual cultures. It is often the case that Black women's bodies are not given such treatment because of the overwhelming body of archival misrepresentations of Black women's selves, bodies and worlds. The work it took to produce the documentary therefore reinforces a productive (mis)understanding of Black French womanhoods in contemporary France. I am indebted to what Gershon Shaked – scholar and critic of Hebrew literature – coined as 'productive misunderstanding'. According to Shaked, the perceived difference between the body on stage or on screen and the audience member can result in deeper, more meaningful understanding of the Other: 'Understanding another culture means constantly grasping the differentness of one's fellow man, and it is bound up in a constant effort to translate differences to our own world of experience, to bring the distant near, make the past present, and the incomprehensible understood.'[7] The viewing audience is therefore engaged in this back and forth of cultural translation in order to make Black women's perceived differences relate to their worlds. Therefore, the productive misunderstanding stems from the recognition of this difference and the work of translating these differences to one's own world.

Niang, as a Black woman at work, makes aesthetic choices that anchors Black presence and work in the Parisian landscape. By this,

I mean that Niang's work makes visible Black women's labour in the city of lights. Niang cleverly juxtaposes Parisian spaces with Black female bodies. For instance, the documentary follows one of its subjects, Iris Beaumier, as she moves around Paris from the metro to the Place de la République and Quais de Seine. While following her through Paris, Iris Beaumier is seen watching white women on advertisement posters and being reflected an image of Blackness with which she may not associate: one of the poor Africans who need help from white passers-by. Many of the other Black 'Mariannes' of the documentary also appear in this Parisian landscape, especially in places dedicated to memorialising aspects of French republicanism. For instance, several shots show the Place de la République, where French citizens are known to congregate after terrorist attacks to commemorate victims (as was the case for Charlie Hebdo). In this way, Niang pushes back against the tendency to make Black bodies invisible. Another technique she uses is to put Black subjects in focus while blurring white people in the shot. Consequently, Niang does more than provide a historical and contemporary record of Black presence in France: she captures and recentres Black women's presence in Paris.

Mariannes Noires made waves on social media when the film appeared. A number of French audience members took to Twitter to specifically voice their outrage about the title. For many, Marianne, the symbol of France and the Republic, is a neutral figure and should therefore not be Black. These comments invoke the long tradition of using white women as muses for sculptures of Marianne; among these muses are the film actresses Brigitte Bardot and Catherine Deneuve and the music icon Mireille Mathieu. All of them embody the role of 'posers' and are therefore passive, while the women in Niang's documentary assume active agents, subjectivities in movement. The fact that whiteness is seen as the norm or neutral suggests that Marianne in reality represents white France. Therefore, when Marianne is depicted as a Black woman, many object that she contradicts France's norm of neutrality and universalism.[8] The meaning of neutrality here is a jab at French universalism, which implies that 'whiteness' is the default neutral subject position, as Niang states in an interview.[9] When whiteness is used as a symbol of universalism, it reinforces the idea that Black people do not bear the same human traits as white people and that no one can relate to them and their experiences. Therefore, the question of who can represent France as a universal subject under-lies the portrayal of Black women taking up space in the film and forging their own unique *traces*, thus disrupting this pervasive narra-tive. I will now discuss how two of the seven 'Mariannes Noires' in the film take up space in their professional lives.

First, Fati Niang is the creator and CEO of 'Black Spoon', the first African food truck in Paris, which is the epitome of *tracée* into the culinary field. When Fati appears on the screen, she is in La Défense, the main business district of Paris. In the background, just out of focus, is her food truck. Niang speaks about the difficulties she faced when starting and growing her business. Not only is Fati Niang's food an African food truck located in Paris, it also is located in La Défense. While many told her that she would never make it or that her business would not last, she is now the first and only African food truck in this elite business district. Her testimony shows the obstacles she overcame as a woman of colour, including the patronising tone in which the doubts were expressed. It also reveals some less obvious manifestations of the fear of Black bodies taking up space in France and of what in France is known as 'communautarisme'.[10]

Second, these less obvious manifestations of fear and racism confirm what Fatima El-Tayeb has written about the experience of embodying the stranger in public space, whereby their presence needs constant justification through permits or official paperwork proving their belonging and legitimacy.[11] The opposition to Fati Niang's ambitions was closely linked to her attempt to take up space in an upscale business district where she was thought not to fit. This opposition also highlights that Black female labour is made invisible and relegated to service sectors such as cleaning and restaurant work.[12] In other words, the assumption that her Blackness would be 'out of place' in such an upscale place betrays the less obvious assumption that Black women in general could never appeal to the elite business clientele of La Défense.[13] The derogatory remarks that Fati Niang faced when she expressed her ambition served as clear reminders about how society implicitly regulates which bodies fit and where.

Finally, Niang's critics were also sceptical of her ability to appeal to a certain clientele in La Défense because of her African fusion-inspired menu. The documentary, however, shows Black, Asian and white customers in business attire lined up in front of 'Black Spoon' during their lunch break. This evidence, along with Fati Niang's testimony, contradicts the idea that her food truck is a venture that appeals only to a particular identity-based community.[14] Niang's *tracée* into the culinary world has proved her critics wrong: her African gastronomy venture appeals to people of all races and ethnicities. This diversity mirrors Fati Niang's own identity. In fact, she sees the food truck as 'un prolongement de moi' ('an extension of myself') (00:27:10) and as a representation of the mixing of her African and French cultures. This view is consistent with an important trope in many literary texts written by Black women,[15] that food and flavours are one of the domains of society in which cultural mixing occurs most easily.

The second example of a Black woman who takes up space at work is the gallery owner Elizabeth Ndala, who defines herself as 'a pure French product' (00:04:54). Her *tracée* consists of being one of the few Black women-owned galleries in Paris. Elizabeth Ndala is introduced to the documentary's viewers as she is leaving a Parisian café. As she is walking by tables, a white man in the foreground turns his head to follow her exiting body. As brief as it is, this moment anchors Ndala in a French reality, represented by the café, while also inscribing her body directly in the white gaze of the customer. However, what follows re-establishes Ndala as a subject of the gaze. The camera follows her through the streets of Paris. She stops at a door in the seventh arrondissement. Ndala fumbles for her keys and opens the door to her own art gallery in the heart of Paris, situated in the same arrondissement as the Musée du Quai Branly, thus geographically representing a physical *tracée*, one deviating from institutional art collecting and showcasing. The camera scans the interior of the gallery, where colourful paintings of African masks and Black women's bodies by a variety of feminist artists are on display. By portraying Ndala as an art acquirer entering her gallery, surrounded by African art, the documentary reverses the white-on-Black gaze commonly found in paintings and visual productions. This scene also challenges the long-standing dynamic of white collectors of African art. Ndala curating her own collection in conversation with the female African authors she features thus elevates and shifts the conversation around substitution of African art by the nearby Musée du quai Branly.

With her gallery in the background, Ndala says, 'jamais j'aurais dû être galleriste' ('I was never supposed to be a gallerist') (00:25:50). She thought instead that she would have to 'rester soit acheteuse soit chef de produit marketing dans un travail qui m'apportait la sécurité finalement.' ('keep [her] job as a buyer, or a head of marketing, a job that would bring [her] security at the end of the day') (00:25:50). Although she was never supposed to occupy the space where she is now, her gallery honours Black feminist artists, art from a Francophone-African perspective, and women and queer artists, thus providing an oppositional gaze.[16] Ndala attributes her success not to her African origins or her French origins, but to the little girl within her who dreamed of having her own gallery: 'Mais je ne suis pas sûre que ce soit lié à ma culture ni française ou ni congolaise. Je pense que c'est lié vraiment à ma personnalité, à mon tempérament. Et c'est la petite fille qui était en moi en fait qui avait plein de rêves qui s'est dit "mais là, tu ne vis pas la vie que tu avais rêvée"' ('But I don't think that it's linked to my culture, neither French nor Congolese. I think it's linked to my personality, and my temperament. And actually the little girl in me who was full of dreams, who said "hey, you don't have the life that you dreamed about"') (00:26:10). This statement humanises Black women by showing the multiplicity of their lives, their choices, their characters and personalities along with their childhood dreams and aspirations, when often Black subjects are deprived of such representation growing up. The evocation of childhood dreams and imagination is a theme that comes back at the end of the documentary, when a little Black girl is asked what she would do to help people if she were the queen of the world. The multi-dimensionality of Black women is celebrated in this documentary, from childhood dreams to professional aspirations, *Mariannes Noires* helps its audience get a holistic picture of what it is to be a Black woman working to achieve one's dreams, and the *tracées* to these dreams.

Taking Up Speech: Visual and Speaking Texts

Above, I showed how the documentary portrays Black women's professional work as anchored in the Parisian landscape. In what follows, I will show how Niang also seeks to subjectivise Black women by showing them speaking in public for professional reasons. In this way, she explores how Black women produce and navigate verbal discourses about race and gender in their work. To do so, I will discuss two subjects of the documentary: Isabelle Boni-Claverie and Maboula Soumahoro. In analysing these women's filmic productions and academic voices, I will show how the documentary gives a voice to a group of Black women in France that is often overlooked: Black women who belong to the middle class.

Mariannes Noires illuminates middle-class Black women's struggles in their professional lives. This focus is innovative because films, television shows and popular books often focus on lower-income Black people and perpetuate stereotypes about criminality, labour in the service industry, undocumented status, and so on.[17] This tendency obscures the lives of France's middle-class Black women who have achieved a certain level of economic stability and yet continue to experience racial discrimination. The documentary, in contrast, shows that the experience of race is still a unifying factor in Black French women's lives. It gives a voice to 'ordinary women' of the middle class and shows how their Blackness appears in their Frenchness.

The filmmaker Isabelle Boni-Claverie illustrates the silencing and invisibility of Black upper middle-class women in French society due to the popularity of stereotyped narratives. In the documentary, Boni-Claverie speaks about her filmmaking process and explains that *Trop noire pour être française?* arose from her personal experience to show that despite economic and professional success, she still experiences racism in her everyday life. Her point is that the discrimination she faces pertains to race, not class. *Mariannes Noires*'s use of a few clips from Boni-Claverie's documentary renders her work and her voice doubly visible, as part of Niang's project of drawing attention to the lives and work of upper middle-class Black women in France.

Similarly, another subject of the documentary, the researcher, professor and public intellectual Maboula Soumahoro, testifies to the difficulties that she encounters when she speaks up in the public sphere. Although she is a well-published academic who has enjoyed success at prestigious institutions such as Columbia University in the United States, she confesses that she has faced many difficulties in finding a tenured position and in speaking up. Soumahoro explains that during interviews, her interlocutors often skew the conversation towards her 'activism' and not her qualifications and her work. During one job interview, one of the first questions she was asked was 'Tell us about your militancy'. This micro-aggressive statement assumes that Soumahoro is a militant and directs the conversation away from her credentials, implying that she does not belong in academia because of her supposed militancy. Despite all this, Soumahoro's scholarship on Black France has resonated far beyond France: for instance, she is often invited to the United States to speak as an expert on Black France. As an institution, French academia has fought long and hard to keep Soumahoro and Black women in general in isolation in the field of Black French studies while also reminding them that even in the bastion of republican *'égalité des chances'* ('equal opportunity') embodied by the university, they are not in the right environment.

When Soumahoro is invited into other performative spaces, such as television programmes, her body and self still fall under scrutiny. In her book, *Le triangle et l'Hexagone,* Soumahoro describes the many factors that exclude her from public space, even though she is a public intellectual. She writes that her skin, her hair and her corpulence are all at play when she takes up speech.[18] Soumahoro explains that the first attributes that people read pertain to her outward appearance; whatever she says after that is understood as coming from her racial identity as a Black person. Her interlocutors therefore fail to recognise the intersection of the multi-dimensional identities she carries, as being not only a Black woman, but also a Black woman intellectual. This double process of intimidation and delegitimisation functions as emotional racialised labour (what Soumahoro calls 'la charge raciale' ('racialised emotional labour') in her book).[19] When Soumahoro is called a 'militant', she is not only devalued but also, as she says in the documentary, delegitimised – her authority is called into question.

Soumahoro also states that when she chose to focus on Black French people in France, she knew she would not be able to aspire to the highest positions in French academia, that 'it's kind of shooting yourself in the foot but for me, it's the only job that's worth it' (00:34:12). In other words, choosing to work on racial issues in France, where the word 'race' is proscribed means abandoning the dream of rising high in the ranks of the academic world in France. Continuing to speak up about these societal issues, and thus forging a clear *tracée* away from white epistemologies on French academic benches, has direct repercussions on people's careers.

Despite the disadvantages of being a Black scholar of race in France, Soumahoro demonstrates her *tracée* by choosing freedom in the pursuit of self-fulfilment. She describes her work as a duty to herself and as part of her pursuit of self-actualisation: 'Pour moi, au-delà du fait de parler des Noirs, au-delà de tout ça, c'est une question de liberté, je fais ce que je veux, j'ai pas à être limitée par ma race, par mon appartenance raciale, par mon sexe' ('For me, beyond the question of talking about Blackness, it's a basic question of freedom, of being able to do what I want, and to not be limited by my race, my racial origins, my sex') (00:31:12). Soumahoro's testimony on screen is therefore less a response to the criticism and disparagement of her adversaries than it is an affirmation of her freedom to take up space in and contribute to French academia.

The Black women in Niang's documentary have different personalities and different backgrounds, but they have all experienced difficulties at the intersection of their identities. Whether the challenge is to integrate French academia or to make visible the struggles of middle-class Black women, Black women at work must constantly prove their merit, their right to belong and their competency. Are there alternate pathways towards happiness, towards the elimination of self-doubt and towards the rejection of the judgemental white gaze? In the final section, I will discuss how entrepreneurship functions as a *tracée* to self-fulfilment, self-actualisation and Black excellence in the example of the entrepreneur Aline Tacite, the owner of an afro hair salon.

Making Space

Located in Bagneux, right outside Paris, 'Boucles d'Ebène' ('Ebony Curls') is a Black hair salon owned by Aline Tacite. When Tacite is shown on screen, she explains that she started Boucles d'Ebène because she had difficulty finding products suited to her hair and salons with healthy hair practices. Indeed, Black afro and natural hair have a long history of being depreciated and unappreciated, especially in France. In the documentary, Tacite points to this long history of Black hair's depreciation by white French society. She draws on Antilleans' experiences from the BUMIDOM period,[20] where women and men alike sought to integrate into white society by altering their physical traits to fit in. This led to Black French women and men to internalise this hate and transmit to the next generation that their hair was a source of shame.[21] In a sense, Tacite's decision to wear her hair naturally was a radical act of self-acceptance, and her business grew out of this act. Boucles d'Ebène began as a response to the increasing demands of Black French women who wanted to accept their hair and who they were. In addition, Tacite saw this as an opportunity to educate thousands of women thanks to her other initiatives, such as the Boucles d'Ebène conference. This biennial conference hosts many natural hair influencers, hair practitioners and celebrities who come together to educate Black women around best hair practices. Boucles d'Ebène was one of the first platforms to offer such a well-rounded forum of afro hair education; it was followed by the Natural Hair Academy, which takes place annually in Paris. As Tacite stepped into her professional role and exploited her *savoir faire* around afro hair, she forged a *tracée* to Black excellence that has not only brought her professional success but also benefited the many women who visit her salon and attend her conference and in the process are educated in self-acceptance and self-actualisation.

Tacite's public advocacy for natural afro hair began in 2004 and was revitalised with a TEDx talk in 2017,[22] in which she spoke about why natural hair needed to be reclaimed and why negative images associated with Black hair (wool, untameable, coarse, among other things) remain in the French imaginary today. The hair salon, therefore, is not just the place where she does her work; it is also where she teaches self-love and where women speak together about their knowledge, fear and insecurities. In her entrepreneurship *tracée*, Tacite has explicitly spoken about French society's depreciation of afro hair. By creating her own business and her own path, she has escaped the demand to fit in and let go of her 'hairitage' or 'héritage capillaire',[23] with the result that she has also helped her community. Her business involves more than economic transactions. Therefore, this vision of entrepreneurship resists a capitalist model which sees lives, in particular Black women's lives, as disposable and puts profit above all things. Tacite's *tracée* thus inscribes a different path in a capitalist society.[24] Beyond the economic transactions behind Tacite's business, it also consists of 'hairitage' transactions. The documentary, for instance, shows Tacite advising and educating her clients on their hair. She looks at them in the mirror and addresses them with a smile on her face. In this moment, the documentary captures the simple experience of having one's beauty reflected back. When Tacite looks at her clients in the mirror and, as a natural hair advocate, teaches them to care for their hair, she illustrates the self-love and self-acceptance that are needed in a society that consistently refuses to reflect Black women's beauty back to them. By filming Tacite at work in her salon, the documentary testifies to the genuine care that goes into caring for afro hair and hints at the ramifications of this care for self-esteem.

Mariannes Noires as Black Excellence?

Mariannes Noires shows that Black women in France do much more than simply exist. As I have discussed, it portrays Black women at work as embodiments of modern-day 'Mariannes'. It also shows how Black women at work counter the invisibility of Black middle-class women in France. Finally, the documentary suggests that entrepreneurship is another kind of *tracée* that Black women take as they seek to forge ahead in fields that were not designed for them. In other words, entrepreneurship can be seen as a way to author one's own life and destiny. Regardless of the *tracée* chosen by these Black women at work, these '*Mariannes noires*' exercise the freedom to pursue their childhood dreams and self-fulfill the careers that they have set their minds to, all of this, despite overt and covert racism and sexism.

Given this, should we interpret *Mariannes Noires* as a proponent of a form of exceptionalism known as 'Black excellence'? Over the past few years, the term 'Black excellence' has become a trendy way to refer to exceptional Black leadership, creativity and artistry. The viewer of *Mariannes Noires*, then, may assume that this documentary is a portrait of Black excellence: a tribute to seven Black women who have excelled in their fields. Indeed, because humanising representations of ordinary Black women at work are so rare in France, the subjects of *Mariannes Noires* may appear to be extraordinary. But while all of these women can and should be called 'Mariannes', we should not assume that their behaviour is exceptional for Black people. In fact, Niang likes to insist that their pathways in life are ordinary: 'Ce film, c'est pour montrer le quotidien, loin de l'image des femmes noires qu'on a l'habitude de voir à l'écran ... Ce sont des femmes lambda. Elles passent pour extraordinaires car on ne les montre pas assez' ('This movie is to show the daily lives, far from the images of Black women we are used to seeing on screen ... They are ordinary women. They look extraordinary because they are not seen enough').[25] As Niang says and shows in the documentary, she portrays the ordinary moments, the casual encounters, walking in the streets, sitting at a café. The ordinary, that often lacks in the representation of Black women. As Niang argues, there are many like them who live their ordinary lives daily and who pass as extraordinary because, as I have shown earlier, they are absent from the repertoire of visual productions.

However, *Mariannes Noires* undertakes this work of picturing evidence and continues to establish a serious record of Black aesthetics. The documentary successfully provides an aesthetic record of Black womanhoods anchored in Paris, while also showing these women at work in their fields. The professional *tracées* they have undertaken allows them to land where no one would have seen them coming because of the double oppression they are fighting. However, this did not deter them from achieving their professional successes and, by reconnecting to their childhood dreams, the Mariannes in the documentary offer a unique vantage point from which we can reimagine Black womanhoods both in and out of the professional realms.

Works Cited

Boni-Claverie, Isabelle (dir.), *Trop Noire pour être Française?* ARTE France, Quark Productions, 2015.

Chamoiseau, Patrick, and Raphaël Confiant, *Lettres Créoles: Tracées Antillaises et Continentales de La Littérature: Haïti, Guadeloupe, Martinique, Guyane, 1635–1975* (Paris: Hatier, 1991).

Condé, Maryse, *Mets et Merveilles* (Paris: JC Lattès, 2015).

Dubois, Régis, *Les Noirs dans le cinéma français* (Paris: Editions Lettmotif, 2012).

El Tayeb, Fatima, *European Others: Queering Ethnicity in Postnational Europe* (Minneapolis MN: Minnesota University Press, 2011).

Germain, Félix, *Decolonizing the Republic: African and Caribbean Migrants in Postwar Paris, 1946–1974* (East Lansing MI: Michigan State University Press, 2016).

hooks, bell, *Black Looks: Race and Representation* (New York: Routledge, 2015).

Knox, Katelyn, *Race on Display in 20th and 21st century France* (Liverpool: Liverpool University Press, 2016).

Laurent, Sylvie, and T. Leclère (eds), *De quelle couleur sont les Blancs? Des 'petits Blancs' des colonies au racisme anti-Blancs* (Paris: La Découverte, 2013).

Lepelletier, P., 'Darmanin se dit contre les rayons de "cuisine Communautaire" dans les supermarchés: "Ça m'a toujours choqué"', *Le Figaro*, (21 October 2020), *www.lefigaro.fr/politique/darmanin-se-dit-contre-les-rayons-de-cuisine-communautaire-dans-les-supermarches-ca-m-a-toujours-choque-20201021* (accessed 30 November 2021).

Maïga, Aïssa (ed.), *Noire n'est pas mon métier* (Paris: Éditions du Seuil, 2018).

Miano, Léonora, *Soulfood Equatoriale* (Paris: Editions du Nil, 2009).

Montlouis-Gabriel, J., 'Interview with Amandine Gay on "Ouvrir la voix": Visibility and Representation in Afro-Feminine Landscape of France', *The French Review*, 92/3 (March 2019), 180–9.

—— 'Ouvrir La Voix (Amandine Gay): Opening One's Eyes to Today's Afropeans', *Essays in French Literature and Culture*, 56 (2019), 109–242.

—— 'Reading "Hairstories" and "Hairitages' in Léonora Miano and Rokhaya Diallo's Works', *ELA, Etudes Littéraires Africaines*, 47 (August 2019), 85–99.

Niang, Mame-Fatou, *Identités Françaises: Banlieues, féminités et universalisme* (Leiden: Brill Rodopi, 2020).

—— 'Mame-Fatou Niang: "Les femmes noires passent pour extraordinaires car on ne les montre pas assez"', *Le Bondy Blog*, (17 October 2017), *www.bondyblog.fr/culture/mariannes-noires-ces-femmes-passent-pour-extraordinaires-car-on-ne-les-montre-pas-assez/* (accessed 26 November 2021).

Niang, Mame-Fatou, and Kaytie Nielsen (dir.), *Mariannes Noires*, Round Room Image, 2016.

Shaked, Gershon, 'The Play: Gateway to Cultural Dialogue', in Hanna Scolnicov and Peter Holland (eds), *The Play Out of Context: Transferring Plays from Culture to Culture* (Cambridge: Cambridge University Press, 1989), pp. 7–24.

Sméralda, Juliette, *Peau noire, cheveux crépus: Histoire d'une aliénation* (Saint-Denis: Publibook 2012).

Soumahoro, Maboula, *Le triangle et l'Hexagone: Réflexions sur une identité noire* (Paris: La Découverte, 2020).

Tacite, Aline, 'La révolution de soi commence à la racine des cheveux (Personnal Revolution Begins at the Root of Hair)', TED, 2017, *www.ted.com/talks/aline_tacite_la_revolution_de_soi_commence_a_la_racine_des_cheveux?language=fr* (accessed 26 November 2021).

Vergès, Françoise, *Un féminisme décolonial* (Paris: La Fabrique éditions, 2019).

Notes

1 Mame-Fatou Niang and Kaytie Nielsen (dir.), *Mariannes Noires*, Round Room Image, 2016.

2 Patrick Chamoiseau and Raphaël Confiant, *Lettres Créoles: Tracées Antillaises et Continentales de La Littérature: Haïti, Guadeloupe, Martinique, Guyane, 1635–1975* (Paris: Hatier, 1991), p. 12.

3 *Maronnage* is the French term for the practice of enslaved runaways, also called 'maroons' to go and live freely in the mountains.

4 Isabelle Boni-Claverie (dir.), *Trop Noire pour être Française?* ARTE France, Quark Productions, 2015.

5 In her book, Mame-Fatou Niang includes extra interviews with the movie participants. In it, Marianne Noire Isabelle Boni-Claverie states that to film a successful film about *banlieue* actors and actresses, a film-maker must embrace stereotypical representations, in *Identités Françaises: Banlieues, féminités et universalisme* (Leiden: Brill Rodopi, 2020), p. 252.

6   Mame-Fatou Niang's work will also be joined by Amandine Gay's *Ouvrir la voix* (2016), who shows a freeing perspective of Black womanhood in France (and in Belgium) and offers different pieces of the mosaic that is Black womanhood in contemporary France. While *Ouvrir la voix* follows a very similar pattern in terms of following Black womanhoods, her trajectory in producing the film, however, was quite different: since she was continually refused funds from the French National Centre for Cinema to produce her film, she had to use her own money to do so. For more on this see, Johanna Montlouis-Gabriel, 'Ouvrir La Voix (Amandine Gay): Opening One's Eyes to Today's Afropeans', *Essays in French Literature and Culture*, 56 (2019), 109–242 and Johanna Montlouis-Gabriel, 'Interview with Amandine Gay on "Ouvrir la voix": Visibility and Representation in Afro-Feminine Landscape of France', *The French Review*, 92/3 (March 2019), 180–9.

7   Gershon Shaked, 'The Play: Gateway to Cultural Dialogue', in *The Play Out of Context: Transferring Plays from Culture to Culture*, Hanna Scolnicov and Peter Holland (eds), (Cambridge: Cambridge University Press, 1989), pp. 7–24.

8   For more on whiteness as universal and neutral, see Katelyn Knox, *Race on Display in 20th- and 21st-century France* (Liverpool: Liverpool University Press: 2016); and S. Laurent and T. Leclère (eds), *De quelle couleur sont les Blancs? Des 'petits Blancs' des colonies au racisme anti-Blancs* (Paris: La Découverte, 2013).

9   Mame-Fatou Niang, 'Mame-Fatou Niang: "Les femmes noires passent pour extraordinaires car on ne les montre pas assez"', *Le Bondy Blog*, 17 October 2017, *www.bondyblog.fr/culture/mariannes-noires-ces-femmes-passent-pour-extraordinaires-car-on-ne-les-montre-pas-assez/* (accessed 26 November 2021).

10   As per Katelyn Knox, '*Communautarisme* refers to asserting a community or minority identity and is seen as divisive in France, though it is selectively applied to racial, ethnic, and religious identities and not usually regional French identities', in Knox, *Race on Display*, p. 165.

11   Fatima El Tayeb, *European Others: Queering Ethnicity in Postnational Europe* (Minneapolis MN: Minnesota University Press, 2011), p. 23.

12   Françoise Vergès, *Un féminisme décolonial* (Paris: La Fabrique, 2019), pp. 7–9.

13   Evidently, Black women's bodies have long been exposed without their consent in the French public space via spectacles of colonial expositions in the Hexagon. That Black women's presence is sought to be erased from the public space goes in a similar movement as these colonial spectacle whereby Black women should be behind the scenes, not front and centre.

14   This eerily echoes French Interior Minister Gérald Darmanin's October 2020 comments about food and communitarianism, see in particular *www.lefigaro.fr/politique/darmanin-se-dit-contre-les-rayons-de-cuisine-communautaire-dans-les-supermarches-ca-m-a-toujours-choque-20201021* (accessed 30 November 2021).

15 For more on food as *métissage*, see in particular Maryse Condé, *Mets et Merveilles* (Paris: JC Lattès, 2015) and Léonora Miano, *Soulfood Equatoriale* (Paris: Éditions du Nil, 2009).

16 bell hooks, *Black Looks: Race and Representation* (New York: Routledge, 2015), pp. 115–6.

17 Aïssa Maïga (ed.), *Noire n'est pas mon métier* (Paris: Editions du Seuil, 2018), pp. 5–10; Niang, *Identités françaises*, pp. 215–6; Régis Dubois, *Les Noirs dans le cinéma français* (Paris: Editions Lettmotif, 2012).

18 Maboula Soumahoro, *Le triangle et l'Hexagone: Réflexions sur une identité noire* (Paris: La Découverte, 2020), p. 89.

19 Soumahoro explains racialised emotional labour as the double responsibility racialised people take on. The first one being to endure discriminatory situations, and the second to reassure and not trouble the dominant class. Soumahoro, *Le triangle et l'Hexagone*, pp. 135–6.

20 State-sponsored programme, the BUMIDOM – the *Bureau pour le Développement des migrations dans les départements d'Outre-Mer* – sought to recruit more than 70,000 workers from overseas *départements* and facilitated their coming to France with promises of 'better jobs'. See, in particular, Félix Germain, *Decolonizing the Republic: African and Caribbean Migrants in Postwar Paris, 1946–1974* (East Lansing MI: Michigan State University Press, 2016), p. 79.

21 Juliette Sméralda, *Peau noire, cheveux crépus: Histoire d'une aliénation* (Saint-Denis: Publibook, 2012), pp. 59, 151.

22 A. Tacite, 'La révolution de soi commence à la racine des cheveux (Personnal Revolution Begins at the Root of Hair)', TED, 2017, *www. ted.com/talks/aline_tacite_la_revolution_de_soi_commence_a_la_racine_des_ cheveux?language=fr* (accessed 26 November 2021).

23 The term 'hairitage' was used widely by bloggers, activists, song writers and African-American scholars. To see this term defined and used in the context of French literary and cultural studies, see Johanna Montlouis-Gabriel, 'Reading "Hairstories" and "Hairitages" in Léonora Miano and Rokhaya Diallo's Works', *ELA, Etudes Littéraires Africaines*, 47 (August 2019), 85–99. The French term 'héritage capillaire' has been used and coined by Léonora Miano, 'Palma Christi', in M. Le Bris and A. Mabanckou (eds), *L'Afrique qui vient* (Paris: Hoëbeke, 2013), pp. 65–110.

24 Vergès, *Un féminisme décolonial*, pp. 5–7.

25 Niang, 'Les femmes noires passent pour extraordinaires'.

Conclusion

SIHAM BOUAMER AND SONJA STOJANOVIC

This volume, organised in three parts around various workplace expressions calling forth metaphors of the 'door' ('behind closed doors', 'revolving doors' and 'opening doors'), concludes that sometimes these doors need to be 'blown off' entirely to allow women to 'take up space'. It starts with Polly Galis's chapter, which considers, through an analysis of Albertine Sarrazin's experiences in the late 1950s and early 1960s, the escape from various types of confinement (prison, domestic work and some forms of sex work); and it ends with Johanna Montlouis-Gabriel who explores how several Black women recently portrayed in the documentary *Mariannes Noires* (*'Black Mariannes'*) (2016) adopt alternative ways, which she terms *tracées*, to create their own career paths. We hope that by starting and concluding this volume with the image of 'openness' in mind – with multiple iterations of women's work struggles and victories in between – it will foster more dialogue on the current state of scholarship in contemporary French studies and the needed continuation of the conversation on women's labour, with a specific focus on those whose voices are often invisibilised.

We recognise that there is a general lack of access to the publishing, media and cinema industries in France for writers and filmmakers who are women of colour, disabled and queer. We are hopeful that this volume will contribute to many women artists and writers gaining (more) scholarly recognition, yet, at the same time we must also acknowledge our own shortcomings in the invisibilisation of certain women's experiences through the selection of contributions for this volume. We would have wished to cover a wider array of cultural products such as, for example, various art or digital forms. While the volume examines a wide range of work

activities, including sectors where women's roles are often under-
mined, the important labour of women in healthcare or politics, to
name a few, merits highlighting. The chapters adopt an intersectional approach to call attention to the complexity of women's
experiences in work spaces; however, multiple structural barriers
that continue to contain or limit women to certain roles deserve
further scrutiny.

Our goal with this volume was to provide a broad overview of the
representations of women at work, with the hopes that it will prompt
scholarship that widens the range of occupations, work and experiences studied. This could be done – paradoxically perhaps – by
narrowing the scope or genre of texts: a volume on the question of
migrant workers or activists and a focus on a specific visual medium
would yield less monolithic views. All in all, what this volume demonstrates is that there is a lot more work to be done in the area of labour
studies in French cultural productions. As Sara Ahmed has repeatedly emphasised, it is vital that women continue to 'take up space',
this volume can be only one small contribution to conversations that
must keep happening.

On a final note, gaps are due partly to the circumstantial context
of the shaping of this project. While this volume's inception pre-
dates the Covid-19 pandemic, the entirety of its writing and editing
fell squarely within it. Dealing with the lack of access to archives and
the burden of additional care work, some anticipated contributors
were not able to be part of the project. However, these omissions also
point to the fact that white and heteronormative experiences are
still being centred in academic spaces, including, to some extent, by
this volume. The global health crisis also brought to the fore many
issues that resonate deeply with our contributors – this is notably
evidenced by various references in the included chapters to the
disproportionately negative effects that the pandemic has had on
women in all areas of life. Reading and writing about long-docu-
mented issues of domestic, care and emotional work hits differently
in the context of the pandemic; when we started pursuing this
project, we knew that the topic of women and work was important
and timely – we just didn't realise quite how much.

Index